P9-DZZ-379

Nationalism and Development in Africa

James Smoot Coleman, 1919–1985

Nationalism and Development in Africa

Selected Essays

JAMES SMOOT COLEMAN
Edited by Richard L. Sklar

NO LONGER
the property of
Whitaker Library

[redacted]

University of California Press
BERKELEY LOS ANGELES LONDON

106070

University of California Press
Berkeley and Los Angeles, California

University of California Press, Ltd.
London, England

© 1994 by
The Regents of the University of California

The photograph of James Smoot Coleman that appears as a frontispiece to this book was taken by Doris Johnson-Ivanga. Reproduced by permission of the archive of the office of International Studies and Overseas Programs, University of California, Los Angeles.

Library of Congress Cataloging-in-Publication Data

Coleman, James Smoot.
Nationalism and development in Africa : selected essays / James Smoot Coleman ; edited by Richard L. Sklar.
p. cm.
Includes bibliographical references and index.
ISBN 0-520-08374-1 (alk. paper).—ISBN 0-520-08376-8 (pbk. : alk. paper)
1. Africa—Politics and government—1960– 2. Nationalism—Africa. I. Title.
JQ1879.A15C64 1994
320.96—dc20 93-25774
CIP

Printed in the United States of America
9 8 7 6 5 4 3 2 1

The paper used in this publication meets the minimum requirements of American National Standard for Information Sciences—Permanence of Paper for Printed Library Materials, ANSI Z39.48-1984. ♾

To Ursula
as Jim would have wished

Contents

Acknowledgments

The editor wishes to express his deep appreciation to Dr. Elwin V. Svenson, now retired from his position as Vice-Chancellor—Institutional Relations at UCLA, for his encouragement and support. Acknowledgments are also due to the following individuals: Norma Farquhar, Editor, International Studies and Overseas programs, UCLA, who obtained permissions to reprint the essays and supervised preparation of the work; Marina Preussner, who typed the entire manuscript, reconciled texts, and revised the footnotes in accordance with a uniform style; Carolina Wieland, who assisted with the final editing at UCLA and prepared the index; and Monica McCormick of the University of California Press, for her perceptive professional editing.

Editorial Note

The essays in this volume originally appeared in scholarly journals and books published in various countries. In order to bring consistency to their overall presentation, variant spellings, minor stylistic divergences, and the disparate handling of references have been standardized. While no attempt was made to check all of the original references, wherever feasible missing information has been supplied, corrections made, and updates furnished for works that were cited by Coleman as being "in press." In addition, the author's own handwritten corrections on those of his offprints available to the editor have been honored.

Since the original publication of some of these essays, certain words and expressions that were common at the time have acquired negative connotations. For example, the term *Negro* is considered highly inappropriate today. A few other expressions will strike today's reader as being arcane. Although these instances of dated terminology are relatively infrequent, the editor believes that Coleman himself would not neglect to mention his awareness of the continuous modernization of our speech, thought, and writing.

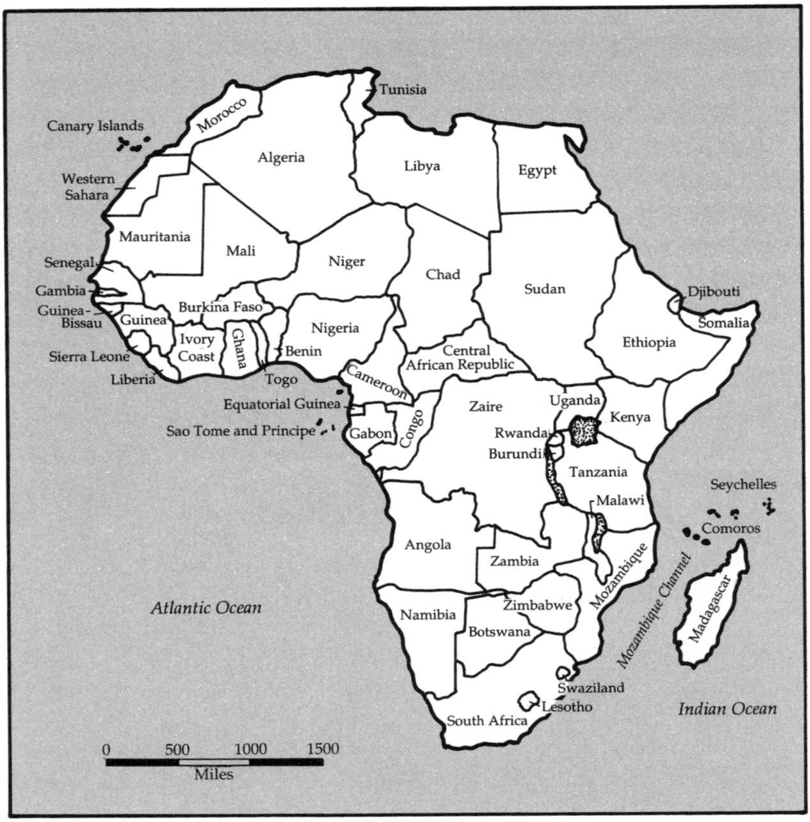

Map 1. Present-day Africa

Changes in Country Names

Colonial Name	*Independence Name and Date*
Basutoland	Lesotho, 1966
Belgian Congo	Rep. of Congo; Zaire since 1971
British Togoland	merged with Ghana at independence, 1957
Cameroons (formerly Kamerun)	Cameroon, 1961
Central African Federation	dissolved in 1963 into Nyasaland, Northern and Southern Rhodesia
Dahomey	Rep. of Dahomey, 1960; Benin since 1975
French Guinea	Guinea, 1958
French Sudan	Mali, 1960
French Togo	Togo, 1960
Gold Coast	Ghana, 1957
Middle Congo	The Congo, 1960
Northern Rhodesia	Zambia, 1964
Nyasaland	Malawi, 1964
Portuguese Guinea	Guinea-Bissau, 1974
Ruanda	Rwanda, 1962
Somaliland	Somalia (formed from British and Italian Somaliland), 1960
Southern Rhodesia	Zimbabwe, 1980; (previously Rhodesia, 1965–1979)
South-West Africa	Namibia, 1990
Spanish Guinea	Equatorial Guinea, 1968
Tanganyika	Rep. of Tanganyika, 1961; united with Rep. of Zanzibar to form Tanzania, 1964
Ubangi-Chari	Central African Republic, 1960
Union of South Africa	Rep. of South Africa, 1961
Upper Volta	Rep. of Upper Volta, 1960; Burkina Faso since 1984
Urundi	Burundi, 1962
Zanzibar	Rep. of Zanzibar, 1963; united with Tanganyika to form Tanzania, 1964

Introduction

A Perspective on the Essays

Richard L. Sklar

A generation ago it was not uncommon for a man of letters to be described as a renaissance man, meaning that the gentleman in question was truly cultured, cosmopolitan, and broadly attuned to the world of knowledge. Nowadays, however, the term "renaissance man" has a slightly archaic and nonscientific ring about it. We simply lack a suitable term or phrase for the universal and international scholar who can be cultured, cosmopolitan, and supremely scientific all at once. We stand in silent awe of such architects and prototypes of a universal civilization—*homo universalis*.

James Smoot Coleman was *homo Americanus* who became *homo universalis*. He personified the idealism that flourished in the United States during the Second World War and its immediate aftermath, when the United Nations appeared to embody the best hope of humankind. In 1947, following four years of service in the General Staff Corps of the U.S. Army and completion of his undergraduate education at Brigham Young University, he went to Harvard for graduate study in political science. There his own genius found its vocation with others who believed that the time had arrived to recreate the human and social sciences on a truly universal, nonethnocentric basis. If, as they believed, prejudice and oppression were the offspring of ignorance, surely freedom in the world would be promoted by science and knowledge. Like his main mentor at Harvard, Rupert Emerson, James Coleman became an *engagé*, meaning deeply sympathetic, student of nationalism in the colonial world.

The influence of Rupert Emerson is a guideline for this exploration of Coleman's contribution to the study of African nationalism. Emerson was the only scholar ever to have been president of two different area studies associations in the United States (or elsewhere, to my knowledge), namely, the Asian and African studies associations. For Coleman, he was both mentor and moral exemplar. But he was not Jim's only mentor in matters of nationalism at Harvard. A second guideline for this analysis is the influence of Karl W. Deutsch. Like Coleman, Deutsch wrote his own dissertation under the supervision of Emerson at Harvard. Deutsch was destined to become one of the finest political scientists of the twentieth century, and to be elected president of both the American and the International political science associations. If Emerson was Jim's guidepost for freedom, Deutsch was the guidepost of reason. If Emerson was the exemplar of passion, Deutsch was the paragon of dispassionate science.

And Coleman himself? Why, he combined those qualities in his own life and work more completely and evenly than any scholar I have ever known. His was a distinctive combination of passion and science. He was, like Emerson, wholeheartedly devoted to African freedom and development for exclusively human reasons. Yet he was ever mindful of his obligation to science, to method, to dispassionate analysis, and to respect for the court of science regardless of its judgments of the causes that he cherished.

I wish to suggest that an Emersonian/Deutschian duality of passion and science was the secret of Coleman's immense contribution to the study of African nationalism. I suggest that his preeminence in that field is specifically attributable to the exact balance of these qualities in his work. His work stands alone because it alone does not tip either way. The rest of us in African studies are tippers one way or the other. Most of us probably tip toward science; some toward passion. Jim alone did not tip.

Think of his seminal essay, "Nationalism in Tropical Africa" (Chapter 2), published in the *American Political Science Review* in 1954. With Deutschian methodicity he dispassionately dissects, inventories, and classifies a multitude of factors that have contributed to the rise and growth of African nationalism. He builds on Deutsch like Charles Darwin, that paragon of empirical science, built on the great classifiers of his time. The essay is a Deutschian prolegomenon to his future masterpiece on the natural history of nationalism in Nigeria; but it concludes, remarkably, with three pages of pure Emersonian zeal, as if the Emersonian lay preacher in his mind had insisted upon a hearing. There is a veritable burst of racially sensitive realism about the blindness of colonial administrators; a reverberation from the depths of nationalist feeling; a truly passionate commentary, like a personal signature. And then there is an abrupt final sentence about the value of interdisciplinary cooperation. At the end of a powerful, passion-laden passage, who in the world would care about "interdisciplinary cooperation"? Coleman, himself, cared and he would not let his readers forget it. He believed, and taught, that the march to freedom had to be disciplined by science.

The essays in Part 1 (Chapters 1–6) of this volume are concerned with the related topics of nationalism and national political integration in the nascent African states. All but the last essay appeared during the first phase of Coleman's scholarly career, culminating in 1958 with the publication of his masterpiece, *Nigeria: Background to Nationalism.*[1] Chapter 1 is a "summary" of his widely noted paper on ethnic group associations in Nigeria. Published in the proceedings of a 1952 conference of social scientists in Nigeria, it has been cited often as a basic source for the sociology of Nigerian nationalism. Coleman's work, like that of Deutsch, demythologized nationalism by showing that movements for freedom from alien control were based on the perceived interests of individuals who were, themselves, subject to the powerful impulses of modernizing social change. Coleman understood that modern Africans would not necessarily reorient their values to accord with those of the elite nation-builders. He was acutely aware that social integration is basically psychological and that few Africans really identified with the new states, which had been created as colonial entities in response to European, rather than African, initiatives. Their very names and tokens of sovereignty would have relatively little affective significance for most Africans. Hence the processes of "reintegration" would not be coterminous with the territorial boundaries of the emergent African states. Subnational separatism and tendencies toward ethnic stratification are the nearly universal challenges to African statecraft. With prescient sobriety, Coleman anticipated the strains and upheavals that were destined to rend the fabric of African societies shortly after the attainment of independence (Chapters 4 and 5).

Part 1 concludes with Coleman's mature and masterly reflection on the problem of national integration, entitled "Tradition and Nationalism in Tropical Africa" (Chapter 6), written during 1966–67 but published in 1975 in a festschrift for Rupert Emerson. It is well known that traditional elites have supported modern nationalism in some instances and opposed it in others. Can such variations be explained by a general rule? Coleman identifies two determinants, rooted in traditional political culture, of modern political behavior, namely, the degree of achievement-orientation resulting from traditional-status mobility and the degree of traditional hierarchism. With the help of these clues, reformulated as "working hypotheses," he concludes that high degrees of status mobility and low degrees of hierarchy, in combination, foster assertive nationalism on behalf of political units which maximize individual opportunities. Coleman himself insists upon the tentative nature of these conclusions, given the fact that few "respectably scientific" psychohistorical studies, pertinent to the subject of nationalism, have been accomplished in Africa. Yet he strongly commends those few which had come to his attention and takes the scientific evidence as far as it will go toward a complex and sophisticated theory of African nationalism. His own mark in pursuit of that goal would not be far distant from the outermost limit of scientific knowledge.

Three of the four essays which constitute Part 2 (Chapters 7–10) are related to the second phase of Coleman's intellectual odyssey: his contribution to the theory of development and modernization. During this period, roughly 1958 to 1970, he coauthored four books of lasting value to the emergent field of development studies.[2] Coleman fostered a school of thought, identified with the Committee on Comparative Politics of the Social Science Research Council, whose adherents were inclined to use the concepts of development and modernization interchangeably on the plausible ground that some forms of modernization, based on universal values, were desired by opinion leaders in all societies. These thinkers have been criticized, with some fairness, for their ethnocentric, Western-cultural biases. As a group, however, they readily acknowledged the validity of that criticism in principle, none with more awareness than Coleman of the ethnocentric pitfalls in this field of scholarship.[3] The basic ideas of these thinkers endure precisely because they were principled pluralists who respected the right of all societies to choose for themselves the forms and values of their social institutions. Wisely, and unlike some of their trenchant critics, they did not attach arbitrary and restrictive definitions to the ideas of development and modernization. These terms were properly understood as twentieth-century equivalents for the older idea of progress.

The concept of modernization, in particular, has been used by social scientists of the current era to encompass all of the social transformations which accompany the rise of industrial civilizations—economic, familial, legal, political, and so forth. In his essay on the specifically "political aspects" of modernization (Chapter 8), originally written for the *International Encyclopedia of the Social Sciences,* Coleman explicates the idea of political modernization with reference to three basic characteristics: (1) the process of differentiation, which connotes the specialization of roles; (2) the ethos of equality; and (3) the growth of capacity to control the environment—human and natural. These features of the modernization process, subsequently identified by Coleman as "dimensions" of the "development syndrome,"[4] correspond to the goals which have been articulated by planners, leaders, and social theorists in all societies. Differentiation implies social complexity, hence increased opportunity for personal achievement and recognition based on knowledge and skill. Equality, as Coleman averred, is the very "ethos of modernity," while the growth of capacity implies increasingly efficient combinations of human and material resources. Incautious declamations of the demise of modernization theory, pronounced (mainly during the 1970s) from standpoints perched on intellectual stilts, are remembered today with puzzlement, if at all.

Ten years after the publication of his principal works on modernization and development, Coleman circulated a brief defense of modernization theory as part of an unfinished manuscript.[5] He prepares his defense by contrasting the uncompromising hostility of "rejectors" with "revisionists," who contend that the "core" of the theory "does have enduring utility as a description of something in the real world." He then endorses a "subtle distinction" made by the revisionists which appeared to him to preserve the practical value of the idea of modernization. The saving distinction is

> between the *empirical* observation that most Third World leaders seek what they believe to be modernization, in any of its variant images, on the one hand, and the imperative that normatively they *should*, or by the laws of history inevitably *will*, seek a particular image of modernity, on the other. That those leaders may seek to emulate and to model what they consider to be modern (or "Western") in other cultures is a fact, which cannot be suppressed merely because of the hypersensitive, guilt-ridden ideological belief by some moderns that it is demeaning or neocolonial; after all, the alleged chief culprit, the United States, has been one of the most indiscriminate borrowers in history, not the least in the fields of science and higher education.

Coleman's revisionist defense of modernization theory is neither evasive nor dogmatic. It squarely confronts the issues of ethnocentricity, imperialism, and class domination. Its subject is no longer wedded to functionalist methodologies, which tend to evade the issues of social and imperial domination. While such methodologies are by no means excluded by the revisionists, they are no longer obligatory. Revised modernization theory, by whatever name its distinctive combination of differentiation, equality, and capacity may be known, has been enriched with the ingredients of Marxism, cultural relativism, and political realism. It has even retaken the high ground of moral concern which had been lost temporarily to more doctrinaire beliefs.

In 1967, Coleman contributed an article entitled "The Resurrection of Political Economy" (Chapter 7) to the first number of a journal published by the Arts and Social Science faculties at Makerere University College in Uganda, where he had been head of the Department of Political Science and Public Administration during the previous year. As Michael F. Lofchie has observed, that particular article "immortalized" the journal (which has long since ceased publication) in which it appeared.[6] It may still be one of the better starting points for those who wish to journey toward a balanced political economy of development, one that would not rely disproportionately on economic concepts and methods of analysis, as if political scientists had little disciplinary wisdom of their own to contribute. Although Coleman promoted the revival of political economy in development studies, his own methods of political analysis were traditional and unaffected by the mathematical methodologies of economic science.

Many of Coleman's colleagues and peers were puzzled by his decision, in 1967, to resign from his positions at UCLA as both professor of political science and founding director of the African Studies Center to continue his service, begun in 1965, as associate director of the Rockefeller Foundation's University Development Project and its representative in East Africa and Zaire. In those capacities, he also organized and directed the Institute for Development Studies at the University of Nairobi (1967–71) before moving his home and principal base of operations to Kinshasa, Zaire. He devoted thirteen years to the task of university-building in Africa, returning to UCLA in 1978 as professor of political science and overall director of international studies. Why did he withdraw from American academia at the height of his intellectual influence and professional prominence? Michael Lofchie's explanation is surely correct: "Jim decided that building institutions in Africa was more important than doing so in this country."[7] But there may have been more to the intellectual reason for his partial withdrawal from the competitive world of professional social science. There may have been a touch of intellectual dissonance, arising from the transition between the first two phases of his intellectual odyssey, between the way he felt about his early research on nationalism and his subsequent contributions to the theory of development. Nationalism worked; as Coleman wrote in his classic article, the colonial nationalists were able "to evict the imperial power and to enthrone themselves." Postcolonial development was another matter. It did not work nearly as well and seemed to need all the help it could get. Furthermore, there were good reasons to doubt whether abstract theorizing about the problems of development really helped to identify them clearly or cope with them effectively. In the 1960s, a growing number of earnest scholars appeared to believe that American-based political and social science hardly helped at all. Time alone would tell how right, or wrong, they were. Coleman had his own doubts about the vaunted yet debatable "modernization paradigm," which he had helped to construct. While he did not yield to the force of extreme criticisms motivated by ideological zeal, he often agreed with specific arguments advanced by dissenters from the litany of modernization. In fact, he was renowned for his encouragement of dissident, independent, and nonconformist scholarship. If, as many believed, Coleman was an exemplar of liberal social science in developmental studies, he "was also, with logical consistency and deep conviction, a great patron of radical and revolutionary scholars."[8]

One essay in this volume, "The Concept of Political Penetration" (Chapter 9), exemplifies Coleman's belief in ideological dialogue. Modernization theorists had introduced the idea of political penetration as a functionalist category for central planning and other state-directed strategies of development. It is the sort of topic that lends itself readily to collaborative research by scholars of diverse ideological orientations. For instance, it accommodates the socialist vanguard idea as felicitously as the idea of a modernizing oligarchy; subtly refined, it can even be reconciled with empowerment of the poor. Under Coleman's guidance, scholars of divergent philosophical and methodological persuasions engaged in a research project on rural development in East Africa, initiated in 1967 and culminating with a volume of essays published ten years later.[9] His own lead essay succinctly explains the concept of political penetration, lucidly summarizes cogent objections to it, and distinguishes between types of penetration in postcolonial Africa. This appears to be Coleman's last essay conceived as a functionalist contribution to modernization theory, a culmination of his second phase, according to my periodization. Henceforth, he would assess modernization theory with philosophical detachment, but his own involvement in its formulation had become history.

He did produce one more theoretical essay, coauthored with C. R. D. Halisi, which ponders the evolution of American political science in the field of African studies and the response of African political science. Prepared for presentation at the silver anniversary (twenty-fifth annual meeting) of the African Studies Association (U.S.A.) in 1982, and published in 1983, this paper (Chapter 10) introduces an original thesis. Coleman and Halisi teach that political science in relation to Africa cannot be separated from the intellectual legacy of colonial rule; that it comes down to earth in a realistic form only when it attains a state of awareness of the colonial legacy and its influence. Otherwise, they suggest, the abstractions of political science in relation to Africa are, like brilliant polar lights, awesome to behold but without the power of terrestrial illumination.

The organizing principle of this exceptionally thoughtful essay is the philosophical antinomy of universalism versus relativism. Each side of the antinomy is represented by a conspicuous tendency in both American and African political science. American political science aspires to global acceptance, but it is betrayed by a disagreeable streak of ethnocentrism. African political science has a strong protectionist and separatist tendency, but it still reaches out for universalizing syntheses which would be able to transcend the restrictive legacies of colonial rule. The needs and limitations of each continue to stimulate their fruitful interaction.

The three essays in Part 3 (Chapters 11–13) of this volume capture many of Coleman's reflections on higher education in the Third World, primarily in Africa. This subject largely absorbed his intellectual energies during the final twenty years of his professional life. For thirteen years, from 1965 to 1978, he was also immersed in the practical tasks of university development in Africa.[10]

Chapter 11 is addressed to the academic freedom and responsibilities of foreign scholars employed by African universities. Coleman discerns a characteristic, but not invariable, reluctance on the part of authoritarian regimes in Africa to demean national universities through flagrant assaults on academic freedom. In return for a circumscribed, but still reasonable, degree of autonomy, scholars tend to censor themselves. Furthermore, they rationalize their conformity to official values as the token of their commitment to the idea of a so-called developmental university. This essay marks the first appearance in Coleman's published works of that optimistic conception destined to become the axial theme of his later thought.

Coleman identifies the idea of the developmental university as a distinctive product of the mid-twentieth-century modernization movement, specifically related to the epoch of national planning for societal development (Chapter 13). Its genesis cannot be dissociated from the transnational "donor community," which Coleman personally represented in Africa by virtue of his role as a representative of the Rockefeller Foundation's successive University Development and Education for Development programs in Third World countries. In this anthology, his thought on government-university relationships in Africa is represented by a study of Zaire, coauthored with Ndolamb Ngokwey (Chapter 12).[11] In the last analysis, Coleman agrees with realists who contend that universities cannot become reliable engines of development for society until they, themselves, develop as credible educational institutions.

By the end of Coleman's term of service with the Rockefeller Foundation, his dedication to the idea of developmental universities in Africa had become an act of faith rather than an expression of empirical logic. In country after country, African universities today scarcely pretend to lead, or even guide, the march toward societal development; instead, they are swamped by rising tides of bankruptcy and disillusionment. Absenteeism, expatriation, and the defection of scholars to far more lucrative careers in the world of business and government are the witnesses and judges of widespread academic decay. However, Coleman's essays still reflect the cautious optimism of a less dismal phase of African university development than that which became manifest during the latter 1980s. For instance, he never lost his faith in the potential achievements of those "many exceptional individual scholars" who were trained during his "seemingly vain effort" to establish a viable university in Zaire.[12]

Coleman's intellectual odyssey, from his empirical study of African nationalism to the theory of modernization, and then to the idea of the developmental university, monitored a stream of social thought which flowed abundantly through the latter twentieth century for a period of thirty-three years.[13] Specifically, his work promoted universalist thought, as opposed to ethnocentricity or cultural parochialism, in the social sciences. Universalism is not synonymous with intellectual toleration or respect for the multiplicity of human cultures. Its theoretical progeny have justified repression in the name of progress as readily as they have fostered the democratic ideal of equal opportunity for all. Coleman's universalist intellect never forgot the crucial distinction between principles and theories. He rarely, if ever, allowed the shadow of a grand theory to obscure his paramount interest in normative rules of conduct and valued outcomes. His example, as evident in this anthology as it is in his other published works and the memory of his professional life, quickens the quest for a truly universal science of society.

NOTES

1. James S. Coleman, *Nigeria: Background to Nationalism* (Berkeley: University of California Press, 1958).

2. *The Politics of the Developing Areas* (Princeton: Princeton University Press, 1960), coeditor and coauthor with Gabriel A. Almond; *Political Parties and National Integration in Tropical Africa* (Berkeley: University of California Press, 1964), coeditor and coauthor with Carl G. Rosberg, Jr.; *Education and Political Development* (Princeton: Princeton University Press, 1968), editor and coauthor with Jeremy S. Azrael et al.; *Crises and Sequences in Political Development* (Princeton: Princeton University Press, 1971), coauthor with Leonard Binder et al.

3. Coleman, "The Development Syndrome: Differentiation—Equality—Capacity," in Binder et al., pp. 73–74.

4. Ibid., pp. 74–75; see also Leonard Binder, "The Crises of Politi-

cal Development," in Binder et al., pp. 3–72, for his correlation of crisis theory with the "modernization syndrome" of equality, capacity, and differentiation.

5. This typescript, entitled "Development: The Concept and Its Indicators," was circulated as Chapter III of a lengthy "Agenda Paper," entitled "Partial First Draft of a Manuscript on Foreign Aid and University Development in the Third World," by James S. Coleman, prepared for a meeting convened under the auspices of the Rockefeller Foundation at Bellagio, Italy, in April 1981. Passages from this paper, not including the passage at this juncture in the text, were incorporated by Coleman in Chapter 13 of the present anthology.

6. Michael F. Lofchie, "In Memoriam: James Smoot Coleman, 1919–1985," *African Studies Newsletter*, Spring 1985, p. 5, published by the African Studies Center, University of California, Los Angeles.

7. Ibid.

8. Richard L. Sklar, "Obituary: James Smoot Coleman," *West Africa*, May 20, 1985, p. 991.

9. L. Cliffe, J. S. Coleman, and M. R. Doornbos, eds., *Government and Rural Development in East Africa: Essays on Political Penetration* (The Hague: Martinus Nijhoff, 1977).

10. In 1978, Coleman was reappointed professor of political science at UCLA, where he also served as overseer of international studies until his death in 1985, at the age of 66. In 1984, he was designated director of UCLA's newly created Office of International Studies and Overseas Programs.

11. Three companion pieces have been omitted from this anthology because they are less clearly relevant to the study of African politics: James S. Coleman, "Some Thoughts on Applied Social Research and Training in African Universities, *The African Review* 2 (1972), pp. 289–307; Elwin V. Svenson and James S. Coleman, "The U.C.L.A. Experience with Foreign Programs," *Human Rights Quarterly*, 6 (February 1984), pp. 56–67; James S. Coleman, "Professorial Training and Institution Building in the Third World: Two Rockefeller Foundation Experiences," *Comparative Education Review*, 28 (May 1984), pp. 180–202.

12. Coleman, "Professorial Training and Institution Building in the Third World," p. 202.

13. In addition to the thirteen essays originally published between 1952 and 1984, and republished in this volume, the book listed in note 1, the five coauthored books listed in notes 2 and 9, and the three essays listed in note 11, Coleman's publications include the following works: "The Emergence of African Political Parties," in C. Grove Haines, ed., *Africa Today* (Baltimore: Johns Hopkins Press, 1955); pp. 225–256; "A Survey of Selected Literature on the Government and Politics of British West Africa," *American Political Science Review*, 49 (December 1955), 1130–1150; *To-*

goland (New York: Carnegie Endowment for International Peace, 1956); "America and Africa," *World Politics*, 9 (July 1957), 593–609; "The Role of the Military in Sub-Saharan Africa," in John J. Johnson, ed., *The Role of the Military in Underdeveloped Countries* (Princeton: Princeton University Press, 1962), pp. 359–405, coauthor with Belmont Brice, Jr.; "The Foreign Policy of Nigeria," in Joseph E. Black and Kenneth W. Thompson, eds., *Foreign Policies in a World of Change* (New York: Harper and Row, 1962), pp. 379–405; "Nationalism or Pan-Africanism," in The American Society of African Culture, *Pan-Africanism Reconsidered* (Berkeley: University of California Press, 1962), pp. 50–75, coauthor with David E. Apter; *Education and Training for Public Sector Management* (New York: The Rockefeller Foundation, 1977), coeditor with Joseph E. Black and Laurence D. Stifel; *Social Sciences and Public Policy in the Developing World* (Lexington, Mass.: D. C. Heath, 1982), coeditor and coauthor with Laurence D. Stifel and Ralph K. Davidson; *African Crisis Areas and U.S. Foreign Policy* (Berkeley: University of California Press, 1985), coeditor and coauthor with Gerald J. Bender and Richard L. Sklar.

1

NATIONALISM AND POLITICAL INTEGRATION IN AFRICA

1 The Role of Tribal Associations in Nigeria

The tribal association is a form of group activity which has emerged into prominence in Nigeria during the last thirty years. It is an organizational expression of the persistence of the strong feeling of loyalty and obligation to the kinship group and the town or village where the lineage is localized. These associations are known by a variety of names: e.g., Naze Family Meeting, Ngwa Clan Union, Owerri Divisional Union, Calabar Improvement League, Igbirra Progressive Union, Urhobo Renascent Convention, etc. Although based mainly on kinship groups indigenous to Southern Nigeria, branches of tribal associations exist in every multitribal urban center, including Muslim areas of the Northern Region, Fernando Po, and the Gold Coast.

These associations were first organized spontaneously in the new urban centers which have grown up as a result of the general social, economic, and educational development during the past three decades. The extension of the railroad and post and telegraph systems, the expansion of the trading activities of the European firms, and the growth of a multitribal junior civil service—the members of which were subjected to service in any part of Nigeria and the Cameroons—resulted in thousands of educated Southern Nigerians being resident for extended periods in alien communities abroad. The rise of new or the expansion of old industries (the plateau tin mines, the Enugu coal fields, the rubber and timber industries in Benin Province, and the plantations in Calabar and Cameroons Provinces) re-

Reprinted from *Proceedings of the Second Annual Conference of the West African [Nigerian] Institute of Social and Economic Research, Ibadan, Nigeria,* no. 1-2 (April 1952), pp. 61–66.

quiring a labor force which would not be provided by the indigenous peoples intensified the twin processes of mobility and urbanization.

This general ferment produced forces which have tended to break down tribal barriers; yet the kinship tie has remained obdurate and has asserted itself in the form of the tribal association. The new urban cities either were artificial and lacking in civic consciousness (e.g., Minna, Gusau, Kaduna, Nguru, Jos, Enugu, Aba, Sapele, and Tiko), or they were completely dominated by inhospitable indigenous groups which treated the expatriates as unwelcome intruders (Ibadan, Kano, Makurdi, Onitsha, Calabar, and Victoria). The relative freedom of association permitted in Nigeria by the British administration, coupled with the feeling of loyalty and obligation to the tribal homeland and the human impulse for "brothers abroad" to come together for mutual aid and protection, were the original bases of this process of association-formation.

At a very early date the members of these associations abroad endeavored to export to their rural homeland the enlightenment, modernity, and "civilization" they encountered in urban centers. This new drive, which is still a powerful force today, was the result of (1) the feeling of obligation and responsibility toward the homeland, which is a striking characteristic of African social organization; (2) an acute awareness of the wide gap between the higher standards of living and greater amenities of the urban centers (particularly the European quarters therein) and the poverty of their rural village; and (3) their receipt of a steady wage which enabled them to undertake programs of community development. The Nigerian age of the "idea of progress" and of improvement unions had dawned.

Since the early 1930s the organizational development of tribal associations has taken two main forms: diffusion and integration. The idea of unions has been highly contagious and has spread rapidly from the urban centers in three directions: (1) to the rural communities of the expatriate groups where "home branches" have been formed; (2) to ethnic groups previously inarticulate (Idoma, Tiv, Birom, Bakweri, etc.); and (3) to special interest groups within the kinship organization (women's associations, students' associations, farmers' associations, etc.). At the same time this process of diffusion was occurring, a program of conscious integration by federation was pursued. This integrative effort had three phases: (1) the federation of all branches abroad; (2) the federation of federated groups abroad with a home branch; and (3) the formation of all-tribal federations in a pyramidal structure commencing with the primary association (the extended family among the Ibos and the large urban towns among the Yorubas) and passing upwards through the various levels of the social structure (clan) or the territorial organization (division or province) of the tribe concerned. The first all-tribal federation was the Ibibio Welfare (now State) Union, organized in 1928. It was only toward the end of World War II that the Edo National Union, the Ibo Federal Union, and the Egbe Omo Oduduwa, among others, were formed. In the postwar period the idea of an all-tribal organization has spread to the Tiv, Igbirra, Biroms, Urhobos—in fact, virtually to all tribes in Nigeria except those in the Muslim areas of the far North. Since 1947 many of the larger all-tribal unions have adopted the name "State" or "National" (Ibo State Union, Ibibio State Union, Edo National Union, etc.), largely, it is believed, as a result of the prevalence of a school of thought which held that a federal system for Nigeria should be based on ethnic groups.

Although the initiative and impetus in the process of association-formation came from the educated elements abroad (who have always retained the leadership), the membership normally included all elements on the socioeconomic literacy scale, from the illiterate peasant or daily-paid laborer to the wealthy trader or titled native ruler or Lagos barrister. There have been several exceptions, of course, where the tribal union was the exclusive preserve of the young school boys, the rabble-rouser, or the opportunist. Membership has always been exclusive (restricted to members of the kinship group), but within the in-group it is inclusive, affiliation being considered a duty, the shirking of which in most cases would result in ostracism.

The many functions—social, economic, and political—performed by these associations during the past quarter century have not been generally recognized nor appreciated. The social functions have been and will continue to be the most important:

1. Mutual aid and protection in the urban centers of temporary residence and employment. This normally includes sustenance during unemployment, solicitude and financial assistance in case of illness, and the responsibility for obsequies and repatriation of the family of the deceased in the event of death.

2. Acceleration of the acculturation process. The new tastes, ideas, and aspirations (including material wants and political consciousness) acquired by the "sons abroad" have been and are communicated to the home villages through the tribal unions. Paradoxically, however, the associations have also tended to retard acculturation by providing a medium for the perpetuation of many aspects of the traditional culture (use of vernacular, traditional dances, celebrations, and ceremonies, and adherence to customary ideas of social morality and discipline) among the expatriate groups. This interaction of the forces of modernity and traditionalism has cushioned the impact of Western ideas and material culture. The urbanized

Nigerian is not as "detribalized" as early observers described him. Through the tribal association he has been able to retain those elements of the traditional culture which are still meaningful to him.

3. Medium for reintegrating the individual employed in an impersonal urban city by permitting him to have the essential "feeling of belonging." The urbanized Nigerian has not been as vulnerable to the disorganizing effects of urban life as his counterpart in Europe and America.

In a more positive sense, the tribal associations have played a very significant part in the material improvement of the rural villages. Accustomed to the principles of self-help and community responsibility, captivated by the idea of progress, conscious of their unfavorable position vis-à-vis other ethnic groups, and dissatisfied with the prewar laissez-faire attitude of Government regarding material progress, the members of these associations have undertaken ambitious projects for the development of their home towns and villages. The greatest achievements have been in the field of education. Smaller unions have built primary schools and sponsored scholarships to secondary schools, while the larger federated unions have financed the construction of "national" or "state" secondary schools as well as the sending of promising young men abroad for higher studies. This contribution by the wage-earning elements abroad has assisted in the leveling up of development in that money has been pumped in to the rural "depressed" areas.

Prior to postwar constitutional reforms the younger educated elements were largely excluded not only from the local councils of the urban centers of temporary residence and from the local government of their home districts, but also from the councils for the central government. It was inevitable under such conditions that these groups would assume a political role. Having grown up during a period when "politics" was frowned upon, most unions disclaimed any interest in political affairs. In actual fact, however, they have performed several useful political functions:

1. They have been a powerful influence for the democratization of native authority councils. By means of petitions, press agitation, and mass meetings they have stimulated many reforms. Official policy has been one either of toleration or of active encouragement of the associations, but always insistent that efforts for reform must be channeled through the Native Authority. The methods by which the associations have exerted their influence are several: joint meetings of members of the Native Authorities and of leaders of the association; nomination of certain union leaders to be members for the councils; chiefs and senior Native Authority members being made patrons of the associations; and interviews between

leaders of the union and the local district officer, the resident, chief commissioner, or even the governor when on tour.

2. In the multitribal urban centers for many years the associations were the recognized basis for representation on Township Advisory Boards or Native Authority Councils as well as the accepted agents for tax collection. In this way they simplified and facilitated administration.

3. They have been a forum for political expression and for the rise to positions of leadership of the younger educated elements. It is significant that the overwhelming majority of the recently elected members of the Eastern and Western Houses of Assembly were prominent leaders of their local tribal associations.

4. They have been the organizational foundation of national political parties (e.g., the NCNC [National Council of Nigeria and the Cameroons]).

5. Above the level of the primary association, the divisional, provincial, and all-tribal federations have played very active roles in postwar development planning and in constitutional review. It is at the all-tribal level, however, that the question of tribalism becomes most acute. There can be no question that the political activities of such associations contribute toward separatism, intertribal tension, and the growth of subnationalism.

During the last few years, two important developments have occurred which may significantly alter the future role of these associations:

1. The emergence of a new group of intellectuals with a very genuine national or regional outlook who are either indifferent or hostile to such associations because of the evils of parochialism and tribalism.

2. The revolutionary reforms in local government. The most significant change—in addition to the democratization of local councils—is that the new local government bodies will possess powers to borrow money and levy rates for material development. A taxpayer will hesitate to make a voluntary contribution to an educational scheme sponsored by his town or clan union when at the same time he is required to pay a five-shilling education rate levied by his own local council.

Notwithstanding these significant changes affecting very directly the political and developmental functions previously performed by the unions, the "sons abroad" will no doubt continue to form associations for mutual aid and protection, and they will still have a vital interest in welfare and improvement of their home villages.

2 Nationalism in Tropical Africa

Postwar uprisings and nationalist assertions in Tropical Africa—that part of the continent south of the Sahara and north of the Union—have directed increased attention toward the nature and implications of the awakening of the African to political consciousness. Among scholars this neglected area has long been the preserve of the scientific linguist or of the social anthropologist; only recently have American sociologists, economists, and political scientists developed an active interest in its problems.[1] As a consequence, apart from certain efforts by anthropologists to popularize their findings and insights, we have been obliged to rely primarily upon the somewhat contradictory accounts of colonial governments seeking to explain imperial connections, or of African nationalists determined to achieve self-government and the good life of which national self-determination has become the symbol.[2] Thus, we have been placed in the uncomfortable position of having to formulate opinions and policy and to render judgments without sufficient knowledge, or, what could be worse, on the basis of evaluations provided by participants in the nationalist struggle. There is, therefore, a very real need for independent and objective research regarding the character and probable course of African nationalist development.

What Is African Nationalism?

Not the least burdensome of our task is the problem of correlating or distinguishing between the generally accepted political concepts elaborated

Reprinted from *American Political Science Review* 48:2 (June 1954), pp. 404–426, an article adapted from a paper discussed at the Conference on Problems of Area Research in Contemporary Africa, Princeton University, October 14–16, 1953, sponsored jointly by the National Research Council and the Social Science Research Council under a grant from the Carnegie Corporation.

with specific reference to developments in the Western world (i.e., state, nation, nationality, nationalism) and the conceptual tools developed by the Africanists. The latter have tended to feel that the traditional concepts and methods of the political scientist are unserviceable in the study of the political structure and life of preliterate societies.[3] Yet, notwithstanding the importance of the lineage, clan, or tribe; the role of the diviner, the chief, or the age-grade society; or the wide variations in the organization of power within such societies, the concept and the institution of the modern nation-state, toward the creation of which African nationalism tends to be directed, is distinctly Western in its form and content. It is as exotic to Africa as Professor Toynbee has suggested that it is to the rest of the non-European world.[4] Nevertheless, just as the Indian National Congress has largely created an Indian nation, so African nationalists are endeavoring to mold new nations in Africa (e.g., "Ghana," "Nigeria," and "Kamerun").

On the level of abstraction at which the political scientist is accustomed to roam, a nation is not a loose catch-all term denoting a larger grouping of tribes (e.g., Zulus, Basutos, Mende, Baganda, or Hausa); rather, it is a posttribal, postfeudal terminal community which has emerged from the shattering forces of disintegration that characterize modernity. This does not mean that the Hausa peoples of Northern Nigeria cannot become a nation, nor does it mean that the "national" consciousness of the ordinary Hausaman must reach the level of intensity of the average Frenchman before there is a nation. It does suggest, however, that there must be a much greater awareness of a closeness of contact with "national" compatriots as well as with the "national" government.[5] This closeness of contact on the horizontal and vertical levels has been a distinctly Western phenomenon, for the obvious reason that it is the result of modern technology.

Not only is a political scientist quite precise in his use of the concept "nation," but in poaching on the insights of the Africanists he also finds it difficult to place under the cover of "nationalism" all forms of past and present discontent and organizational development in Africa. Thus, it is believed useful at the outset to distinguish the following:

A. *Traditionalist Movements*

1. Spontaneous movements of resistance to the initial European occupation or postpacification revolts against the imposition of new institutions, or new forms of coercion, referred to herein as "primary resistance."
2. Nativistic, mahdistic, or messianic mass movements, usually of a magicoreligious character, which are psychological or emotional outlets

for tensions produced by the confusions, frustrations, or socioeconomic inequalities of alien rule, referred to herein as "nativism."[6]

B. Syncretistic Movements

1. Separatist religious groups, which have seceded and declared their independence from white European churches either because of the desire for religious independence or because the white clerics were intolerant regarding certain African customs; hereafter referred to as "religious separatism."[7]

2. Kinship associations, organized and led by the Western-educated and urbanized "sons abroad" for the purposes of preserving a sense of identity with the kinfolk in the bush and "brothers" in the impersonal urban center, as well as of providing vehicles for pumping modernity—including the ideas and sentiment of nationalism—into the rural areas.[8]

3. Tribal associations, organized and led by Western-educated elements, usually in collaboration with some traditionalists, who desire to resurrect, or to create for the first time, a tribal sentiment ("tribalism") for the purpose of establishing large-scale political units, the boundaries of which will be determined by tribal affiliation (i.e., those who accept the *assumption* of common blood and kinship) and the forms of government by a syncretism of tribal and Western institutions.[9]

C. Modernist Movements

1. Economic-interest groups (labor unions, cooperative societies, professional and middle-class associations) organized and led by Western-educated elements for the purpose of advancing the material welfare and improving the socioeconomic status of the members of those groups.

2. Nationalist movements organized and led by the westernized elite, which is activated by the Western ideas of democracy, progress, the welfare state, and national self-determination, and which aspires either (a) to create modern independent African nation-states possessing an internal state apparatus and external sovereignty and all of the trappings of a recognized member state of international society (e.g., Sudan, Gold Coast, Nigeria, and possibly Sierra Leone); or (b) to achieve absolute social and political equality and local autonomy within a broader Euro-African grouping (e.g., French and Portuguese Africa) or within what is manifestly a plural society (e.g., except for Uganda, the territories of British East and Central Africa).[10]

3. Pan-African or transterritorial movements, organized and led by the westernized elite, frequently in association with or under the stimulus

of American Negroes or West Indians abroad, for the purposes of creating a global *racial* consciousness and unity, or of agitating for the advancement and welfare of members of the *African* race wherever they may be, or of devising plans for future nationalist activity in specific regions.[11]

Once these very arbitrary analytical distinctions are drawn, it should be stressed that none of the categories can be treated in isolation. Each of the movements is in one way or another a response to the challenge of alien rule, or to the intrusion of the disintegrating forces—and consequently the insecurity—of modernity. The recent so-called nationalism in Central Africa has been a mixture of primary resistance by the chiefs and traditionalists of Northern Rhodesia and Nyasaland and the nationalist agitation of the westernized elite. Until the project of federation became an active issue, African movements in this area were confined principally to religious separatist groups, tribal associations, or, in the case of Northern Rhodesia, labor unions.[12] On the West Coast, where nationalism is far more advanced, traditionalist and syncretistic movements have not been and are not absent. In some instances, kinship associations and separatist religious groups have been the antecedents of nationalist organizations; in others they have provided the principal organizational bases of the latter (e.g., the National Council of Nigeria and the Cameroons was first inaugurated as a federation mainly of kinship associations, and the African National Congress of the Rhodesias and Nyasaland was the product of fusion of several African welfare societies). In certain cases unrest or protest of a nativistic flavor has been instigated by nationalists for their modernist ends; in others nationalists have claimed such uncoordinated uprisings, as well as purely economic protest movements, to be manifestations of nationalism, when in reality the participants were unaware of such implications.

One of the interesting differences between prewar and postwar nationalism on the West Coast of Africa is that in the former period nationalism tended to be (as Lord Lugard insisted) the esoteric pastime of the tiny educated minorities of Lagos, Accra, Freetown, and Dakar; whereas in the latter period these minorities, greatly expanded and dispersed in new urban centers throughout the interior, have made positive efforts to popularize and energize the nationalist crusade in two ways.[13] The first has been to preach education, welfare, progress, and the ideal of self-government among the masses, largely through the nationalist press, independent African schools, and kinship and tribal associations. The aim here has been, in the words of one of their leading prophets, Dr. Nnamdi Azikiwe of Nigeria, to bring about "mental emancipation" from a servile colonial mentality.[14] The second method has been to tap all existing nativistic and religious tensions and economic grievances among the tradition-bound masses, as well as the grievances and aspirations of the urbanized clerks and artisans, and channel the energies thus unleashed into support of the nationalist drive. The technique here has been (1) to make nationalism, and in particular its objective of self-government, an integrating symbol in which even the most disparate goals could find identification; and (2) to politicize—one would like to say nationalize—all existing thought and associations. Until recently, many observers, including colonial administrators, tended to live in the prewar climate of opinion and therefore underestimated the power which had thus been harnessed to the nationalist machine.

In the case of the Mau Mau movement in Kenya we are confronted with a complex mixture of nationalism, with a strong traditional bias on the part of the westernized leaders, and nativism, manipulated by the leaders, on the part of the masses. Both have been generated to an especially high level of intensity as a consequence of the acute and largely unassuaged sense of frustration on the part of the westernized elite, growing out of the very bleak outlook arising from the almost total absence, until recently, of meaningful career and prestige opportunities within either the old or the new systems, and on the part of the masses, resulting from the land shortage and the overcrowding on the reservations. The presence of a sizable Asian "third force," which virtually monopolizes the middle-class sector, and which has been and is politically conscious, provides a new variable of no little significance in the tribal situation. The fact that the pattern of organization and the strategy and tactics of the Mau Mau revolt indicate a higher level of sophistication than sheer nativism would imply suggests that our analytical categories need further refinement or qualification.

A particularly striking feature of African nationalism has been the literary and cultural revival which has attended it. A renewed appreciation of and interest in "African" culture has been manifested, in most instances by the most sophisticated and acculturated Africans (e.g., Mazi Mbono Ojike's *My Africa*; Dr. J. B. Danquah's studies of the Akan peoples of the Gold Coast; Jomo Kenyatta's *Facing Mount Kenya*; Fily-Dabo Sissoko's *Les Noirs et la Culture*; Léopold Sédar Senghor's *Anthologie de la Nouvelle Poésie Nègre et Malgache*; the French African journal *Présence Africaine* edited by M. Alioune Diop; and the writings of Antoine Munongo in the Belgian Congolese journal *Jeune Afrique*).[15] In some cases this cultural renaissance has had a purely tribal emphasis; in others it has taken a neo-African form, such as the African dress of Dr. Nnamdi Azikiwe, nationalist leader in Nigeria. It has usually been accompanied by a quest for an African history which would in general reflect glory and dignity upon the African race and in particular instill self-confidence in the Western-educated African sensitive to the prejudiced charge that he has no history or culture. In short, there has emerged a new pride in being African. In French areas, the accent until recently has been upon French culture and literature, but there are increasing signs of a shift to African themes amongst the French African literati. The important point is that African nationalism has this cultural content, which renders more difficult any effort to separate rigidly the cultural nationalism of the urban politician from the nativism of the bush peasant.

Yet the differences are important to the student of African nationalism. Primary resistance and nativism tend to be negative and spontaneous revolts or assertions of the unacculturated masses against the disruptive and disorganizing stranger-invader. They are a reflection of a persistent desire of the masses to preserve or recreate the old by protesting against the new. Syncretism is different in that it contains an element of rationality—an urge to recapture those aspects of the old which are compatible with the new, which it recognizes as inevitable and in some respects desirable. Whereas all forms of protest are politically consequential, at least to colonial administrators, only nationalism is primarily political in that it is irrevocably committed to a positive and radical alteration of the power structure. In brief, nationalism is the terminal form of colonial protest.

Another reason for distinguishing between the various categories of assertion, which are basically differences in goal orientation, is not only to provide some basis for judging the nature of the popular support of a nationalist movement during its buildup, but also to have some means of predicting the stability and viability of the political order established by the nationalists once they achieve self-government. The governments of Pakistan, Burma, India, and Indonesia have each been plagued by internal tensions arising from what are fundamentally South Asian variants of traditionalism and tribalism. If a colonial nationalist movement comes to power atop a wave of mass protest which is primarily, or even in part, nativistic in character, this would have a direct bearing upon the capacity of the westernized leaders of that movement not only to maintain political unity and stability but also to carry out what is at the core of most of their programs—rapid modernization by a centralized bureaucratic machine. Any thorough study of the anatomy of a nationalist movement, therefore, must seek to determine the linkages and compatibilities between the goal orientations of the several forces from which that movement derives its élan and strength.

Factors Contributing to the Rise of Nationalism

It is far easier to define and describe nationalism than it is to generalize about the factors which have contributed to its manifestation. Put most briefly, it is the end product of the profound and complex transformation which has occurred in Africa since the European intrusion. It is a commonplace that the imposition of Western technology, sociopolitical institutions, and ideology upon African societies has been violently disruptive of the old familistic order in that they have created new values and symbols, new techniques for the acquisition of wealth, status, and prestige, new groups for which the old system had no place. The crucial point here is not that nationalism as a matter of fact happened to appear at a certain point in time after the "Western impact," but rather that the transformation the latter brought about has been an indispensable precondition for the rise of nationalism. Nationalism, as distinguished from primary resistance or nativism, requires considerable gestation. A few of the constituent elements have been:

A. Economic[16]

1. *Change from a subsistence to a money economy.* This change, consciously encouraged by colonial governments and European enterprise in order to increase the export of primary products, introduced the cash nexus and economic individualism, altered the patterns of land tenure and capital accumulation, and, in general, widened the area of both individual prosperity and insecurity.

2. *Growth of a wage-labor force.* This development has resulted in the proletarianization of substantial numbers of Africans, which has weakened communal or lineage responsibility and rendered those concerned vulnerable to economic exploitation and grievances.

3. *Rise of a new middle class.* Laissez-faire economics and African enterprise, coupled with opportunities for university and professional education, have been factors contributing to the growth of a middle class. This class is most advanced in Senegal, the Gold Coast, and Southern Nigeria, where it has developed despite successive displacement or frustration by the intrusion of Levantines and the monopolistic practices of European firms.

B. Sociological[17]

1. *Urbanization.* The concentration of relatively large numbers of Africans in urban centers to meet the labor demands of European enterprise has loosened kinship ties, accelerated social communication between "detribalized" ethnic groups, and, in general, contributed to "national" integration.

2. *Social mobility.* The European-imposed *pax,* coupled with the development of communications and transport, has provided the framework for travel, the growth of an internal exchange economy, and sociopolitical reintegration.

3. *Western education.* This has provided certain of the inhabitants of a given territory with a common lingua franca; with the knowledge and tools to acquire status and prestige and to fulfill aspirations within the new social structure; and with some of the ideas and values by which alien rule and colonialism could be attacked. It has been through Western education that the African has encountered the scientific method and the idea of progress with their activistic implications, namely, an awareness of alternatives and the conviction that man can creatively master and shape his own destiny.

C. Religious and Psychological[18]

1. *Christian evangelization.* The conscious Europeanization pursued by Christian missionary societies has been a frontal assault upon traditional religious systems and moral sanctions. Moreover, the Christian doctrine of equality and human brotherhood challenged the ethical assumptions of imperialism.

2. *Neglect or frustration of Western-educated elements.* Susceptibility to psychological grievance is most acute among the more acculturated Africans. Social and economic discrimination and the stigma of inferiority and backwardness have precipitated a passionate quest for equality and modernity, and latterly self-government. Rankling memories of crude, arrogant, or insulting treatment by a European have frequently been the major wellspring of racial bitterness and uncompromising nationalism.

D. Political

1. *Eclipse of traditional authorities.* Notwithstanding the British policy of indirect rule, the European superstructure and forces of modernity have tended to weaken the traditional powers of indigenous authorities and thereby to render less meaningful precolonial sociopolitical units as objects of loyalty and attachment. There has been what Professor Daryll

Forde calls a "status reversal"; that is, as a result of the acquisition by youth of Western education and a command over Western techniques in all fields, there has been "an increasing transfer of command over wealth and authority to younger and socially more independent men at the expense of traditional heads."[19]

2. *Forging of new "national" symbols.* The "territorialization" of Africa by the European powers has been a step in the creation of new nations, not only through the erection of boundaries within which the intensity of social communication and economic interchange has become greater than across territorial borders, but also as a consequence of the imposition of a common administrative superstructure, a common legal system, and in some instances common political institutions which have become symbols of territorial individuality.[20]

These are a few of the principal factors in the European presence which have contributed to the rise of nationalism. As any casual observer of African developments is aware, however, there have been and are marked areal differences in the overt manifestation of nationalism. Such striking contrasts as the militant Convention People's party of the Gold Coast, the conservative Northern People's Congress of Nigeria, the pro-French orientation of the African editors of *Présence Africaine,* the cautious African editors of *La Voix du Congolais,* and the terroristic Mau Mau of Kenya are cases in point.

There are a number of explanations for these areal variations. One relates to the degree of acculturation in an area. This is a reflection of the duration and intensity of contact with European influences. The contrast between the advanced nationalism of the British West Coast and of Senegal and the nascent nationalism of British and French Central Africa is partly explicable on this basis.

A second explanation lies in the absence or presence of alien settlers. On this score the settler-free British West Coast is unique when contrasted to the rest of Africa. The possibility of a total fulfillment of nationalist objectives (i.e., *African* self-government) has been a powerful psychological factor which partly explains the confident and buoyant expectancy of West Coast nationalists. On the other hand, as previously noted, the tendencies toward accommodation or terrorism in the white-settler areas is a reflection of the absence of such moderating expectancy.

Certain African groups exposed to the same forces of acculturation and the same provocation have demonstrated radically different reactions. The

Kikuyu versus the Masai peoples of Kenya, the Ibo versus the Hausa peoples of Nigeria, and the Creole and Mende of Sierra Leone are cases in point. It is suggested that the dynamism, militancy, and nationalist élan of the Ibo peoples of Nigeria are rooted partly in certain indigenous Ibo culture traits (general absence of chiefs, smallness in scale, and the democratic character of indigenous political organization, emphasis upon achieved status, and individualism). Much of the same might be said for the Kikuyu peoples of Kenya.

Differing colonial policies constitute another cause of these areal differences. Nationalism is predominantly a phenomenon of British Africa, and to a lesser extent of French Africa. Apart from the influence of the foregoing historical, sociological, and cultural variables, this fact, in the case of British Africa, is explained by certain unique features of British colonial policy.

It was inevitable that Britain, one of the most liberal colonial powers in Africa, should have reaped the strongest nationalist reaction. A few of the principal features of British policy which have stimulated nationalism deserve mention.

1. *Self-government as the goal of policy.* Unlike the French and Portuguese who embrace their African territories as indivisible units of the motherland, or the Belgians who until recently have been disinclined to specify the ultimate goals of policy, the British have remained indiscriminately loyal to the Durham formula.[21] In West Africa, this has enthroned the African nationalists; in Central and East Africa, the white settlers.

2. *Emphasis upon territorial individuality.* More than any other colonial power, the British have provided the institutional and conceptual framework for the emergence of nations. Decentralization of power, budgetary autonomy, the institution of territorial legislative councils and other "national" symbols—all have facilitated the conceptualization of a "nation."[22]

3. *Policy on missionaries and education.* The comparative freedom granted missionaries and the laissez-faire attitude toward education, and particularly postprimary education, has distinguished and continues to distinguish British policy sharply from non-British Africa.

4. *Neglect, frustration, and antagonism of educated elite.* Not only have more British Africans been exposed to higher education, but the British government until recently remained relatively indifferent to the claims and aspirations of this class, which forms the core of the nationalist movements.

5. *Freedom of nationalist activity.* The *comparative* freedom of activity (speech, association, press, and travel abroad) which British Africans have

enjoyed—within clearly defined limits and varying according to the presence of white settlers—has been of decisive importance. It is doubtful whether such militant nationalists as Wallace-Johnson of Sierra Leone, Prime Minister Kwame Nkrumah of the Gold Coast, Dr. Nnamdi Azikiwe of Nigeria, Jomo Kenyatta of Kenya, and Dauti Yamba of the Central African Federation, could have found the same continuous freedom of movement and activity in Belgian, Portuguese, and French Africa as has been their lot in British Africa.[23]

All of this suggests that African nationalism is not merely a peasant revolt. In fact, as already noted, nationalism where it is most advanced has been sparked and led by the so-called detribalized, Western-educated, middle-class intellectuals and professional Africans; by those who in terms of improved status and material standards of living have benefited most from colonialism; in short, by those who have come closest to the Western world but have been denied entry on full terms of equality. From this comparatively affluent—but psychologically aggrieved—group have come the organizers of tribal associations, labor unions, cooperative groups, farmers' organizations, and, more recently, nationalist movements. They are the Africans whom British policy has done most to create and least to satiate.[24]

This brief and selective treatment of a few of the factors which have contributed to the African nationalist awakening suggests certain avenues which might be profitably explored and more fully developed by subsequent research. Specifically, what is the relationship between the nature and intensity of nationalism and the degree of urbanization, the degree of commercialization of agriculture, and the size and geographical distribution of the wage-labor force and salariat? In short, what is the causal connection between "detribalization" and nationalism? Certain aspects of such an inquiry could be subjected to statistical analysis, but the results could only be suggestive, and in some instances might be positively deceptive. In the case of urbanization, for example, the highly urbanized and acculturated Yoruba peoples of Nigeria for nearly a decade lagged far behind the Ibo peoples in nationalist vigor and élan. Ibadan, the largest urban center in Tropical Africa, has been until recently one of the most politically inert towns of Nigeria. Again, in terms of the proletarianization of labor and urbanization resulting from European industrialism and commercial activity, the Belgian Congo is one of the most advanced territories, but one in which nationalism is least in evidence.[25] Freetown, Sierra Leone, one of the oldest nontraditional urban centers, became a haven of respectability and conservatism, being eclipsed by the less developed Protectorate in the push toward nationalist objectives. Urbanization has been an im-

Table 1. Commercialization and Nationalism in Certain African Territories

	Percentage of Cultivated Land Used by Africans for Commercial Production (1947–1950)[a]	*African Wage Earners as Percentage of Total African Population (1950)*[b]	*Degree of Overt Nationalism*
Gold Coast	75%	9.0%	Advanced
Belgian Congo	42	7.6	None
Nigeria	41	1.2	Advanced
Uganda	33	3.9	Nascent
Kenya	7	7.6	Nascent

[a]Source: E. A. Keukjian, "Commercializing Influence of the Development of Exports on Indigenous Agricultural Economics in Tropical Africa," unpub. diss. (Harvard Univ., June 1953); United Nations, Economic and Social Council (15th session) *World Economic Situation, Aspects of Economic Development in Africa.* New York, Document E/2377, March 20, 1953.

[b]Source: United Nations, Department of Economic Affairs. *Review of Economic Conditions in Africa (Supplement to World Economic Report, 1949–50).* New York, Document E/1910/Add.1 Rev.1-ST/ECA/9/Add.1, April, 1951, p. 76.

portant ingredient in the nationalist awakening, but it has been a certain type of urban development—mainly the impersonal and heterogeneous "new towns"—which has occurred in conjunction with other equally decisive factors.

In the case of the relationship between the degree of commercialization of land and labor and the degree of nationalism, the figures set forth for the Gold Coast in table 1 suggest either a causal connection or a parallel development. Yet in turning to similar figures for other territories—especially the Belgian Congo and Nigeria—it is clear that the relationship between commercialization and nationalism, important though it may be, must be considered and interpreted in the light of other variables.

Again, the fact that the nationalist movements have been organized and led by intellectuals and the so-called middle class suggests a relationship between nationalism and the number of Africans with higher education, the size of per capita income, the degree of the individualization of land tenure, the size of middle-class and professional groups (i.e., independent traders, produce middlemen, farmers employing labor, druggists, lorry owners, lawyers, doctors, etc.), and the degree of vertical mobility with-

Table 2. Christianity and Nationalism in Certain African Territories

	Percentage of Christians to Total Population	*Percentage of Protestants to All Christians*	*Percentage of Catholics to All Christians*	*Degree of Overt Nationalism*
Belgian Congo	37%	29%	71%	None
Nyasaland	26	49	51	Nascent
Gold Coast	15	58	42	Advanced
Angola	15	22	78	None
Kenya	10	51	49	Nascent
Nigeria	5	67	33	Advanced

Source: *World Christian Handbook* (London, 1949).

in the emergent socioeconomic structure. In any event, the insights of an economist are indispensable for a complete anatomy of African nationalism.

The Christian missionaries have been blamed frequently for their ruthless assault upon native religious systems and the thoroughgoing Europeanization, conscious or implicit, in their evangelization. This has suggested the formula: missionaries—"detribalization"—nationalism. Yet the postwar figures shown in table 2 do not bear out this assumption.[26] Missionaries have been important catalytic agents in the transformation of African societies, but the causal connection between their activities and nationalist assertion cannot be established by mere quantitative analysis. The figures in table 2 hint at a possible causal relationship between preponderant Protestant evangelization and advanced nationalism (viz., Gold Coast and Nigeria) and preponderant Catholic evangelization and the absence of nationalism (viz., Portuguese Angola and the Belgian Congo). Yet this connection must be examined in the light of other relevant factors, such as the degree of control and direction extended to missionary societies by colonial governments; the freedom allowed such societies to establish schools—particularly secondary schools—and to determine the curriculum; the tolerance accorded antiwhite or anticolonial sects (e.g., the Jehovah's Witnesses are permitted in most of British Africa but proscribed in non-British Africa); the latitude allowed African sects of a syncretistic, revivalistic, or puritanical character; the extent to which evangelical bodies have *Africanized* their church organization, the priesthood, and the propagation of the gospel; and, finally, the strength of Islam.

The corrosive influence of Western education has been a significant ingredient in the rise of nationalism. Yet the Belgian Congo claims a higher percentage of literacy than any other colonial territory in Africa.[27] In order to establish a relationship we must move beyond the superficial analysis of literacy statistics and ask the following questions:

1. *The nature of the curriculum.* Has it been and is it literary and based upon the model of a European grammar school, or is it practical and designed to train the student to be a good farmer, artisan, or clerk in European employ, and incidentally to limit his sophistication and contact with unsettling ideas? Is instruction conducted in the vernacular or in a European language?

2. *Opportunities for postprimary education.* Are secondary schools (particularly those operated by missionary societies or by enterprising and nationalist-minded Africans such as Eyo Ita in Nigeria or Jomo Kenyatta in Kenya) allowed to mushroom into existence, or are they carefully planned and rigidly controlled by the colonial government as to both number and curriculum? What are the opportunities for study in universities abroad? What is the latitude granted students to determine their own careers? Here we touch upon a crucial factor: in 1945, Freetown, Sierra Leone, and Lagos, Nigeria, each had more Western-type secondary schools than all of the non-British territories in Africa combined. In 1952 over four thousand Africans from British territories were studying in universities and technical schools abroad and nearly one thousand in territorial universities in Africa, whereas only a handful had such opportunity or inclination in Belgian and Portuguese Africa. This is in part a reflection of the existence of a larger African middle class in British Africa, but it is also the result of the unique British attitude regarding the relationship between higher education and the emergent African leadership. French policy and practice, despite differing assumptions, most closely approximate those of the British.[28]

3. *Openings of careers for the talented.* The stability of any political or social order is determined by this factor. Is there any planned relationship between the output of the schools and opportunities for satisfying employment or careers? In French and Belgian Africa, colonial governments have maintained a stringent control over the supply-demand situation as between postprimary schools and the requirements of government and the developing economy. In British Africa there are hundreds of thousands of unemployed or underemployed "Standard VI" boys clustered in the coastal towns and urban centers of the interior.

The most potent instrument used in the propagation of nationalist ideas and racial consciousness has been the African-owned nationalist press. In Nigeria alone nearly one hundred newspapers or periodicals have been published by Africans since the British intrusion, of which twelve dailies and fourteen weeklies—all African owned—are currently in circulation. The crucial role performed in the nationalist awakening by African journalistic enterprise on the British West Coast is well known.[29] Until the publication of *Afrique Noire* (organ of the Rassemblement Démocratique Africain of French West Africa) there was nothing in non-British Africa which even closely approximated this development. And even this journal is no match for the pungent criticism and racial consciousness one finds in the pages of Dr. Nnamdi Azikiwe's *West African Pilot* in Nigeria.[30] Needless to say, the nationalist press is one of our major sources of data regarding nationalist motivation, objectives, and organization. It is not the number of newspapers published which is significant, but rather the volume of circulation and areal distribution, the news and editorial content and the nature of the appeal, the types of readers, the existence of competitive papers sponsored by colonial governments, the financial stability of the paper, and other factors which would reflect its impact and influence upon the ideas, aspirations, and activities of those literate groups predisposed toward nationalism.

These are but a few of the more important factors in the rise of nationalism which require evaluation and weighting before the student of comparative colonial nationalism can go beyond the mere description of the history and anatomy of a particular nationalist movement. There is great danger in doing a disservice to scholarly research in Africa if one generalizes on the basis of observations made and data assembled in one territory. As has been suggested, there are certain general predisposing and precipitating causes of modern nationalism which are applicable to the whole continent; yet once these are mentioned, it is necessary to examine each area of nationalist activity for that special combination of factors which explains the origin, strength, and orientation of its nationalist movement.

Factors Conditioning Nationalist Development

Normally, a colonial nationalist movement directs its efforts toward the attainment of two main objectives: (1) the achievement of self-government and (2) the creation of a cultural or political sense of nationality and unity within the boundaries of the area of the nation to be. Nationalists are obliged to adopt the second objective because imperial powers either did not or could not establish political boundaries which embraced only one self-conscious effort to build nations. The nationalist dilemma is that in most cases pursuit of the primary goal (self-government) lessens the likelihood of achieving the secondary goal (cultural and political unity).

Put another way, the drive behind African nationalism in many instances is not the consciousness of belonging to a distinct politicocultural unit which is seeking to protect or assert itself, but rather it is the movement of racially conscious modernists seeking to create new political and cultural nationalities out of the heterogeneous peoples living within the artificial boundaries imposed by the European master. Their task is not only to conduct a successful political revolution and capture power, but also the painful job of national political integration. And, as Professor Crane Brinton has shown, the lessons of history are that nation-building is the product of both consent and coercion, and usually the latter.[31] It is the colonial power, of course, which has had a monopoly over the means of coercion.

The major factor conditioning the development of a particular nationalist movement, therefore, is the degree of internal politicocultural unity, tolerance, or compatibility amongst the peoples of the area moving into its national era. Disunities can exist in a given territory for a variety of reasons:

1. Traditional precolonial hostilities and cultural incompatibilities, such as exist between the Kikuyu and Masai peoples of Kenya, or the Ibo and the Tiv peoples of Nigeria. In some instances these have been exacerbated as a result of imperial policies, in others as a consequence of the mere fact of lumping them together and endeavoring to impose territorial uniformity.

2. Tensions between groups resulting from unevenness in development, acculturation, and the acquisition of modernity. These can be the product of original cultural differences (i.e., the variations between groups in their receptivity and adaptability to modernity—e.g., the Ibo and Hausa); historical circumstances (i.e., differences in the duration and intensity of the European impact—e.g., the Creoles of Freetown vs. the Mende peoples of the Protectorate of Sierra Leone); or of constitutional reforms pointing toward African self-government. One could argue that Ibo-Yoruba hostility in Nigeria is the product of all three factors. Just as the advance toward independence precipitated a cleavage between Muslims and Hindus in India, so has the development of nationalism and the move toward self-government in Africa brought to light a multitude of disunities. Fear of domination by the more advanced and acculturated groups, European or African, is one obvious explanation.

3. Tensions between the westernized elite—the nationalists—and the traditionalists and the masses. This nationalist disability has tended to be exaggerated in the past, usually by imperial spokesmen endeavoring to repudiate the nationalists or to isolate them from the traditionalists. The

intensity of the cleavage varies widely according to circumstances. In several areas such as the Protectorate of Sierra Leone, Northern Territories of the Gold Coast, Western and Northern Nigeria, amongst the Kikuyu in Kenya, and in Northern Rhodesia and Nyasaland, the educated nationalists and some leading traditionalists have cooperated in varying degrees.

4. Differences within the ranks of the westernized elite. These disagreements—and one is struck by their persistence, strength, and virulence—may arise from several causes, including normal competition for power and prestige or honest differences over aims, timing, or methods to be employed in the nationalist drive. Such differences as separate Messrs. Fily-Dabo Sissoko and Mamadou Konate in the French Sudan; Lamine Gueye and Léopold Senghor in Senegal; Félix Houphouet-Boigny and Kouame Binzème in the Ivory Coast; Prime Minister Kwame Nkrumah and Dr. J. B. Danquah in Gold Coast; the Sardauna of Sokoto, Obafemi Awolowo, and Dr. Nnamdi Azikiwe in Nigeria; Eliud Mathu and Jomo Kenyatta in Kenya; and Harry Nkumbula and Godwin Lewanika in Central Africa have very materially affected the course and strength of nationalism in the territories concerned.

These nationalist disabilities are the product of a complex mixture of hard historical and cultural facts, of changes introduced and differentials created by the Western intrusion, as well as of provocations of the nationalist drive itself. The success of any nationalist movement will in large measure depend upon the extent to which these internal tensions are softened or dissipated. The latter will depend, in turn, upon the degree of repressive opposition, or unwitting or intentional cooperation, of colonial governments; upon the development of panterritorial political associations, the membership of which is rooted in all ethnic groups and in which there is free vertical mobility into the "upper crust" which that membership constitutes; upon the emergence of panterritorial economic-interest groups (e.g., middle-class associations or labor organizations); and upon many other sociological processes (out-group marriages, commensality, etc.) which Professor Karl W. Deutsch has suggested are essential building blocks of any new national community.[32]

It would be naive and unhistorical to argue that a large measure of politicocultural integration is required—as distinguished from being desirable—in order for a nationalist movement to succeed in wresting self-government from an imperial power. Most successful colonial nationalist movements have been organized and led by small minorities which have been able either to gain the support of the masses or to capitalize upon their inertia and apathy. It would be unrealistic, however, to contemplate the success of a movement which did not have at least a minimum of unity or tolerance within the "upper crust," even though it be of the sort displayed by the unstable truces negotiated from time to time between the Sardauna of Sokoto, Mr. Obafemi Awolowo, and Dr. Nnamdi Azikiwe, the regional leaders in Nigeria.

Some of these forces contributing toward integration are measurable and provide rough indices upon which the research scholar can base predictions of the development of a particular nationalist movement. In an interesting new theory regarding the growth of nations, Professor Deutsch has suggested certain criteria which might be profitably employed in seeking to determine the prospects of success of a nationalist movement in its nation-building endeavors.[33] His central thesis is that cases of successful political integration in history show a number of patterns which seem to recur. As he puts it, a nation "is the result of the transformation of people, or of several ethnic elements, in the process of social mobilization." The prospects of success are indicated by the completeness of that transformation and the intensity of social mobilization around the symbols of the new national community. A nation is not only a subjective affirmation of will of zealous nationalists; it is also the product of the operation of powerful objective forces, several of which have been mentioned.

Thus far it has been assumed that the leaders of nationalist movements in Africa will seek to build new national communities out of the diverse human materials located within the artificial boundaries of the existing colonial territories. This was precisely what happened in Latin America (Spanish imperial provinces), in the Middle East (European and Turkish regions), and in Southeast Asia (Dutch Indonesia, Burma, and in a qualified way, British India). In the case of British Africa, where nationalism is most advanced, this same tendency for nationalism to follow boundaries established by the imperial power rather than those coincident with precolonial sociopolitical groups is in evidence (e.g., Gold Coast and Nigeria). On the other hand, in many areas the situation is still relatively fluid. Togoland nationalism has been predominantly an Ewe affair, and the Ewes are a transterritorial group stretching from the Gold Coast to Dahomey. Separatist sentiment in Northern Nigeria is an example, *par excellence*, of incomplete social mobilization. This, when coupled with growing Yoruba and Ibo self-consciousness, suggests that earlier pan-Nigerian nationalism may be eclipsed and Nigeria may ultimately become three or more states. Until the recent decision to give the Southern Cameroons greater autonomy within the emergent Federation of Nigeria, Cameroonian nationalists were wavering between remaining an integral part of the Eastern Region of Nigeria, or seceding and joining with the nationalists in the French Cameroons in an endeavor to create a Kamerun nation based upon the artificial boundaries of the short-lived German Kamerun.[34] In Kenya, Mau Mau and all earlier protonationalist movements have been predominantly Kikuyu endeavors, even though the name Kenya has been employed. In Tanganyika, the Chagga Cooperative movement may be the basis for a Chagga separatism; and in Uganda, it is questionable whether pan-Uganda integrative forces can erase the "national" separatism implicit in the Buganda Kingdom. Again, in Central Africa, will the territorial separatism symbolized by the Northern Rhodesian and Nyasaland National Congresses be eclipsed by the common sentiment and institutions growing out of the new Federation?

In the case of French Africa, dissimilarities in colonial policy (i.e., assimilation and direct rule) have tended to produce a somewhat different situation. Yet since the reforms of 1946, as a result of which each of the territories of the two federations of French West Africa and French Equatorial Africa received their own representative assemblies, territorial nationalist movements have tended to eclipse the pan-French African Rassemblement Démocratique Africain in much the same fashion as Nigerian, Gold Coastian, and Sierra Leonian nationalist movements have replaced the earlier National Congress of British West Africa. Thus one finds the Parti Républicain de Dahomey, Parti Progressiste Sudanais, Union Démocratique du Tchad, and similar organizations in each of the territories. The future "national" orientation of nationalist forces in French Africa would seem to depend upon the extent to which pan-Federation forces and institutions, such as Grands Conseils, or the assimilationist forces of the French Union, such as the metropolitan parties and labor movements projected overseas, operate to retard the growth of territorial symbols and sentiment. One thing, however, seems certain: French Africa, because of the French policy of assimilation and direct rule, is less likely to encounter such movements as the Egbe Omo Oduduwa of the Nigerian Yorubas, the Kikuyu Central Association in Kenya, and the Bataka movement in Uganda.

In general, it would seem that where nationalism manifests itself in considerable strength, it is evidence that disintegration of the old and social mobilization around the symbols of the new order have occurred on a scale sufficient to weaken or destroy attachments and loyalties of the nationalists to precolonial sociopolitical units, either because they have been crushed and are beyond memory or because they are unattractive or manifestly unsuitable as "nations" in the modern world of nation-states. The European presence has done much toward the creation of new nations, the "national" sentiment of the nationalists being a reflection of this.

A few of the many factors which might be observed and evaluated in order to determine the probable success, as well as the territorial implications, of an African nationalist movement or nation-building endeavor are as follows:[35] (1) the degree of internal social mobility, economic interchange and interdependence, intermarriage and commensality, and the intensity and level of social communication among the ethnic groups comprising a given territory; (2) the location of population clusters and "core areas," as well as of "subnational" regions of more intense economic interchange or of cultural focus; (3) the powers and functions of "subnational" political institutions (i.e., regional, tribal, etc.), and the degree of meaningful participation in them by the Western-educated elements; (4) the rate at which "national" institutions and activities are capable of attracting and absorbing new social strata from all ethnic groups into the "national" life (e.g., the ethnic composition of the central administrative and technical services); (5) the centrality and nationalness of educational institutions, particularly the professional schools and universities; (6) the degree of panterritorial circulation of nationalist newspapers and literature and the extent to which these play up "national" events and personalities; (7) the differentials in the material development, the per capita income and wealth, the acquisition of modern skills and knowledge, and the concentration and capacity for accumulation of capital amongst the different subnational areas and ethnic groups;[36] (8) the ethnic makeup of the Western-educated categories, and particularly of the active membership of nationalist or protonationalist groups; (9) the development and extent of usage of a transtribal panterritorial language, be it English, French, Portuguese, Swahili, or Hausa; (10) the compatibility of the "detribalized" basic personality types produced by the indigenous cultures; (11) the extent to which the territory concerned embraces total cultural groups, or, put another way, the degree to which artificial colonial boundaries have bifurcated ethnic groups whose division may be the source of later irredentism; and (12) the rapport between the Western-educated nationalist elements and the traditionalists, including the existence of nativistic tensions or economic grievances which the nationalists could manipulate or exploit in their mobilization of mass support.

Results obtained from inquiries along these lines would go far to explain the present orientation of a nationalist movement as well as possible future trends. And yet an emphatic note of caution should be sounded: objective forces of integration and disintegration are powerful determinants in the nation-building process, but so also are subjective factors.[37] By all laws of geography and economics Northern Ireland should belong to Eire, and East Pakistan to the Republic of India—but they do not. By the same laws, the Gambia should belong to Senegal, French Guinea to Sierra Leone and

Liberia, Mozambique to the Central African Federation, and so forth; and yet present trends suggest that such will not be the case. The principal sources currently operating to shape Africa's emergent nations are either tribalism or a nationalism following artificial imperial boundaries; and, with few exceptions, neither of these is directed toward the creation of political units which the geographer or economist would classify as ideal. In this respect, of course, Africa is not unique.

The foregoing raises the crucial question of whether it is possible for the peoples of Africa, in their own interest, to avoid the balkanization implicit in the full application of the national principle to their continent. So long as the rest of the world is organized according to that principle, and so long as the national idea universally embodies aspirations which cannot be satisfied by other forms of human organization, the answer would seem to be in the negative. The quest for racial equality and acceptance is as important an ingredient in the African revolt as is the desire to determine one's own destiny. Rightly or wrongly, self-government within the confines of the sovereign nation-state has become the supreme symbol of the equality of peoples. The only possible alternative would be broader Euro-African political groupings or self-governing plural societies in which emergent African leaders could play what they would feel to be an equal role. In the light of the persistence of national self-determination as a symbol, and particularly in view of the growing strength and contagion of African nationalism, the future of such multiracial experiments will depend in a large measure upon the rapidity with which European governments and leaders provide for such a role.

Special Problems of Research into African Nationalism

There is perhaps no other type of research venture capable of evoking stronger feeling than an inquiry into colonial nationalism. The word nationalism in a colonial milieu has tended to be treated as the equivalent of sedition, or even treason. And this for good reason: by definition, colonial nationalists are seeking to bring about a radical alteration in the power structure, namely, to evict the imperial power and to enthrone themselves. From the moment it makes its presence known, therefore, a nationalist movement is, in effect, engaged in a civil war with the colonial administration, the constitutionality of its methods varying according to the liberality of the colonial regime and the moderation of the nationalist leaders.

As regards colonial officialdom, an American undertaking a study of

African nationalism is handicapped by the fact that in large measure the African nationalist awakening is the product of American influences. Since the turn of the century, American Negro religious sects have contributed no little to religious secessionism, particularly in South and West Africa. The Garveyism of the early 1920s had an influence among sophisticated Africans which has tended to be overlooked or minimized. Since 1919 a growing number of American Negro intellectuals have taken an increasingly militant stand on African colonialism. Anti-imperialist sentiment in the United States, especially during World War II, was the source of considerable inspiration and delight to budding African nationalists, as well as the cause of no little acrimony between wartime allies. The Atlantic Charter, the Four Freedoms, and public statements by Mr. Willkie and President Roosevelt have bulked large in postwar African nationalist literature. The most important American contribution, however, has been the impact of our culture upon African students who have studied in America. Many of the important pioneers in the African awakening were profoundly affected by their American experience. Of this group the late Dr. J. E. K. Aggrey and Prime Minister Kwame Nkrumah from the Gold Coast, and Professor Eyo Ita and Dr. Nnamdi Azikiwe from Nigeria are the most prominent and best known. During World War II the number of African students in America was less than twenty-five; since 1945 it has increased to over five hundred. With few exceptions these students have been and are strong nationalists, many of them having become leaders upon their return to Africa. In the eyes of colonial officialdom, therefore, an American inquiry into nationalism tends to raise certain doubts.

There has been a tendency in the past for American visitors making quick tours of Africa to rely mainly upon the white colonial administration for an appraisal of nationalist sentiment and activity. This is unfortunate in many respects. In the first place, it is most likely that any information bearing on nationalism is locked up in classified files. Second, most colonial administrators have tended to be antinationalists, even though many in British West Africa have adapted themselves to working with nationalists toward a mutually agreed goal of effective self-government. Their evaluation of nationalism is bound to be colored by their preconceptions and vested interests or by their honest fears regarding the welfare of the bush peasant, for whom they tend to have a preference and a strong paternal affection. Third, circumstances have tended to place them too close to events or too far removed from the people. Their growing preoccupation with headquarters administration and development schemes, the social impediments, created frequently by the presence of white wives and families, to effective and continuous contact with the masses, and almost total lack of rapport or confidence between nationalists and administrators, have given the latter many blind spots. Their past miscalculations of nationalist strength and trends tend to confirm this. In short, instead of being used as informants, a role they are not anxious to perform, they should be objects of study. Their fears, their adjustments, and their efforts to suppress, retard, manipulate, or encourage nationalism are all relevant in a complete study of the many interacting factors present in a nationalist situation.

Unlike the field anthropologist, who consciously seeks to work among the traditionalists, the student of political nationalism is concerned mainly with the attitudes, activities, and status of a political nationalist-minded Western-educated elite. Here one is in a world very different from that of officialdom or the traditionalists. It is a world of great idealism, crusading zeal, and high resolve, as well as one of suspicion, hypersensitivity, and exaggeration. It has its careerists and opportunists and its chronic nonconformists; but it also has its emergent statesmen, its enterprising industrialists, and its distinguished scholars. Only here can one get a partial glimpse into the depth of nationalist feeling, the sources of inspiration and ideas, and the key elements in nationalist motivations. Yet there are distinct limitations to the interview technique, not the least important of which is the possession of a white skin. Moreover, a colonial nationalist movement must have its *arcana* as well as its propaganda.

In the quest for knowledge regarding African nationalism, the most fruitful as well as unprovocative avenues to explore are those already indicated in earlier sections. African nationalism is something more than the activities of a few disgruntled journalists and frustrated intellectuals to whom Lord Lugard referred in his *Dual Mandate*. It is the inevitable end product of the impact of Western imperialism and modernity upon African societies; it is also the inevitable assertion by the Africans of their desire to shape their own destiny. Imperial systems are disintegrating, new nation-states are emerging, and new forms of political organization transcending the national state are under experiment. These political aspects of African nationalism, however, are but the surface symptoms of a great ferment about which we know very little. The study and analysis of the many complex factors in this unfolding drama provide not only a stimulating challenge to the social sciences, but also a compelling invitation to greater interdisciplinary cooperation.

NOTES

1. Two notable prewar exceptions were Professor Raymond Leslie Buell and Dr. Ralph J. Bunche.

2. As an excellent example of the application of the insights of anthropology to the problems of political development in this area, see William R. Bascom, "West and Central Africa," in Ralph Linton, ed., *Most of the World* (New York: Columbia University Press, 1949), pp. 331–405. For a historian's appraisal, see Vernon McKay, "Nationalism in British West Africa," *Foreign Policy Reports*, 24 (March 15, 1948), pp. 2–11.

3. M. Fortes and E. E. Evans-Pritchard, eds., *African Political Systems* (New York: Oxford University Press, 1940), pp. 4 ff. Insofar as traditional concepts and methods are concerned, ethnocentrism has been freely confessed by political scientists in recent self-criticism. See David Easton, *The Political System* (New York: Alfred J. Knopf, 1953), pp. 33 ff.; also "Report of the Inter-University Summer Seminar on Comparative Politics, Social Science Research Council," *American Political Science Review*, 47 (September 1953), pp. 642–643. Amongst the modernists in political science one finds the argument that the political scientist should not be rejected too readily since he has developed skills and acquired insights that might well shed new light on the political process and pattern of government of preliterate societies after the anthropologist has exhausted his resources. Another argument, rather different, is that such societies might profitably be regarded as microcosms in which the political scientist can discern with greater clarity the essentials of government that might be obscured in the more complex studies, especially in terms of their implications for policy formulation. See Ithiel de Sola Pool, "Who Gets Power and Why," *World Politics*, 2 (October 1949), pp. 120–134.

4. Arnold Toynbee, *The World and the West* (New York: Oxford University Press, 1953), pp. 71 ff. It is difficult to accept without qualification Professor Toynbee's argument that the "national state" was a "spontaneous native growth" in Europe. One could argue that the centrally minded, nation-building elites of emergent Asia and Africa are but the present-day counterparts of the centralizing monarchs of early modern Europe.

5. Royal Institute of International Affairs, *Nationalism* (London: Oxford University Press, 1939), pp. 1–7; Karl W. Deutsch, *Nationalism and Social Communication* (New York: John Wiley & Sons, 1953), pp. 1–14.

6. Nativism is here used in its broad and universal sense, as defined by the late Professor Ralph Linton: "Any conscious, organized attempt on the part of a society's members to revive or perpetuate selected aspects of its culture." See his "Nativistic Movements," *American Anthropologist*, 45 (April-June 1943), p. 230. The concept thus includes traditionalist movements in either the European or non-European world. This point is stressed because of the understandable sensitivity of many educated Africans to the root word "native," which as a result of the colonial experience tends to carry with it the connotation of inferiority. See also A. LeGrip, "Aspects actuels de L'Islam en A.O.F.," *L'Afrique et l'Asie*, no. 24 (1953),

pp. 6–20; Katesa Schlosser, *Propheten in Afrika* (Braunschweig: Albert Limbach Verlag, 1949).

7. Daniel Thwaite, *The Seething African Pot* (London: Constable, 1936), pp. 1–70; George Shepperson, "Ethiopianism and African Nationalism," *Phylon*, 14 (First Quarter 1953), pp. 9–18; Hilda Kuper, "The Swazi Reaction to Missions," *African Studies*, 5 (September 1946), pp. 177–188; Jomo Kenyatta, *Facing Mount Kenya* (London: Martin, Secker & Warburg, 1953), pp. 269–279.

8. James S. Coleman, "The Role of Tribal Associations in Nigeria," *Proceedings of the Second Annual Conference of the West African Institute of Social and Economic Research, Ibadan, Nigeria, April, 1952* [Chapter 1, this volume; ed.]. See also *East Africa and Rhodesia*, October 5, 1951, p. 106: "Nairobi is the happy hunting ground for the organizers of tribal associations, as there are to be found in the city representatives of practically every tribe in East and Central Africa." Also K. A. Busia, *Report on a Social Survey of Takoradi-Sekondi* (Accra: Government Printer, 1950).

9. Most advanced amongst the Yoruba, Ibo, Ibibio, Ewe, Buganda, and Kikuyu peoples.

10. The difference between the goal orientations of the two categories of movements is partly the result of the objectives of differing colonial policies (i.e., the British policy of self-government and differentiation versus the French, Portuguese, and in a qualified sense the Belgian policies of assimilation and identity) and in part the result of the presence or absence of a settled white population. Confronted with the overwhelming obstacles to the full realization of African self-government, African leaders of the African Congress have tended not to define their ultimate objectives, preferring to act empirically. The strength and persistence of the automatic drive is reflected, however, in their reported attraction to the original Gore-Brown partition plan adopted by the European Confederate party. See David Cole, "How Strong is the African National Congress," *New Commonwealth*, 27 (January 4, 1954), p. 9.

11. For a variety of reasons these movements have thus far apparently accomplished little more than to dramatize their existence at infrequent ad hoc conferences. Until recently the initiative tended to be taken by Americans or West Indians of African descent (e.g., Marcus Garvey, W. E. B. DuBois, and George Padmore), although in the early 1920s there was a National Congress of British West Africa organized by the late Casely Hayford of the Gold Coast. Also, M. Blaise Diagne, a Senegalese, was President of the first Pan-African Congress in Paris in 1919. For recent pan-African nationalist activity in British West Africa, see *West Africa*, December 12, 1953, p. 1165; and for British Central Africa, see Cole, "How Strong is the African National Congress," p. 9.

12. See Ian Cunnison, "The Watchtower Assembly in Central Africa," *International Review of Missions*, 40 (October 1951), pp. 456–469.

13. Sir F. D. Lugard, *The Dual Mandate in British Tropical Africa* (Edinburgh, London: W. Blackwood & Sons, 1923), pp. 83 ff.

14. Nnamdi Azikiwe, *Renascent Africa* (Accra: The Author, 1937).

15. See Rosey E. Pool, "African Renaissance," *Phylon*, 14 (First Quarter 1953), pp. 5–8; Albert Maurice, "Union Africaine des Arts et des Lettres," *African Affairs*, 50 (July 1951), pp. 233–241; Alioune Diop, "Niam n'goura," *Présence Africaine*, no. 1 (November-December 1947), pp. 1–3. The cultural revival is the product of four forces: (1) reflection and introspection on the part of educated Africans, frequently those confronted with the stimulating contrasts of a foreign environment while abroad; (2) the American Negro renaissance which commenced in the 1920s; (3) encouragement and sponsorship of European governments and unofficial organizations such as the International African Institute; and (4) support of missionary societies such as the United Society for Christian Literature in the United Kingdom.

16. L. P. Mair, "The Growth of Economic Individualism in African Society," *Journal of the Royal African Society*, 33 (July 1934), pp. 261–273; Allan McPhee, *The Economic Revolution in British West Africa* (London: G. Routledge & Sons, 1926); G. Wilson, *An Essay on the Economics of Detribalization in Northern Rhodesia*, Part I (Livingstone: Rhodes-Livingstone Institute, 1941). Cf. Karl Polanyi, *Origins of Our Time* (London: V. Gollanz, 1946); P. C. Lloyd, "New Economic Classes in Western Nigeria," *African Affairs*, 52 (October 1953), pp. 327–334.

17. J. D. Rheinallt Jones, "The Effects of Urbanization in South and Central Africa," *African Affairs*, 52 (January 1953), pp. 37–44.

18. William Bascom, "African Culture and the Missionary," *Civilisations*, 3:4 (1953), pp. 491–501.

19. Daryll Forde, "The Conditions of Social Development in West Africa," *Civilisations*, 3:4 (1953), pp. 471–485.

20. See R. J. Harrison Church, *Modern Colonization* (London: Hutchinson's University Library, 1951), pp. 104 ff.; Robert Montagne, "The 'Modern State' in Africa and Asia," *The Cambridge Journal*, 5 (July 1952), pp. 583–602.

21. Regarding Belgian policy, see Pierre Wigny, "Methods of Government in the Belgian Congo," *African Affairs*, 50 (October 1951), pp. 310–317. Wigny remarks that "Belgians are reluctant to define their colonial policy. They are proud of their first realizations, and sure of the rightness of their intentions" (p. 311). Since this was written, there have been some very dramatic changes in Belgian policy, especially regarding the educated elite, the potential nationalists. The great debate in Belgian colonial circles on "le statut des Congolais civilisés" was terminated by four decrees of

May 17, 1952, according to which educated Congolese are assimilated to Europeans in civil law. Regarding Portuguese policy, see Marcelo Caetano, *Colonizing Traditions, Principles and Methods of the Portuguese* (Lisbon: Agência Geral do Ultramar, 1951). The keynote of the policy is the "spiritual assimilation" of the Africans to a "Portuguese nation dwelling in European, African, Asiatic and Indonesian Provinces." The African *civilisado* is thus a citizen of Portugal.

22. Partly in response to nationalist pressures, the French Government has recently initiated certain measures of financial devolution to French West Africa. See G. Gayet, "Autonomies financières françaises," *Civilisations*, 3:3 (1953), pp. 343–347. These measures may enhance the powers of the territorial assemblies to the point that the latter might ultimately become the foci for territorial nationalisms.

23. The stringent police measures adopted recently in Kenya and Nyasaland, the special press laws which have long been in effect in British East and Central Africa, and the obstacles to nationalist activity which have existed in the Muslim areas of Northern Nigeria do not necessarily invalidate this comparative historical generalization.

24. The thesis here is that there are at least four ingredients in the psychology of colonial nationalism, and that British policy in Africa has come closest toward inculcating or providing them: (1) an awareness of the existence or possibility of alternatives to the status quo, a state of mind produced by Western education and particularly by study and travel abroad; (2) an intense desire to change the status quo; (3) a system within which the major alternative to the status quo—self-government—has the status of legitimacy; and (4) an area of relative freedom in which that legitimate alternative may be pursued.

25. The Belgian policy of stabilization of labor in the urban centers of the Congo, in which 83 percent of the men have their families with them, is one of the several factors which may help to explain this.

26. *World Christian Handbook* (London: World Dominion Press, 1949).

27. United Nations, *Non-Self-Governing Territories*, vol. 3, *Special Study on Education* (January 1951), Document ST/TRI/SER.A./5/Add 2.

28. By decree of April 16, 1950, the Institut des Hautes Etudes was established at Dakar; and on January 1, 1952, there were 1,640 scholarship holders in continental France, of whom 572 were pursuing higher education; Roger Pons, "French Union," *Civilisations*, 3:4 (1953), pp. 575–583. On the British educational policy in Tropical Africa, see *African Education* (Oxford: The Nuffield Foundation and the Colonial Office, 1953). The Belgians within the past few years have dramatically reoriented their policy regarding higher education for the Congolese. Since 1952 Congo students have been admitted to the Albert I College at Leopoldville; the first Negro University of the Congo is scheduled for opening in 1954; and

recently the Belgian press has drawn attention to the admission to Louvain University of a Negro student from the Congo; Joseph M. Jadot, "Belgian Congo," *Civilisations*, 3:4 (1953), 599–602.

29. Compare with the number of African-owned-and-edited dailies and weeklies (combined total) in the following territories: *British Africa*: Gold Coast (17), Uganda (8), Sierra Leone (7), Gambia (3); *French West Africa* (10); and none, insofar as is known, in Belgian, Portuguese, or Spanish Africa, or in Kenya, the territories of the Central African Federation, or in the Union of South Africa.

30. On the other hand, there appears to be no newspaper in British West Africa comparable with the European-owned-and-edited journal of French West Africa entitled *Les Echos de l'A.O.F.*, which "week after week passionately attacks the administration." See Thomas Hodgkin, "The Metropolitan Axis," *West Africa*, January 9, 1954, p. 6.

31. Crane Brinton, *From Many One* (Cambridge: Harvard University Press, 1948).

32. Karl W. Deutsch, "The Growth of Nations," *World Politics*, 5 (January 1953), pp. 168–196.

33. Ibid.; see also Deutsch, *Nationalism and Social Communication*, pp. 81 ff.

34. *West Africa*, January 30, 1954, p. 87.

35. For several of the concepts used here the author is indebted to the works of Professor Karl W. Deutsch, previously cited; see especially his *Nationalism and Social Communication*.

36. It could be argued, for example, that apart from historical and cultural factors, the difference in the per capita income of the three regions of Nigeria (£26 for the Western Region, £16 for the Northern Region, and £23 for the Eastern Region) is of no little significance in the recent and current drive for greater regional autonomy. See A. R. Prest and I. G. Stewart, *The National Income of Nigeria*, abridged ed. (Lagos: Government Printer, 1954), pp. 14–16.

37. Given suitable conditions, including a politically favorable milieu and the proper techniques, there would seem to be no reason why subjective factors such as loyalties, attitudes, and attachments to national or subnational symbols, could not to some extent be measured.

3 Current Political Movements in Africa

One of the most striking features of the African political awakening has been the mushroom appearance of an unexpectedly large number and wide variety of sociopolitical movements and associations. Although these movements differ markedly in their degree of organization, solidarity, and objectives, there has been a tendency to lump them together indiscriminately into one of two categories. In the eyes of most African nationalists they are considered as simply different aspects—but emphatically integral parts—of a rational and single-minded "struggle for freedom"; whereas to many resident Europeans or colonial administrators they are regarded simply as either irrational and atavistic reversions to barbarism or as manifestations of manipulated discontent on the part of self-seeking and exploitative minorities of *déracinés*. It is the purpose of this essay to discuss and analyze briefly the origin, development, and differing characteristics of these movements and to note the impact they have had upon colonial policies.

Background to African Awakening

Most forms of politically relevant group activity in contemporary Africa are in one way or another the product of the stimulation or provocation of (1) the dynamism of the Idea of Progress, the processes of commercialization and industrialism, and other distinguishing attributes (that is, individualism, rationalism, and secularism) of that historical cluster of phenomena known as "Westernism"; and (2) the confusions, frustrations, and bitterness produced by the carriers of the "Western impact," a paternalistic

Reprinted from *The Annals of the American Academy of Political and Social Science, Contemporary Africa: Trends and Issues*, 298 (March 1955), pp. 95–108.

colonial system, an intensive and at times intolerant Christian evangelization, and comparatively unenlightened agents of Western economic enterprise. These two sets of factors, one stemming from the provocative challenge of a technologically advanced intrusive culture and the other from a variety of superimposed alien institutions, have combined to create social situations which lay the basis for the birth and development of political movements.

These "ripe" situations are distinguished by at least three special elements. One has been the staggering blow modernity has dealt the structure of authority, systems of belief, and the cohesiveness of traditional African societies. Indiscriminate missionary education, the relatively uncontrolled operation of Western economic forces, and the adaptability and impatient drive for self-transformation on the part of many African peoples have produced situations of profound disorganization, instability, tension, and insecurity. Another element has been the accumulation of both material and psychic grievances that have been and are bitter and pervasive. Some of these are the inevitable transition pains of societies undergoing rapid change. Others are natural human reactions to avoidable situations of hopelessness and denial arising from unimaginative colonial policies. Still others simply reflect an agonizing awareness by Africans of painful facts of life—that a deep gulf exists between African socioeconomic realities on the one hand and the new wants and aspirations generated by culture contact on the other. This despair is matched in intensity only by their passionate conviction that with African self-government and forced industrialization they can rapidly bridge the gap. Finally, there has been an upward thrust of new leadership cadres from the more westernized groups acutely distressed by their own insecurity and bitterly aggrieved over the disabilities and inequalities of alien rule.

PLAY OF EXTERNAL INFLUENCES

These situational factors of social disorganization, accumulated grievances, and the emergence of a new and claimant leadership are only part of the background; a variety of external influences have intruded or operated either to further ripen the situation or more particularly to inspire, assist, provide direction, or activate the emergent leadership cadres. The most important carriers of these influences have been (1) Africans who have traveled or resided abroad, especially as students at universities in Europe and the United States; (2) the printed word, particularly in the form of literature directed to target groups in Africa by interested organizations abroad as well as through the medium of the African-owned nationalist press; and (3) those non-African individuals and groups within and without Africa who for various reasons have undertaken to champion what they have claimed to be the cause or interests of the Africans.

Among the many sources from which influences have originated, four deserve special mention: the metropolitan country, the United States, Soviet Russia, and India. The role played by unofficial organizations and political parties of the metropolitan country in the African political awakening has been vastly underestimated. The activities of such groups as the Fabian Colonial Bureau, and later the Africa Bureau, have won for its leaders the affection of most African nationalists and the hostility of not a few administrators as well as of most of the white settlers of East and Central Africa. The current activities of the more militant Congress of Peoples Against Imperialism and the recently launched Movement for Colonial Freedom are representative of continuing stimulus provided by unofficial organizations in the United Kingdom to Africans temporarily resident there as well as in the African territories. A similar function has been performed by political parties and the labor federations in metropolitan France.

Unofficial organizations and influences operative in and from the United States have also played an important historical role. Nationalist leaders such as Premier Nnamdi Azikiwe (Nigeria), Prime Minister Kwame Nkrumah (Gold Coast), Dr. Hastings Banda (Nyasaland), Mr. Peter Mbiyu Koinange (Kenya), and Dr. E. B. Kalibala (Uganda), and scores of other political leaders and activists throughout British Africa are graduates of American universities. Many American religious sects (Negro and white), as well as militant Negro movements such as Marcus Garvey's Universal Negro Improvement Association (which still survives) and the procommunist Council on African Affairs, have also had their effect.

The Soviet Union has supported nationalist development in Africa as part of its global strategy to create situations of instability and weakness within the Western world, to train and indoctrinate communist leadership cadres with the expectation that by manipulating mass discontent and nationalist symbols they could seize power in African Soviet Republics, and, in general, to carry out Lenin's dictum to attack the West through its dependent territories. The instruments in this program have been many and varied. The seducement of African students in England and France by British and French communists has been the most direct. Other approaches have included the irresponsible use of United Nations organs to harass colonial powers and build up the image of the Soviet Union as savior of the colonial peoples, university scholarships or summer "vodka tours" to African students for study or travel behind the Iron Curtain, the establishment of liaison between procommunist international front organizations (for example, the World Federation of Trade Unions and the International Students Union) and African student groups and labor organizations, and the effort to feed propaganda through procommunist African newspapers or other literature outlets in Africa.

As a vanguard in the struggle against British colonialism, India has exerted a remarkable influence. It has been and remains a symbol of the successful achievement of independence, and success stories in situation of intense aspiration can serve as powerful stimuli. The Indian National Congress has been both an inspiration and the model for organization founders in Africa. Moreover, Indian minorities in South and East Africa, who continue to look to India for guidance, have had a very direct and important influence upon African political developments, including in some instances active organizational collaboration.

Here then were two sets of circumstances conducive to the appearance of political movements: (1) the prevalence among most African societies of what might be called "transitional crisis"—an exploitable and highly inflammatory condition marked by a sort of generalized malaise and sense of frustration, an instability of expectations, and a predisposition toward almost any form of action or radical change that promised tension release, direction and focus, and a set of apparently realizable goals; and (2) the play of a variety of special external influences which served to aggravate those situations and to inspire and agitate the minds of the new politically claimant elite.

PRECIPITATING FACTORS

In addition to these predisposing and external influential factors, there have been certain special circumstances or unique events that have precipitated the birth of political movements. At least three of these deserve mention.

One refers to situations of uncertainty and doubt regarding the legitimacy, effective power, or stability of political authority. Developments during and since World War II—such as imperial self-criticism and pledges of constitutional reform, the shortage of administrative staff, victorious independence movements elsewhere, and the emphatically anticolonial character of postwar world opinion—all tended to raise doubts, to reveal weaknesses, and either to set in motion a process of political change or to create the assumption and expectation of change.[1] In short, the mere existence of political uncertainty, whether from a collapse or weakening of government power or from the assumption or fact of political change, has provoked political ferment and organizational development aimed at radical change.[2]

A second type of precipitant has been the actual or threatened intrusion or imposition of some new disability or set of coercions, real or imaginary, involving deeply felt needs such as land, security, or status. Indeed, any change considered detrimental—even the abolition of clitoridectomy—might become a symbol for arousing and focusing generalized discontent. Colonial legislation and other official action prejudicial or believed to be prejudicial to African land rights, as well as measures involving, or believed to involve, new taxes, have been among the most common provocations to mass action and organizational formation. Again, constitutional changes, whether projected or in progress, which have been and are disadvantageous (or appear to be so) to the interests, integrity, or aspirations of one group (class, tribe, or race) vis-à-vis another group have also been crucial stimuli to formal political activity. For example, the Uganda National Congress became more active as a result of the apprehensions created over the project to integrate the Buganda Kingdom into a Uganda state and by the crisis resulting from the deposition of the *kabaka* (king). Similarly, both the Nyasaland and the Northern Rhodesian African Congresses were energized by their vision of potential disabilities Africans would acquire in a Central African Federation infected by the native policy of Southern Rhodesia. Indeed, there are few politically relevant movements in Africa today that have not been triggered by some variant of one of these factors.

A third and perhaps most decisive precipitant has been the appearance of an unusual African leader—a messiah, hero, or national leader, possessed of something akin to Weber's charisma. It has been this uncommon type of leader, himself frequently the product of the most tortured cultural ambivalences, who has been able not only to mobilize, channel, and focus aspirations and mass discontent upon a fixed set of objectives such as self-government or "Africa for the Africans," but also to incite surprisingly large numbers of Africans to "political" action by articulating their aspirations through the manipulation of modern or traditional symbols or through the exploitation of situations of acute political uncertainty or threatened disabilities.

Varying Patterns of Political Movements

Although most African political movements have common roots in the conditions created by modernity and the colonial experience, and tend to acquire shape, focus, and élan under certain similar circumstances, there have been and are wide differences. These differences can be found in their goals, the symbols they employ, the social background of leadership cadres, the instruments and techniques for securing and maintaining discipline among followers as well as support or acceptance among the masses, and the degree and nature of formal organization. Moreover, most movements can be further distinguished by determining where they fall, according to the above criteria, between such sets of polar extremes as traditionalist-modernist, rational-irrational, programmatic-opportunistic, constitutional-terroristic, and materialistic-idealistic. Yet the complex blending of old and new that one finds in these movements places positive limits upon even the most rigorous and systematic efforts designed to establish clear-cut categories.

In each political movement one finds a different mixture of interacting factors drawn from the following:

1. The precolonial situation, including the nature of authority patterns of indigenous African societies, the fluidity of intergroup and intragroup relationships at the beginning of colonial rule, and the historical circumstances under which that rule was imposed.

2. The colonial experience, including especially the differential play of forces of acculturation, the survival of traditional structures of authority and forms of association, the degree of exposure to unsettling external influences, and the size and political orientation of those groups most affected and aggrieved by alien rule.

3. The contemporary limits to political activity, with special reference to the rigidity of colonial policy and institutions, the freedom of the milieu in terms of political expression, and the realizability of political aspirations of the new claimant elites.

These several variables have been and are the important determinants of the form, structure, and orientation of African political movements. Each movement, however, is highly relative to the historical situation in which it is rooted as well as the milieu into which it is born.[3] Once these necessary reservations are made, stressing both the complexity and relativeness of these phenomena, a more detailed treatment of three selected types can be made, namely: the messianic, tribal, and territorial movements.

MESSIANIC POLITICORELIGIOUS MOVEMENTS

Among the several responses that have been made to situations of tension, deprivation, and frustration produced by culture contact, the so-called messianic movement is perhaps the most inscrutable and difficult to categorize. The history of sub-Saharan Africa during the past fifty years is filled with accounts of such movements, and several are currently either openly or covertly active, or they are simmering beneath the surface, or perhaps even some are in gestation. Although there are many variations among these movements, they share certain common attributes. One is that although basically religious in their origin and symbolism, most of them have tended to acquire a strong political significance in that the extinction of the European presence is considered to be a prerequisite for the realization of their vision of the good life. Another is that a "prophet" or "messiah," or a millenary dogma, serves to provide a sense of purpose, direction, and certitude. A third common element is the promise and expectation of a radical "transformation" in the form of either a return to an old or the realization of a new "golden age." These attributes account for that type of xenophobic, fanatical, and nonprogrammatic anti-Europeanism which messianic movements represent and which distinguishes them rather sharply from the more organized and westernized "nationalist" movements.

Certain special situations tend to be linked with the occurrence of these movements in sub-Saharan Africa. The peoples involved very frequently have been subjected to intensive Protestant evangelization marked by considerable sectarian competition and rivalry. Circumstances of acute despair and confusion, political denial and hopelessness, or economic insecurity have frequently prevailed. In particular, outlets for meaningful political expression have tended to be absent. These movements are far more common in British East and Central Africa, the Belgian Congo, and in French Equatorial Africa before the postwar political reforms—areas where the presence of white settlers or the prevalence of a rigid paternalism precluded any significant sense of political self-realization or hope on the part of Africans. Finally, the movements have tended to be phenomena of *particular* African tribes or cultural groups rather than Africans in general. Thus, the Dini ya Msambwa of western Kenya has been confined almost exclusively to the Bukusu and Suk tribes; the Mau Mau is an affair of the Kikuyu; Kimbangisme in the Belgian Congo and Amicalisme and Kakisme in French Equatorial Africa are expressions of the Bakongo; and so forth.[4]

Despite these coincidences there are significant variations in the character and orientation of the differing politicoreligious movements subsumed under the general rubric "messianic." At least three might be broadly distinguished:

1. Puritanical movements such as, on the one hand, the episodic, highly localized, and thus far inconsequential Mahdist movements among the Islamized groups of the western Sudan and, on the other hand, Christian

revivalist and prophet-led movements which attack witchcraft, idols, and shrines, and many traditional African customs.[5]

2. Chiliastic movements of the "Watchtower" variety which preach that "the Kingdom is at hand in this generation," in which there will be "a complete absence of all the ills of this world." Their political significance is strikingly revealed by the fact that they are banned in most African territories.

3. Nativistic movements, whether of the "rational" (self-transforming) or of the "magical" (divine intervention) types, which aim to recapture certain aspects of traditional tribal culture.[6]

TRIBAL POLITICAL MOVEMENTS

The concept of the detribalized African, useful though it may be in referring to social change at the most general level, is a very inadequate tool for the description and critical analysis of specific African political phenomena. The concept tends to evoke the distorted image of polar extremes, "tribalized" witch doctors and secret societies on the one hand and "national congresses" on the other, with very little connection between the two. This is indeed a gross distortion of African realities: with few exceptions most Africans, including diviners and barristers, stand somewhere between the two extremes. Moreover, few reflective Africans today would argue on behalf of either the inevitability or desirability of complete westernization. Eclecticism is the dominant strand in current African political thought. Old Africa is slow to die, and one of the reasons is the respect New Africa has for it.

Thus, the proportion of traditionalism to modernism in any given movement is not fixed or stable, and in any case both ingredients are normally present. While the messiahs, leaders, and activists tend to be modernists—in the sense of coming from the ranks of those groups most exposed to Westernism—their own personalities, as well as the movements they lead, are complex mixtures of both the old and the new. This relativeness of the content of nonmessianic movements makes classification both difficult and arbitrary. For analytical purposes the most useful criterion for distinguishing between the varying forms is the unit of focus of politically relevant activity: (1) the tribe (used in a generic sense to refer to the largest of any indigenous African political grouping) or (2) the territory (the artificial political unit created by the imperial powers, such as Uganda and Nigeria).[7]

In the case of tribal movements, differences in scale and size of the traditional unit provide the most useful criterion for broadly distinguishing two levels of organization, namely, kinship associations and pantribal movements. Kinship associations are found in large numbers in nearly every urban, mining, or industrial center of sub-Saharan Africa. Functionally, they are not unlike the cultural associations formed by first-generation American immigrants in large impersonal eastern cities of the United States. They have sprung into being as a consequence of the persistence of the strong feelings of loyalty and obligation to the kinship group (family, lineage, or clan) or to the village where the lineage is localized.

Most kinship associations commence as simple mutual aid, protection, or self-help societies; but many tend to take on highly important political functions. In the case of the local politics of the village or town of origin, the branches organized by the "sons abroad," as well as the "parent" branch organized by hometown activists, become centers for local political action on the part of the educated elements. In the case of politics above the local level these associations perform a variety of highly significant political functions: they have been and are fountainheads for dissemination of political—particularly "nationalist"—ideas in the interior, training grounds for cadres of political activists, vehicles for the emergence of new "tribal" or "national" leadership, as well as the primary organizational cells for pantribal unions and territorial political movements.

Pantribal movements have been organized attempts to foster a feeling of loyalty and unity toward, and to advance the prosperity and welfare of, the tribe. The latter refers to the widest sense of conceivable community above that of the kinship group but below the level of the territory. These movements have been launched initially for several very different purposes, few of which were strictly political in origin.[8] Many sprang into being simply as a result of the stimulus of competition, the power of suggestion, or the urge for imitation. There was a phase in Nigerian political development, for example, when it was considered fashionable for all "progressive" Africans to found their own national or state (that is, tribal) union. Finally, there have been some cases where a pantribal institution emerged as the logical capstone to autonomous kinship associations which had been founded independently and over a period of time in several widely dispersed cities and towns.

These pantribal unions have been a phenomenon mainly of British Africa, a fact for which at least three explanations may be given: (1) the prevalence of greater freedom of association; (2) the policy of deliberate tribal preservation (indirect rule), as well as strong official encouragement of movements for pantribal (as distinguished from territorial) integration and consciousness; and (3) the official attitude toward the Western-educated elements as manifested both in the earlier exclusion of those elements from the central apparatus of colonial government and in the more recent effort to channel their energies into local government.

Once formed and in being, pantribal unions have tended to become politicized. This is in part the result of the official policies just enumerated. It is also the result of the gravitation of the politically conscious educated elements to their tribe of origin not only because of the persistence of tribal loyalties and obligations or their new appreciation of African culture but also because the tribe could provide them with a relatively secure political base, a fairly reliable personal following, and masses whose aspirations, belief systems, grievances, and tensions they knew intimately and therefore could most easily and legitimately appeal to or manipulate. Moreover, in many cases tribal unions have taken on the political functions of organized pressure or bargaining groups on behalf of tribes placed in a minority or disadvantaged position as a consequence of constitutional developments at the territorial level. Finally, tribal unions were "organizations in being," which territorial politicians found highly useful not only as a structure in which they could climb to positions of leadership in territorial politics but also as an immediately available, developed organizational apparatus and a cadre of political activists.

Although divisive in terms of the development of a territorial consciousness and loyalty, most pantribal unions have been incomparable instruments for wide-scale integration of peoples never before united. Two remarkable examples of this have been the Ibo State Union and the Kikuyu Central Association. Both of the large tribes which these unions represent (Ibo, 5 million; Kikuyu, 1 million) are distinguished by a high degree of decentralization of indigenous authority; in neither case was there a tradition or a memory of a preexisting unity or statehood. Yet in each instance the pantribal union, by focusing upon certain genuine cultural similarities such as language or common ceremonies, or upon certain shared disabilities or grievances, or simply by being led by a "national" hero, has been able to create an Ibo or a Kikuyu "tribal" consciousness transcending former localisms, at least among certain strata of the population.

TERRITORIAL POLITICAL MOVEMENTS

The line between tribal and territorial movements is not sharp (see table 3). Indeed, Dr. Nnamdi Azikiwe, Premier of the Eastern Region of Nigeria, was for long simultaneously president of the Ibo State Union and of the panterritorial National Council of Nigeria and the Cameroons. Yet there is one crucial difference between the two movements: the fact that the target of the territorial movement is the capture of, control over, or participation in the central institutions of power and government of the territory. In the pursuit of these objectives, two types of territorial organizations have emerged: (1) the nationalist movement, which among other things agitates for a constitutional order that will make such control and participation possible; and (2) the political party, which seeks to achieve and hold power, via the electoral process, in the constitutional order thus established. Accordingly, insofar as it wins political concessions from the colonial power, a territorial nationalist movement progressively takes on the attributes of a territorial political party. This is precisely what has occurred in the ideal conditions of British West Africa, where nationalist movements have been long in gestation and favored with a situation which made a transformation to a political party possible.

In French Tropical Africa a rather different, if not a reverse, development has occurred. Although prewar French policy effectively prevented the emergence of nationalist movements, the dramatic extension of citizenship and suffrage to Africa under the 1946 Constitution called political parties suddenly into being for the purpose of electing candidates for office in the new institutions. With the passage of time these territorial "electoral" parties have tended to take on certain attributes of a nationalist movement, although none—except for certain parties in the trust territories—has seriously advocated secession.

In the plural societies of British East and Central Africa a very different situation has developed. There the racial composition of the population, the social forces at work, and the political climate have been such as to rob Africans of the usual objective of a nationalist movement (independence or political equality) as well as a constitutional order in which political parties could meaningfully participate. As a consequence of this absence of function and hope, not only are political movements far less developed but also there is a strong predisposition toward conspiratorial and messianic movements.

Several factors have operated to focus African political energies and passions upon territorial, as distinguished from tribal, movements. In the modern world mere "bigness" has a seductive attraction. It is not only a symbol of power, equality, and respectability but also a means by which to "make one's voice heard." Largeness in scale is also considered essential for rapid industrialization and economic development. Also, except for such large cultural groups as the Yoruba, Ibo, Ewe, Hausa, Baganda, and Kikuyu, few African tribes are so constituted or situated in the eyes of educated Africans themselves as to become independent national states. Again, in some instances simple imitation and emulation, or the irrepressible expansiveness of thought and aspirations characteristic of a

Table 3. Principal Political Associations in Contemporary Sub-Saharan Africa

Group A: Territories of British West Africa

	Political Associations
Gambia	Democratic Party Gambia Moslem Congress
Sierra Leone	*Sierra Leone People's Party National Council of the Colony of Sierra Leone
Gold Coast	*Convention People's Party Ghana Congress Party Moslem Association Party Northern People's Party National Liberation Movement
Togoland (British)	*Togoland Congress Convention People's Party All-Ewe Conference
Nigeria	*Action Group
Western Region	National Council of Nigeria and the Cameroons[a]
Northern Region & Northern Cameroons	*Northern People's Congress Northern Elements Progressive Union Middle Belt People's Party Middle Zone League National Council of Nigeria and the Cameroons
Eastern Region	*National Council of Nigeria and the Cameroons National Independence Party United National Party
Southern Cameroons (British)	*Kamerun National Congress Kamerun People's Party

Note: This list is not exhaustive. It includes only those territorial movements that are constitutional and have some sort of formal organization. It therefore excludes tribal, messianic, and subversive political movements. The Belgian and Portuguese territories are omitted because of the absence therein of the conditions necessary for formal political associations to have a meaningful existence. The closest approximation would be such pressure-group associations as the *Fédération des Associations de Colons du Congo et du Ruanda-Urundi* (Fédacol) or the *Union des Colons du Ruanda-Urundi* (Ucorudi).

* Identifies the political party which received the highest vote in the most recent election to the representative assembly of the territory or state concerned.

[a] The NCNC controls a majority of the seats from the Western Region in the Central Nigerian House of Representatives.

Table 3 (*continued*)

Group B: Territories of French Tropical Africa

	Metropolitan Parties	African Parties
French West Africa		
Mauritania	Rassemblement du Peuple Français[b]	*Union Progressiste Mauritanienne (IOM) Entente Mauritanienne[c]
Senegal	Section Française de l'Internationale Ouvrière[d]	*Bloc Démocratique Sénégalais (IOM)
Sudan	Rassemblement du Peuple Français	*Parti Progressiste Soudanaise (SFIO) Union Soudanaise (RDA)
Guinea	*Rassemblement du Peuple Français Section Française de l'Internationale Ouvrière	Indépendants d'Outre-Mer (IOM) Union Forestière Union du Maude Rassemblement Démocratique Africain
Upper Volta	Rassemblement du Peuple Français	*Indépendants d'Outre-Mer (IOM) Union Voltaïque Amicale Voltaïque Union du Lobi
Ivory Coast	Rassemblement du Peuple Français Section Française de l'Internationale Ouvrière	*Rassemblement Démocratique Africain
Niger	Rassemblement du Peuple Français	*Union du Niger Indépendant (IOM) Rassemblement Démocratique Africain
Dahomey	Rassemblement du Peuple Français	*Parti Républicain Dahoméenne (IOM) Groupement Ethnique du Nord Union Progressiste Dahoméenne
Togoland (French)		*Union des Chefs du Nord Togo Parti Togolais du Progrès (IOM) Comité de l'Unité Togolaise Mouvement de la Jeunesse Togolaise

[b] Formal name of the Gaullist movement.

[c] The abbreviations indicate the parliamentary group or broader association to which the party is attached (*apparanté*) or allied, i.e.: IOM: *Indépendants d'Outre-Mer*, an organization of overseas *parlementaires*; SFIO: *Section Française de l'Internationale Ouvrière*; RDA: *Rassemblement Démocratique Africain*, a pan-French African political movement having its greatest strength in the Ivory Coast; RDA-PC: signifies that the U.P.C. identifies itself with the pro-Communist wing of the RDA.

[d] Formal name of the French Socialist Party.

Table 3 (*continued*)

Group B: Territories of French Tropical Africa (continued)

	Metropolitan Parties	*African Parties*
French Equatorial Africa		
Chad	Rassemblement du Peuple Français	*Union Démocratique Tchadienne (RPF) Rassemblement Démocratique Africain
Middle Congo	Rassemblement du Peuple Français Section Française de l'Internationale Ouvrière	*Parti Progressiste Congolais (RDA)
Ubangi-Shari	Rassemblement du Peuple Français	*Mouvement d'Évolution Sociale de l'Afrique Noire
Gabon	Rassemblement du Peuple Français	*Indépendants d'Outre-Mer (IOM) Défense des Interêts Locaux Union Gabonaise
Cameroons (French)	Rassemblement du Peuple Français Section Française de l'Internationale Ouvrière	*Évolution Sociale Camerounaise Union des Populations du Cameroun (RDA-PC) Renaissance Camerounaise Bloc Démocratique Camerounaise

Table 3 *(continued)*

Group C: Territories of British East and Central Africa and the Union of South Africa

	European Associations	*Arab/Asian Associations*	*African/Colored Associations*
British East Africa			
Kenya	Elected Members' Organization United Country Party Federal Independence Party	Kenya Indian Congress Kenya Muslim League Central Arab Association	African Members' Association
Zanzibar	—	Arab Association	—
Uganda	Uganda Chamber of Commerce	Asian Association Uganda Muslim Union	Uganda National Congress Uganda National Congress Youth Association Uganda People's Party All-Uganda Party
Tanganyika	Tanganyika European Council	Asian Association Muslim Association	Tanganyika African Association
British Central Africa			
Nyasaland	Convention of Associations Nyasaland Association	Nyasaland Asian Convention	Nyasaland African Congress Nyasaland Chief's Union Nyasaland African Progressive Association
Northern Rhodesia	*Federal Party[e]		N. R. African National Congress N. R. All-African Convention Euro-African Society
Southern Rhodesia	*United Rhodesia Party Confederate Party[e] Independent Labour Party Independent Rhodesia Party		Southern Rhodesia African Association
Union of South Africa	*Nationalist Party United Party Labour Party Liberal Party Union Federal Party	South African Indian Congress	African National Congress Bantu National Congress Non-European Unity Movement Coloured People's National Union Coloured People's Congress All-African Convention African People's Organization

[e]The Federal Party and the Confederate Party are also the majority and minority parties, respectively, in the Legislative Assembly of the new Federation of Rhodesia and Nyasaland.

"liberation" mood, are not negligible factors. Moreover, the social groups most actively working for change have frequently been those which circumstances have placed closest to the territorial superstructure (students and teachers, clerks, and artisans employed by colonial government and foreign firms, and so forth), or those elements, such as traders and merchants, who have benefited most from a broad area of economic interchange. All of these groups find it comparatively easy, if not attractive, to think and act in "territorial" terms. Furthermore, there is the obvious fact that only a territorial movement can seriously challenge the power and legitimacy of a colonial government. Perhaps the most decisive factor, however, has been the coercive influence of territorial representative institutions—Legislative Councils, Regional Assemblies, Assemblées Territoriales, or Grands Conseils—which have compelled African political leaders to organize and act with a territorial frame of reference if they want to act meaningfully.[9]

In many situations there exists an uneasy alliance between tribal and territorial movements. All of the knotty problems—and potential instability—implicit in the existence of incipient national separatism in a multinational state are in evidence. While in the early stages tribal movements were useful, if not indispensable, organizational props to leaders of territorial movements, many of these leaders have become irritated by, if not fearful of, the "pressure group" fickleness of tribal unions representing minority groups. Moreover, some of these tribal leaders fear that they will be challenged by the leadership that might rise through the structure of the larger pantribal unions. The more centrally minded Jacobins among these leaders detest these *corps intermédiaires* because they represent a constant threat to "national" territorial unity and a potential obstruction to rapid social and economic change. These centrifugal and centripetal pressures are among the most critical forces at work in many parts of Africa today.

Effect of Political Movements on Colonial Policies

Just as there tends to be a polarization of attitudes concerning the cause and nature of African political movements, so are there extreme views regarding the actual effect they have had and are having on colonial policies. African nationalists tend to view that little or no change would have occurred had it not been for the intense pressure they generated from below. Imperial spokesmen argue, however, that most postwar reforms in colonial policy were self-produced, or that in any event the changes are but current applications of traditional principles. Both are partially correct.

Certainly, apart from the revolutionary sociopolitical forces asserting themselves within Africa, World War II produced profound changes in the world climate of opinion regarding colonialism as well as in imperial attitudes and policies.

There can be little doubt, however, that the unexpected appearance of highly organized and disciplined mass movements under a new militant leadership, such as the Convention People's Party of the Gold Coast or the Action Group of the Western Region of Nigeria, has forced a drastic revision in imperial calculations far beyond West Africa. These movements revealed in startling fashion that, given determined and skillful leadership and "ripe" situations, tremendous social forces could be tapped and channeled into political activity. This revelation dealt a devastating blow to the major assumption underlying all previous policy regarding the African peoples, namely, that they constituted an inert mass that could be manipulated and molded at will—and indefinitely—by the alien intruder.

The impact of these movements upon policy has varied greatly. On the British West Coast since 1945 there has been a continuous interaction between African nationalist movements insatiably pressing for new increments of power and prudent and responsive British administration conducting a delaying action, a process which has now reached the stage where self-governing African states will soon be entering the mainstream of world affairs. In French Tropical Africa a separatist nationalism, except in Togoland and the Cameroons, has not developed; but political parties operating as pressure groups within and without the National Assembly are compelling a greater devolution of power to the African territorial governments and assemblies than either the Napoleonic tradition or the policy of assimilation would normally envisage. In British East and Central Africa, African movements, whether in the form of the terroristic Mau Mau or the National Congresses of Uganda, Northern Rhodesia, and Nyasaland, have compelled a far more liberal interpretation of the concept of partnership than European settlers would have thought conceivable five years ago. Moreover, for the time being the gravitation of total power into the hands of resident white settlers has been arrested, at least in Kenya, Uganda, and Tanganyika. Finally, in the Belgian Congo, the extraordinary attention paid during the last few years to the problem of the status and future of the *élite noire* is a reflection not only of the existence of pressures from burgeoning social forces within the Congo but also of the strong impact that political movements in neighboring French and British areas have had upon official Belgian calculations.

In sum, while there is little doubt that the rise and maturation of African political movements has undermined smug prewar assumptions, the variation in the impact of such movements nevertheless does, as noted above, point up the crucial importance of colonial policies during the initial stages in determining the form and direction taken by these movements striving for new relationships beyond colonialism. In Africa, as elsewhere in the non-European world, policies of avoidance and repression are not only sterile but in the long run quite futile. Once unleashed and in motion, social energy is irrepressible and uncompromising in its quest for direction and expression. Policies of responsiveness and constructive guidance offer the possibility that such expression will be responsible, purposive, and creative. Meanwhile, the ubiquitous and cynical agents of a new imperialism are abroad armed with special skills and seductive formulas for the manipulation of unsatisfied social energy and incipient political movements.

NOTES

1. These situations of political doubt and confusion have been primarily a phenomena of British Africa—in part because of the self-liquidating theory of self-government and in part because of the more intensive open self-criticism generated by British democracy. The paternalism that has prevailed in Portuguese and Belgian territories, and to a qualified extent in French areas, has tended to forestall or to distinguish any serious questioning of the political order. The remarkable number and type of political movements which have appeared in Togoland and the Cameroons under French trusteeship is explained in part by the fact that they are the only areas of French Tropical Africa where both the legitimacy and the ultimacy of French authority are seriously in doubt.

2. As Gaetano Mosca would argue, a period of renovation has commenced which permits "all to aspire to the most exalted positions and some to attain them . . . [and] once such a movement has set in, it cannot be stopped immediately." See his *The Ruling Class* (New York: McGraw-Hill, 1939), pp. 67–68.

3. The decisive casual variable in some movements may be the social structure of the indigenous culture; in others it may be the degree and character of missionary enterprise; while in others it may be simply the absence of competition from other politically claimant races.

4. This tribal focus of messianic movements does not invalidate the distinction made in this essay between such forms of expression and tribal movements discussed subsequently. Moreover, the tribal bias is not an invariable characteristic, as evidenced by the infectious spread of Mau Mau and multitribal nature of the Maji-Maji Rebellion in Tanganyika. See R. M. Bell, "The Maji-Maji Rebellion in the Liwale District," *Tanganyika Notes and Records*, 28 (January 1950), p. 38.

5. For example, the Kyoka movement in north Angola (1872), the Harris movement of Liberia and the Ivory Coast, the Second Elijah movement in Nigeria (1914), and more recently Kimbangisme-Amicalisme-Kakisme in the Belgian Congo and French Africa.

6. As in the case of all analytical types, there are no pure nativist movements. The classification signifies rather a conscious traditionalist orientation and is sufficiently broad to include such contemporary expressions as the Dini ya Msambwa and the Mau Mau of Kenya, with certain qualifications. Indeed, the spirit of nativism is reflected in the oft-quoted dedication in Jomo Kenyatta's book, *Facing Mount Kenya* (London: Martin, Secker & Warburg, 1953): "To Moigoi and Wamboi and all the dispossessed youth of Africa: for perpetuation of communion with ancestral spirits through the fight for African freedom, and in the firm belief that the dead, the living, and the unborn will unite to rebuild the destroyed shrines."

7. Except for Basutoland and Swaziland there are no African territories that are coterminous with tribe; hence by our criterion, except in cases of tribal pretentiousness or imperialism, there are no tribal movements that have a territorial focus; and by definition there are no territorial movements with a tribal focus. This is true despite the fact that the Ibo have predominated in the National Council of Nigeria and the Cameroons, the Yoruba in the Action Group of the Western Region of Nigeria, the Baganda in the Uganda National Congress, and the Kikuyu in the proscribed Kenya African Union.

8. For example, the Ibo Federal Union of Nigeria was originally founded by Western-educated Ibo leaders to mobilize the resources of the Ibo peoples in a heroic drive toward self-transformation through Western education. The pan-Yoruba Egbe Omo Oduduwa was launched initially as a cultural organization "to foster the study of the Yoruba language, culture and history." The all-Ewe conference was organized to unite the Ewe peoples through the elimination of restrictive colonial frontiers. The pan-Chagga Kilimanjaro Native Cooperative Union had a purely economic origin, as suggested by its title. The Kavirondo Welfare Association came into being for the specific purpose of presenting the African land case before a British Commission of Inquiry. The Descendants of Kintu in Uganda, however, was founded as an oppositional movement of the Baganda against the Mengo ruling classes in the Buganda Kingdom—an obviously political purpose.

9. French Africans find it easier to think and act politically in "territorial" terms not only because of the French system but also because of the French policy of direct rule. The effect of this policy is strikingly revealed in the different political orientation of African modernists in Dahomey, where the French extinguished the Kingdom of Dahomey, and in Uganda, where the British preserved the Kingdom of Buganda.

4 The Problem of Political Integration in Emergent Africa

Under the pressure of a variety of external influences, as well as internal forces generated by the impact of modernity and the provocations of alien rule, the steel grid of European colonialism is gradually being lifted from the face of Africa. Intergroup and class tensions and disunities, long masked by the relatively stable pattern of relationships which characterized prewar colonial Africa, are being progressively and dramatically brought to light. Some of these situations of actual or potential conflict are rooted in precolonial conditions; others are the product of circumstances and forces created by European colonialism. Still others are the inevitable result of the conditions under which imperial control is being relinquished. Most of them portend chronic political instability as well as a bleak outlook for the development of democratic government.

There are at least three respects in which the circumstances of colonial liquidation are particularly relevant to the problem of political integration. One concerns the form and scale of political organization: traditional African politicocultural units, and the colonial territorial systems into which they happened to be grouped by the accidents of imperial history, are being replaced arbitrarily by modern large-scale states. The second refers to political institutions: in most of these emergent units there has been an uncritical adoption of the majoritarian institutions of parliamentary democracy and the unitarian institutions of the centralized state. The third concerns the nature of political authority: traditional African elites

Reprinted from *Western Political Quarterly* 8:1 (March 1955), pp. 44–57, an article adapted from a paper discussed in Comparative Government Panel 2 of the Fiftieth Annual Meeting of the American Political Science Association, held in Chicago, Illinois, September 9–11, 1954.

and the colonial bureaucracies under which they have served are being eclipsed, and almost by default power is passing progressively into the hands of new westernized African elites or resident European settlers.

These changes in the scale of political organization, in the structure of political institutions, and in the character of the governing elites have either aggravated or they have created three principal types of situations of nonintegration, namely, (1) disunities between indigenous African cultural groups arbitrarily bunched together in emergent multitribal African states; (2) tensions between the several racial communities that make up the plural societies of the emergent multiracial states; and (3) socioeconomic disparities between the emergent political elites—African or European—and the relatively inert African masses.

In terms of both political stability and the development of democratic institutions, most of the important political problems in emergent Africa are related to these three different situations of tribal, racial, and class nonintegration. A classificatory scheme considered as a useful, if not indispensable, ordering device for the description and analysis of the political aspects of these problems and situations is set forth in table 4 and map 2.

There are several obvious political approaches to the problem of integration. One would be to avoid the problem altogether merely by retaining the essential "steel grid" features of colonialism, open or disguised. In essence this has been the course followed in the Belgian and Portuguese territories, albeit with differing theoretical and legal rationalizations. A similar result has been achieved in the case of Southern Rhodesia, and latterly the new Federation of Rhodesia and Nyasaland, by means of the wide devolution of power from the imperial government in the United Kingdom to the European settlers in Africa. Critics argue that for the vast bulk of the population this is not really "decolonization" but rather a simple geographical shift in the locus of colonial authority.

Another political approach may be found in the role played by powerful political leaders, nationalist movements and political parties, and territorial political institutions, as instruments and new modes of integration. One authority has suggested that the charismatic leadership exercised by Prime Minister Kwame Nkrumah may in the long run prove to be the really critical factor in the successful transition of the Gold Coast from a British colony to an effective and stable parliamentary democracy.[1] Territorial political movements such as the Sierra Leone Peoples' Party, the Bloc Démocratique Sénégalais, the Northern Rhodesia National Congress, and the Federal Party of the new Central African Federation, have been and remain incomparable vehicles for enlarging the scale of political activity.

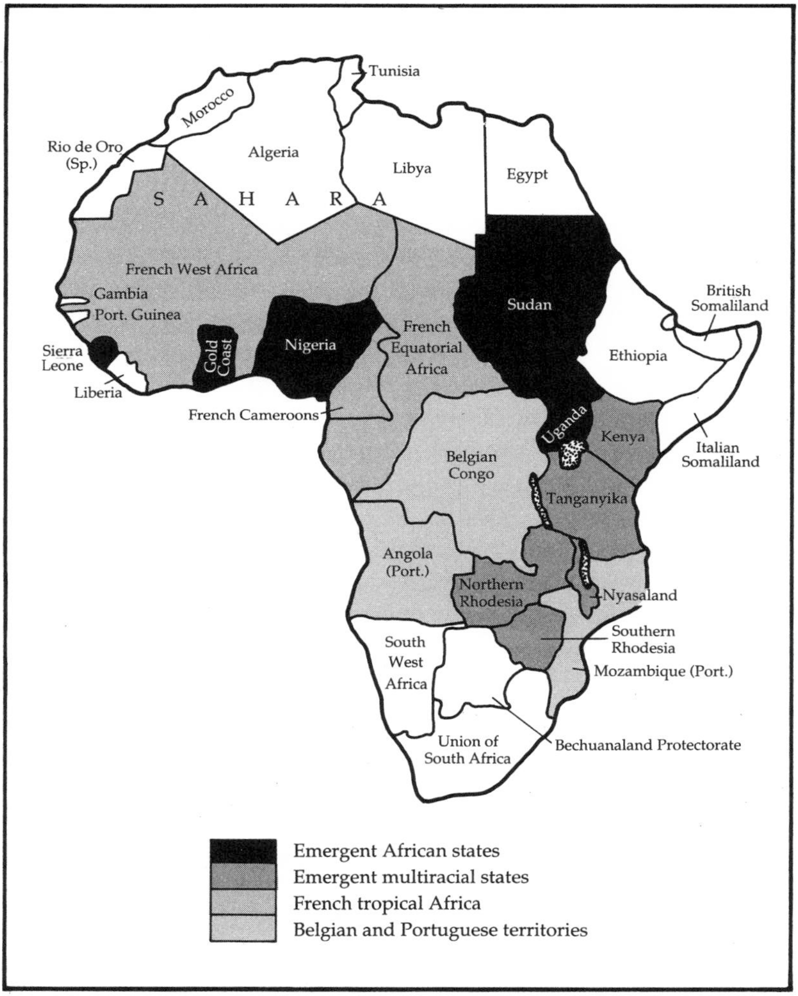

Map 2. Principal territories and states in emergent Africa, 1954

Table 4. Classification of Principal Territories and States in Emergent Africa

	Europeans	*Asians*	*Levantines*	*Arabs*	*Coloreds*	*Africans*
Emergent African states[a]						
Sudan		(Approx. 35,000 nonindigenous peoples)				8,350,000
Sierra Leone	1,000	—	2,000	—	—	2,000,000
Gold Coast (excluding Togoland)	4,000	—	2,500	—	—	4,111,500
Nigeria (excluding Cameroons)	6,000	—	3,500	—	—	31,202,000
Uganda	3,500	35,000	—	1,500	—	4,917,500
Emergent multiracial states[b]						
Tanganyika	16,500	36,500	—	35,000	—	7,590,000
Kenya	30,500	98,000	—	35,000	—	5,253,000
Federation of Rhodesia and Nyasaland						
Nyasaland	4,000	6,000	—	—	2,000	2,453,500
Northern Rhodesia	43,000	3,000	—	—	1,000	1,930,000
Southern Rhodesia	160,000	8,500	—	—	6,000	2,130,000
French tropical Africa[c]						
French West Africa	63,000	?	?	?	?	17,144,500
French Equatorial Africa	20,000	?	?	?	?	4,386,500

Undetermined[d]						
Belgian Congo	80,000	1,000	—	—	1,000	11,789,000
Portuguese Angola	79,000	?	?	—	26,000	4,006,500
Portuguese Mozambique	48,000	14,000	—	—	25,000	5,640,000

Note: The criteria of classification of the above territories include the stated political objectives of colonial policy, the current political orientation revealed by recent events, and the ethnic composition of the territorial population. "Emergent Africa" refers to that broad grouping of territories situated south of the Sahara and north of the Union (see map 2). This areal focus is admittedly quite arbitrary; in many respects the problems of political integration in plural societies referred to herein are found in their most acute form in the excluded geographical extremes—Tunisia and Morocco in French North Africa, and the Union of South Africa. Smaller territories, such as the Gambia and Somaliland, and independent states, such as Ethiopia and Liberia, are also omitted.

[a]British territories of nonwhite-settlement advancing to self-government under *African* leadership. Uganda is included in this category because of the recent official assurance that it is destined to be predominantly an "African" state.

[b]British territories of white settlement advancing towards self-government under multiracial or *white-settler* leadership. Nyasaland, otherwise a possible candidate for independent African statehood, falls in this category because of its inclusion in the new European-dominated Federation of Rhodesia and Nyasaland.

[c]French territories assimilated to France in which Europeans and Africans participate in common Euro-African institutions in metropolitan France as well as in Africa. Togoland and Cameroons under French Trusteeship are not included. As a result of their special international status, as well as the unsettling influence of autonomist developments in neighboring British territories, separatist Togolese and Cameroonian nationalist movements, aspiring to independent African statehood, have emerged.

[d]These territories are currently devoid of Western-type political activity—and therefore the acute problems of political integration discussed herein—as a consequence of the paternalistic and authoritarian character of the Belgian and Portuguese colonial systems. While their future political orientation is uncertain, the population composition of these territories would seem to point towards a multiracial formula. Constitutionally, Angola and Mozambique are overseas provinces of Portugal.

Furthermore, territorial assemblies and legislatures, centralized bureaucracies, and other territory-wide institutions have been structures that have fostered—indeed forced—progressive integration.

In the short run these political factors are decisive; perhaps in the long run they may be the major determinants. Yet there are economic and cultural factors that have been and will continue to be of crucial importance in the aggravation or the solution of those politically consequential situations of tension and malintegration previously mentioned. It is the purpose of this paper to focus primarily upon these latter factors in terms of the following: (1) the state of economic development; (2) the role of indigenous African culture; and (3) the impact of certain external influences.

The State of Economic Development in Africa

In societies such as those in Africa that are undergoing rapid change, there is a close relationship between economic development on the one hand and territorial integration and class stratification on the other.[2] The present state of economic development in Africa is most easily assessed in terms of the degree of commercialization of agriculture, labor, and services. The several processes embraced within the concept "commercialization" (cash-cropping, wage-earning, individualization of land tenure, urbanization, etc.) constitute a combined assault upon the structures and values of traditional African societies. The power of the chief or elders as custodians of the land, the cohesiveness of the lineage as the primary socioeconomic unit, and the integrity of the indigenous social structure within which rank, status, and role are determined mainly by age and religious position—all tend to be undermined by the corrosive impact of the cash nexus and the expanding market economy. In short, commercialization leads to social disintegration, which is the painful but necessary first step in the historic transition from small communal economies of folk societies to large-scale, highly diversified, industrial economies characteristic of and required by the modern state.[3]

Once these general propositions are noted, certain important reservations and qualifications must be made. Even where most advanced, commercialization (as distinguished from industrialization) has not invariably extinguished, or even seriously challenged, traditional loyalties and obligations. In some instances, such as the wealthy Yoruba of Western Nigeria and the Ganda of Uganda, Western economic developments and prosperity have done little to weaken—indeed, in some respects they have positively strengthened—lineage and tribal attachments. In other instances, the staggering challenge presented by the new economic forces, coupled with other acculturating influences, has led to greater clan or tribal cohesion either by provoking a blind and aggressive reaction or by stimulating a heroic drive aimed at self-transformation.[4]

It is normally assumed that the processes of commercialization not only tend to dissolve old ties and institutions but that they perform the positive function of fostering reintegration. Examples of the latter include the evolution of new patterns of economic interdependence and the growth of occupational or class associations binding together peoples previously divided by tribe or race. From available evidence it is clear that these developments do not necessarily occur around the symbols or within the boundaries of emergent political units. A cocoa economy has helped to unite most of the Gold Coast; but it has been a divisive factor in Nigerian unity. In Uganda, a panterritorial cotton economy has done little to break down the sectional separatism of the Buganda Kingdom. Moreover, associational development does not necessarily promote intertribal or interracial cooperation or unity; indeed, in many instances the new groupings become the instruments for sharpening and the structures for formalizing latent antagonisms and tensions. Thus, in French *Afrique noire* Euro-African labor federations are in some respects the vehicles for achieving a broader racial or territorial unity, yet the Chambers of Commerce remain a divisive sanctuary of the European traders. In Northern Rhodesia the African Mineworkers' Trade Union is an incomparable agency for dissipating intertribal antagonisms amongst the African miners; but like the Mine Workers' Union (European) it is also an organization of racial separatism in terms of Northern Rhodesian society. Again, the powerful Kilimanjaro Native Cooperative Union has tended to unite the Chagga tribe; yet it is also an instrument for Chagga separatism in terms of Tanganyika unity.

The processes of commercialization have produced a restratification in most African societies.[5] The African *nouveaux riches*, the European *colons*, and the Levantine and Indian middle-class merchants have tended to replace the elders and traditional prestige groups in the upper levels of the class structure. With certain exceptions and variations these new socioeconomic groups are also the politically claimant elites in the emergent states.[6] Where they exist side by side in plural societies there is a continuing struggle between these unassimilated racial elites regarding control over, or participation in, the centralized government power being relinquished by the colonial bureaucracies.[7]

In the light of available evidence the following general propositions regarding commercialization are advanced:

1. In the balance, commercialization has not yet occurred on a scale sufficient for fragmented economic units to be welded together into large-

scale exchange economies which might thereby become decisive factors in the integration and unity of the emergent states. Moreover, in many instances commercialization has either preserved or aggravated old divisions and tensions, or it has created new ones as a result of the unevenness of its incidence, in terms both of areal and class distribution of its material benefits and power potential.

2. In response to many pressures, including especially the passionate drive for rapid modernization, and an increasing attraction toward *étatisme* as an instrument for its achievement, the processes of commercialization—and latterly of industrialization—are being accelerated and extended in depth. It remains an open question whether this development will intensify or soften existing tribal, racial, and class cleavages. Much will depend upon the vision of colonial administrators and the new elites, as well as the development of a viable exchange economy.[8] Recent trends suggest that situations of malintegration may get worse before they are finally resolved.

The Influence of Indigenous African Culture

The myth that the African had no history or culture in precolonial times, as well as the belief that his culture could not—indeed ought not—survive the disintegrative effects of the slave-trade, modernity, and colonialism has been effectively demolished by the cultural anthropologists as well as by recent events and situations.[9] The seemingly insoluble Ewe-Togoland imbroglio, the persistence of tribalism in Nigeria, the separatism of the Baganda in Uganda, and the surprising strength of the Mau Mau movement in Kenya have all served to dramatize both the tenacity and the determinative importance of indigenous cultural traits, institutions, and patterns of political behavior.[10]

The effect of the indigenous culture upon the problem of integration could be examined in terms of several criteria. The following four are believed particularly significant: (1) the persistence of traditional patterns of land tenure, capital accumulation, and agricultural practices as obstacles to social mobility, commercialization, and the development of large-scale integrative economies;[11] (2) differences in the adaptability of traditional African societies to modernity which, as a result of the growth of disparities in the level of material development, give rise to new intergroup tensions generated by the competitive struggle for power within the new order; (3) the continuity and strength of indigenous cultural determinants in the personality formation, political expectations and behavior, and attitude toward authority of the members of the westernized elites—in short, psychocultural factors of differentiation;[12] and (4) the survival of indigenous sociopolitical units as foci for the loyalties, ambitions, and energies not only of the traditionalists but also of the present and upcoming generations of modernists. This latter phenomenon is the one most directly and immediately relevant to the process of nation-state building.

The persistence of the tribe, archaic state, or areal culture as a symbol of group unity and individual self-identification, as well as an attractive medium through which to achieve self-realization, is the result of a variety of complex factors. One explanation is found in the comparatively short duration and the uneven impact of Western influences. African urbanization, for example, has been a fairly recent phenomenon characterized by the sudden growth of a few very large coastal or mining centers whose hinterlands have only indirectly and very incompletely felt the play of acculturating influences.[13] Another factor has been the "indirect rule" policy of deliberate preservation of traditional political systems, a policy pursued with varying zeal and success by all African colonial powers with the qualified exception of France.[14] Still another element has been the surprising manner in which the traditional systems have been able to attract and to absorb the new westernized elites.

The attraction of these new elites to their cultural groups of origin has been strengthened by two ingredients in African nationalism. One of these is the "back to Africa" cultural movement spearheaded by the westernized groups. In many cases this has been the result of a new and deeper appreciation of their own culture acquired through travel and study abroad. In others it takes the form of petulant and aggressive exaggerations stemming from a bitterness over having been excluded from full participation in white European culture which they have endeavored to emulate. In still others, this historical-cultural revival is part of a program to explode myths and refute arguments regarding African capacity for self-government. As Dr. Onwuka Dike, a distinguished Nigerian historian, has put it: "so long as the African is regarded as a man without a culture and without a history, doubts concerning his ability to govern himself will find credence."[15]

A second element involves the quest for status. In the competition for power and the status it will bring in the new order, these new elites tend to gravitate to their ethnic or racial group of origin as a base and springboard from which to assert their leadership in the larger political order. As "sons of the soil" they can not only make special claims to legitimacy; they are also in a better position to manipulate and control the unacculturated masses of their own group through the adaptation or perversion of traditional magicoreligious symbols and sanctions with which they are familiar.[16]

Another important determinant in the survival of traditional systems as meaningful political units is related to the scale and structure of indigenous political systems. Africans coming from small autonomous local communities or from widely dispersed tribal societies have tended to adapt themselves more readily to the symbols of and membership in modern large-scale political units. Conversely, the loyalties and sentiments of Africans coming from archaic state systems have tended to be less malleable, particularly where those systems were preserved under indirect rule (e.g., the Hausa-Fulani states of Northern Nigeria and the Buganda Kingdom of Uganda). Indirect rule has been—and by definition was bound to be—more effective in the case of archaic states. The task of reintegration in modern Africa states has been and will be easiest in those areas which have been under direct rule, where the old order was crushed or ignored, or in those areas where stateless village and tribal societies predominated.[17]

In general, the following propositions are advanced:

1. That with few exceptions, indigenous African culture has been of transcendent importance in determining the foci of the political attachments and activities of the westernized modernists. In many situations it will continue to be a dominant factor not only because of its indestructibility or intrinsic utility but also as a consequence of its deliberate perpetuation by the modernists either as a means by which to inculcate individual and group pride, or as a useful source of issues which can excite the masses and which can, therefore, be profitably exploited and manipulated in election campaigns and territorially based opposition movements. Recent separatist tendencies in the Gold Coast (e.g., the National Liberation movement in Ashanti and the Northern Peoples' Party in the Northern Territories) are highly significant cases in point.

2. That in the case of emergent African states, indigenous culture in other instances will progressively become less determinative as a consequence of increased commercialization, the integrative influence of new central political institutions, the growth of new transtribal occupational and political associations, and the broader outlook of upcoming elites attracted to large-scale units on rational grounds. These processes are relatively slow; moreover, they presuppose the uninterrupted existence of some form of strong, central government pursuing a positive program of nation-building, whether that government be in the hands of a colonial bureaucracy, a Euro-African diarchy, or an African elite with a "national"

outlook. In the absence of such conditions, a general disintegration and sorting out would undoubtedly occur.

3. That in the case of emergent multiracial states dominated by European settlers, as well as those areas remaining in a colonial status, the centrifugal tendencies of communalism and tribalism amongst Africans will tend to be held in check by the overriding sentiment of racial consciousness generated by common African opposition to the dominant minority, whether of the settler or metropolitan type.

The Impact of External Influences

There have been a variety of external influences that have contributed to and continue to affect the course of African political developments. Important among these are the differing impact of the United States, the West Indies, India, and South Africa upon the growth and spread of nationalism, the unsettling consequences of the United Nations activity regarding the African trust territories, the remarkable influence of the Moral Rearmament movement amongst the new African elites, and the nascent penetration of labor unions and student groups by international communism. Each of these has been and will continue to be highly significant.[18] Three other factors command attention, however, because of the special bearing they have had upon the problem of integration: (1) Christianity; (2) Islam; and (3) the political thought and institutions of the metropolitan countries.

Perhaps more than elsewhere in the non-European world, Christian missionaries in Africa have constituted the vanguard in the penetration of Western culture and power. This Christian influence, and particularly the unsettling nonconformity of Protestantism, has profoundly affected political developments.[19] With few exceptions the westernized African elites leading nationalist or terrorist movements and claiming power in the new order are products of mission schools. The existence of a vernacular literature—a potentially divisive factor, considering Africa's linguistic mosaic—is the result of painstaking missionary scholarship or sponsorship.[20] Protestant sectarianism and the encouragement of tolerance of local church autonomy have been and are responsible for seemingly endless schisms and proliferation of sects. Moreover, as a result of its emphasis upon conversion of the individual, as well as its heavy European cultural bias, Protestant evangelism has tended to widen the cultural cleavage between the new elites and the non-Christian masses.[21]

The extent of Islamization and the potentiality of Islam as an integrative or divisive factor in political developments in Tropical Africa have tended to be underestimated. In part this is due to the fact that most secular political activity has been dominated by the new Christianized elites. Actually, Islam has spread its influence, albeit unevenly, over more than half this vast area, leaving what Westermann has called "a thin but influential layer of Mohammedan culture."[22] Moreover, under the stimuli of modernity and Westernism, the idea of nationalism, and the fear of domination by the Christianized minorities, a new Islamic political leadership is commencing to assert itself in many areas. The potentialities of increased intergroup tension on grounds of religion, therefore, are considerable. This is particularly true in two types of situations: (1) territorial separatist movements in the case of those emergent states embracing within their boundaries distinct areas that are predominantly Islamic; and (2) communal parties in those areas where Moslems are in a minority. Both developments have already become important political factors.[23]

Western forces of acculturation operating in Africa have been channeled through the medium of the national cultures of the several European colonial powers. In particular, the political attributes of the metropolitan country—its distinctive political theory, institutions, and patterns of behavior—have not only shaped and conditioned colonial policy; they also have been crucial determinants of the institutional structure of the emergent states and the political assumptions, expectations, and behavior of the new elites.[24] The implications of this metropolitan influence can be noted by comparing the situation in British and French territories as regards local government and central executive power.

The British preoccupation with the development of institutions of local government is one of the outstanding political facts of contemporary Africa. The effort is not simply a modernized version of indirect rule, an imperial or white-settler stratagem designed to retard or to halt the agitation for or the devolution of power to centrally minded African nationalists. Nor is it based solely upon the conviction or faith that strong local government can be made a constitutional safeguard against African authoritarianism, or can serve as an interim training ground in parliamentary democracy and public finance. These are certainly ingredients. Yet the policy is in large measure simply an automatic projection to Africa of traditional British political theory and practice regarding local government in the United Kingdom. Conversely, French indifference or resistance toward local government reform in *Afrique noire* is as much the uncritical extension to Africa of the "statist" and centralist tradition of metropolitan France as it is a special imperial device for discouraging African autonomy. In any event, laudable though it may be on many counts, the British policy tends to perpetuate indigenous cultural cleavages and to foster separatist movements within the new states.

At the central level the main precipitants of tension have been formal constitutional steps taken to replace imperial power with the majoritarian and unitarian institutions of parliamentary democracy and the modern centralized state. Each move in this direction has tended to sharpen or provoke group tensions, as well as accelerate the efforts of competing groups to capture or limit power at the center. This phenomenon is most pronounced in British Africa because of the unique British policy of granting territorial self-government within the framework of parliamentary institutions in which power is concentrated in an all-powerful central executive. The limited measure of devolution within the French Union, coupled with the very different form and function of political representation in French African territories, has been far less provocative.

It could be argued perhaps that imperial withdrawal under circumstances of intense intergroup conflict would act as the catalyst forcing and accelerating either a reintegration of or tolerance among the competing groups. As the threshold of self-government is crossed, leaders might be induced or feel compelled to accept and participate in the new order. In any event, in the transition from colonialism to varying patterns of self-government, a general sorting out of peoples and the achievement of a new stability, by consent or coercion, would seem to be an inevitable development. It is highly debatable whether this reintegration and stabilization can ever be brought about effectively under imperial tutelage. It is possible, however, that it will occur under new forms of oligarchy or authoritarianism in which the African elites or European settlers are the state builders.

The following two propositions are advanced regarding external influences:

1. Colonialism in Africa has been the medium for the indiscriminate diffusion of Western ideas and institutions. Dominant among these is the modern state. Most current efforts to erect modern states in the heterogeneous cultural and racial milieu of African territories are producing situations that either defy a peaceful solution or invite authoritarianism. Notwithstanding this unripeness or incompatibility of the cultural context, it would seem that the process of state formation will proceed inexorably not only because the modern state remains the unchallenged symbol of personal and group freedom, but also because of the belief that it provides the only respectable and legitimate arena for the exercise of power, the realization of democracy, and the attainment of economic prosperity. In sum, the modern state tends to be the supreme norm. Hence Euro-African

institutions and political relationships in contemporary Africa that fail to satisfy the prestige, power, and welfare aspirations of upcoming African elites will probably collapse under the onslaught of a separatist African nationalism.

2. State formation and colonial liquidation in Tropical Africa are taking place in a climate of opinion and institutional environment quite different from that which prevailed in the other major areas formerly under European imperialism. Under the pressure of world opinion and an African nationalism saturated with mid-twentieth-century ideas of social democracy, the welfare state, and mass participation in politics, sobered and repentant colonial governments have pursued for nearly a decade various schemes of political, economic, and social development. The crucial point is that the broad dissemination of democratic ideas to the masses and the progressive mobilization of new social strata are both occurring *before* the termination of the European presence and the stability it has enforced. These special elements in the African situation are bound to produce a unique pattern of politics and Euro-African relationships in the postcolonial period.[25] In short, it is unlikely that nascent African states such as the Gold Coast or Tanganyika will follow the pattern of political development characteristic of areas which achieved their independence in an earlier preindustrial and predemocratic period.

NOTES

1. David E. Apter, "Political Democracy in the Gold Coast," in Calvin W. Stillman, ed., *Africa in the Modern World* (Chicago: University of Chicago Press, 1955), pp. 115–139.

2. The reciprocal relationship between economic development and political integration is emphasized in a report by a study group of the Royal Institute of International Affairs in *Nationalism* (London: Oxford University Press, 1939), pp. 239–240: "Economic interests and the social groups representing these interests belonged to the most influential forces which promoted the rise of the nation-state and the first awakening of national consciousness. Yet in achieving a certain institutional and psychological unity, the young nation-state, for its part, reshaped the inherited economic organization and the human energies employed in its working." Cf. Karl Deutsch, *Nationalism and Social Communication* (New York: John Wiley & Sons, 1953), pp. 31–43.

3. For a recent appraisal of the progress and problems of commercialization in Africa, see United Nations, Department of Economic Affairs, *Enlargement of the Exchange Economy in Tropical Africa* (March 12,

1954), Document E/2557ST/ECA/23. For West Africa see Daryll Forde, "The Conditions of Social Development in West Africa," *Civilisations*, 3:4 (1953), pp. 471–485. For East and Central Africa see Audrey L. Richards, ed., *Economic Development and Tribal Change* (Cambridge: W. Heffer & Sons, 1954).

4. See Vincent Harlow, "Tribalism in Africa," *Journal of African Administration*, 7 (1955), pp. 17–20; for the Yoruba see P. C. Lloyd, "New Economic Classes in Western Nigeria," *African Affairs*, 52 (October 1953), pp. 327–334, and for the Ganda people of Uganda see Richards, *Economic Development and Tribal Change*.

5. One of the crucial differences between the pattern of development that is taking form in emergent Africa and that of Latin America centers upon the social and political consequences of commercialization. Professor Sanford A. Mosk has noted that the processes of commercialization in Latin America tended "to strengthen and solidify the economic power of the landed aristocracy. Inevitably, political oligarchy was also strengthened." See "An Economist's Point of View," in W. W. Pierson, ed., "Pathology of Democracy in Latin America: A Symposium," *American Political Science Review*, 44 (1950), pp. 118-129. With the qualified exception of the plural societies, the results have been very different in Tropical Africa for at least three reasons: (1) the preservation of indigenous patterns of land tenure; (2) the intrusion of a nonpolitical middle class (Indians in East and Central Africa and Levantines in West Africa); and (3) the reversal in status of social and political élites produced by the indiscriminate education of Africans by Christian missionary societies.

6. Exceptions include the ubiquitous Hausa traders who are spread throughout the Western Sudan, as well as the West Coast Levantines who have accommodated themselves very readily to the new African leadership. One of the reasons for the weakness of nationalism in Northern Nigeria is the inability of the Western-educated militants to gain active financial support from the northern middle class—the Hausa traders.

7. In a series of reports published before the Mau Mau uprising, an urban sociologist engaged in field work in Kenya concluded that there were many economic factors working toward racial integration, and that, provided the Europeans did not use their political power to exclude Indians and Africans, it seemed likely "that economic classes common to all races will evolve." Mary Parker, "Race Relations and Political Development in Kenya," *African Affairs*, 50 (January 1951), pp. 41–52. There is, of course, every likelihood that in African plural societies economic developments may create a sizable African middle class which would become increasingly discontented, nonintegration-minded, and politically assertive, rather than satiated and accommodating toward the white-settler oligarchy. See A. S. Kruger, "South Africa's Native Middle Class," *New Commonwealth*, October 14, 1954, pp. 387–389. Evidence from Brazil, heretofore the model

of successful racial integration in a plural society, suggests that when such a development occurs, lines become more rigid and integration becomes less of an operative ideal. See Ralph L. Beals, "Social Stratification in Latin America," *American Journal of Sociology*, 58 (1953), 327–340.

8. The conspicuous consumption and lack of social responsibility of many elements among the African *nouveaux riches* is disquieting, yet there are also increasing signs in more stabilized situations of a growing sense of public service. Cf. Paul A. Baran, "On the Political Economy of Backwardness," *The Manchester School of Economic and Social Studies*, 20 (1952), pp. 66–84.

9. For anthropological appraisals of African cultural and linguistic survivals see M. J. Herskovits, *The Myth of the Negro Past* (New York: Harper & Bros., 1941), and Joseph H. Greenberg, "Studies in African Linguistic Classification," *Southwestern Journal of Anthropology*, 5 (1949), pp. 309–317.

10. On the Ewe situation see United Nations, Trusteeship Council, *Special Report of the United Nations Visiting Mission to Trust Territories in West Africa, 1952, on the Ewe and Togoland Unification Problem* (November 7, 1952), Document T/304. On the Baganda see Colin Legum, *Must We Lose Africa* (London: W. H. Allen & Co., 1954), and on the role of Kikuyu culture in the Mau Mau see L. S. B. Leakey's two books, *Mau Mau and the Kikuyu* (London: Methuen & Co., 1953), and *Defeating the Mau Mau* (London: Methuen & Co., 1954), as well as J. C. Carothers, *The Psychology of the Mau Mau* (Nairobi: Government Printer, 1954). For a very penetrating study of the role of Malgache culture in the Madagascan rebellion of 1947, see O. Mannoni, *Psychologie de la Colonisation* (Paris: Editions du Seuil, 1950).

11. For an examination of the general problem see "The Cultural Aspects of Economic Growth," in Bert F. Hoselitz, *The Progress of Underdeveloped Areas* (Chicago: University of Chicago Press, 1952), pp. 73–175; Eugene Staley, *The Future of Underdeveloped Countries* (New York: Harper & Bros., 1954), pp. 199–273. For specific treatment of African problems see *Enlargement of the Exchange Economy in Tropical Africa*, pp. 39–54.

12. A particularly intriguing area of inquiry, for example, would be a study of the political temperament and behavior of westernized Ibos of Nigeria in terms of the early conditioning influence of traditional Ibo culture. See M. M. Green, *Ibo Village Affairs* (London: Sedgwick & Jackson, 1947), pp. 139–148, 235 ff.

13. Jean Comhaire, "Some African Problems of Today," *Human Organization*, 10 (1951), pp. 15–18. For a case study of the sociopolitical influences of an urban center upon its hinterland see Edwin S. Munger, *Relational Patterns of Kampala, Uganda* (Chicago: University of Chicago Press, 1951).

14. Earlier comparative studies that are as yet unmatched in excellence are L. P. Mair, *Native Policies in Africa* (London: George Routledge & Sons, 1936), especially pp. 118–260, and Malcolm Hailey, *An African Survey* (London: Oxford University Press, 1938), pp. 345–545. For more recent appraisals of French policy see K. E. Robinson, "French West Africa," *African Affairs*, 50 (April 1951), pp. 121–131. For British policy see Malcolm Hailey, *Native Administration in the British African Territories*, 4 vols. (London: H. M. Stationery Office, 1950); and for Belgian policy see A. F. G. Marzorati, "The Belgian Congo," *African Affairs*, 53 (April 1954), pp. 104–112, and the excellent quarterly *Bulletin du Centre d'Etude des Problèmes Sociaux Indigènes*.

15. K. Onwuka Dike, "African History and Self Government," *West Africa*, February 28, 1953, p. 177. Cf. Gunnar Myrdal, *An American Dilemma* (New York: Harper & Bros., 1944), pp. 749–754, regarding the quest for a history and culture on the part of American Negro intellectuals. For African expressions see K. Ozuomba Mbediwe, *British and Axis Aims in Africa* (New York: W. Wendell Malliet & Co., 1942); A. A. N. Orizu, *Without Bitterness* (Toronto: McClelland & Stewart, 1944); Mbonu Ojike, *My Africa* (New York: Longmans, Green, 1946); D. C. Osadebay, *Africa Sings* (London: Arthur H. Strekwell, 1952); and Jomo Kenyatta, *Facing Mount Kenya* (London: Martin, Secker & Warburg, 1953). A highly exaggerated historical reconstruction is set forth in Amanke Okafor's "West African Background," in Basil Davidson and Adenekan Ademola, eds., *The New West Africa* (London: G. Allen & Unwin, 1953), pp. 20–55.

16. This tendency to gravitate to one's original tribal base is illustrated by the very close relationship between Premier Nnamdi Azikiwe and the Ibo State Union, between Premier Obafemi Awolowo and the all-Yoruba Egbe Omo Oduduwa, and between Jomo Kenyatta and Kikuyu tribal movements.

17. Cf. Godfrey Wilson and Monica Wilson, *The Analysis of Social Change* (Cambridge: Cambridge University Press, 1945). One factor, among several, contributing to the very considerable unity achieved in the southern Gold Coast, is that despite the existence of archaic states, either indirect rule was never fully established, or it proved unworkable.

18. For communist penetration of Africa see Vernon McKay, "Communist Exploitation of Anti-Colonialism and Nationalism in Africa," in C. Grove Haines, ed., *The Threat of Soviet Imperialism* (Baltimore: Johns Hopkins Press, 1954), pp. 258–273; and the article by Max Yergan, "The Communist Threat in Africa," in C. Grove Haines, ed., *Africa Today* (Baltimore: Johns Hopkins Press, 1955), pp. 262–280.

19. See William Bascom, "African Culture and the Missionary," *Civilisations*, 3:4 (1953), pp. 491–501; R. Oliver, *The Missionary Factor in*

East Africa (London: Longmans, Green, 1952); L. P. Groves, *The Planting of Christianity in Africa* (London: Lutterworth Press, 1948).

20. William E. Welmers, "African Languages and Christian Missions," *Civilisations*, 3:4 (1953), pp. 545–561; and Hailey, *An African Survey*, pp. 68–102.

21. The individualism of Protestantism is found not only in its tenets but also in its missionary strategy. The aim has been not to Christianize a people *en masse*, but to gather together a flock of converted individuals. See H. Kraemer, *The Christian Message in a Non-European World* (London: Edinburgh House Press, 1938).

22. Diedrich Westermann, *The African To-day and To-morrow* (London: Oxford University Press, 1949). See also George W. Carpenter, "The Role of Christianity and Islam in Contemporary Africa," in C. Grove Haines, ed., *Africa Today* (Baltimore: Johns Hopkins Press, 1955), pp. 90–113. A recent authority estimates that somewhat less than one-half of the population of West Africa is nominally Muslim; see Alphonse Gouilly, *L'Islam dans l'Afrique Occidentale Française* (Paris: Larousse, 1952), pp. 291–292.

23. The sharp cultural cleavage between the peoples of the Muslim areas of the Western Sudan and the non-Muslim areas of the Guinea Coast is the basis for varying degrees of separatist sentiment in that broad belt of territories stretching from French Guinea to the French Cameroons. In the more developed southern centers in these territories Muslim parties have emerged as a new factor in the developing political situation. Moreover, there are deep cleavages amongst the Muslim elements, particularly between the vast mass of orthodox Sunni Muslims, following Maliki law, and the adherents of the Ahmadiyya movement. See specially J. H. Price, "Islam in the Gold Coast," *West Africa*, December 18, 1954, p. 1188.

24. For a brief survey of the conditioning influence of metropolitan political theory see H. A. Wieschhoff, *Colonial Policies in Africa* (Philadelphia: University of Pennsylvania Press, 1944), pp. 25–61. For a recent comparative study see Philip Garigue, "Changing Political Leadership in West Africa," *Africa*, 24 (July 1954), pp. 220–232.

25. This does not necessarily mean that the prospects for democratic government are any better under such circumstances of rigorous and intensive indoctrination. Arguments against widespread participation in politics are not necessarily undemocratic, especially in what might be called "premature" situations. Cf. W. H. Morris Jones, "In Defense of Apathy," *Political Studies*, 2 (1954), pp. 25–37, and Reinhard Bendix, "Social Stratification and Political Power," *American Political Science Review*, 46 (1951), pp. 357–375.

5 The Character and Viability of African Political Systems

America's principal interest in Africa's political systems is that they be democratic and stable. No other goals would be compatible either with the declared aims and the known aspirations of the African peoples, or with the expressed ideals and the national interest of America. Immediate strategic interests or the imperatives of rapid economic and social development may require greater stress on order and stability, and the present prospects for achieving either goal in most of Africa appear quite remote. Nevertheless, the development of democracy and the maintenance of stability remain as long-range objectives. We will therefore focus upon those forces and situations in contemporary Africa having a bearing on their realization.

Once these objectives are declared, we must emphasize at once that stability does not mean the rigid maintenance of a static society. Nor does democracy mean the presence of any particular set of formal institutions. For us, stability can mean only that governments are sufficiently responsive to popular pressures to ensure that change is orderly and that political authority itself is maintained. For us also, the minimum elements in democracy are freedom from alien rule, the existence of effective and regularized restraints on the exercise of political power, and a political climate in which dissent and opposition are not only tolerated but are provided a legitimate functional role in the political process. Stable African democracies could emerge from quite different social and historical circumstances than those characteristic of Western societies. Indeed, we should not be insensitive to the possibility that special conditions found in devel-

Reprinted from Walter Goldschmidt, ed., *The United States and Africa* (New York: The American Assembly, 1958; 2nd ed., 1963), pp. 27–62.

oping African societies, or that a unique, possibly accidental, sequence and convergence of historical events could serve as functional equivalents to those circumstances with the development of contemporary Western democracies.

Variety of the African Political Scene

The popular image of colonial Africa has tended to be one of a vast, undifferentiated continent. Now that the African peoples have lifted the steel grid of colonialism from more than three-fourths of the face of their continent and have thrust themselves onto the world stage, the complexity and diversity of both the old and new Africa become strikingly evident. True, Africa is a single continent; but the voices, the situations and problems, and the forms of political organization are many and varied.

Africa's diversity is nowhere more strikingly revealed than in the prevailing and emergent forms of government under which the African people live and are seeking to work out their destinies. All the classical types of polities are represented, ranging from a medieval monarchy, through black and white oligarchies and static colonial regimes, to new tutelary democracies and single-party mobilization systems. An awareness and understanding of this political multiformity are important to enable the outsider to comprehend and interpret current political events and to sensitize policymakers and their critics to the limitations and opportunities presented by the different political systems. Policies welcomed and successful in one country may be rejected and totally inappropriate for another. Such political diversity obviously must be fully appreciated for any realistic assessment of the prospects for democracy and stability.

Despite the extraordinary diversity of African political systems, certain general types may be seen which share sufficient similarities to permit some form of classification. The criteria of classification have varied during the past two decades. Prior to and immediately following World War II, African territories were classified according to the imperial power exercising control. By the mid-1950s, the character of the emergent political forms introduced a new and crucial variable. Today, however, the basic distinction is between (1) independent African states (including the two historic African states of Ethiopia and Liberia, and the new and emergent African states that have won or consolidated their independence during the past decade, or now stand on the threshold of receiving it); and (2) colonial and European settler oligarchies (Portuguese Angola and Mozambique, Southern Rhodesia, and the Republic of South Africa), which constitute the final bastion of entrenched European colonialism and minority racial domination in the modern world (see map 3).

Independent African states constitute a comparatively novel type of polity among contemporary political systems. What sets them off as a type—and there are exceptions—is not that they are *sui generis*, but that they represent in the most extreme form those generic attributes of most new states in the developing areas, namely, economic underdevelopment, cultural pluralism, and shortage of high-level manpower. African states tend to cluster at the bottom of any ranking of countries by the conventional indices of economic development. Few countries reflect such a high degree of cultural fragmentation, or are so heavily dependent upon the external world for expatriate technical and administrative personnel. Among other things, this means that the burdens of modernization and the problems of political integration that their political systems confront are more awesome, and the likelihood of success less predictable, than elsewhere.

HISTORIC AFRICAN STATES

The Republic of Liberia and the Kingdom of Ethiopia share most of the foregoing attributes, yet they stand apart from other African states. They are not only the two oldest independent states in Africa, but, except for the brief Italian occupation of Ethiopia, they escaped the colonialism that engulfed the rest of the continent. This unique experience has meant that, alone among African peoples, they have enjoyed the dignity and national pride which go with a long history of national independence. But they have missed the economic and educational development and the widespread popular demand for rapid modernization that colonialism brought to most of Africa. Their economies, social structures, and political systems have remained relatively static for the past century, although recently there have been substantial changes. The two systems are both oligarchies dominated by a culturally distinct minority: in Liberia, it is the Americo-Liberian aristocracy; in Ethiopia, the Amhara ruling class.

The power structures and political process within these ruling oligarchies are quite different. In Ethiopia, the emperor is, in theory and in fact, the supreme source of all power. There are no regularized restraints upon his power, for the constitution and all modern political institutions are his own creation, and all the political actors are his appointees. There are no parties or pressure groups, and no independent or opposition newspapers. A cult has been built around the present emperor, who has consolidated

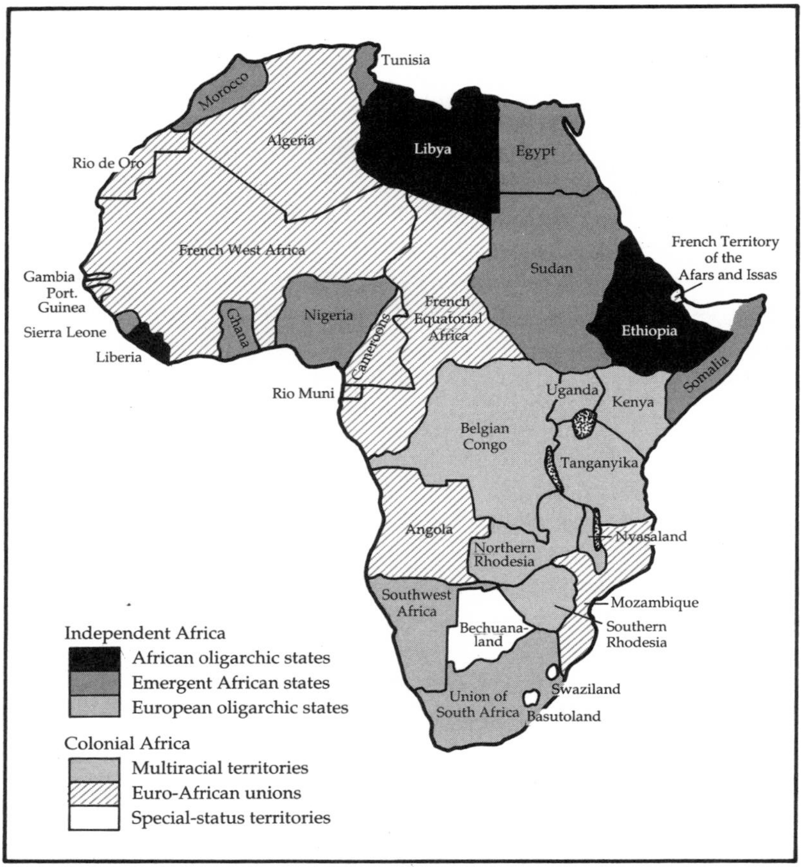

Map 3. Geographical distribution of political systems in Africa, 1963

and maintained his power through the shrewd appointment and manipulation of subordinates and foreign advisers. In Liberia, political institutions and the political climate are democratic in theory. In fact, however, the political process is controlled by the Americo-Liberian oligarchy in Monrovia through the True Whig Party, which has dominated the political scene since 1870. Opposition parties have appeared, but as Thomas Hodgkin observes, "opposition remains an affair of cliques . . . [and], as in any one-party State, there is a tendency for opposition to be confused with heresy." Under the presidency of Mr. William Tubman—in office since 1943—the system is relatively stable, but only qualifiedly democratic within the oligarchy.

Several factors should be kept in mind in considering the continued stability and progressive democratization in Liberia and Ethiopia. The first of these is that, in contrast to South Africa, the Liberian and Ethiopian oligarchies are not closed systems. The original Americo-Liberian founding families have assimilated to a considerable degree with the tribal peoples in the Liberian hinterland. In Ethiopia, no rigid social or official bar has been set against the advancement of members of the conquered tribes and their acceptance in the Amhara ruling group. In both governments, some of the high officials come from tribal groups traditionally dominated by the oligarchies.

Second, the present leaders, President Tubman of Liberia and Emperor Haile Selassie of Ethiopia, are themselves among the principal driving forces toward the modernization and integration of their societies, and both have made cautious gestures in the direction of eventual democratization. As several of the more stable democracies in the world today came about through the progressive democratization of former oligarchies, it might be that it is easier to democratize a stable but adaptable oligarchy than to stabilize an excessively egalitarian society. In any event, whether the present trends in Liberia and Ethiopia continue depends largely on the successors to Tubman and Selassie.

A third point concerns the social and political consequences of the current programs of economic expansion and development in these hitherto stagnant societies. Such development may serve only to strengthen and enrich the present dominant class, as happened in the early stages of the commercialization of the economies of certain oligarchic societies in Latin America. In the long run, however, economic change and growth are bound to unleash a process of social change and movement, which in turn will have its own internal dynamic and should lead to fundamental changes in social structures. For example, neither country now has an indigenous middle class, or a wage-earning class of any significance. Indeed, one of the explanations for the self-perpetuative quality of these oligarchic systems is that heretofore there have been no opportunities outside government employment for the acquisition of status, wealth, or power. Economic development should operate to change this.

A final consideration is the future political role and pretensions of the new university-educated elites emerging in both countries. Until recently, very few Liberians had received a university education. The majority of the first generation of university-trained Ethiopians, who were just beginning to assert themselves in the social life of the country, were murdered by the Italians in the massacres of 1937. During the last decade, however, several hundred Liberians and Ethiopians have been sent abroad by their governments to study in universities, and more are being sent each year. Others are pursuing higher studies in the new universities of Liberia and Addis Ababa. Most of these university graduates are employed by their respective governments in comparatively high status positions, and this is likely to continue. These men constitute a distinctly new class, whose importance is out of proportion to its size and whose future political orientation will be decisive in the political development of the two countries.

This new class may acquire a vested interest in the existing oligarchies and become their strongest defenders and perpetuators, but it is more likely that in due course elements within this elite will be the primary sources of political ferment and change. Not all belong to the oligarchy by origin, and the attractions of becoming national leaders of their "oppressed" groups may be overwhelming. While they assume a posture of defensive pride in their systems in their relations with outsiders, most of them are thoroughgoing modernists who are known to be dissatisfied with the pace and direction of change and the limited role they are allowed to play. This was dramatically revealed in the abortive coup led by Ethiopian intellectuals against the present regime, during the emperor's absence from the country in December 1960. The coup failed because key leaders in the army decided at the last moment to remain loyal to the regime. They supported the objectives, but disagreed with the timing of the revolt.

New and Emergent African States

Since the end of World War II, twenty-nine former African dependencies have become sovereign states, and three more (Kenya, Nyasaland, and Northern Rhodesia) are clearly destined for early self-government under indigenous political leadership. The implications—both external and internal—of this sudden and massive increase in the number of sovereign entities in Africa are profoundly significant. The impact of this array of new states upon international organization and politics is discussed in Chapter 3;[1] here we are concerned with the common characteristics and patterns of internal political development of these states. Before turning to these, however, a few observations on the character of the colonial legacy are in order.

THE COLONIAL LEGACY

The most striking characteristic shared by the new states is their recent emergence from the colonial experience. However history might judge modern Western colonialism in Africa, there is little question that it created the present political entities; it has given them distinct legal personalities, and except for Portuguese and Spanish-dominated areas, it has operated to produce—albeit in varying degrees and in some respects unwittingly—a set of conditions conducive to the modernization and the democratization of their societies. The new and emergent states of Africa have had comparatively greater exposure to modernity than have Liberia and Ethiopia, which missed the colonial experience. This is shown by higher levels of economic development, more widespread education, the emergence of new classes (such as an educated salaried group, a nascent middle class and proletariat, cadres of political and opinion leaders, and a small core of trained civil servants), and a whole array of aspirations of a distinctly modern character. Another characteristic is the wider popular involvement in modern social and political processes, as a result of the development of mass nationalist movements as the vehicles for the attainment of independence (see table 5). Moreover, in the terminal stages of colonial status most colonial governments earnestly sought to introduce massive social change and to endow the emergent political systems with democratic institutions. As a result of this social and political mobilization under colonialism and the drive for independence, a number of elements—the declared national goals, the dominant political symbols, the social expectations, and the standards for judging political action in the postindependence period—became ultrapopulist and ultrademocratic in character. In these and other respects, it could be argued that the colonial experience has greatly enhanced the democratic potential of the new states.

On the other hand, these positive elements are largely negated by other aspects of the imperial legacy. One is the comparative recency and brevity of the very developments noted above. At most, they have occurred on any meaningful scale only during the last decade. Indeed, in the former Belgian Congo, no serious efforts to develop an indigenous administrative

Table 5. Africanization and Party Patterns in Emergent African States (excluding North Africa)

			Number of Parties		Representation by Party Type in National Legislature		
	Africanization of the Higher Civil Service	*Percentage of Electorate voting in last election*	*Contesting last election*	*Represented in National Legislature*	*National Parties*[a]	*Sectional, Tribal and Religious Parties*	*Indepen-dents*
Sudan	[b]	[b]	[b]	6	62%	28%	10%
Ghana	52%	50%	6	6	80	18	2
Federation of Nigeria	53	[c]	[b]	11	46	51	3
Western region	56	68	6	2	100	0	0
Eastern region	52	[b]	[c]	3	92	6	2
Northern region	[b]	[b]	[b]	5	3	97	0
Southern Cameroons	[b]	[b]	[b]	3	0	100	0
Sierra Leone	[b]	[b]	[b]	2	87	0	13
Somaliland	37[d]	[c]	10	4	98	2	0

[a] A national party is one which seeks support in most or all of the constituencies in the emergent state, or (for Nigeria) in more than one region.

[b] Data not available.

[c] Elections partly indirect.

[d] Refers only to the degree of Africanization of the higher posts of the judiciary (magistrates) and administration (chiefs of departments and services, prefects, and district commissioners and delegates).

and political capacity were made until the disastrous headlong rush to independence in the six months preceding the transfer of power in July 1960. The simple fact is, of course, that none of the colonial powers intended to create modern self-governing democratic states in Africa. Western racialism and ethnocentricity perpetuated a widespread belief that the European "presence" in Africa was permanently necessary and desirable. When postwar African nationalism forced a change and imposed a timetable aimed at early independence, procedural and institutional innovations of a "democratic" character were launched on a "crash program" basis. Thus, although most new African states have possessed all of the paraphernalia and pretensions of democratic government at the time of independence, their leaders and peoples have had extremely limited experience with modern democratic institutions. Since survival of such institutions depends heavily upon acceptance and commitment by a people accustomed to their use and confident in their ultimate effectiveness in satisfying wants and attaining goals, the significance of the democratic component of the colonial legacy can be vastly exaggerated.

The critical factor is not that the African peoples have had only a limited experience with the institutions and procedures of democracy; rather, it is that a colonial milieu is not one in which the idea and spirit of democracy—that cluster of attitudes and feelings supportive of the democratic process—can be acquired. On the contrary, a colonial regime is essentially one of bureaucratic authoritarianism, in which government is viewed as the initiator of all public policy, as well as the source of all amenities and of most good jobs. A colonial government rules through petition and administration, and not through political competition and compromise. The public does not participate in the political process; it is "administered" by a bureaucratic elite, which by the system's definition knows what is best. The present generation of African leaders and citizenry was socialized into this type of political system (see table 6). It is most likely that their orientation, attitudes, and feelings toward the present system, and their perception of their role within it, have been determined far more by the type of governmental process they observed during the period of "pure" colonialism than by the last-minute "democratic" innovations made immediately prior to independence.

SOME GENERAL CHARACTERISTICS OF NEW AFRICAN STATES

Three characteristics common to most of the new states are particularly significant for an understanding of contemporary political structures and

Table 6. Patterns of Racial Participation in the Central Organs of Government in British Multiracial Territories in Africa
(All figures given as percentages)

	East Africa			*Federation of Rhodesia and Nyasaland*[a]			
	Uganda	*Tanganyika*	*Kenya*	*Federation*	*Nyasaland*	*Northern Rhodesia*	*Southern Rhodesia*
EUROPEANS							
In population	0.1	0.3	0.8	3.1	0.2	2.2	7.1
In legislative	35	52	62	80	78	85	100
In executive	64	55	71	100	100	100	100
In civil service	[c]	83.5	[c]	100	89	[c]	100
AFRICANS							
In population	99.0	98.6	96.2	96.6	99.6	97.6	92.5
In legislative	50	24	24	20	22	15	0
In executive	27	30	14	0	0	0	0
In civil service	[c]	4.5	[c]	0	10	[c]	0
ASIANS[b]							
In population	0.9	1.1	3.0	0.3	0.2	0.2	0.4
In legislative	15	24	14	0	0	0	0
In executive	9	15	14	0	0	0	0
In civil service	[c]	12	[c]	0	1	[c]	0

[a] Percentages relating to population are for the Federation as a whole; those relating to the Central Organs of Government are for federal institutions only.
[b] Asian includes Arabs, Coloureds, and other non-Europeans.
[c] Figures not available.

trends: (1) their lack of integration; (2) their internal organizational weakness; and (3) their comparative smallness.

Lack of integration Africa's new states are examples par excellence of the "unintegrated" political systems that have precipitatedly emerged from modern colonialism. Internal discontinuities and divisions are many and varied, but three have particular political significance: tribal and sectional tensions, the traditionalist-modernist dichotomy, and the yawning gap between the affluent new political elite and the class of clerks, teachers, skilled artisans, and students who have been, or manifestly will be, less successful in obtaining the fruits of independence.

Political integration is made difficult by the cultural heterogeneity and artificial boundaries that are common characteristics of most national societies in their early formative stages. They are particularly marked in African states, largely because during the scramble for Africa, the metropolitan countries arbitrarily bunched together diverse precolonial African societies into colonial administrative units. Moreover, not only are the peoples within states divided by tribe, religion, and differences in level of development, but several of the international boundaries cut across ethnic groups and thus divide formerly homogeneous cultural communities. Some of these obstacles to integration are illustrated by the accompanying maps of six African states (see map 4).

Colonialism exerted a unifying influence by "holding the ring" within which objective forces of integration, such as more intensive social intercourse and economic interchange, could operate; by imposition of a common administrative, legal, and educational system; by creating a nationally minded educated class; and by simply being the common enemy against which nationalist movements were able to organize a "national" opposition. But, as African colonialism has been comparatively short-lived, these integrative influences have been uneven and limited. Moreover, certain colonial policies—particularly the British policy of "indirect rule"—tended to preserve and exacerbate tribal or regional separatism.

"Tribalism" has been identified by many observers of the African scene, both academic and popular, as the major obstacle to national unification in new states. This is a gross oversimplification of the complex process of integration in Africa and reflects the loose and indiscriminate use of the term "tribe" (as well as the persistence of the notion that the tribe is Africa's only form of social organization) in much discussion of that continent. To be sure, there are many tribes, in the strictly anthropological sense, in Africa. Moreover, the number of persons in Africa who are still living in, or have only recently come from, predominantly tribal societies

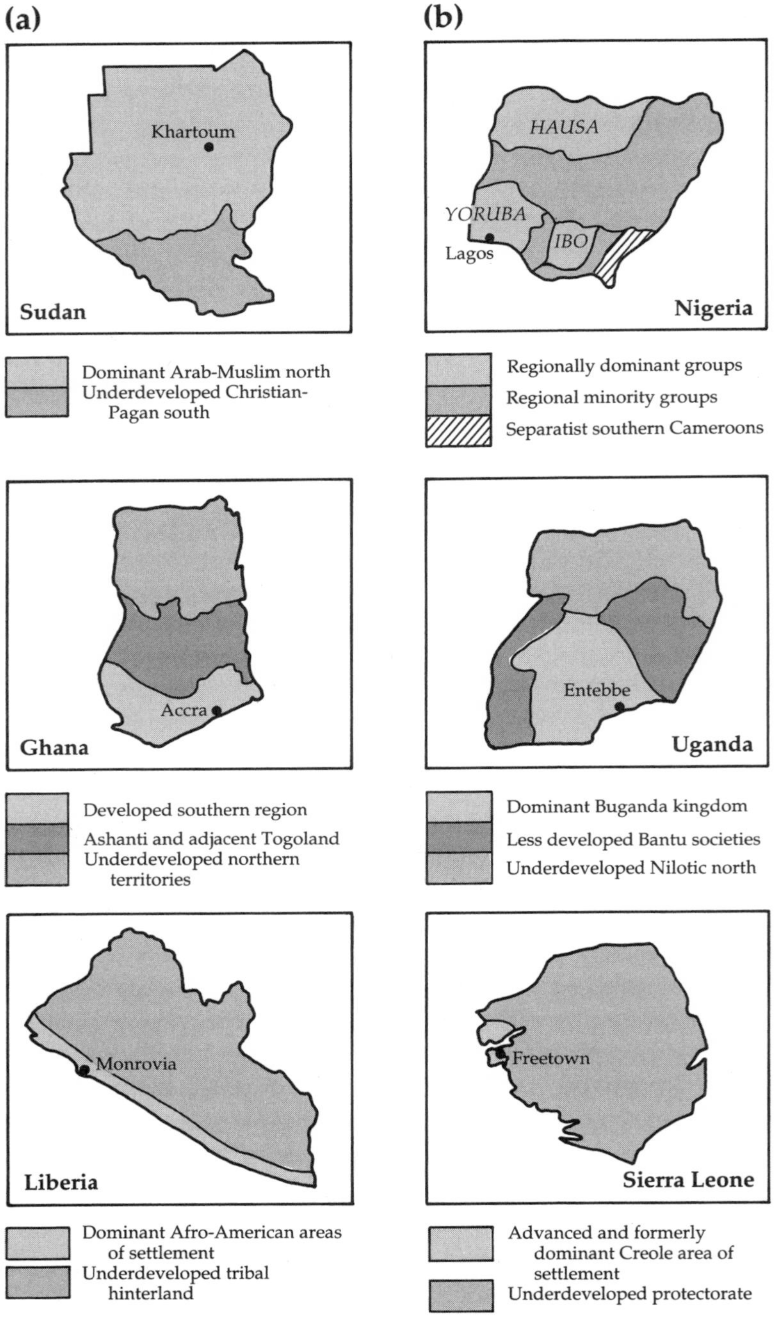

Map 4. Cultural and regional obstacles to integration, 1963, (a) in some African states, and (b) in some emergent societies

is undoubtedly larger than in any other major region in the contemporary world. Yet there are other types of human aggregation and ethnic grouping in Africa that can be called tribes only in the sense that Toynbee refers to all nations as tribes. Many large African ethnic groups, such as the Hausa, who number more than ten million, or the Somali, who number more than two million and occupy an area nearly the size of Texas, would be called nationalities or nations, if located in Europe. The distinction made here between tribes and nontribes in Africa is not a frivolous semantic quibble; it is essential for any sound understanding and analysis of such phenomena as political separatism, irredentism, and regional nationalisms found throughout the continent.

Once these observations are made, it would be incorrect to conclude that genuine tribalism is an unimportant factor in African politics. The general trend for national leaders to condemn any manifestation of tribalism—which, following the loose language of non-Africans, they also use to denote ethnic differences—is fair evidence that it must still be a relevant factor. The size of the ethnic group concerned is an important variable. The fact that Governor-General Nnamdi Azikiwe of Nigeria (an Ibo), Tom Mboy of Kenya (a Luo), and President Joseph Kasavubu of the Congo (a Mukongo) are identified with large ethnic groups is highly significant in the politics of their respective countries. On the other hand, the tribal origin of such men as President Kwame Nkrumah of Ghana, Kenneth Kaunda of Northern Rhodesia, and President Julius Nyerere of Tanganyika, is an irrelevant consideration in their countries because the ethnic groups concerned are small or have never constituted a threat to other groups. Again, for a variety of historical, economic, and geographical reasons, certain groups bifurcated by international boundaries are the source of considerable instability, both within and between new states (e.g., the Ewe, between Ghana and Togo, and the Somali, between Somalia, Ethiopia, and Kenya). Yet other divided groups of not dissimilar size and of equally variant social structure (e.g., the Yoruba, between Nigeria and Dahomey, and the Hausa, between Nigeria and Niger) have so far not created a political problem of any kind. It is not the multiplicity of tribes within a state that is necessarily an obstacle to the creation of a broader nationality—in fact, the larger their number and the smaller their size, the better. It is rather the large ethnic groups—the Foula in Guinea, the Ashanti in Ghana, the Yoruba in Nigeria, the Baganda in Uganda, and the Bemba in Northern Rhodesia—that complicate the task of building a national entity. Thus, although the internal stresses and strains of the new states are very profound indeed, the extent to which tribalism is a contributing cause varies considerably and makes generalization difficult.

Even in those situations in which tribalism, ethnic origin, and regional nationalisms are the source of continual internal tension, we should bear in mind that neither stability nor democracy requires complete uniformity or homogeneity. As R. H. S. Crossman has argued, "The stability of any democracy depends not on imposing a single unitary loyalty and viewpoint but on maintaining conflicting loyalties and viewpoints in a state of tension." Indeed, it is not impossible that, provided a measure of national unity is achieved, the tribal and sectional pluralism of African states could make dictatorship less possible by providing countervailing power centers which cannot be coerced and regimented into a single authoritarian system. Ironically, however, one of the factors nudging several African leaders toward greater authoritarianism, as will be noted subsequently, is the constant threat (real or imaginary) that dissident tribal, ethnic, or regional groups pose to the integrity of the new states. This has been particularly true in the Sudan, Ghana, and Guinea. In Nigeria, however, it could be argued that the tensions between the three regions, each the political core area of a major cultural group, and each unable either to dominate or to separate from the others, has created a structured, multiparty system that is largely responsible for the fact that, at the federal level, Nigeria is unquestionably the most free and open polity in independent Africa.

Social and economic developments that are gaining momentum and could minimize the disruptive effects of tribal or regional separatism include the expansion of the wage earning and commercial sectors of the economy, great social mobility, and the appearance of a new generation of leaders who are more emphatically "national" in outlook. In short, those historic processes which have been integrative elsewhere are also at work in Africa.

A second obstacle to national integration in the new states is the tension between the forces of traditionalism and modernism. Here two issues should be distinguished: (1) the extent to which traditional social systems are a deterrent to the modernization of the economy and societies, and to the integration and democratization of the new political systems; and (2) the character of the relationship between traditional elites (chiefs, emirs, elders) at the head of the indigenous political systems and the modern secular political elites controlling the new states. The popular view that there is an inherent opposition between traditionalism and modernism is false; traditional systems have varying capacities to accept and assimilate modern innovations. Many societies are inherently resistant to change; others, like the Buganda Kingdom, have been able to "traditionalize" innovation with great ease and rapidity; still others, like the conservative and authoritarian Hausa emirates, can be effectively employed by the new secular elites as instruments for economic development. Yet a capacity to accept or to facilitate modernization in the economic and social spheres—thereby furthering the modernizing objectives of the new states—does not necessarily mean that the traditional society concerned will readily accept integration into the new national society. The Baganda of Uganda, and the Chagga of Tanganyika, for example, have been able to absorb modern innovations very rapidly; yet each presents a separatist threat to the political unity of the new states of which they are a part. Indeed, the very capacity of a traditional system to adapt means a capacity to persist—which is exactly what most centralizing, Jacobin-minded national elites do not want.

The extent of the cleavage between traditional and modern elites in the new states has varied considerably in different countries. The problem has been most pronounced in former British and Belgian dependencies, where under the policy of indirect rule, traditional elites were recognized, given status, and used not only as agents in the colonial administrative process, but also as imperial instruments to counter and negate the nationalist activities of the rising educated elites. In a few areas (Nyasaland, Northern Rhodesia, and Western Nigeria), close links were established during the agitational period between radical educated nationalists and traditional rulers. In other instances (Northern Nigeria, Mauritania, Sierra Leone, and the Cameroons) the conservative educated elite governing the new states has close family ties with important elements in the traditional elite. In most cases, however, suspicion and hostility of varying intensity have characterized the relationship between the two sets of elites.

The secular nationalist elites have, with the few exceptions noted, inherited central power, and have used that power progressively to curtail, neutralize, or extinguish the residual authority or influence of the traditionalists. Even in such cases as Nyasaland, where the relationship was fraternally cordial, or Northern Nigeria, where the educated sons of the traditional aristocracy assumed control over the regional government, the same process of centralization at the expense of the traditionalist elites has occurred. This has been most dramatically demonstrated by the recent action of the regional government of Northern Nigeria in removing from office two of the area's most powerful emirs (Kano and Gwandu). Although this general trend toward centralization is everywhere evident, in several of the new and emergent states the acute tensions between the two elites have yet to be resolved.

A third source of conflict in the new states is the persistence after independence of the gap between the comparatively affluent governing class and the mass of the people, but most particularly the clerk-teacher-artisan class. One of the most striking, and vulnerable, aspects of the social structure of colonial societies was the yawning gulf between the standard of living, perquisites, and social status of the members of the alien governing elite and of the indigenous subaltern clerk class whose aspirations and frustrations were particularly intense. In most African states, there has been little change since independence in the size and nature of the gap, or in the atmosphere of tension, fear, and envy between the two categories separated by it. The only change has been that the nationalist veterans of the agitational period, themselves recruited mainly from the clerk class, have been catapulted into the offices and homes rapidly vacated by the departing alien governing class.

Plans for economic and social development and for increased educational opportunity are all directed toward the creation of a social structure in which these gross discrepancies will be eliminated. But these are "long haul" measures, and over the next decade one can anticipate little change unless drastic measures are taken. In the meantime, two related postindependence trends operate to intensify the disaffection and political explosiveness caused by the gap. One is the growing discontent in those new states where saturation has already begun to be reached in the upper stratum of the social structure. A new generation of secondary school and university graduates, arriving on the scene in ever increasing numbers, is acutely aware that it will undoubtedly not have the opportunities of the present generation to climb rapidly to high positions of power and affluence. Moreover, in the government service—the source of most prestigious jobs—these graduates are compelled to accept junior positions, working under persons with little education and training, and frequently of very limited capacity. As the rate of upward mobility is progressively curtailed, discontent in the government service could assume proportions equalled only by the frustration felt by junior African clerks working under Europeans during the colonial period.

A second, and politically even more explosive, category of disaffected persons is the primary "school leavers," one of the most serious social—and, in due course, political—problems the governing elites of the new states may have to confront. For most of these states, independence meant the launching of vast new programs of educational development. Ironically, despite the almost limitless needs for trained manpower, the economies of the new states and the number of postprimary educational facilities are not expanding at a rate sufficient to provide career opportunities for the tidal wave of primary school leavers now commencing to hit the job market. The unemployment levels in this category are alarmingly high in many urban centers. The school leavers flocking to the cities create a high potential for mob action, and constitute a social category vulnerable to political manipulation by rival groups. Indeed, it is this very category which provided the mass base for agitational meetings and nationalist demonstrations in the preindependence quest for power by the present governing elites.

Internal organizational weakness The weakness of central authoritative institutions, and the limited development of an indigenous bureaucracy, army, and police force are among the more arresting internal structural characteristics of the new African states. They are a reflection, as already noted, of European colonial systems that neither anticipated nor desired early termination. Africanization of higher administrative, technical, and managerial positions was not seriously pursued until the very last "crash program" phase of colonial rule. Ironically, the departure of experienced personnel, and their replacement by raw recruits with limited training and experience, has been occurring simultaneously with a great expansion in the scope of government and a staggering increase in the demands made upon it. It is indeed truly remarkable that the fragile administrative structures of the new states have thus far avoided complete collapse.

That they have not has been due to several ameliorating factors. One is that despite the headlong rush toward full Africanization, many senior colonial officials have remained on in key roles, in some cases on pension, in most instances on contract (see table 7). Although acutely sensitive to the pressures for Africanization, leaders of African governments have very realistically faced up to their administrative unpreparedness and weakness, and have agreed to generous arrangements to cover personnel willing to remain on for a transitional period. Former colonial powers have also made generous provision for financial assistance and career guarantees to maximize the retention or recruitment of experienced administrators and technicians. The French government, for example, has recruited and subsidized a large number of *conseillers techniques* for all former French dependencies that have requested them. Moreover, upon conclusion of their service to the African governments, these advisers are assured careers in the French home civil service. The United Nations Organization and its specialized agencies and the large American foundations have also provided substantial financial and technical assistance for the establishment of institutes of public administration and accelerated in-service training programs. The African governments themselves have tailed their scholarship programs to ensure that the products from universities or technical training institutions, both in the home countries and abroad, will be channeled

Table 7. Africanization and Party Patterns in French Tropical African Territories
(All figures given as percentages)

	Africanization of the Higher Civil Service		*Representation by Party Type in Territorial and Federation Assemblies*		
	State	*Territorial*	*Trans-territorial Parties*	*Territorial Parties*	*Sectional and Tribal Parties and Independents*
Federation of French West Africa (8 territories)	23	70	73	20	7
Federation of French Equatorial Africa (4 territories)	7	41	38	57	5
Autonomous Republic of Togoland	29	72	0	0	100
Trust Territory of the Cameroons	8	80	0	0	100

into the most critically short categories. Finally, a significant number of those Africans who have entered the higher civil service have had extensive experience as clerks in the administration during the colonial period. This latter fact has tended to be undervalued. Certainly their presence has provided a measure of continuity.

The strong postindependence drive for rapid Africanization in the new states has undoubtedly resulted in a decline in efficiency and probity in government. Moreover, there is bound not to be a normal age spread within the administrative hierarchy. Europeans of various ages, at different rungs in the career ladder of the higher civil service, have been replaced by Africans all of roughly the same age. When all positions are Africanized, there could be virtual stagnation for nearly a generation, because of the absence of normal attrition and the consequent "promotion freeze." Thus there is a danger of an acute shortage of career outlets for the upcoming generation. Only the development of new and attractive careers in both government and the private sector could prevent the political instability such a situation would create.

Military establishments have been the last of the authoritative structures of government to be created in sub-Saharan Africa. Among the new states, only the Sudan, Senegal, and the Congo could claim at the time of independence to have a national army of any significance. This very fact illuminates the internal organizational weakness of the new states. In each of these three countries, the military establishment has played a decisive role in the political life of the country since independence. It has had more than a little impact upon the thinking not only of national political leaders, but also of the new cadres of army officers commanding the small but expanding national armies in other new states. Given the serious internal tensions, and the comparative fragility of other authoritative structures and central institutions, national armies are obviously destined to exert a profound influence on the future course of internal political development. (The fragility of the central institutions of the new states is strikingly revealed by the fact that it required no more than a platoon of disgruntled soldiers to overthrow the Olympio government in Togo and establish a successor regime.)

Each of the new sovereign states, large or small, is seeking to create some type of national military establishment of its own. States like the Sudan and Senegal inherited seasoned military units already bearing the name of the country concerned; in other states, such as Ghana, Nigeria, and Tanganyika, leaders have had to build a national force from segments of former interterritorial forces fragmented in the process of independence (e.g., the West African Frontier Force and the King's African Rifles); still others have started with nothing at all. Whatever the colonial legacy, the new states confront three internal problems of considerable political significance: the problem of ethnic balance in recruitment, the problem of civilian supremacy, and the problem of intraservice unity and discipline.

During the colonial period, the pattern of recruitment for defense forces primarily reflected imperial needs and security calculations, but also the fact that men from certain tribes or ethnic groups were predisposed to seek military careers and made better soldiers to boot. Thus, for example, the majority of recruits in Nigeria and Ghana came from the northern areas of those two countries, partly because in the eyes of the British government those areas were politically more reliable, and partly because men from northern ethnic groups actively sought life in the colonial defense forces. Again, in Kenya and in Uganda, the number of Kikuyu and Baganda soldiers is insignificant; yet the Kikuyu and the Baganda are numerically the largest, and politically the most important, ethnic groups in those countries. This same pattern of differential recruitment for African military—and police—units prevailed throughout colonial Africa. This has meant that the governing elites of the new states have been confronted with a gross imbalance in the ethnic and regional composition of the national armies they are seeking to create.

The imbalance was confined mainly to enlisted ranks, because of the reluctance of the colonial powers to create an indigenous officer corps. The 25,000-man Force Publique of the former Belgian Congo, for example, had no indigenous officers at the time of Congolese independence—which, incidentally, accounts for much of the chaos that followed. In the postindependence crash program to create a corps of African officers, leaders have faced the problem of ethnic imbalance in another form: because of regional differences in the availability of secondary education, the recruitment of officer cadets for military schools on the basis of merit alone would obviously favor candidates from ethnic groups in the educationally more developed regions. This ethnic imbalance in the composition of the new national armies has been a matter of grave concern to the governing elites. President Nkrumah of Ghana, for example, was confronted at independence with an army composed predominantly of northerners, yet it was in the north that his personal position, as well as that of his party, was least secure. He was forced to retain expatriate officers in top command positions after independence while enforcing the principle of ethnic and regional balance in recruitment, and maintaining a special concern with the political orientation and reliability of the new officer corps.

As national armies become stronger in Africa's new states, it is doubtful whether the Anglo-American principle of civilian supremacy over the military will prevail. It is certainly an element in the colonial legacy, and it is also part of the ethos of military academies such as Sandhurst, where a sizable number of the new African army officers have received their training. Yet the model is not untarnished (e.g., the French Army in Algeria), and in any event, much of Tropical Africa, particularly those areas under French and Portuguese control, was ruled in quasi-military fashion with military officers carrying their titles (e.g., *commandant du cercle*) while occupying higher administrative positions. Moreover, an increasing number of African officers are receiving their military training in Soviet bloc countries, or from Soviet personnel in African countries.

It could be argued that the civilian elites now in the process of creating the new armies are in a position to devise a variety of safeguards to ensure civil primacy, but these can hardly remain once the military emerges as a semiautonomous structure. In fact, there are many elements in the situation which invite or compel army officers to use their organizational strength to seize or seek control over government: the puritanical impulse to cleanse the country of the corruption of civilian leaders; the fragility and impotence of civilian-controlled structures to modernize the society, to preserve national unity, to maintain internal security, or to attain development goals; and, of course, the simple age-old impulse to enjoy power. Whatever the motive, African peoples, accustomed by colonialism to bureaucratic authoritarian government and desirous of rapid modernization, might well be attracted to army rule, if only for a transitional period.

National armies in Africa's new states are regarded not merely as standby forces for defense and internal security, but as integral parts of the whole national modernization effort. The extent to which they can serve constructively in this heroic task, either as adjuncts of civilian power or as controllers of the government, will depend upon the degree of internal unity and discipline they can achieve. Experience in the Sudan, Senegal, and the Congo, however, has demonstrated that the cohesiveness of the African army can be seriously threatened not only by ethnic conflicts, but also by tensions between senior and junior officer groups, and by rival factions within the army that have ethnic, ideological, or constituency links with rival factions in the governing party or competing groups within the society. The fact that the new armies are being developed on a crash-program basis, and therefore lack strong service traditions, maximizes the likelihood that tensions within the society will be reflected in the ranks of the army, particularly in the absence of a countervailing and restraining ethos of professionalism. Thus, military rule in Africa would not necessarily mean political stability, much less accelerated modernization.

Smallness in scale Africa is the continent par excellence of the "microstate." The majority of its political entities (twenty-five out of forty-five) have populations of less than three million. Only three countries (Nigeria, Egypt, and Ethiopia) have populations in excess of twenty million. The political fragmentation of the colonial period has altered very little in the transition to independent statehood. With few exceptions, African leaders in each of the artificial entities created by colonialism have sought and attained separate sovereign statehood under the slogan "independence first, then unity." This has occurred despite the artificiality of colonial boundaries, the unintegrated character of the societies embraced within those boundaries, the brevity of colonial rule, and the strong ideological commitment of African leaders to the idea of African unity.

The reasons for the continuation of Africa's political fragmentation are many and varied. They include the disinclination of the colonial powers to combine neighboring territories, or to regroup them along more rational lines (although colonialism did reduce the number of separate units from more than seven hundred to under fifty); the many practical considerations that made it expedient for African leaders to seek independence within the confines of the existing territory, and particularly to "territorialize" what in origin was a general racial nationalism; the need to inculcate "national" loyalties and to protect "national" interests once independence has been won; and the rapid and inevitable development of vested private and group interests once a sovereign unit has been created. In all these respects, of course, Africa is not unlike other former colonial continents; its only claim to uniqueness is that it has more land, is more sparsely populated, and was divided up into more units.

The argument for relatively large political entities is usually made on the grounds that this encourages economic growth and the maintenance of international peace. The political fragmentation of a region into a multitude of microstates is not only a deterrent to economic growth but maximizes the likelihood of interstate conflicts. Economic development is impeded because of the obstacles to mobility of goods and services, and because a disproportionate share of the national income must be diverted to government and administration. The probability of interstate conflicts increases, because there are a greater number of interacting sovereign units, each with its own national interests and army. As one contemplates the emerging pattern in Africa, it becomes clear that these general propositions are applicable to its array of new microstates.

However, several ameliorating factors should be taken into consideration. In the precarious postindependence period, the new elites are highly vulnerable, and the smallness in scale makes it easier for them to cope with the awesome problems of administering, unifying, and developing the societies of which they have charge. Also, federation or unification would not necessarily result in greater economy; it might mean simply that another higher and overarching set of expensive governmental structures would be established, as has happened in the only two examples thus far—Somalia and Cameroon. Moreover, African states are working on a number of functional economic relationships and collective security arrangements to minimize the disadvantages of fragmentation. It is possible that economic necessity and ideological predisposition will lead to new patterns of cooperation. Finally, we should be ever mindful that many African states are "micro" only in terms of the size of their present population. Science, technology, and improved standards of living all point to an impending population explosion in Africa.

THE CONSUMMATION OF FREEDOM

The single most important factor serving to explain postindependence political developments in the new African states is their burning drive to consummate freedom. African leaders are agonizingly aware that legal independence has not substantially altered the fact that they are heavily dependent on the rest of the world. President Sekou Touré has stated the case very eloquently:

> The anticolonial struggle was not brought to an end on September 28, far from it! It has merely been taken up again, more powerfully than ever, under its double aspect of the struggle against the remnants of the colonial regime.

To African nationalists neocolonialism does not mean the imposition of new forms of alien control from outside Africa; rather, it is the persistence of residual European influence in Africa itself. Moreover, it is not direct political control or influence that is the irritant, but the omnipresent cultural influence of the West, which saturates all aspects of life, and daily reminds the African of the ignominy he suffers for having blindly aped all aspects of an alien system, and for continuing to depend upon that system. As Touré put it, the demand is for "integral decolonization":

> When we say "Decolonization" we mean we want to destroy the habits, conceptions and ways of conduct of colonialism. We are determined to replace them with forms that are Guinean forms, conceived by the people of Guinea, adapted to the conditions, to the means, to the aspirations of the people of Guinea.

Although Touré has stated the argument more bluntly than other leaders, he is unquestionably the apostle of a new generation of African nationalism.

The practical political implications of this impulse to consummate the "African revolution" go far beyond mere Africanization of the civil service. They involve increasing state intervention into the schools and universities, to ensure Africanization of the curriculum, and into the economy, to maximize local control and initiative. They necessitate a self-conscious eclecticism in the adaptation of inherited political forms and in the fashioning of new procedures and institutions. Not only will the altered forms be something that can be called uniquely African, or Ghanaian, or Guinean, but the ideology and the rationale underlying the new forms will be identified as distinctly African. This is seen not only in such vague concepts as "African personality" and "Négritude" but more importantly in such notions as "African socialism." It will be several decades before this psychological revolution is consummated; in the meantime, the powerful quest for cultural identity and pride that it reflects must be accorded a political significance it has often not received.

THE ONE-PARTY TREND

The dominance of the one-party system is the most distinctive political feature of all newly independent states in sub-Saharan Africa. There are only two exceptions: the Republic of the Sudan, where the ruling military power has outlawed all parties, and the Federation of Nigeria, which has in effect three competing one-party regional systems, none of which has been, or is likely to be, able to control the whole. Elsewhere, there is either only one party by law (Mali, Guinea, Ivory Coast, and Chad), or one party overwhelmingly dominates the system. In all cases where competing parties existed at the time of independence, there has been a seemingly inexorable consolidation of control by one dominant party. Moreover, the process of consolidation is continuing in all of those states where it is not completed, and in those states on the threshold of independence, there is every indication that the same process is in motion.

There is one major explanation for this remarkable phenomenon: the extraordinary—indeed virtually limitless—power possessed or inherited by the majority party at the time of independence. This party may have already legally secured a monopoly over the political system (e.g., the Parti Démocratique de Guinée [PDG] in Guinea and the Parti Démocratique de la Côte d'Ivoire [PDCI] in the Ivory Coast), or it may have controlled only slightly more than half of the votes in the most recent preindependence elections (e.g., Togo and the Cameroons). In either event, the end result has tended to be the same. The task of consolidating power has been relatively easy in the former countries. Majority parties in the second category, that is, those who had not been able to preempt the political arena or monopolize nationalist symbols prior to the transfer of power, have had greater difficulty, but eventually their overwhelming predominance in the system has become nearly as complete.

A majority party that is the legal successor to a departing colonial regime inherits, or by default acquires, almost unparalleled power and freedom of action once it becomes the government of the day. It inherits the full panoply of legal powers and statutes, of coercive and punitive procedures, carefully developed by a colonial regime that was, as previously noted, bureaucratic authoritarianism in its purest form. It is also legatee to the enormous powers possessed by a government in a society in which virtually all services (roads, communications, schools, hospitals, water supplies, and scholarships), and most good jobs, are under the control of the governing party. The discriminatory use of these latter powers is among the more decisive elements responsible for the phenomenon known as the "vanishing opposition." When the power of deprivation of services and patronage is insufficient to persuade opposition elements to cease activity and to join the governing party in a vast *parti unifié*, or united front, then the more classical forms of persuasion or neutralization—imprisonment of opposition leaders, harassment by contrived allegations, censorship, and curtailment of political liberties—can be, and in several instances have been, employed.

The governing party in the immediate postindependence period not only inherits the massive legal powers possessed by the former colonial regime, as well as the vast patronage powers of the government of a welfare state, but it also functions in a virtual institutional vacuum. As we have noted, other central authoritative structures are weak, fragile, or nonexistent. The bureaucracy is in a state of violent transition, armies are either in an organizational state or are nonexistent, and national legislatures and parliaments have not yet had the chance to develop into significant central institutions. Because of the internal organizational weakness of other potential power centers, governing political parties have tended to emerge by default as the single authoritative structures in the new states.

Endowed with such comparatively unfettered power, the leaders of dominant parties have moved progressively toward the one-party system, in response to a variety of factors and pressures. One of these is the character of the opposition. In all but a few instances, opposition groups have tended to fall into one of three categories, each of which could reasonably be regarded as a threat to the integrity or independence of the new state: (1) groups identified closely with the interests of the former colonial power or its agents (e.g. the Conakat Party in Katanga); (2) groups based upon tribal, ethnic, or regional sentiment; and (3) groups linked with hostile regimes or movements in neighboring states. Thus, acceptance of the idea of a "loyal opposition," fundamental to the Western concept of democracy, has been difficult, because most opposition movements have ultimately sought support from "disloyal" sources.

Another consideration furthering one-party rule is the magnitude of the task of modernization. Most African leaders would support Walt Rostow's assertion that "the building of an effective centralized national state has been almost universally a necessary condition for [economic] take-off." In their eyes, the monolithic single party is the only structure *in being* which will enable them to overcome internal disunities and create a stabilized political community, mobilize the human and material resources of their country, and otherwise attain those basic preconditions for economic growth. As in all developing areas, authoritarianism—whether of the communist, Kemalist, or "guided democracy" variety—offers many attractions as a means for accelerating the pace of modernization and economic development, and for integrating and stabilizing the new national societies.

Single-party rule also maximizes the likelihood that the present governing elite will be able to perpetuate itself in office. This is, of course, a timeless and universal impulse among all ruling groups. In the contemporary African context, however, the wide gap in the social structure intensifies the struggle of the elite to remain on top and to resist at all costs the long fall back to the meager and drab existence of the clerk class, whence most of them have come.

These are a few of the considerations that help to explain the marked trend toward single-party regimes in the new states. Since most of the present generation of African leaders have been exposed to Western political values and are hypersensitive to the fact that they are being judged by Western democratic standards, they have made a special effort to justify and to rationalize the one-party system. In addition to the various practical considerations discussed above (i.e., the disloyal character of opposition movements and the imperatives of modernization), party theoreticians have argued that the single party is a distinctive institutional pattern expressive of African culture. The argument is that in traditional African democracy there was no concept of an opposition within a society; a person was either an integral part of the society or an alien. Moreover, decision-making was a process of "talking it out" until unanimity was reached, a tradition African Marxists have hailed as supportive of the principle of "democratic centralism." The latter also argue that in traditional African societies there are no classes; hence, Marxism in Africa means "African socialism"—a heresy with which Moscow and Peking find it difficult to cope. Obviously, however, given the cultural pluralism of precolonial Africa, one can find a traditional cultural analogue and justification for any type of political system, ranging from the most egalitarian democracy to the purest form of despotism.

African apologists or rationalizers of single-party government seek to validate it on other than traditional grounds. For African Marxists—and most leaders in French-speaking Africa, and not a few in English-speaking Africa, are declared Marxists—the single monolithic Party, reaching from the Central Committee of the Political Bureau down to the smallest village cell, needs no rationalization. It is the only valid form of political organization in a mobilization regime. Democracy, they claim, is found within the Party. A second and less doctrinaire argument is that in developing societies there exists a singularity of focus upon, and commitment to, agreed national goals; therefore, competing parties are an unnecessary luxury, diverting national energies and confusing the national will. In balance, whatever the theoretical defense, it is clear that for the predictable future the notion of a formal opposition party in Africa's new political systems will continue to be regarded either as unwelcome or heretical.

Colonial and European Settler Oligarchies

One of the characteristic features of British colonial policy in the past has been the willingness to devolve political power into the hands of resident white settlers, in those territories where the size and demands of the white community made such action necessary or expedient. This policy was largely founded on the belief that white British subjects had the right to responsible local government wherever they might reside, and that they would be as objective and humane as colonial officials in carrying out the burdens of trusteeship for the African masses. The European minorities in the Republic of South Africa and in Southern Rhodesia were the beneficiaries of this policy. In 1910 and 1923, respectively, they were given responsible government—South Africa as a Dominion (in 1931 it became fully independent), and Southern Rhodesia as a "self-governing colony."

Since the acquisition of internal self-government, the European oligarchies in these two countries have consolidated their positions of control over the African community through a long series of differentiating legislative enactments. Such measures have included the delimitation of separate European and African areas, laws to control the movement and residence of Africans, a legalized industrial color bar, the denial of African representation or participation in the central organs of government, and systems of "direct" European administration. Their positions were made even more secure by instituting stringent systems of social control and employing a variety of both subtle and overt devices designed to prevent or frustrate any serious challenge by the African community. In most of these measures, Southern Rhodesia has tended to follow the lead of the Republic of South Africa.

Southern Rhodesia The political systems of Southern Rhodesia and South Africa are essentially similar in that they are oligarchical, are based upon the fundamental assumption of white supremacy, and receive the support of the overwhelming majority of Europeans in the two countries.

Beginning in 1953, however, there was a naive hope among some persons that Southern Rhodesia might be progressively democratized, and its racial caste system broken down, as a result of its being a constituent unit of the new Federation of Rhodesia and Nyasaland. The constitution of the Federation was based on the principle of interracial "partnership," and provided for African participation in the central organs of government. From the very beginning, however, the Federation was destined to fail because of the violent opposition of Africans in Nyasaland and Northern Rhodesia. The rapid growth of nationalism and the rise to power of a new generation of militant leaders finally compelled the British Government to agree, early in 1963, to a dissolution of the Federation and to the ultimate independence under African leadership of the two northern territories. These developments provoked an equally violent reaction from the European oligarchy in Southern Rhodesia, manifested immediately in the victory at the polls of the Rhodesian Front Party—a European right-wing racist movement—over the United Federal Party, the so-called "pro-partnership" group. Throughout 1962 and early 1963, the Southern Rhodesian government banned all African nationalist organizations and enacted sweeping new security laws. The British agreement to secession by Nyasaland and Northern Rhodesia provoked an immediate demand for independence by the European oligarchy in Southern Rhodesia, and the threat of unilateral action if Britain refused. Thus, by mid-1963, Southern Rhodesia had emerged as one of the several racial tinder boxes of European-dominated southern Africa.

The Republic of South Africa Although the European oligarchies in both Southern Rhodesia and the Republic are determined at all costs to preserve their supremacy, the Republic is in an infinitely better position to do so. It is comparatively wealthy, it has industrialized rapidly, possesses its own munitions industry, and more than 3 million Europeans call the country their home. The ruling oligarchy is relatively secure in its power, and is employing the entire machinery of the state to perpetuate a political system that is undemocratic in fact as well as in constitutional theory. Three points deserve consideration: the question of democracy within the oligarchy; factors affecting the stability of the present system; and the long-run prospects for a progressive democratization of that system. There can be little question that, except for certain features, the political process within the white oligarchy has in the broadest sense been democratic. One of the exceptions is the lack of open dissent and discussion within the ruling Nationalist Party. The special history and psychology of the Afrikaner community has produced a strong determination on the part of its leaders not only to create the impression of monolithic unity but by various subtle measures to enforce such unity within the ranks of Afrikanerdom. This has further accentuated the historic tendency for membership in each of the two major parties to be predominantly of one nationality.

Other features, far more disquieting in the eyes of critics, are found in the actions of the Nationalist Party leadership since it came to power in 1948, namely, the lack of respect for normal constitutional restraints in carrying out certain aspects of its apartheid program, the "Afrikanerization" of the higher civil service and key posts in the foreign service, army, and police, and government intrusions in the realm of higher education. Critics maintain that these measures have led to what is in effect an Afrikaner dictatorship, not only over the non-European majority but also over the non-Afrikaner elements in the oligarchy. Sympathizers stress the basic agreement within much of the European community on government policies, including in particular the maintenance of white supremacy.

Most persons outside the Republic of South Africa now regard the situation as one pregnant with impending disaster. Yet, there is the possibility that a measure of sentimentality leads to an underestimation of the strength of several elements of police state stability in the present system. The strongest of these is the extraordinarily stringent system of social and police control over actual or potential African political leaders and dissident Europeans in particular and over the non-European community in general. Backed by a comprehensive array of "security" acts, the authorities have been able to immobilize nationalist-minded African leadership and to make it virtually impossible for meaningful, united, and sustained political action to be organized in the non-European community.

The stability of the present regime is further strengthened by its policy of building up the traditional, largely rural, Bantu sector. Whether intended or not, this has the effect of sharpening existing cleavages and hampering unity of action between the African rural mass and the more nationalistic and educated urban leadership. Moreover, many policies of the present government have either the active or tacit support of a majority of the Europeans, and whatever organized liberal opposition exists is politically weak, if not impotent. In sum, from a short-run standpoint the present regime is stable.

The prospects of an ultimate racial holocaust are made virtually certain by the intransigence of the overwhelming majority of Europeans regarding the principle of white supremacy; the fact that most politically minded Africans have passed the point of no return and will not accept any arrangement other than majority (i.e., African) domination; and the determination, and increasingly the capacity, of independent African states to give ever-increasing assistance, ranging from refuge and operational bases for guerrilla groups to military training and supply. The tragedy is that there is no higher or external legal authority, such as that of the United Kingdom Government over Kenya or of the United States Government over the American South, which could enforce progressive democratization.

Portuguese Africa Portugal was the first, and is now the last, major colonial power in Africa. Until the outbreak of the nationalist rebellion in northern Angola, in 1961, the Portuguese system gave the appearance of being remarkably stable, albeit an authoritarian stability. Even the limited successes of the rebellion, however, revealed the basic weakness of the Portuguese system. The fact that there had previously been no overt nationalist movement in Portuguese territories is explained by the thoroughgoing policy of repression and exile for dissidents, the extremely limited opportunities for higher education, and the lack of contact between most Portuguese Africans and "free" political systems. Since 1960, however, the emergence of independent states on the northern borders of Angola and Mozambique has transformed the situation. Dar-es-Salaam has become the headquarters for resistance groups organized for agitational and guerrilla activity in Mozambique, and Leopoldville performs a similar function for Angolan groups. The independence of Nyasaland and Northern Rhodesia will unquestionably lead to an acceleration of such resistance activity. The African leaders of all the neighboring independent states are publicly committed to a policy of support for the resistance groups.

The Portuguese response to these unexpected challenges has been characteristically Portuguese: a few paper reforms legally abolishing the status known as *Assimilado* (after three hundred years no more than 0.3 percent of the Angolan population had achieved that status in any event), new economic development plans, and a new labor code; but there is little visible evidence of the radical transformation in approach and reform the situation demands. On the contrary, existing systems of social and police control have been tightened, and security forces and the number of white settlers from metropolitan Portugal have vastly increased. The point of gravest concern is that the Portuguese system will collapse precipitately like the Congo before any serious steps will have been taken to prepare even a handful of Portuguese-speaking Africans to handle the awesome tasks of government. Like Southern Rhodesia and South Africa, Portuguese colonialism in Africa not only imposes upon the liberal West one of its most agonizing moral problems, it has created a situation so pregnant with disaster that a peaceful solution, or one that does not leave a residue of racial bitterness that can affect the West's relations with Africa for generations to come, appears impossible.

Implications for American Policy

America cannot have a monolithic policy in Africa. Our major objective of democratic and stable political systems, although apparently hopelessly unrealizable in the predictable future, remains applicable throughout the continent. But we must pursue this objective through variant policies adapted to the different political situations.

In the new and emergent African states, we must be sympathetic to and understanding of the actions of leaders and governments related to the quest for the consummation and consolidation of African independence. We must be tolerant of the various forms of government and economy in Africa, recognizing the special circumstances that make their forms different from our own, and possibly necessary during a transitional period. We should also realize that the goals of democracy can be achieved through different types of institutions and cultural forms.

We must recognize that there are limits to which the political systems of the new states can be constructively assisted by external agencies. The political system of every independent country reflects a unique alignment of internal forces and a distinctive way of making decisions and maintaining order. Moreover, the leaders and peoples of the new states are understandably sensitive to outside judgment on the way in which they manage their affairs. This does not mean that we must withhold comment or censure in cases of authoritarian excesses; it does mean that we should ensure that our judgment is free from ethnocentrism and historical prejudice, and make certain that it is based on facts and is not premature.

The major direct contribution that both the private and public sectors of American society can make to assist the political development of the new states, and yet not be vulnerable to the charge of intervention, is to expand opportunities for higher education and professional training for Africans, particularly in the fields of public administration and political economy. This would improve the qualifications of the new political and bureaucratic elites, and thereby increase their capacity to cope with the many critical problems of nation-building and development discussed in this chapter.

We must categorically affirm our complete opposition to the continuation of the colonial and European oligarchies of southern Africa, but at the same time offer to facilitate and assist in every way possible the painful process of adjustment required. Through private diplomatic channels, as well as in the United Nations, we should apply the greatest possible pressure for reform upon the governments concerned. The problems of transition in these areas are staggering, but the costs and lessons of the Congo tragedy should remind us of the painful consequences of inaction. It should also impress upon us the paralysis our government will inevitably suffer when racial conflagrations in these areas finally erupt and invite or compel external intervention. The Katanga imbroglio revealed with stark clarity the existence in American society of powerful forces that oppose our government's pursuit of a positive and creative policy in situations where the survival of a dominant white minority, or substantial American private economic, or national strategic, interests are involved. Katanga was the catalyst which activated and joined together a melange of ultraright and oppositional fringe groups (e.g., anti-United Nations, anti-foreign aid, pro-isolationist, pro-white supremacy, pro-big business), backed by a well-financed Katanga lobby with a surprising influence in prominent congressional circles. Yet Katanga is but an eye-opener to the far greater domestic opposition our government will confront once intervention in South Africa becomes an immediate policy issue.

NOTES

1. Vernon McKay, "Changing External Pressures on Africa," in Walter Goldschmidt, ed., *The United States and Africa*, 2d rev. ed. (New York: Columbia University Press, 1963), pp. 74–112. [Note added and reference completed by the editor; no other references are given in the original.]

6 Tradition and Nationalism in Tropical Africa

Introduction

The relationship between tradition and nationalism in Tropical Africa is generally regarded as having been a negative and mutually antagonistic one. African tradition has connoted, among other things, conservatism, subservience, and dependence, smallness in scale, parochialism, and rule by an illiterate gerontocracy. African nationalism, by contrast has implied progress, independence, expansion in scale, and leadership by youthful and educated modernists. Whereas elsewhere tradition may have inspired nationalism, in Africa it has tended to be regarded—most militantly by the nationalists themselves—as one of the causes of national humiliation and as the main obstacle to modern nationhood. Divisive tribalism, stagnating customs, and obstructive chieftainships of traditional Africa were considered, along with colonialism itself, as the chief enemies of nationalism. In a word, futurism, not traditionalism, has been the ethos of African nationalism.

The crude characterization of the relationship, although not unreasonable when painting with a broad brush, seriously oversimplifies the complex realities of both African tradition and African nationalism as well as their frequently subtle relationship. Our purpose here is to examine this relationship with special emphasis upon the ways in which tradition was a factor affecting nationalism in the preindependence period.

Reprinted from Martin Kilson, ed., *New States in the Modern World* (Cambridge, Mass., and London: Harvard University Press, 1975), pp. 3–36.

THE CONCEPT OF TRADITION

The concept of tradition has acquired a bewildering variety of meanings. It is pointless, therefore, to discuss its relationships to nationalism without some conceptual clarification and precision. At the outset four types of tradition ought to be distinguished:

Typological tradition The widespread use of Max Weber's ideal-type construct,[1] together with the equally common use of a simplified transition model[2] and of dichotomous and pattern-variable modes of analysis[3] in the study of change and modernization of whole societies—the emerging preoccupation of most social sciences—have tended to create or to perpetuate a grossly oversimplified and stereotyped image of the nature of tradition in the developing areas, and particularly in Africa. These analytical devices have many advantages.[4] Moreover, the study of change compels one to specify a baseline, and some concept of a "traditional society" is understandably the usual baseline used.[5] Also, when one is making broad sweeping comparisons of a vast array of complex phenomena a high level of abstraction is probably inevitable. The end result, however, has been an image of a uniform, homogeneous, and static traditional African society, whose attributes characteristically include a predominance of ascriptive, particularistic, and diffuse patterns, nonlegal rational bases of authority, limited mobility and differentiation, and so forth. Indeed, one gets the impression that the trait list of ideal-typical traditionality is derived not from the observation of concrete "traditional societies" but simply from a specification of the polar opposites of a trait list of typological modernity derived from a generalization about contemporary industrialized societies in the West. The extensive and frequently uncritical use of these analytical devices has contributed no little to confused thinking and dubious generalizations about the nature of tradition in Africa.

Stereotypical tradition This is by far the oldest type of characterization of tradition in Africa. In a brilliant analysis of stereotypes about Africa, Igor Kopytoff has noted:

> The scarcely human beings in the writings of antiquity give way in the early Age of Exploration to stable polities ruled by kings and nobles. Where Arab travelers saw virtue in relation to Islamic influence, the European Enlightenment, alienated from its own social order, created the virtuous, because untouched, "noble savage" from whom Europe could learn in its quest for regeneration. The latter images are more familiar, for many of them are still with us.

> Unbridled lawlessness coexisted with robots in the iron grip of unchanging custom, and witch-ridden paranoiacs under tyrannous chiefs vied with happy villagers living in communal harmony. The common thread here is ethnocentrism . . . the universal tendency of all people to perceive other culture patterns through the categories and concerns of their own. The resulting myths may be positive or negative.[6]

One is naturally concerned about the extent to which the ostensibly social scientific formulation of typological tradition discussed above has been influenced by the ethnocentric image of African tradition derived from the highly varied and frequently contradictory stereotypes by which the external world has characterized Africa over the centuries.

Mythopoeic tradition This tradition refers to the generalized, and equally ethnocentric, flattering images African nationalists and Afrophiles hold and seek to propagate about African tradition. The images are invariably positive; they frequently are consciously created to counter pejorative stereotypes. Indeed, as nationalistic interpretations of tradition they are themselves expressions of nationalism. They are a near universal accompaniment of nationalism. As Max Radin put it: "In antiquity as in modern times a sense of nationalism may create characteristics not only for persons but for entire groups . . . tradition assists in building a national ideal and therefore helps to create the complex of nationalism. A national ideal usually means a flattering self-portrayal on the part of a people in which certain traits are singled out as especially characteristic."[7]

Empirical tradition This tradition is the complex of existential "attitudes, beliefs, conventions and institutions rooted in the experience of the past and exerting an orienting and normative influence on the present."[8] Whether or not a particular tradition exists at a given point in time is an empirical question but one that is admittedly very difficult to answer.

These four distinctions are only analytical, but they are important ones to make. A mythopoeic tradition can become a stereotype and elements in it can even become part of the trait list of a typological tradition. A flattering stereotype regarding African tradition developed externally can be, and has been, expropriated by African nationalists and made part of their mythopoeic tradition. In any event, we are here primarily concerned with the last three types—with how external pejorative stereotypes of African tradition have reinforced nationalist protest, with how African nationalists have been affected by or have sought to create a mythopoeic tradition, and with how elements in the empirical African tradition affected the rise and pattern of development of African nationalism.

Before turning to these issues, the concept of tradition requires further examination. One point concerns the vexing question of which "experience of the past" is to be regarded as "traditional." The dilemma is put succinctly by Thomas Hodgkin:

> During the first phase [of Africa's interaction with the West] African governments and peoples—in particular those which, like Dahomey, Segu, Samory's military empire, Bornu under Rabeh Zubayr, Mahdist Sudan, were involved in organized and active resistance to European penetration—were naturally concerned to preserve their established institutions, values, and ways of life. These institutions and values cannot properly be described as "traditional," since the nineteenth century was in certain respects a revolutionary period in African history, and the regimes which resisted European aggression most effectively were in many cases either the products of revolutionary upheavals or attempting to carry out policies of internal reform and modernization. Moreover these regimes had already been exposed, in some instances over a long period of time, to Western influences.[9]

Similar uncertainty regarding the "traditional" is created by the new traditions introduced and the old traditions transformed during the colonial period. In former British Africa, for example, efforts were made to introduce the institution of chieftainship among many groups in which it was not indigenous. In many cases these efforts failed; but in some instances the innovation caught on and presumably became part of the tradition of the group concerned. Again, the idea of a "Kamerun" nation acquired the power of a tradition as evidenced by its revival after thirty years and subsequent influence upon nationalist development in the two trust territories.

One might argue that the only reasonable position in the face of these confusions is to recognize the ambiguities in Africa's traditions produced by its mixed-up precolonial past and arbitrarily to specify that the state of affairs prevailing in African societies at the time of the formal imposition of colonial rule would be regarded as the baseline traditional order.[10] But this overlooks the fact, underscored by Kopytoff, that the institutional framework within which most Africans were operating during the most intensive nationalism—was "a blend of precolonial and postcolonial institutions." He adds that "for the actors in a given social system, the analytical difference between what may be called 'traditional' and other elements may not be relevant, for nontraditional elements have become a part of the present social mythology and shape the expectations of people."[11] Indeed, in many situations it is impossible to distinguish precolonial tradition from the amalgams of tradition emerging out of the experiences and innovations of the colonial period and then specify their respective relationship to nationalism.

A further complicating factor is that contradictory, or at least noncongruent, traditions can exist as different levels or in different aspects of activity of even a single homogeneous society. This fact, Kopytoff notes, is what has made modern anthropology "extremely skeptical of the utility of shorthand descriptions of whole societies," not to mention embryonic nations or whole continents or races.[12] In this same vein Hodgkin has brought out the multivalence of the Islamic tradition in Africa. Whether the conservative authoritarian tradition, or the radical reformative tradition of Islam will be articulated by a given movement or institutional arrangement is probably situationally determined. The fact is, of course, that sacred Islamic scripture, like the Bible, can be interpreted to support either tradition.[13]

A final general point about the concept of tradition is that there is considerable variation in the responsiveness and adaptive capability of the traditions of indigenous African societies. Such diversity in the response pattern of traditional orders elsewhere is now well established in the works of Evon Vogt, Herbert Blumer, and others.[14] A traditional order can reject, tolerate, assimilate, or exploit an innovation; and, as well, elements of tradition can themselves be exploited by a modernizing movement. This latter phenomenon has been termed a "reinforcing dualism" by Robert Ward and Dankwart A. Rustow.[15]

THE CONCEPT OF NATIONALISM

There is no point to an elaborate definitional exercise on the vexing concept of "nationalism" and "nation" in the African context; the literature on this issue is already too extensive, the issues and the realities are fairly well known, and in the final analysis one has to be arbitrary, as I must be here. In one short sentence Professor Jacob Ajayi illuminates what we mean by nationalism: "In contrast to nineteenth century Europe where the basic aim of nationalism was to fit people who shared the same culture and language into a nation-state, the fundamental yearning of African nationalism has been to weld peoples speaking different languages and

Table 8. Types of Collectivity

Collectivity of Reference	*Working Concept for Sentiment and Activity Manifest by/for Collectivity*
Race, continent, or subcontinent (Negro race, the African continent, *Afrique noire*)	Pan-Africanism
Colonial territory (new state; presumptive new nation: e.g., Ghana, Congo, Kenya, Senegal)	Nationalism
Subterritorial collectivities	
Nationalities, either *historic* (ethnolinguistic collectivities with previous political unity: e.g., Baganda, Barotse, Bakongo; or without such unity, e.g., Kikuyu, Ewe, Ibo) or *situational* (large-scale collectivities acquiring identity and self-consciousness through supertribalization: Bangala, Baluhya, etc.)	Ethnic nationalisms (ethnicity)
Tribes (small-scale ethnolinguistic, kinship-defined collectivities)	Tribalism (micronationalism)
Regions and localities	Regionalism or localism
Any collectivity which asserted itself against alien rule prior to the emergence of an organized territorial nationalist movement as the presumptive successor regime (e.g., primary resistance, nativistic or traditionalistic movements, independent churches, etc.)	Protonationalism

having different traditional cultures into one nation state."[16] For our purposes the concept "nationalism" and allied concepts will be used according to the schema shown in table 8.[17]

These working definitions provoke three observations. One is that by arbitrarily confining the concept of "nationalism" to the colonial territory as the collectivity of reference one makes the negative relationship between tradition and nationalism a function of the definition. This is true, but only in part. In the modern world nationalism is generally regarded as attaching to the nation-state, and with only a few exceptions it has been the artificial colonial territories which have become the new states creating their own nations. The history of postcolonial Africa only serves to reinforce and confirm this historic phenomenon.[18] Second, in broad historical perspective one must recognize the existence of a variety of forms of self-assertion and resistance among the African peoples which were just as "anticolonial" as the more organized forms of territorial nationalism. It was undoubtedly concern over this point—that is, that scholars overlooked or ignored earlier protest movements as a result of how they defined their phenomenon—that led Hodgkin to include under the rubric of "nationalism" any and all forms of protest from the beginning of colonialism.[19] Recognizing the validity of his argument has led us to include here the category "protonationalism" to cover these earlier phenomena, which were manifestly more closely linked to African "tradition."

A third observation concerns the extraordinary complexity one encounters in defining and classifying subterritorial collectivities and their corresponding modes of self-assertion. The task would be simple if they all fell into the categories either of historic traditional kingdoms (for example, Buganda, Barotse, or the Northern Nigerian emirates) or of such small-scale "traditional tribes" (in the purely anthropological sense) as Colonel Gowon's Birom of Northern Nigeria. The fact is that the overwhelming majority of subterritorial collectivities fall in an indeterminate intermediate category. Some large-scale aggregations had an ethnolinguistic basis for being a distinct identity (for example, Yoruba, Ibo, Hausa, Kikuyu, Luo, and so on), but their self-consciousness as an entity is largely the product of developments during the colonial period, including particularly the rise of territorial nationalisms. Other large-scale aggregations, which had little or no objective ethnolinguistic basis for a distinct identity, acquired a self-consciousness as a result of the phenomenon of "supertribalization" or "ethnic redefinition" described by Wallerstein, Mercier, and Young.[20] Indeed, in some instance, new self-conscious "ethnic" collectivities emerged that were based solely upon artificial administrative units.[21]

The foregoing underscores the fact that a subterritorial ethnic collectivity is not, as Emerson said of a nation, a preordained entity which, "like Sleeping Beauty, needs only the appropriate kiss to bring it to vibrant life."[22] In a large measure, subterritorial "ethnic" consciousness, like nationalism itself, is situationally induced and determined and therefore ultimately definable only in subjective terms. As Mercier, drawing on Nadel, put it:

> It is impossible to answer always by "yes" or "no" such questions as: Is the ethnic group defined by the common origin of its members? Is it a culturally homogeneous unit? Is it linguistically homogeneous? Does it have a common way of life? Is it a politically organized unit, or, at least, a whole where cooperation between constituent elements is intense and constant? S. F. Nadel concluded that the ethnic reality can never be objectively delineated. An eth-

> nic group is identical with the theory which its members have of it.[23]

Given this indetermination it is manifestly difficult to say that a particular ethnic collectivity, or the ethnic consciousness which it expresses, is in any meaningful sense "traditional."[24]

The genesis and the evolution of African nationalism have been significantly affected by, and in turn have affected, at least three different aspects of what we will loosely call African tradition, namely, traditional ethnic grouping (with all of the qualifications already noted); traditional political elites; and traditional political cultures. Viewing African nationalism as the dependent variable, we are primarily concerned here with how these three elements of traditionality affected its development.

Nationalism and Traditional Ethnic Groupings

THE PRIMACY OF THE TERRITORY AS THE NATION

The persistence of popular attachments to traditional ethnic groupings has been regarded by most nationalists and their external supporters as antithetical to nationalism.[25] This is not so only because such groupings were by definition subnational but because of the uncritical belief that the continuation of such attachments prevented the development of a positive sense of identification with the territorial nation nationalists were seeking to create. The concept, the feasibility, of multiple loyalties were not recognized. Most nationalists, Jacobinic rather than Burkean in their orientation, were ideologically determined to eliminate all *corps intermédiaires*. There were some notable exceptions—Chief Obafemi Awolowo of Nigeria and Joseph Kasavubu of the Congo being cases in point. Awolowo, for example, argued that Nigeria's "ultimate goal" should be an arrangement whereby "each group, however small, is entitled to the same treatment as any other group, however large."[26] Kasavubu and other Abako leaders, Lemarchand notes, "conceived of the Congolese nation as an aggregate of distinctive loyalties based on 'ethnic, linguistic, and historical' affinities . . . [and] favored the maintenance and preservation of all intermediate groups."[27] Both men, be it noted, were leaders simultaneously of a large nationality group (the Yoruba and Bakongo respectively) and of national political parties operating within the framework of the emergent territorial nation. In balance, however, most nationalist leaders were hostile, rhetorically at least, to what they viewed as parochial ethnic groupings, to what Tom Mboya has called "negative tribalism."[28]

The African nationalists' animus toward traditional ethnic groupings is understandable once the larger territory became the sole focus for their nation-building efforts. But why did the territories become the focus? The usual explanation has been the manifest unsuitability of Africa's traditional units for modern independent statehood coupled with the strong attraction of nationalists to larger-scale polities. The goals of African nationalists, Professor Ajayi has observed, were "the creation of larger, economically and technologically developed nations able to take their places on a basis of equality with other nations in the world."[29] The key word here is probably "equality." As Ali Mazrui has argued: "Nationalism in Africa is still more egalitarian than libertarian in its ultimate aspirations . . . whereas the Americans proclaimed 'equality' in pursuit of independence, the African nationalists have now sought independence in pursuit of equality. . . . Perhaps it is useful to coin a term like 'dignitarianism' for such a movement."[30] Others of "dignitarian" persuasion, such as Margery Perham, attribute the special African passion for equality and racial acceptance to the "sense of humiliation upon realizing their own retarded position among the peoples of the world. . . . Denied so many of the things which have given birth and nourishment to nationalism elsewhere, Africans, it seems, are obliged to draw upon [this] one main source."[31] To Thomas Hodgkin such "psychoanalytic" explanations betray a "residual intellectual colonialism" which only serves "to strengthen the common, but mistaken Western view that Africa is a special case, its revolution unlike other revolutions in human history."[32]

The nationalists' preference for the colonial territory over the traditional ethnic group as the nation-to-be cannot be convincingly explained solely—or even mainly—by their quest to achieve equality and dignity through large-scale polities. If this were so how does one explain the host of microstates which independent Africa presented to the international community and the willful neglect of unparalleled opportunities to join the modern state system within the framework such large-scale polities as ex-French *Afrique noire* (for which a suitable African name could easily have been found), or the Mali or East African federations? Surely there are other, more significant, determinants of their choice. Political necessity was obviously one important factor. The realities of the power structure, as well as the variable colonial policies and practices of the different imperial countries, made it necessary for nationalists to seek independence within the political unit in which fate had placed them, and this was the territory. It was this sheer practical necessity to seek independence within the existing power unit which made the territory the focus, rather than any subterritorial ethnic group or supraterritorial entity.

The choice of the territory over the traditional group was further strengthened by the far greater opportunity it presented for rapid upward social mobility and political ascendancy of a rising class of new modernizing elites. Margery Perham's query of 1937 (referring to Nnamdi Azikiwe) underscores the limited career opportunities for the new class available in most traditional African societies: "But what scope . . . can the rudimentary Ibo groups offer to one of the tribe who has spent ten years at American universities accumulating academic qualifications?"[33] Thus, their choice was not simply based on the judgment that traditional groups would not be viable modern states for realizing the collective equality and dignity of the African peoples involved; an equally compelling explanation is that such groups patently did not offer the career opportunities and prospect of high status for an aggressive, upwardly mobile new class in the same way as did the territory. The admittedly typical case of Buganda, which did offer such upward mobility and thereby deflected the focus of Buganda nationalism from the territory to the traditional kingdom, is the striking exception that confirms the point.[34] In the same vein the history of Zambian nationalism would have been considerably different had the political structure and culture of the Barotse Kingdom provided similar scope and opportunity for individual self-realization of the Lozi members of its rising educated class.[35]

A final point is that analysts have probably tended to underestimate the extent to which territories did acquire a personality and an integrity of their own during the relatively brief period of colonialism, and were in fact—and not just aspiration—embryonic nations, despite the accidents of their creation and the artificiality and irrationality of their boundaries. Identities can be crystallized fairly quickly by situational pressures, vested interests, career calculations, and the myriad other forces that operate to differentiate terminal political communities. As Ajayi put it, "As the European administrations became more and more effective, the colonial boundaries, arbitrary as many of them were, began to acquire some significance for the African. Each territorial unit was becoming the focus of some national loyalty of its own."[36]

VARIABILITY IN THE ROLE OF ETHNICITY IN NATIONALISM

There have been many factors which have affected the strength and determined the role of ethnicity in the development of territorial nationalism, but at least three variables are particularly significant: the ecology and political structure of traditional societies; the nature of colonial policies regarding traditional ethnic groupings; and the ethnic pattern of the territory. In comparing the phenomenon of tribalism in West Africa (particularly Nigeria), on the one hand, and East and Central Africa (Congo excluded) on the other, Peter Lloyd hinted that its manifestation may in part be a function of more highly developed peasant agriculture. The societies in West Africa, he observes, "are peasant societies; many of the farmers grow a crop for export and a very small proportion of the population lives in the modern town or works as wage labour. . . . The rural areas are here better developed with schools and dispensaries. Pride in one's natal area might well grow in Central Africa if rural development is hastened."[37] Assuming the argument regarding differences between the two areas is valid (and there is much evidence that it needs serious qualification), the notion that there is a correlation between vigorous peasantry and extreme localism is a familiar one in the comparative study of nationalisms. One collaborative group of scholars put it this way: "Peasants remain completely untouched by the intellectual and political elements of modern nationalism. Their distinctive dresses and customs are local rather than national; they dislike not only the foreigner but also the men from the next village; . . . left to themselves, they will never produce a national movement."[38] This inherent localism of the agrarian peasant may or may not be the basis for an ethnic nationalism in conflict with a territorial nationalism—much would depend upon the size of the ethnic group concerned. However, the problem is more complicated than this, because heightened ethnicity in Africa has tended to be a nonpeasant, mainly urban, phenomenon.

Another proposition is that which postulates a positive correlation between those traditional societies with a history of previous political unity and the assertion of an ethnic nationalism. Hodgkin put the proposition this way: "Ethnic loyalties tend, or have tended, in fact, to be strongest among peoples like the Hausa-Fulani in Northern Nigeria or the Yoruba in Western Nigeria, the Ashanti in Ghana, the Moshi in Upper Volta, who had behind them, in the precolonial period, well-developed powerful states, which were not in any intelligible sense 'tribal.'"[39] The interesting and comparative study of Buganda and Ashanti by David Apter provides further support to this line of argument.[40] A related proposition advanced by Parkin and Banton, at first seemingly—but, in fact, not—contradictory to the preceding one, posits a positive correlation between politically uncentralized traditional societies (that is, those which have had no history of political unity or centralization) and the predisposition to form urban ethnic associations.[41] Ian Lewis has challenged this proposition on the basis of other evidence and advances an alternative situational explanation for the variability in the formation of such associations. The crucial factors leading to their formation, he argues "are less the pre-existing political systems of those concerned than their overall political circumstances at any point in time in the urban situation." In those urban situations where the members of a particular ethnic group are "treated as outsiders and constitute a sensitive minority, and whose traditional tribal structure—*whatever its type*—is not sufficiently closely associated with the town in which they live to meet their needs satisfactorily," they will form such associations.[42] The fact is that once ethnic oppositions within a territory are aggravated, ethnicity is a phenomenon manifest by all of the interacting collectivities and usually with equal intensity. Indeed, on balance it would be difficult to decide which of two contrasting types of traditional societies, the Ashanti and the Ibo, for example, were more ethnically self-conscious in the development of territorial nationalism in Ghana and Nigeria respectively.

Explanations for the variability in the manifestations of ethnicity in nationalist development usually place considerable weight upon the policies and practices toward ethnic groupings of the colonial powers. Certain general facts are widely recognized and require no discussion, namely, that there were declared differences in policies associated with the concepts of direct rule (France) indirect rule (Britain), and quasi-indirect rule (Belgium and Portugal); that these policies were not uniformly applied nor uniformly successful, and in many instances there was little to differentiate the actual patterns of colonial rule; and that where indirect rule was applied in a thoroughgoing manner (for example, the Buganda and Barotse kingdoms) there has been greater ethnic self-consciousness among the groups involved than where direct rule (the deliberate efforts to extinguish ethnic identity) was practiced. Thus, in general, ethnicity is markedly less visible in ex-French Africa than in ex-British Africa. Beyond this the only safe generalization one can make is that at most the different colonial policies accentuated or minimized predispositions but were not in themselves the decisive, or necessarily even the most significant, determinant of ethnicity, despite much nationalist rhetoric about "divide and rule."[43]

Ethnicity as a factor in nationalist development in a given territory has been accentuated or attenuated according to the particular patterning of its ethnic groups. This fact underscores once again the role of the situation as both a precipitant and determinant. The effect of ethnic patterns can be analyzed in terms of types of ethnic patterns, ethnic stratification, and the cumulation of ethnic differentiation with other processes of differentiation. Clifford Geertz has suggested a typology of what he calls "concrete patterns of primordial diversity."[44] Adapting his typology to the African situation, at least five patterns are discernible: the uniethnic pattern, represented only by Somalia, Lesotho, and Swaziland, in which the intended divisions are intraethnic in character; the bi-ethnic pattern, in which one group is dominant over one or more other groups within the territory (for example the Watutsis in preindependent Ruanda); the "duopoly" pattern,[45] of which the Matabele and Mashona of Rhodesia are the best example; the tripolar pattern, found in Nigeria (Hausa, Yoruba, and Ibo) and Kenya (Kikuyu, Luo, and the political aggregate of the remaining groups); and the multiethnic pattern, of which Tanzania, Zambia, and the Congo are illustrative.

Ethnic self-consciousness has tended to be more pronounced, and more prone to escalate, in those situations where the relationship among groups was one of ethnic stratification (the bi-ethnic pattern) rather than ethnic coexistence (the multiethnic pattern).[46] Territories having a pattern of duopoly or a tripolar pattern were, as in all situations of bi- or tripolarity, vulnerable to the delicate balance of their ethnic duality or plurality suddenly giving way to a polarization into total ethnic bloc opposition or rivalry. Only in the case of the multiethnic pattern have there been opportunities to avoid rigid confrontations, partly because of the absence of actual or threatened domination by one group, but mainly because of the amenability of such situations to ethnic bargaining, shifting ethnic alliances in the classical balance of power syndrome, or the shrewd use of ethnic arithmetic by nationalist leaders so disposed.

Ethnic stratification characterized the relationship of many groups throughout Africa at the time of the formal imposition of colonial rule and the present territorial boundaries. In only a few cases (for example, former Ruanda, Urundi, and Zanzibar) was the system of ethnic stratification coterminous with the territorial boundaries. In all other cases it was limited to the relationships among groups in only parts of the territories (for example, Northern Nigeria and the Hima kingdoms of Uganda). One of the paradoxes of British colonial policy was the deliberate perpetuation of preexisting stratifications, while at the same time allowing full scope for the operation of other destratifying influences (education, urbanization, mobility, economic change) which frequently had their greatest impact on grounds in the lower strata of the prevailing stratification systems. Thus, one found in most British territories a dual process at work; on the one hand, efforts were made to preserve established systems of ethnic stratification within a context of social change; and, on the other hand, modernizing forces were allowed to spawn new, upwardly mobile elements pushing aggressively into the top stratum of an emerging territorial stratification system. As these territories entered their nationalist era a massive process of restratification was already in progress—previously dominant ethnic groups confronted or were already caught up in a radical downward "status reversal," while previously subordinate groups had already acquired or had the vision of obtaining high status in the emerging territorial social structure and polity. This juxtaposition of the frustrations of the *nouveaux pauvres* and the aggressiveness of the *nouveaux riches* greatly intensified ethnic self-consciousness and rivalry, which the growth of nationalism only served to exacerbate.

Individuals were, of course, the direct beneficiaries in this process of restratification, but because of the phenomenon of "cumulation," differentiation within the new territorial stratification system tended to fall heavily upon ethnic lines. "The paramount fact," Mercier notes, "is that modern differentiations arising from the degree of economic and educational development, the nature of religious transformations, etc., *cumulate* with traditional differentiations."[47] As is well known, modernizing status-producing influences such as education and the commercialization of land and labor have had an uneven impact upon African societies, and for a variety of reasons (geographical location, cultural receptivity or resistance to innovation, overpopulation, adequacy of the traditional societies to provide scope for new elites, and so on) differentiation within the new territorial stratification systems has fallen heavily along ethnic lines.[48] This is one important reason why modernizing nationalism, in the short run at least, heightens rather than diminishes interterritorial ethnic nationalism. As Zolberg notes, "cross-pressures that might inhibit conflict" are weak or nonexistent.[49]

Certain types of ethnic mix, ethnic stratification, and ethnic restratification resulting from cumulation provide the basis for ethnic self-nationalism itself which, ironically, intensified and escalated ethnic subnationalisms. "Where there is original unity," Emerson notes, "nationalism serves further to unite; where there is a felt ethnic diversity, nationalism is no cure."[50] The reasons for the positive correlation between the development of territorial nationalism and the escalation of subterritorial ethnic nationalisms are now fairly well known and documented: ethnic groups provided the most secure political base for territorial "national" leaders, and it was to this base that they almost invariably gravitated in the competitive territorial arena;[51] urban ethnic associations, frequently linked to more comprehensive panethnic movements, provided the original organizational infrastructure of many territorial nationalist movements, and few of the latter were ever able to emancipate themselves from this dependence;[52] as territorial nationalism grew in strength and achieved some of its objectives (universal suffrage and, through elections, greater representation and presence in central government, as well as accelerated socioeconomic modernization), these very achievements intensified ethnic nationalisms for the obvious reasons of competition, fear of ultimate domination by one ethnic group, and increased ethnic differentiation through cumulation;[53] and colonial powers frequently aided and abetted ethnic movements and associations as a counterbalance to or disintegrator of territorial nationalism.[54] That this is not a peculiarly African phenomenon but one generic to all new states in the process of birth is now well established.[55]

These are ways in which ethnic self-consciousness negatively affected and was affected by territorial nationalism. However, there are other ways, as Wallerstein, Mercier, and Sklar have shown, in which ethnicity contributed to national integration and to nationalism. Mercier argues that "nationalism and tribalism are not always two radically opposed types of movements. In the new states, ethnic identity does not always have a centrifugal effect. . . . Ethnic diversity can, in many different ways, contribute to unification to be utilized towards that end."[56] Wallerstein's case in support of this thesis is that urban ethnicity tends to reduce the kinship tie, that urban ethnic groups are instruments for resocialization and keeping the class structure fluid, and that they also serve as outlets for political tensions by making it possible for aggrieved individuals to challenge persons rather than the office they occupy.[57] To these integrative functions Zolberg adds the contribution urban ethnicity makes to secularization, and by introducing a secular political loyalty, which inevitably operated to undermine traditional structures and to facilitate the institutions of new forms of government.[58] This latter thesis is not unrelated to Sklar's proposition that Yoruba pantribalism, being supratribal and cosmopolitan, was like Jewish Zionism in its innate secularity and capacity to produce "a sense of 'national' identity among peoples who are ethnically or tribally diverse but culturally related."[59] And because Yoruba pantribalism provided the main support for a "nationalist" territorial party it thereby contributed to the movement for national independence.

The essence of these arguments would seem to be that urban ethnicity and pantribalism are supratribal and secular, and therefore nontraditional, phenomena. Therefore, to the extent that people are emancipated from essentially kinship-defined ethnic groups (the real tribes) and acquire through supertribalization a new secular identity with a larger "nontraditional" aggregate, the bond with traditionalism is thereby weakened or extinguished and those concerned are more open and flexible to new, possibly multiple, and certainly larger-scale affiliations. But the fact remains that the ethnic redefinition that produces such supertribes or self-conscious pantribal nationalities is still a subnational phenomenon. And one could argue both logically and from the actual pattern of nationalist development in Africa that it has not been the "ethnic" obstacles to the emergence of territorial "national" identities, but the supertribalized collectivities (the Mongo and Bangala in the Congo) or the large-scale and newly self-conscious nationalities (Yoruba, Ibo, Kikuyu, Luo, and so on) that have been the main problem. To elevate, expand, and redefine ethnic identity to larger subterritorial aggregates, no matter what their scale, is still not solving the problem. And as Zolberg concludes, "from the point of view of participants in the system, the contributions of conflict and ethnicity to national integration are less visible than the obstacles they created."[60]

A second line of argument is Sklar's thesis that ethnicity in the form of communal partisanship contributed to the diffusion of nationalism because the competing communal groups could be manipulated by competing national parties to further the movement for national independence. Traditional communal rivalries were exploited by rival nationalist groups in their effort to cumulate and articulate grievances of any kind and thereby deepen their influence in the countryside. Terence Ranger has illuminated this same process of nationalization of parochialism in his study of the Lozi. Several leading UNIP (United National Independence Party) territorial nationalists in preindependence Zambia were from the Lozi aristocracy, sons of still prominent personalities in the traditional elite of the Barotse Kingdom who were, during the critical period of the nationalist struggle for independence, in opposition to the then paramount chief. Ranger concludes: "The sweeping victory of UNIP candidates in the 1962 elections in Barotseland should have come as no surprise. Arthur Wina and Mubiana Nalilungwe . . . offered a traditional form of leadership to the Lozi voters, even though one now in opposition to the paramount rather than in alliance with him."[61] These and numerous other examples of territorial nationalist manipulation and penetration of traditional communal conflict illuminate the way in which traditionalism provided channels for political communication and situations facilitating political mobilization. As Sklar put it: "Millions of tradition-bound people were drawn through the medium of communal partisanship into the mainstream of political activity when they accepted the leadership of progressive nationalists. Therein lies its historic significance. Communal partisanship, based on psychological commitments to the traditional values of tribal groups, was utilized by nationalist leaders to mobilize mass support in rural area and old towns."[62]

Nationalism and Traditional Political Elites

In a discussion of the rise of African nationalism Margery Perham once asked why "almost no traditional authorities have come forward as nationalists . . . [because] it might have been expected that the almost universal and deep-rooted institution of chieftainship would have supplied, as it were, readymade leaders. . . . In most parts of Africa, however, chieftainship [tended] to wither at the first breath of a national movement."[63] Her two explanations are familiar ones, namely, the close association of most chiefs with, even integration within, the ruling power, which thereby tainted them as "imperialist stooges"; and the fact that chiefs were "chiefs of tribes" and therefore not only symbols but perpetuators of subnational ethnic parochialisms, which territorial nationalism was determined either to domesticate or to suppress.

The hostility of radical nationalism to the traditional political elites was not due simply to the fact that they were perceived to be—and in most places were in fact—part of the colonial administrative establishment nationalists were seeking to overthrow and capture. Rather, it was that chiefs were considered to be positively antinationalist by conviction and by their actions—or inaction. For one thing, the goals of nationalism seemed to be regarded by chiefs as hopeless. As Tom Mboya lamented, chiefs were "convinced through the administrative set-up that the white man's position was indestructible and no amount of agitation was going to move it."[64] More important, however, they frequently sided openly with, or permitted themselves to be used by, the colonial administrations in explicit opposition to nationalism. In former French Africa traditional elites figured prominently in antinationalist "patron-type" parties (in the sense that they supported continuation of the French presence); they were in fact referred to as *partis de l'administration.*[65] In the Ivory Coast in 1951, for example, the chiefs "openly declared themselves against the RDA (Rassemblement Démocratique Africain) and pledged loyalty to France."[66]

In English-speaking Africa the use of chiefs by the colonial authorities as a counterweight to nationalism was even more pronounced, if only because traditional political elites figured more prominently in the British colonial system. Thus, in Tanganyika in 1956 and 1957 the colonial government set up a "convention of chiefs" specifically to oppose the growing popularity of the Tanganyika African National Union (TANU).[67] Colonial government support of the antinationalist paramount chiefs and the conservative aristocracy among the Bemba and the Lozi in preindependent Zambia are other cases in point. However, the most blatant use of traditional elites to frustrate modernizing African nationalism has been in post-UDI (Unilateral Declaration of Independence) Rhodesia and in South Africa's effort to implement the Bantu Authorities Act.[68] Indeed, the examples of colonialism's instrumental exploitation of chiefs are legion. In generalizing about all the colonial territories which have moved or are moving to independence, Kautsky concluded that "it may in the end be only the colonial government that maintains the old aristocracy in power."[69]

Like most categories and concepts used in generalization about African political developments, the category of "chief" or "traditional elite" tends to be employed in an undifferentiated manner. But, as St. Clair Drake observed, "There are chiefs and chiefs."[70] At least three categories should be distinguished: (1) village-level local chiefs, who throughout the colonial as well as early postcolonial period continued to perform traditional political, familial, and ceremonial functions at the grass roots level; (2) kings, paramount chiefs, emirs, *grands marabouts,* and other traditional heads of large-scale collectivities and indigenous polities (emirates of Northern Nigeria; the Buganda, Barotse, Ruanda, and Burundi kingdoms, the senior *obas* in Yorubaland, and so on); and (3) an intermediate category who were sometimes traditional but usually were "official" creations or clients of the colonial powers. One report described chiefs in this category as owing their recognition "largely to the action of the [colonial] administration, who appointed or recognized influential men of the time and then 'built them up' by giving them legal and moral support."[71] It is mainly this intermediate category which was used instrumentally by colonial administrations to resist nationalism, then subsequently by nationalists (once their ultimate victory was assured), and finally by postcolonial governments of the new African states. A final category includes those educated African nationalists who acquired by various means the honorary title of "chief" or "prince" to enhance their status and legitimacy. This phenomenon was particularly pronounced in Southern Nigeria, although it also occurred elsewhere.

The manipulation of the third category of so-called traditional elites—many, be it noted, with little or no "traditional" legitimacy—by whoever was in power, underscores the inherent weakness and extraordinary opportunism of chiefs once nationalism got under way. The oscillations in the loyalties of the chiefs in the Ivory Coast, recounted by Zolberg, provide an excellent case in point. Between 1946 and 1951 most Ivory Coast chiefs belonged to a secular organization founded by Houphouet-Boigny and called Association des Chefs Coutumiers. As he was president of the RDA (Rassemblement Démocratique Africain), the pan-*Afrique noire* nationalist movement during the last three years of that period, one could say that the chiefs supported the nationalism of the RDA. However, when Houphouet fell out with the French in 1951, the association openly sided with the French administration in opposition to the RDA, as already noted. Subsequently when Houphouet emerged once again as the heir presumptive to French authority in the Ivory Coast the association became a trade union (Syndicat des Chefs) with Houphouet-Boigny as its honorary president.[72] The same back-and-forth movement has characterized the opportunistic shifts, and the party and government manipulation, of chiefs in Ghana and several other African countries.[73] Thus, the role of traditional elites (genuine or spurious) of this intermediate category in the development of territorial nationalism has been largely a function of their opportunistic calculation of "where power lies"—or is likely to lie—in the evolving political system.

The pattern of development was somewhat different in those territories where genuine traditional elites had retained substantial influence during the colonial period. Indeed, so determinative were they in the development of some West African states, that Ken Post has classified development patterns in West Africa "according to the relationship between the traditional and modern elites during the last decisive decade before independence . . . [because] it is this relationship that determined the nature of the political system which emerged at independence."[74] His four categories, adapted here to illustrate patterns outside West Africa as well, are: (1) countries or regions in which the traditional elite (political or religious) remained relatively powerful (Mauritania, Niger, Northern Nigeria, Burundi); (2) countries in which the influence of traditional elites at a critical point in time was decisive in determining victors among competing nationalist heirs to colonial power (former French Cameroun, Senegal, Dahomey, Federation of Nigeria taken as a whole, Uganda, Sudan); (3) countries where the modern nationalist elite found it advantageous to come to terms with, or consciously seek to use, traditional authority (Upper Volta, Gambia, Sierra Leone, Ivory Coast, Western Nigeria, and Congo [Kinshasa]); and (4) those states where residual traditional authority was largely nonexistent or irrelevant (Kenya and Malawi) or where nationalist leadership, sought very early, and reasonably successfully, to reduce or to eliminate the power of traditional elites (Ghana, Guinea, Mali, Rwanda, Tanzania, and Zambia). These were the "agitational period" preindependence patterns. The postindependence syndrome is more singular in character, as evidenced by the respective fates of the Moro Naba, the emir of Kano, the Kabaka of Buganda, and the king of Burundi, to mention the most obvious cases in point.

Although the relationship between traditional elites and modernizing nationalists has tended in general to be marked by distrust and opposition, there have been phases and situations in the development of territorial nationalism when they have made common cause. In most such instances, this occurred as soon as the winds of change convinced the chiefs that ultimate nationalist victory was assured. The "crossing of the carpet" by the chiefs of Tanzania illustrates the power of the bandwagon. Describing the crucial election of 1959 in Tanganyika, Pratt observes that

> Prior to the election, as TANU's strength grew throughout the country, chief after chief hesitated to court unpopularity by declaring himself against TANU. The fence got very crowded as one chief after another climbed on it. Then, in September 1958, TANU very shrewdly named a leading chief as a candidate in the election. With that, the chiefs *en masse* began to make their peace with TANU and quietly to demonstrate or at least assert their underlying sympathy with it. In March 1959, at a meeting of the Convention of Chiefs, created by government as a counterbalance to TANU, the political resolutions passed were indistinguishable from the TANU electoral platform. Thus, the political support of the chiefs for the government was lost.[75]

There are instances, however, where chiefs openly sided with nationalists without opportunism being the prime motive. Thus, most chiefs in former Northern Rhodesia and Nyasaland spontaneously joined with modernizing nationalists to oppose the creation of the now defunct Federation of Rhodesia and Nyasaland. This coming together in a common cause has characteristically occurred in those circumstances where the common threat to both categories (traditionalists and modernists) was so visible and imminent that joint action was inevitable.[76]

There are also instances of nationalists and chiefs collaborating in the early states of protest. This was particularly true in Ghana and Nigeria,[77] as well as in southern Africa. Ranger has pointed out:

> The fact that the first stirrings of modern politics in Northern Rhodesia occurred through an alliance of the Lozi paramounts with the new educated and through contacts with agencies in South Africa and overseas fits neatly enough into a general southern African pattern; . . . early political activity in southern Rhodesia centered around the Lobengula family and its "tribal" appeal for a Matabele National Home and . . . the new educated and even "foreign" middle class Africans supported this movement, while Mary Benson has demonstrated that in South Africa the founders of the Congress movement were allied with the paramounts of Zululand, Swaziland and Basutoland, and regarded themselves as much advisors of these royal families as leaders of a supra-tribal political movement.[78]

Thus, although the political outlook of these early centers of protest later became conservative and parochial, the history of African nationalism would be incomplete were it to ignore what Ranger has called this "bridge period between traditional resistance and full scale modern nationalists politics" and the significant role traditional elites with a modernizing bent played in initial nationalist assertion.[79]

Nationalism and Traditional Political Cultures

Variations in the manifestation and development of nationalism in Africa can also be explained by variations in traditional African political cultures. By the political culture of a particular human group we refer to the ensemble of more or less typical attitudes, beliefs, and values of its members regarding politics and authority. It includes their general orientation toward the political systems as well as their political behavioral dispositions.[80] In more familiar language, it refers to the political aspects of "national character." The psychocultural approach to political analysis, of course, remains controversial. It has serious limitations and dangers. It can easily lead to unscientific stereotyping; there are, as well, extraordinarily difficult methodological problems in specifying the political phenomena. Nevertheless, there is very persuasive evidence that, used with caution and tentativeness, the political cultural variable helps us understand and explain variations in African nationalism that otherwise would remain inexplicable.

In addition to the general limitations to the psychocultural approach, two special problems are encountered in attempting to use it to explain African political phenomena. One is that very few systematic, respectably scientific, psychocultural studies have been made in Africa that are directly pertinent to an understanding of nationalism.[81] Robert LeVine's admirable recent comparative study of the Hausa, Ibo, and Yoruba of Nigeria; Audrey Richard's analysis of the traditional political values of the Baganda; and Ethel Albert's earlier interesting work among the Ruandans and Rundi—these excellent pioneering studies stand out almost alone.[82] The second complicating factor is that because of their great cultural heterogeneity and the relative brevity of their existence as "national" entities, it is difficult to speak meaningfully of the political culture of a new African state as a whole, although Hodgkin and Morgenthau have suggested Mali to be an exception.[83] Our examination of this variable is, therefore, limited to propositions regarding the political culture of traditional African ethnic groups or of the African people in general, and how these might have affected the development of territorial nationalism.

SUBTERRITORIAL POLITICAL CULTURES AND TERRITORIAL NATIONALISM

My working hypothesis is that there have been significant variations in nationalistic assertiveness among ethnic groups inhabiting a colonial territory, that is, some groups have been more assertive and nationalistic than others, and that these variations are in many instances a function of the differences in the political culture of the ethnic groups concerned. The history of the rise and development of territorial nationalisms in Africa amply supports the fact of marked ethnic disproportionality in both the leadership and mass involvement in radical territorial nationalism. The vanguard role played by particular ethnic groups in the evolution of territorial nationalism in several countries is now well known—the Ibo and Knuri (and among the Yoruba, the Ijebu) in Nigeria, the Kikuyu in Kenya, the Bemba in Zambia, the Bamaleke in the Cameroun, the Ewe in Togo are among the most noteworthy. Moreover, in many instances there was an escalation of territorial nationalism as a result of the defensive creation of the less assertive ethnic groups to the leadership and prominence of those groups *culturally disposed* to be more assertive and radical. Thus, in such cases, territorial nationalism, paradoxically, was the ultimate beneficiary of interethnic rivalry provoked and kept alive by an ethnic imbalance in nationalistic assertiveness.

I am not concerned here with the essentially situational explanations for ethnic variability in nationalistic disposition. Sometimes the situational determinant is the sole explanation; at other times it reinforces a cultural disposition or vice versa. Therefore, it is difficult to disentangle the two and say with certitude which is the basic and which is the reinforcing factor. Three of the more common situational explanations for ethnic differences in nationalistic assertiveness are: (1) the more protracted and intensive exposure of the vanguard group to exploitative or socially disorganizing influences (for example, the Kikuyu); (2) overpopulation in the ethnic homeland and the consequent diaspora abroad (for example, the Ibo, Ewe, and Bamaleke); and (3) earlier and more extensive educational and economic development because of geographic location or better endowment in natural resources resulting in some groups acquiring and retaining a competitive advantage over other groups. These and other situationally determined differences have undoubtedly been important, in many instances decisive. For present purposes, however, our concern is with the more enduring "traditional" elements in the political cultures of those ethnic groups which tended to take the leadership in territorial nationalist movements, and here I will focus upon two variables: traditional status mobility and the scale and degree of hierarchism of the traditional political system.

My working proposition is that in the historic transformation of Tropical Africa from colonialism to independence ethnic variations in assertiveness and attraction to territorial nationalism, *ceteris paribus*, correlated positively with ethnic variations in achievement motivation, and drawing on LeVine's theory, these latter differences are explained by variations in the traditional status mobility systems of the ethnic groups concerned.[84] Those ethnic groups whose cultures allowed for and encouraged greater status mobility have greater achievement orientation, which is diffuse. As regards the political aspects with which we are concerned, high achievement orientation meant a far greater predisposition to earlier and more emphatic assertiveness of territorial nationalism. The Ibo of Nigeria, who for nearly a decade were the undisputed carriers of Nigerian territorial nationalism, have been regarded as the archetype of this phenomenon. Now, with the results of LeVine's systematic social psychological probe, these impressions have social scientific formation and explanation. Horton has summed up the common impressionistic view of the Ibo people: "renowned in recent years for the value they set on aggressive competition, the struggle for achievement and the willingness to explore new avenues of power and status."[85] Horton explains it by overpopulation; LeVine more convincingly accounts for it in terms of the traditional Ibo status mobility system based on parental values of individualism and specific training of the child in independence and achievement. He summarizes his results and their implications as follows:

> This investigation indicates that associated with well-known regional variations in levels of economic development and Westernization in Nigeria are individual behavioral dispositions of a deep-seated nature which are probably resistant to change. . . . [They] are not randomly or uniformly distributed among the three major ethnic groups of Nigeria; they vary significantly, and form a distinctive cluster. The cluster consists of achievement motivation, concern with self-improvement, non-authoritarian ideology, a favorable attitude toward technological innovation, and rapid advancement in Western education and the Western type of occupational hierarchy. The Ibo and, to a lesser extent, the Yoruba are high on all of these dimensions; the Hausa are low. . . . One effect of this clustering of dispositions is that those individuals most prepared to occupy the positions of professional, technical, and bureaucratic leadership in the newly formed Nigerian nation are per-

> sons . . . [drawn from those ethnic groups culturally more achievement oriented].[86]

For my purposes the hypothesis derivable from this is that greater assertiveness and leadership in territorial nationalist movements tended to be taken by persons from those ethnic groups having high achievement orientation (associated with an open traditional status mobility system) *in situations where higher status is perceived as being obtainable in a larger territorial status system.* This latter italicized addition to the LeVine hypothesis is required in view of my particular concern with ethnic variations, not in gravitation to ethnic nationalism, but to territorial nationalism. If the traditional Ibo social and political system, as adapted under colonialism, had provided statuses equal to or higher than the emerging status system of Nigeria, it is just as likely that the Ibo would have confined their aggressive energies to building an ethnic nation-state, with no less passion than that of the Baganda in Uganda. The crux of the matter is surely in Horton's phrase "willingness to explore new avenues of power and status," and adding thereto "a greater perceptiveness in identifying such avenues."

A second variable that has been used to account for ethnic differences in support of territorial nationalism has been the scale and degree of hierarchism of traditional political systems. Scale and hierarchism are, of course, separate variables, but for present purposes they can be regarded as characteristically associated in the same system. My working proposition is that the smaller the scale of (that is, the greater the decentralization of authority), and the lesser the degree of hierarchism in, the political system of an ethnic group, the more readily and flexibly disposed the members of that group are to join modern associations (such as territorial nationalist parties and trade unions, as well as panethnic associations). This correlation of a disposition for associational formation and activity with a traditional type of political system was suggested by Ken Post in his study of the Nigerian 1959 election:

> It seems that those communities which in the past had no feeling of relationship with one another, sometimes even speaking different dialects of the same language, have been able to come together more effectively in a modern election than those which traditionally had been contained within some larger unity. . . . Those societies whose traditional political systems were on a small scale, and least hierarchical, were those which in modern elections were best able to come together in support of a political party. . . . where there was a tradition of chieftainship, hierarchical organization, and

> the association of power with office the way was opened to all sorts of disputes which might be taken up by the parties.[87]

The main thrust of Post's argument (as well as that of Banton)[88] is that the combinational and associational disposition of members of smaller-scale, nonhierarchical societies enabled them to unite more easily than societies of the opposite type when faced with an external challenge. In other words, Post suggests that the combinational disposition would be directed ultimately toward greater ethnicity. Our amendment to this proposition is that small-scale nonhierarchical societies do have a greater combinational disposition but that this can be considered separately from the particular aggregate which benefits from it; in a word, it is an "open" or "ethnically neutral" disposition flexible to combine, aggregate, and associate, of which either—or simultaneously both—ethnic group or a nationalist movement of a territory can be beneficiaries.

The fact that both of my propositions regarding ethnic variability—the disposition for achievement and for combination—are drawn from the modern political behavior of the Ibo raises the questions whether they are *sui generis* to the Ibo or whether the two are really not ultimately the same thing, namely, that an open status system and a decentralized nonhierarchical political system are one and the same phenomenon. Not necessarily so. The Baganda have been achievement oriented but not disposed to combination outside Buganda. Also, in another comparative study, Robert LeVine found that two traditional African societies (the Gusii and the Nuer) possessing the same broad structural patterns did not have similar political cultures.[89] The two societies fall into the same type: stateless segmentary (that is, small-scale, nonhierarchical) societies, according to one of the more common structural typologies of traditional African societies. Yet in political culture (attitudes and orientation toward politics and authority) the two societies are polar opposites, the Gusii being strongly "authoritarian" and the Nuer extremely "egalitarian." This suggests that one cannot necessarily infer political culture from political structure.[90] However, this whole range of issues falls in a category of the unexplored in African political studies. At this stage we cannot and should not generalize except in the most tentative and hypothetical way.

AFRICAN POLITICAL CULTURE AND AFRICAN NATIONALISM

We now switch from ethnic variability to ethnic commonality, from particular cultural traits as explanations for differential ethnic assertiveness to generic cultural features as explanations for the distinctive features of a common phenomenon. The actual history of African nationalism has been, of course, the progressive "territorialization" of an original pan-Africanism.[91] So undifferentiated did Lord Hailey consider the phenomenon of self-assertion in Africa that he argued prominence be given "to the use of the term 'Africanism' rather than 'nationalism'" because Africans missed "the dynamic influence of the concept of territorial nationalism."[92] It is difficult, however, to make a convincing case that generic African nationalism is distinguishable from other varieties (European, Asian, Latin American) for cultural, rather than situational, reasons. In any event, I neither have the data, nor is this the place, for macroscopic continental comparisons. Here I am concerned only with identifying possible correlations between certain generically distinctive features of African nationalism. This is clearly a realm for wide-open speculation.

Three common characteristics of African territorial nationalisms are the *eclecticism* in the content of a common nationalist language, the pervasive *populism* in the mass appeals made to mobilize the population, and the *futurism* in the nature of the goals of the nationalist movement. Each of these could find a probable situational explanation. Indeed, Hodgkin argues that the existence of a common language of nationalism reflects "a certain kind of historical situation, certain fundamental human problems to be resolved, [which] tend to stimulate a particular way of thinking about the situation and the problems."[93] Each of the characteristics could also find an explanation in the historic pejorative view that Africans have no culture or tradition, or at least none worth preserving. However, I am interested in the third possibility, namely, can these common features be explained by generic African culture. Here one must turn to Lloyd Fallers, one of the most competent and perceptive macrosociologists of this generation, who has a penchant and talent for the kind of uninhibited generalization we need. He has suggested the existence of two traits generic to traditional African societies: egalitarianism and political primacy. On egalitarianism he has this to say:

> There remained in traditional Africa, even in the larger kingdoms with their elaborate political hierarchies, a kind of egalitarianism that seems to have had two principal roots. One of these was the pattern of kinship and family structure, which is over much of the continent restored upon exogamous unilineal descent groups. Although in the structure of the state persons might stand to one another in highly asymmetrical dyadic relationships of economic and political superiority and subordination, every person tended also to belong to one or more extended, solidary descent groups that cut across such hierarchical structures. Exogamy produced in

> addition, a set of affinal ties knitting descent groups together and inhibiting subcultural differentiation among them. At the village level, rights in land characteristically were heavily concentrated in the hands of kinship or local groups. Thus tendencies toward crystallization of rigid horizontal strata were checked, in spite of the frequent concentration of power and wealth in elite hands.[94]

In addition to these considerations, the ethos of egalitarianism has been further strengthened by the absence in Africa of literary religious traditions, by a so-called "high" culture, which, Fallers notes, could have provided the basis for more clearly differentiated elite subcultures. Here we have a traditional cultural explanation for modern egalitarian populism, as well as for the eclectic version of Marxism called African socialism. The ethos of equality involved here, be it noted, is not that which infuses the "dignitarians" referred to by Ali Mazrui (the passion to be equal with other races); rather it is that egalitarianism defines relationships among the African peoples themselves.

A second generic feature of African culture identified by Fallers is the primacy of the polity:

> In traditional Africa goods and services, both as symbols and as facilities, circulate primarily in terms of political relations, for it is the polity that dominates stratification. . . . Traditional African societies . . . have characteristically exhibited patterns of role differentiation in which political specialization has been more prominent than economic. The ambitions of their members have been directed primarily toward attaining authority. . . . Although direct cultural continuity may be difficult to achieve, some characteristic features of the traditional systems may perhaps persist and give a distinctly African character to the new independent nations. For example, in the new African nations, as in the old, political structures seem likely to continue to dominate economic ones and political elites to retain their pre-eminence.[95]

This is not meant to explain, and culturally validate, Kwame Nkrumah's admonition to "seek ye first the Political Kingdom." It does suggest that to the extent that Fallers's bold and sweeping proposition is valid, there might be a traditional cultural explanation—supportive of other explanations—for the extraordinary political sensitivity of Africans and for the widespread response to political nationalism and to the leadership of nationalist elites.

NOTES

1. Max Weber, *The Methodology of the Social Sciences* (Glencoe, Ill.: Free Press, 1949), pp. 90, 93, in which an ideal-type construct is defined as a "one-sided accentuation . . . by the synthesis of a great many diffuse, discrete, more or less present and occasionally absent *concrete individual* phenomena, which are arranged . . . into a unified analytical construct. In its conceptual purity, this mental construct cannot be found anywhere in reality."

2. For a critique of the transition model widely used in the study of change see Wilbert E. Moore, *Social Change* (Englewood Cliffs, N.J.: Prentice-Hall, 1963), pp. 40–42.

3. The dichotomies (and their application) of Redfield, Maine, Tönnies, Weber, as well as Parsons's pattern variables, are discussed in Bert F. Hoselitz, "Main Concepts in the Analysis of the Social Implications of Technical Change," in Bert F. Hoselitz and Wilbert E. Moore, eds., *Industrialization and Society* (Geneva: UNESCO, 1963), pp. 11–29.

4. See Francis X. Sutton, "Representation and the Nature of Political Systems," *Comparative Studies in Society and History*, 2:1 (October 1959), pp. 1–10.

5. Leonard W. Doob, *Becoming More Civilized: A Psychological Exploration* (New Haven: Yale University Press, 1960), p. 20, states: "Without a baseline changes cannot be sensibly observed. Unless that baseline is cautiously established, however, the outcome will be no better than that provided by the snob in modern society who with little encouragement can indicate the characteristics of peoples less civilized than himself."

6. Igor Kopytoff, "Socialism and Traditional African Societies," in William H. Friedland and Carl G. Rosberg, Jr., eds., *African Socialism* (Stanford: Stanford University Press, 1964), pp. 53–54.

7. Max Radin, "Tradition," *Encyclopedia of the Social Sciences* (New York: Macmillan, 1938), 15:64.

8. *Webster's Third New International Dictionary* (Springfield, Mass.: G. & C. Merriam, 1961).

9. Thomas L. Hodgkin, "The Relevance of 'Western' Ideas for the New African States," in J. Roland Pennock, ed., *Self-Government in Modernizing Nations* (Englewood Cliffs, N.J.: Prentice-Hall, 1964), p. 66.

10. Cf. Cyril E. Black, *The Dynamics of Modernization* (New York: Harper & Row, 1966), who observes: "For the societies of Western Europe, the traditional institutions are those of the Middle Ages, and the challenge of modernity to the traditional system occurred between the twelfth and eighteenth centuries. Comparable traditional periods before the challenge of modernity may be discerned in all other societies. In the least developed societies, the traditional period has lasted until well into the twentieth century" (p. 8).

11. Kopytoff, "Socialism and Traditional African Societies," p. 21. As Joseph Ki-Zerbo, "African Personality and the New African Society," in The American Society of African Culture, *Pan-Africanism Reconsidered* (Berkeley: University of California Press, 1962), p. 274, observed, "Very often the soldier who tries to speak French as it is spoken in Paris will show you the talisman he wore in the fight for the liberation of France. Similarly, during electoral rollcalls, I have often seen candidates call upon both the voice of the people and the intervention of the witch doctors." Peter Lloyd, "Tribalism in Nigeria," in A. A. Dubb, ed., *The Multitribal Society* (Lusaka: Rhodes Livingstone Institute, 1962), p. 134, has noted that the sharp dichotomy sometimes made between town and village life (equating it to traditional and European life) is methodologically unsound for Nigeria, where "the educated and town dwelling African is so patently creating a culture that is neither traditional nor European. He is continually adapting his norms and values according to the demands of urban life and salaried employment."

12. Kopytoff, "Socialism and Traditional African Societies," p. 57.

13. The proponents of both traditions were pitted against each other in the nationalist struggle in Northern Nigeria. See Thomas L. Hodgkin, "A Note on the Language of African Nationalism," in Kenneth Kirkwood, ed., *African Affairs* (London: Chatto & Windus, 1961), pp. 26–27.

14. Evon Z. Vogt, "The Navaho," in Edward H. Spicer, ed., *New Perspectives in American Indian Culture Change* (Seattle: University of Washington Press, 1962); and Herbert Blumer, "Industrialization and the Traditional Order," *Sociology and Social Research*, 48 (January 1964), pp. 129–138.

15. Robert E. Ward and Dankwart A. Rustow, eds., *Political Modernization in Turkey and Japan* (Princeton: Princeton University Press, 1963). "Reinforcing dualism" refers to "the exploitability of traditional institutions, attitudes, and behavior patterns for modernizing purposes" (p. 466).

16. J. F. A. Ajayi, "The Place of African History and Culture in the Process of Nation-Building in Africa South of the Sahara," *Journal of Negro Education*, 30:3 (1961), p. 206.

17. There is nothing novel about this breakdown; it has been used by Rupert Emerson, Paul Mercier, and others. Emerson notes that there are at least three major levels of social and political community: "the traditional societies of the past, the colonial or colonially derived structures of the present, and the several Pan-African aspirations." Rupert Emerson, "Nation-Building in Africa," in Karl W. Deutsch and William J. Foltz, *Nation-Building* (New York: Atherton Press, 1963), p. 97. See also Paul Mercier, "On the Meaning of 'Tribalism' in Black Africa," in Pierre L. van den Berghe, ed., *Africa: Social Problems of Change and Conflict* (San Francisco: Chandler Publishing Co., 1965), p. 484.

18. See John H. Kautsky, ed., *Political Change in Underdeveloped*

Countries (New York: John Wiley & Sons, 1965), pp. 34–45, who notes the general ineffectiveness of unification movements transcending and amalgamating colonial territories as well as movements of secession and fragmentation within those territories (p. 38). Cf. Black, *The Dynamics of Modernization*, and Lucian W. Pye and Sidney Verba, eds., *Political Culture and Political Development* (Princeton: Princeton University Press, 1965), p. 528.

19. Thomas Hodgkin, *Nationalism in Colonial Africa* (London: Frederick Muller, 1956), p. 23.

20. Immanuel Wallerstein, "Ethnicity and National Integration in West Africa," *Cahiers d'Etudes Africaines*, no. 3 (October 1960), pp. 129–139; Mercier, "On the Meaning of 'Tribalism,'" pp. 483–501; M. Crawford Young, *Politics in the Congo* (Princeton: Princeton University Press, 1965), pp. 232–272.

21. Young, *Politics in the Congo*, p. 245, quotes Biebuyck and Douglas that although "administrative units often cut across tribal and linguistic boundaries . . . to some extent their very existence has created solidarities of another kind," and notes that in the years preceding the urban elections in Leopoldville three of the five major ethnic associations bore the name of administrative divisions rather than tribes.

22. Rupert Emerson, *From Empire to Nation* (Cambridge: Harvard University Press, 1960), p. 91.

23. Mercier, "On the Meaning of 'Tribalism,'" p. 487.

24. This variability determined by the situation makes it necessary to qualify Emerson's observation, "Nation-Building in Africa," p. 101, that in Africa the "natural" boundaries are those of the tribes or other traditional groupings.

25. van den Berghe, *Africa: Social Problems*, p. 3, has identified six different meanings of the term "tribe," the collective generally used to refer indiscriminately to all traditional groupings. Three of these meanings relate to the scale of the collectivity ("small localized group," a large-scale ethnolinguistic group, and heterogeneous precolonial states); the other three meanings are "rural" as opposed to "urban," "traditional" as opposed to "modern," and simply anything the "opposite of 'national'."

26. Obafemi Awolowo, *Path to Nigerian Freedom* (London: Faber & Faber, 1947), p. 54.

27. Rene Lemarchand, "The Basis of Nationalism among the Bakongo," *Africa*, 31:4 (October 1961), p. 347.

28. Tom Mboya, *Freedom and After* (London: Oxford University Press, 1963), pp. 70–71. Emerson, "Nation-Building in Africa," p. 105, notes that "tribalism can be dealt with in two fashions—either use of the tribes as the building blocks of the nation or eradication of them as completely as possible, replacing them by a single national solidarity. It is the latter course which is more generally followed."

29. Ajayi, "The Place of African History," p. 211.

30. Ali A. Mazrui, "On the Concept 'We Are All Africans,'" *The American Political Science Review*, 57:1 (March 1963), p. 96.

31. Margery Perham, "The Psychology of African Nationalism," *Optima*, 10:1 (1960), p. 18. Cf. Lloyd A. Fallers, "Equality, Modernity and Democracy in the New States," in Clifford Geertz, ed., *Old Societies and New States* (Glencoe, Ill.: Free Press, 1963), p. 217.

32. Hodgkin, "The Relevance of 'Western' Ideas," pp. 62–63.

33. Margery Perham, *Native Administration in Nigeria* (London: Oxford University Press, 1937), p. 361.

34. See Lloyd A. Fallers, "Despotism, Status Culture and Social Mobility in an African Kingdom," *Comparative Studies in Society and History*, 2:1 (October 1959), pp. 11–32; and David E. Apter, *The Political Kingdom in Uganda* (Princeton: Princeton University Press, 1961).

35. Terence Ranger, "Tribalism and Nationalism: The Case of Barotseland" (unpublished manuscript).

36. Ajayi, "The Place of African History," p. 209.

37. Lloyd, "Tribalism in Nigeria," p. 133.

38. Royal Institute of International Affairs, *Nationalism* (London: Oxford University Press, 1939), p. 274.

39. Thomas Hodgkin, "The New West Africa State System," in Millar Maclure and Douglas Anglin, eds., *Africa: The Political Pattern* (Toronto: University of Toronto Press, 1961), p. 78.

40. David E. Apter, "The Role of Traditionalism in the Political Modernization of Ghana and Uganda," *World Politics*, 13 (1960), pp. 45–68.

41. M. Banton, *West African City: A Study of Tribal Life in Freetown* (London: Oxford University Press, 1957); D. J. Parkin, "Urban Voluntary Associations as Institutions of Adaptation," *Man*, n.s. 1:1 (1966), pp. 90–95. Banton's study was in Freetown and Parkin's in Kampala.

42. I. M. Lewis, "Nationalism, Urbanism, and Tribalism in Contemporary Africa" (unpublished manuscript); italics added.

43. Politics of differentiation by colonial powers (particularly Britain) of major areal clusters of peoples (that is, Northern and Southern Sudan, Northern and Southern Nigeria, and to a lesser extent all along the West Coast of Africa) undoubtedly had a major divisive effect in national development.

44. Clifford Geertz, "The Integrative Revolution: Primordial Sentiments and Civil Politics in the New States," in Geertz, ed., *Old Societies and New States*, pp. 117–118.

45. Herbert J. Spiro, "The Rhodesias and Nyasaland," in Gwendolen M. Carter, ed., *Five African States: Responses to Diversity* (Ithaca, N.Y.: Cornell University Press, 1963), pp. 391–392.

46. David Marvin has noted that "tribal rivalry has been greatest in territories in which one or more tribes have acquired a dominant position,

either through a tradition of successful conquest over surrounding peoples, through having achieved a more or less centralized government, or through having been in a position to exploit the new economic advantages." "Tribe and Nation in East Africa: Separatism and Regionalism," *The Round Table*, 52 (June 1962), p. 255.

47. Mercier, "On the Meaning of 'Tribalism,'" p. 492. Cumulation of differentiations are not simply vertical. In the development of the Copperbelt in Northern Rhodesia the division between (higher status) Lozi and Nyasa clerks and (lower status) Bemba workers did not reflect "some situation of resurgent tribalism or persistence of loyalties and values stemming from a traditional social order," but rather with the cumulation of the differentiations of an "emerging class structure" and ethnic divisions. Ranger, quoting Epstein, in "Tribalism and Nationalism," p. 10.

48. As I have noted elsewhere, "uneven acculturation, resulting in part from the uneven tribal acquisition of Western education and the uneven spread of 'status' employment, produced competitive tensions within the educated categories which were powerful stimulants to tribal as well as territorial nationalism." See James S. Coleman, *Nigeria: Background to Nationalism* (Berkeley: University of California Press, 1958), p. 143. Again, for the Ivory Coast, Aristide R. Zolberg, *One-Party Government in the Ivory Coast* (Princeton: Princeton University Press, 1964), pp. 47–48, has observed that "differentiations between traditional societies have been intensified by the cumulative effect of uneven Western impact and, in recent years, by differential rates of cultural and economic change."

49. Zolberg, *One-Party Government in the Ivory Coast*, p. 134.

50. Rupert Emerson, "Paradoxes of Asian Nationalism," in Immanuel Wallerstein, ed., *Social Change: The Colonial Situation* (New York: John Wiley & Sons, 1966), p. 530.

51. Lewis, "Nationalism, Urbanism, and Tribalism," p. 2, notes: "Politicians who aspire to break down tribal barriers and to erect in their place a new national culture have also, perforce, to utilize the same tribal ties in their search for supporters and power, and to take adequate account of them in their selection of colleagues and allies in governmental and administrative action."

52. The link between urbanization and the growth of ethnic self-consciousness is a familiar syndrome. See Zolberg, *One-Party Government in the Ivory Coast*, p. 143; Wallerstein, *Social Change*, pp. 249–300, makes "The Creation of Urban Ethnicity" a major section of his study.

53. Emerson, "Nation-Building in Africa," p. 106, observes that it is inevitable that ethnic groups "should seek political expression and be used as built-in constituencies when democratic machinery is introduced."

54. This "divide and rule" tactic was used extensively throughout colonial Africa, and currently is being used by the Portuguese in both Angola and Mozambique, and by the South African government in its

Bantustan policy. See John A. Davis and James K. Baker, eds. *Southern Africa in Transition* (New York: Praeger, 1966), pp. 15–16, 160–162.

55. "Indonesian regionalism, Malayan racialism, Indian linguism, or Nigerian tribalism are, in their political dimensions, not so much the heritage of colonial divide-and-rule policies as they are products of the replacement of a colonial regime by an independent, domestically anchored, purposeful unitary state." Geertz, "The Integrative Revolution," p. 121.

56. Paul Mercier, "On the Meaning of 'Tribalism'," p. 486.

57. Wallerstein, "Ethnicity and National Integration."

58. See Zolberg, *One-Party Government in the Ivory Coast*, p. 144.

59. Richard Sklar, "The Contribution of Tribalism to Nationalism in Western Nigeria," *Journal of Human Relations*, 8 (Spring-Summer 1960), p. 411.

60. Zolberg, *One-Party Government in the Ivory Coast*, p. 144. He concludes that few members of the Ivory Coast political elite would accept the validity of the social science hypothesis that racial and tribal pluralism are not incompatible with national integration (p. 285).

61. Ranger, "Tribalism and Nationalism," p. 12.

62. Sklar, "The Contribution of Tribalism," p. 415. The process of nationalist exploitation of traditional communal conflict was not sheer expediential instrumentalism. Sklar argues (p. 413) that as a result of the influence of the manipulating radical nationalist leaders "communal participation parties have assimilated nationalistic principles within their codes of traditional values."

63. Perham, "The Psychology of African Nationalism," pp. 179–180.

64. Mboya, *Freedom and After*, p. 64.

65. Hodgkin, *Nationalism in Colonial Africa*, p. 156. Ruth Schachter Morgenthau, "Single-Party Systems in West Africa," *The American Political Science Review*, 55:2 (June 1961), p. 301, has noted that these patron parties were most active and successful in Mali, Niger, Guinea (until 1956), and Mauritania. It was in these territories, she notes, that the struggle against the colonial power barely masked another struggle, most acute in the countryside, between traditionalists and modernizers.

66. Zolberg, *One-Party Government in the Ivory Coast*, p. 120.

67. Cranford Pratt, "East Africa: The Pattern of Political Development," in Miller Maclure and Douglas Anglin, eds., *Africa: The Political Pattern* (Toronto: University of Toronto Press, 1961), p. 118.

68. See Thomas Karis, "South Africa," in Gwendolen M. Carter ed., *Five African States: Responses to Diversity* (Ithaca, N.Y.: Cornell University Press, 1963), pp. 555–557.

69. Kautsky, *Political Change in Underdeveloped Countries*, p. 42.

70. Quoted in H. Passin and K. A. B. Jones-Quartey, *Africa: The Dynamics of Change* (Ibadan: Ibadan University Press, 1963), p. 27.

71. Colonial Office Summer Conference on African Administration, Eighth Session, 27 August–7 September 1957, *The Place of Chiefs in African Administration*, p. 76. See Morgenthau, "Single-Party Systems in West Africa," pp. 301–302, for a discussion of the nature of the "official chiefs" and their relationship to nationalist parties in former French Africa.

72. Zolberg, *One-Party Government in the Ivory Coast*, pp. 287–288.

73. The most recent illustration of the sheer opportunism of chiefs and crass manipulation of the chiefly office is found in the revelations of the National Liberation Council of Ghana regarding the Nkrumah regime. During the period 1957–1966 the latter had allegedly promoted a large number of subordinate chiefs to the status of paramount chiefs "without regard to traditions and customs." The NLC was therefore demoting all those chiefs concerned.

74. Ken Post, *The New States of West Africa* (London: Penguin Books, 1964), pp. 54–55.

75. Pratt, "East Africa," p. 118.

76. The militant stand taken by Paramount Chief Sabata Dalindyebo of the Tembu tribe in the Transkei against apartheid was identical with that of educated South African nationalists.

77. A West Coast example of this early spirit of collaboration between educated nationalists and traditional elites were the occasional visits made by Chief Ladip Solanke (founder of the West African Students Union) from London to West Africa between 1929 and 1932. Solanke deliberately sought to bring the two elements together. Indeed, Nana Sir Afori Atta of the Gold Coast, and the alake of Abeokuta and emir of Kano, were one-time patrons of WASU. See Coleman, *Nigeria*, pp. 206–207.

78. Ranger, "Tribalism and Nationalism," pp. 7–8.

79. One other way in which traditional elites may have facilitated nationalist development is in being scapegoats for unpopular measures and discontent during the critical period of terminal colonialism during which nationalists acquired increasing power over public policy but still had not achieved independence. Thus, in Ghana during this period the CPP (Convention People's Party) encouraged commoners to destool uncooperative chiefs and, according to Drake, destoolment represented one means "by which local and regional discontent is focused on traditional authority rather than upon the new elites."

80. The concept is used substantially as defined by Gabriel Almond and Sidney Verba in *The Civic Culture* (Boston: Little, Brown, 1965), pp. 12–30; and as further developed by Pye and Verba in *Political Culture and Political Development*.

81. Lystad observes that "Despite the 'psychologizing' that frequently accompanies the analysis of political institutions and processes, and despite the often brilliant insights into psychological, cultural, and value aspects

of African politics within individual countries—insights one intuitively feels must have some validity—the study of national character has hardly begun." Robert A. Lystad, "Cultural and Psychological Factors," in Vernon McKay, ed., *African Diplomacy: Studies in the Determinants of Foreign Policy* (New York: Praeger, 1966), p. 104. See also Robert A. LeVine's comprehensive survey of the literature in his chapter on "Africa," in Francis L. K. Hsu, ed., *Psychological Anthropology: Approaches to Culture and Personality* (Homewood: The Dorsey Press, 1961), pp. 48–92.

82. Robert A. LeVine, *Dreams and Deeds: Achievement Motivation in Nigeria* (Chicago: University of Chicago Press, 1966); Audrey I. Richards, "Traditional Values and Current Political Behaviour," in Lloyd A. Fallers, ed., *The King's Men* (London: Oxford University Press, 1964), pp. 256–293; and Ethel M. Albert, "Socio-political Organization and Receptivity to Change: Some Differences between Ruanda and Urundi," *Southwestern Journal of Anthropology*, 16:1 (Spring 1960), pp. 46–74. The discredited study of J. C. Carothers, *The Psychology of the Mau Mau* (Nairobi: Government of Kenya, 1964), should be mentioned only to further underscore the inadequacy of our existing knowledge.

83. Thomas Hodgkin and Ruth Schachter Morgenthau, "Mali," in James S. Coleman and Carl G. Rosberg, Jr., eds., *Political Parties and National Integration in Tropical Africa* (Berkeley: University of California Press, 1964), pp. 220–221, argue that modern Mali has a "historically grounded sense of identity, which Professor Ki Zerbo has called Mali's 'tradition étatique' [which] is reinforced by the continuity of certain types of social institutions." This "statist" element in Mali political culture presumably has minimized tribalism and facilitated the development of Mali's peculiar brand of puritanical nationalism and its monolithic one-party system.

84. LeVine, *Dreams and Deeds*, pp. 16–21.

85. Quoted in ibid., p. 83.

86. Ibid., pp. 92–93.

87. K. W. J. Post, *The Nigerian Federal Election of 1959* (London: Oxford University Press, 1962) p. 380.

88. Banton, *West African City*, pp. 195 ff.

89. Robert A. LeVine, "The Internationalization of Political Values in Stateless Societies," *Human Organization*, 19:2 (Summer 1960), pp. 51–58.

90. LeVine, ibid., p. 54, concludes from his study that "classifying political systems on the basis of their predominant political values, particularly those concerning authority, yields insights into them which cannot be obtained by a scheme based purely on the broad outlines of political structure."

91. David E. Apter and James S. Coleman, "Nationalism or Pan-Afri-

canism," in The American Society of African Culture, *Pan-Africanism Reconsidered* (Berkeley: University of California Press, 1962), pp. 50–75.

92. Lord Hailey, *An African Survey* (London: Oxford University Press, 1961), p. 271.

93. Hodgkin, "A Note on the Language of African Nationalism," p. 40.

94. Fallers, "Equality, Modernity and Democracy in the New States," p. 180.

95. Lloyd A. Fallers, "Social Stratification and Economic Processes," in Melville J. Herskovits and Mitchell Harwitz, eds., *Economic Transition in Africa* (Evanston, Ill.: Northwestern University Press, 1964), pp. 126, 129, 130.

2

THEORY IN DEVELOPMENT STUDIES

7 The Resurrection of Political Economy

The time has come to recognize the professional respectability as well as the practical essentiality of the ancient and honorable hybrid discipline of "political economy." There are at least three compelling reasons in support of this proposition. One is that the ever-increasing specialization of political scientists and economists has tended to reify what is after all nothing more than an artificial boundary between two categories of social scientists, each concerned with only analytically different aspects of a single concrete whole, namely, human society. In drawing attention to the artificiality of disciplinary boundaries in the social sciences we do not deny the critical importance of specialization and all that it implies; rather, we are merely affirming a nonpurist—and, incidentally, a historically validated—concept of what constitutes an academic discipline, much along the lines of the late Frederick Dunn's definition:

> A field of knowledge does not possess a fixed extension in space but is a constantly changing focus of data and methods that happen at the moment to be useful in answering an identifiable set of questions. It presents at any given time different aspects to different observers, depending on their point of view and purpose. The boundaries that supposedly divide one field of knowledge from another are not fixed walls between separate cells of truth but are convenient devices for arranging known facts and methods in manageable segments for instruction and practice. But the foci of interest are constantly shifting and these divisions tend to change with them, although more slowly because mental habits alter slowly and

Reprinted from *Mawazo* 1:1 (June 1967), pp. 31–40.

> the vested interests of the intellectual world are as resistant to change as those of the social world.[1]

Such a flexible concept of a discipline validates the continuing process of disciplinary hybridization so marked in recent and contemporary social science. There is, for example, widespread acceptance of such hybrids as "political sociology" and "social psychology." Thus, recognition of the hybrid discipline of political economy is supported not only by history—it is after all the oldest of the hybrids—but by current fashion as well.

A second argument is that those comparatively unique historical situations of fairly pure laissez-faire which once encouraged and perhaps even gave some justification for sharp differentiation between the two disciplines have long since been transcended by varying but substantial forms of *étatisme*, either of the "developed" welfare state, or of the modernizing state variety. In either type of polity—indeed, in all intermediate types as well—sound and successful public policy requires the specialized competence and collaboration of both groups of disciplinarians. The interdependence of political, administrative, and economic aspects of modern statecraft must be matched by an interdisciplinary perspective among those scholars essaying to comprehend, analyze, and provide policy guidance for national development.

The third reason is that there already are a significant number of practitioners in both disciplines concentrating in the hybrid area, but unlike such proud hybridists as political sociologists and social psychologists they seem reluctant to declare their special identity. This is true despite the legitimating and fortifying definition in *Webster's Third New International:*

> *political economy* 1: an 18th century branch of the art of government concerned with directing governmental policies toward the promotion of the wealth of the government and the community as a whole; 2*a*: a 19th century social science comprising the modern science of economics but concerned principally with governmental as contrasted with commercial or personal economics; *b*: a modern social science dealing with the interrelationship of political and economic processes.

The principal reason for their reluctance is that in the course of the evolution of political science and economics as separate and increasingly specialized disciplines, the term political economy has tended to become the distinctive appellation for a special branch of economics (i.e., definition 2*a*), and modern politicoeconomic hybrids have, as a consequence, sought to avoid guilt by association. However, as their number and the need for them increases, as inexorably it will, the most logical name for their interdisciplinary identity will and must be reclaimed, and *Webster's* definition 2*b* allowed to prevail.

The Trend Toward Convergence

Independent but complementary and frequently identical, developments have occurred or are in gestation in both disciplines which have greatly facilitated the relaxation of the boundaries that ever-greater specialization over the years has tended to erect. The impact of the Soviet Union and other socialist systems, and more recently the developing areas, has led to a greater convergence of scholarly interest and concern in the two disciplines. The interdependence of economy and polity in such systems is in theory and fact so close that the nature of the relationship could not be ignored even by the arch purists in both disciplines. Moreover, whether specializing in such systems or not, all political scientists and economists *qua* social scientists are, or ought to be, comparativists; thus an explicit concern with the economy-polity relationship in differing systems has been virtually inescapable.

Political science has always been more or less amenable to giving consideration to the effect of nonpolitical variables upon politics. This is partly due to the tendency of its practitioners to regard their profession as the "umbrella" discipline, and partly to the weaker impact of the scientific perspective upon them. The result has been fuzzy boundaries, lack of focus, and extraordinary diversity in schools, approaches, and methods. As a leading political scientist has lamented, at mid-century, "If political scientists are agreed on anything, it is probably on the muddled state of their science. Political scientists are riding off in many directions, evidently on the assumption that if you don't know where you are going, any road will take you there."[2]

During the past two decades, among a new and more scientifically oriented generation of political scientists, there has been a quite extraordinary expansion of interest in and commitment to the developing areas. Already disposed and, by their permissive discipline, allowed to study anything politically relevant (and in the tempestuous decade of terminal colonialism almost everything was politically relevant), they became the proponents and carriers, on a rather massive scale, of an entirely new orientation in the discipline. This orientation was marked by an intensification among them of the macropolitical perspective (national elites, national parties, and the nation-building process tended to be the main foci), and by an explicitly interdisciplinary commitment derived in part from contact with the structural functionalism of anthropological colleagues in the field, and from their perception of the obvious importance of the social, economic, and cultural setting of politics. Their intensive personal exposure to the realities of the developing areas not only strengthened their macropolitical (nation-building) and holistic perspective, as well as their sensitivity in general to the relevance of the setting of politics; it also brought the scholars concerned into direct contact with the major problem of public policy of the postcolonial period, namely, economic development. In due course one or another aspect of the politics of economic development emerged to the fore as dissertation topics and research proposals by a second wave of postwar younger political scientists coming to Africa.

In the meantime, other major reorientations in the discipline of political science were already well under way: (1) the impact of "group theorists"; (2) the increasing popularity within the discipline of functionalism and "systems" theory; (3) the shift from static to dynamic modes of analysis for the study and comparison of patterns of political development in both historical and contemporary perspective; and (4) the reconceptualization of the nature of the polity from that of ultimate physical compulsion to the idea of the creative, purposive mechanism through which societal goals are determined and pursued. Each of these has had evident implications for the role of economic variables in political analysis.

The group theorists alerted political analysts to the significance of economic (pressure) groups in the political system and provided a basic analytical tool for assessing the functioning of the system. The concept "political system" has compelled political scientists to think of the political universe analytically (i.e., as encompassing all politically relevant activity in all institutional spheres) rather than confining the "political" to the narrower concept of "state" and concrete political and governmental structures such as parties, legislatures, and courts. The shift from static or "equilibrium" analysis to dynamic and developmental analysis also nudges political scientists into taking exogenous variables into consideration in their analysis and into relating patterns of development in the polity to those in the society and economy. Finally, although it has been some time since governments in Western countries accepted a continuing responsibility for the function of providing welfare, planning the economy, and using the power of the state to seek and achieve new goals, political scientists until very recently continued to define the political realm either in the simplistic nineteenth-century law-and-order terms of Max Weber—"monopoly of the legitimate use of physical force within a given territory"—or in such equilibratory Parsonian terms as "pattern maintenance," "adaptation," or "integration." As J. Roland Pennock put it:

> Political systems develop their own autonomous political goals and . . . the attainment of these collective goals is one of their major functions, providing an important measure of their development. . . . I shall call these goals "political goods." . . . The degree to which a political system achieves these political goods may be considered yet another dimension of political development.

And one of Pennock's four "political goods" (the other three being the classical maintenance of "law and order," "justice," and "liberty") is "the promotion of economic growth, either indirectly by supplying the necessary infrastructure, by providing conditions that encourage the immigration of foreign capital and expertise, or more directly by governmental 'planning' and enterprise."[3] Today, this is accepted as a proper function of government, and therefore as an integral part of the political scientist's concept of the polity.

The first significant contrast between economics and political science is the greater scientific rigor (both attempted and achieved) of the former. The self-image of most, but not all, economists is that they are the only really "hard" social scientists with a predictive capability. This they can rightly claim, but at a price. It has meant, among other things, a reluctance to include noneconomic variables in their analysis, and an avoidance of being stigmatized as area specialists. The avoidance of noneconomic variables is deliberate. As one leading economist put it, "Society has an economic aspect and this is the element economic science purports to explain, leaving others to other disciplines." The avoidance of the noneconomic realm is brought out in economist Karl de Schweinitz's interesting distinction between economic "development" and "growth," which deserves being quoted at length.

> [Economic] *growth* may be defined as increasing output (GNP) per capita. [Economic] *development* has broader reference to the building of institutions, new lines of production, and the dissemination of attitudes essential for self-sustaining growth. . . . It must be acknowledged at once that economics is concerned more with growth than development and so, paradoxically, does not have much to contribute to the explanation of the origins of growth. Recently it has been taken to task for this "failure," the charge being that while appropriate for growing systems the narrow concerns of economics do not explain much where growth is not taking

> place. . . . These critics ask too much of economics. Unlike Marxian analysis, which attempts to encompass the totality of behavior, it does not pretend to be a complete science of society. Economics is concerned with market phenomena in nationally-integrated economies. Where these do not exist, its analytical techniques are non-operative. . . . However imperfect economics is, it is further advanced as a policy science than the other social sciences. And if it has not been more effective in helping new states realize growth objectives, it is because so many of them have not yet developed institutions conducive to growth. For explanations of this lack of development, however, one should look to political science or sociology, rather than to economics.[4]

Another reason for the economists' tendency to avoid political variables is their close and more continuous link with governments as policy advisers. De Schweinitz's claim that economics is a more highly developed policy science is undoubtedly correct: economists know it, employing governments know it, and other social scientists know it. As a result economists are more acceptable, indeed, more sought after, as social science technicians in the policy formulation process. One obvious consequence—a tendency characteristic of anyone in the Establishment—is to avoid or ignore political variables, usually by the convenient phrase *ceteris paribus*. This tendency is underscored by the fact that even those development economists who readily acknowledge the relevance of the social and cultural context of development, or even psychological variables, frequently exclude those of a political character. Some economic advisers claim that they do not and cannot ignore such variables; they assess them "on the job," so to speak, and react accordingly. What they do reject is the need for the development of a set of integrative theoretical conceptions concerned with politicoeconomic phenomena. It is our contention here that the hybrid discipline of political economy requires such a theoretical framework.

The imperative of disciplinary purity and the constraints of their advisory role help to explain all evident reluctance by economists in the past to involve themselves explicitly with the noneconomic environment. Nevertheless, at least three major reorientations in economics have nudged economists toward a more interdisciplinary perspective. It is, also, particularly interesting and relevant that these parallel three of the new orientations in political science previously discussed, suggesting the operation of certain generic forces in the social sciences. These new emphases in economics are (1) the macroeconomic perspective emerging from the Great Depression and Keynesian Revolution and reinforced by the impact of the developing areas; (2) the shift in focus from static equilibrium models to development; and (3) acceptance of the unavoidability of taking into account the setting or contest ("exogenous factors") within which economic growth occurs.

By the end of World War II macroanalysis in economics was well established. The development of Keynesian ideas made it possible for economists to consider major aggregate variables and to look at an economy as a whole, in the same sense that postwar political scientists were nudged by systems analysis and structural functionalism to look at the polity as a whole. Moreover, Keynesian economics favored a very considerable degree of government regulation and direction of the economy, a point of view highly congruent with the transformative "social engineering" ideology of the political elites of the new states emerging from colonialism. The new holistic orientation in economics was thus linked with their acceptance of the idea that the polity had a creative, purposive, and goal-seeking function.

The second major reorientation has been what Walter Newlyn has described as the "significant shift in the 'centre of content' of the subject of economics itself." A postwar phenomenon, he describes it as follows:

> By excessive concentration on . . . static analysis, economists have lost touch with the bold generalizations of Adam Smith, Ricardo, Malthus and Marx about the basic growth variables. . . . Indeed, during this century economists have had sadly little to say about the "causes of the wealth of nations." The significant shift in the centre of content of the subject . . . has taken place, like many previous changes in the emphasis of economic thought, in response to the social problems of the time. [The latter, including the "immensity of the task of transforming the economies of the underdeveloped countries"] . . . has turned economists away from their preoccupation with the fluctuations of activity in industrial societies to the problems of growth of primitive societies. Economists became once more interested in growth *as a process* to be examined and explained. . . . all economists have suddenly become "development" specialists and, as a result, have become interested in comparative studies of growth. . . . this specialization necessarily means that their comparative method must be applied to the economy as a whole.[5]

Third, many economists, like political scientists, have also come to admit the relevance of the "setting" for economic growth. The decisively persuasive factor has been their encounter with the realities of the developing areas. The first wave of economists drawn to the developing areas saw capital formation as the chief problem, but this simple model of growth inevitably had to be modified because of its woeful inadequacy. Economists were thus compelled, as Manning Nash put it, "to confront the social and cultural system, so to speak, head on," to take systematic account of the context of economic development. This broadening of the spectrum of the economists' world is associated with the work of Walt Rostow (*Stages of Economic Growth*), Arthur Lewis (*Theory of Economic Development*), as well as the various writings of Gunnar Myrdal, Bert Howelitz, Everett Hagen, Simon Kuznets, Albert Hirschman, and many others. They have all turned at some point or other in their analyses to anthropologists, sociologists, and psychologists for a stipulation of the context of development.

The Political Preconditions of Economic Development

The most striking new emphasis in discussions on the nature of politics and the problem of economic development in the developing countries, and particularly in Africa, is the almost unanimous agreement on what has come to be known as the "primacy of the polity." The arguments asserting polity primacy over other institutional spheres tend to fall into two categories: (1) the argument of African cultural continuity, and (2) the argument of situational necessity.

The argument that the primacy of the political sphere in contemporary Africa is rooted in African culture is advanced by Professor Lloyd Fallers:

> In traditional Africa goods and services, both as symbols and as facilities, circulate primarily in terms of political relations, for it is the polity that dominates stratification. . . . Traditional African societies . . . have characteristically exhibited patterns of role differentiation in which political specialization has been more prominent than economic. The ambitions of their members have been directed primarily toward attaining authority, and economic processes have commonly been dominated by the political needs of individuals and groups. Although direct cultural continuity may be difficult to achieve, some characteristic features of the traditional systems may perhaps persist and give a distinctly African character to the new independent nations. For example, in the new African nations, as in the old, political structures seem likely to continue to dominate economic ones, and political elites to retain their preeminence. To be sure, the place of economic processes in society has changed greatly. Whereas in traditional societies an essentially static economy was manipulated for political ends, the new inde-

> pendent states make rapid economic development the principal aim of public policy. . . . The traditional cultural emphasis upon authority coincides with, and perhaps helps to produce, modern conceptions of planning for economic development.[6]

Most anthropologists are reluctant to generalize in this manner about "traditional African culture," largely because of the enormous diversity of indigenous institutional forms and the fact that they personally are intimately familiar with only one or two societies. They are equally adverse to generalize about cultural continuities. However, this particular hypothesis stands as an exciting challenge to the behavioral sciences to validate, qualify, or disconfirm.

The main burden of the argument for the priority of the political sphere over the economy in the developing countries is, however, based on situational necessity. The major elements in this argument are now fairly well known. Walter Newlyn has argued, for example, that the peculiarity of the development problems which face the primitive economies of Africa has convinced economists of the "need for deliberate planning and for governments to play a major role as entrepreneurs in the transformation of the modes of production of such economies." Charles Wolf argues that another reason for the dominance of the political factor is that nationalists in many colonial areas perceived the relationship between political and economic power in causal terms, namely, whoever possesses political power has, and ought to have, control over the economy. A strongly interventionist economic tradition is a major element in the Western colonial legacy to new states. Moreover, in areas of almost total expatriate domination of the economy the determination to use newly won political power to "indigenize" economic power has been understandably strong, indeed, inevitable. This could be done only by an interventionist policy since the "free play of the market" would serve only to perpetuate expatriate domination of the economy. Fairly comprehensive interventionism has also been a consequence of the determination of insecure political elites in new states to maximize their control over what S. N. Eisenstadt has called "free-floating resources." The political value of various forms of patronage (i.e., control over public employment and loans) and of a monopoly over central planning are self-evident.

One of the most explicit and detailed arguments rationalizing the priority of the political realm in the developing areas is that made by economist Wilfred Malenbaum. He notes that in the first decade of discussion regarding economic development in the newly independent countries it was universally assumed that economic growth was mainly a technical and virtually autonomous process, the independent variable affecting all other spheres. Painful experience convinced many economists that the relationship was precisely the reverse. Out of this ordeal of frustration, Malenbaum affirms the following proposition:

> We now know that the primary ingredient of *economic* growth is motivational more than material. [We also know] that the motivation for change in a nation demands some national expression. The attitudes and desires of parts of the nation—including, where relevant, the demands of the market place—must somehow combine to serve as the national expression. This task of combination extends far beyond tasks of organization or of administration. It is essentially and fundamentally a political task, reflecting skilled leadership. . . . [Patterns of economic growth are not possible] unless the political structure, including its leadership, seeks their attainment as explicit and major goals.[7]

The argument that polity primacy is either a political precondition or a correlate of economic development in postcolonial new states is at the heart of the debate over the nature of the development process. Do postcolonial African realities validate this contention? The picture is not entirely clear and the time interval is too short to judge. However, the cases of Ghana and Guinea, where polity primacy unquestionably reached its zenith, might provide some insight. Together with Mali they were the two states with the strongest, and presumably most creative leadership. They were the most self-conscious about the development of a coherent activist ideology, about the creation and maintenance of a highly centralized and monolithic organizational structure with total monopoly over all associations, total assimilation of party and governmental structures, and total fusion of the polity and the economy.

The record of economic development in these two states since independence would tend to disconfirm the hypothesis that there is a positive correlation between polity primacy and economic growth. In Guinea, shortly after independence, the government set up a complete monopoly over both foreign trade and domestic wholesaling. Although the achievements of the new state were quite remarkable, particularly in view of the abrupt withdrawal of the French, there were catastrophic failures in economic policy and planning. There are many explanations for these failures, but as Elliot Berg argues, "the major burden rests with the Guineans themselves."

> The state trading venture was an unmitigated disaster, afflicting the whole economy. An inexperienced Guinean management found itself in charge of what was in effect the largest trading firm in Africa. Despite some gallant efforts, the distribution system rapidly fell victim to a massive administrative muddle. . . . Fundamental reappraisals were hindered by the need to maintain socialist purity, an unwillingness to look coolly at all the alternatives. Official economic discussion in fact became increasingly divorced from reality. . . . The costs of Guinea's false starts cannot be calculated only in terms of wasted resources and foregone growth. Much of the popular enthusiasm for the regime and the dynamism of its leadership has been dissipated. Cynicism and corruption have spread, and signs of disaffection appeared. The moral and political cement binding the state together has been weakened as respect for law, and for the regime, has diminished.[8]

The story is not dissimilar for the much wealthier state of Ghana, whose economy steadily deteriorated between independence in 1957 and the overthrow of the Nkrumah regime in 1966. During that period Ghana's foreign exchange reserves dropped from £170m to nothing; national income per head in 1960 was £G70; by 1964 it had gone up in real terms only to £G76. Personal consumption actually dropped from £G50 to £G47.[9] The list of serious deficiencies in many sectors of the economy traceable in one way or another to the policies of the government is too long to recount here. The main point is that in Africa's two new states, in which there was the greatest determination to fuse the polity and the economy and to establish and maintain the primacy of the polity at its highest level, there has been either a poor or a disastrous record of economic development.

It is easy to concentrate and personalize the blame for these failures. In fact they do not disconfirm the hypothesis that there is a positive correlation between interventionism and economic development in new states. The notion "primacy of the polity" confuses the issue: the polity exerts ultimate authority over the economy in any system, otherwise there is no system, only a state of anarchy. The real issue is the nature and the degree of the control political authority exerts over the economy and, more specifically, the nature of the power relationship between authorities defined as political and those defined as economic. The primacy of the political dimension implies not only that political action (ideas, leadership, organization, and power) transcends and determines development in other institutional spheres but that it operates effectively within the limits imposed by the constraints (e.g., cultural resistance, social rigidities, political opposition) it confronts. Where it attempts to defy or exceed those constraints, economic failure or regression is likely to occur.

Much of the recent literature on economic development reflects near unanimity on the absolute essentiality of an effective system of public administration. The point need not be labored, it is both obvious and well known. Yet there is not complete consensus. Referring to John Kenneth Galbraith's list of four preconditions (one of which was "a reliable apparatus of government and public administration"), Albert O. Hirschman observed that

> whenever development occurs, it does so invariably in the absence of one or several of these "required" components or preconditions. In nineteenth century Germany, it occurred without much primitive accumulation of capital and in Italy without the Protestant ethic, to mention some of the earlier theories on prerequisites; and during the postwar period, Brazil experienced development in the absence of monetary stability, and Colombia even in the absence of public order, not to speak of land reform. . . . Therefore, I continue to advocate that in their research the experts pay special attention to the emergence and possible rationality of new or inverted sequences. When they discover an "obstacle," such as poor public administration . . . their job does not consist in merely advising its removal; they ought to explore also how, by moving the economy forward elsewhere, additional pressure (economic and political) could be brought on the obstacle to give way.[10]

This is useful wisdom distilled from the comparative study of conditions normally associated with economic development, but does it not ignore the peculiarity of the African problem of economic development referred to by Newlyn? Here the need for central, planned, and directed economic development is so manifest, and the dependence of such a process upon an efficient and trained bureaucracy so clear, that while one can share Hirschman's and Gershendron's skepticism that history provide little guidance, one can also insist that the overpowering logic of the African situation makes effective public administration a precondition for economic development.

Economists and political scientists are not only concerned with the identification of political and administrative preconditions of economic development but also with the nature of political constraints and the latitude of political feasibilities in concrete situations. Some of these are generic to African as well as other societies. As they are multiethnic societies, political leaders must be acutely sensitive to the imperative of ethnic arithmetic not only in the allocation of jobs but also in the geographical allocation of resources and in the distribution of the product of economic growth. Heeding this imperative frequently plays havoc with economic rationality, but it is a political constraint of such pervasiveness and magnitude, because it strikes at the very heart of the legitimacy of the governing regime, that economists neglect it at peril to themselves as well as the political leaders they advise.

The Political Consequences of Economic Development

Political economists are concerned not only with how political variables and constraints affect economic development but also with how the latter, as an independent variable, affects political behavior and institutions. This latter dimension will be examined with reference to three rather well-known issues: (1) economic development and political competitiveness; (2) rapid economic growth and political instability; and (3) uneven economic development and political integration.

The statistical evidence (how reliable it may be is still in dispute) unquestionably suggests a close connection between economic development and political competitiveness (a situation close to but not completely synonymous with democracy). Higher degrees of economic development are associated with greater political competitiveness; and, conversely, the lowest levels of economic development tend statistically to be linked with authoritarianism. These studies suggest, be it noted, only a statistical correlation, and not a causal nexus.

The hypothesis that economic growth and political competitiveness are positively correlated has been challenged by Morris Janowitz:

> This type of analysis appears to have limited relevance for understanding, on a comparative basis, the dynamic relationship between economic development and political forms. . . . there is no basis for asserting that, with higher levels of economic development, there is a movement toward more competitive political systems. In fact, among those nations with the highest level of economic development, the absence of democratic competitive systems is more noteworthy than their presence, since competitive systems are concentrated in the middle level of economic development. . . . But the analysis is not without meaning if the general hypothesis is abandoned and the underlying process examined. Authoritarian-personal regimes are heavily concentrated among the nations with low economic development, for these nations are just embarking on

> economic development . . . [However] the basic conclusion is that, with higher economic levels, the outcome is as likely as not to be in the direction of military oligarchy, and perhaps somewhat more likely.[11]

Another critic, Harry Eckstein, has argued that between the great extremes of economic development and economic underdevelopment there is a "large no-man's land where apparently any governmental order, from stable democracy to totalitarianism can exist."[12] We are clearly in the presence of an issue that cannot be definitively resolved, at least not until there is a vast improvement in our statistical data and a greater consensus on the definition of political forms.

There is far greater consensus on the proposition that *rapid* economic growth has political destabilizing consequences. It has this effect because it increases the number of individuals who are *déclassé* ("detribalized" in old Africanist jargon) and most disposed to lead or to follow in a revolutionary movement; it markedly increases the number of gainers (the insatiable *nouveaux riches*) and losers (the bitterly resentful *nouveaux pauvres*), both of whom tend to become alienated; and it vastly expands the numbers caught up in the "revolution of rising expectations."[13] Hagen, however, rejects the contention that there is a positive correlation between economic growth and political instability. The "awakening of the masses," their growing awareness of the possibility of change, he argues, has been brought to them "by the course of history; it is surely almost entirely independent of economic growth."[14] But even if economic growth is one of the contributory causes of this awakening, the remedy is not to curtail or to forego growth. On the contrary:

> Awareness that they are not powerless will surely reach the peasant and worker in the absence of economic change, even if slightly late, and their reaction will be the more extreme if nothing has previously been done to indicate that the world has regard for them. Opportunities for economic growth that reach the discontented groups are surely a counteragent if the accumulated bitterness has grown too great.[15]

The foregoing argument overlooks the disposition and the capacity of individuals and groups to accommodate themselves to the hard realities of life. The "revolution of rising expectations" may indeed lead to a "revolution of rising frustrations," but the latter does not necessarily lead to actual revolution. Any number of examples, historical and contemporaneous, can be found of individuals and categories of persons who, by all objective criteria, should be on the brink of revolutionary violence or bitterly alienated, but who are nonetheless disposed and capable of adjusting themselves to disappointment and only partial fulfillment of their original expectations. This imponderable in human nature is all too frequently overlooked. In the painful choices political leaders must make it is admittedly a calculated risk to base decisions on the assumption of accommodation rather than revolution, but dedicated and inspired (and inspiring) leadership itself can frequently ensure that the dice are loaded in favor of accommodation.

The third selected issue concerns the effect of economic growth upon political integration. This has been brilliantly examined by economist Elliot Berg in his effort to explain postwar political developments in former French West Africa, and particularly to explain why differential political choices were made at certain critical junctures. Berg found the economic factor unquestionably dominant at each crisis point. Underlying these complex political events, he argues, "is a set of economic circumstances which have given shape to the political decisions made; in West Africa, as elsewhere, political choice is conditioned by the nature of the economic environment in which it takes place."[16] The unequal economic development among the various territories of French West Africa was the decisive factor in the political choices which resulted in the subsequent political fragmentations of that vast stretch of the African continent.

Economic growth can also have a politically dysfunctional effect as a result of its uneven impact in an ethnically pluralistic context. It can not only perpetuate, but all too frequently it intensifies tensions among different ethnic, regional, and parochial groups. Before planned economic growth is launched existing groups and regions are not only at a different level of economic development but they have differential capacities for further development. Those already more developed have an inherent advantage over those that are less developed. As Adam Curle has noted, "It is a sad fact that, once the process of development starts in one sector of a society, the inequalities within that society tend to increase. . . . Trade, labour and enterprise are apt to move towards the progressive areas, leaving the poor zones still poorer."[17] The net result of this natural operation of economic forces invariably tends to be heightened ethnicity, and sometimes even political separatism.

It is equally clear that certain patterns of economic growth can and do lead to new class differentiations. There is evidence, for example, that the present agricultural policies of the Uganda government are leading toward the formation of a "rich peasant" class dependent for its position upon such state favors as loans, group farms, and agricultural advice. Similarly, the business-promotion policy of the Kenya government would appear to be consciously directed toward the creation of an African entrepreneurial class. The emergence of these new classes is bound to affect future political processes and the nature of public policy, including particularly economic policy. The post-Arusha efforts of the Tanzanian government, aimed at arresting the process of new class formation, are an interesting example of the use of state authority to prevent members of the new political elite from using their positions of influence to make themselves the new economic elite.

The high degree of de facto *étatisme* characteristic of most new states elevates the process of economic policy-making to a position of central importance. Economic policies are highly determinative of the achievement or prevention of particular economic, political, or social consequences. But economic policies themselves reflect conscious political decisions. Thus, once one accepts the importance of political decisions for economic growth, the way in which economic policies are determined is obviously of crucial significance. The comparative study of the process should provide insight into the kinds of decisions and policies that are politically as well as economically feasible.

The foregoing issues illustrate the many areas of public policy and problems of nation-building where the practical and the theoretical concerns of the political scientist and the economist converge. They provide a basis for a potentially fruitful dialogue, in which one would hope the purism of the economist and the dilettantism of the political scientist might be somewhat reduced. Whether there is enough there yet to resurrect the hybrid discipline of political economy is a question that can be answered only by the practitioners themselves.

NOTES

1. Frederick S. Dunn, "The Scope of International Relations," *World Politics*, 1 (October 1948), p. 142.
2. Heinz Eulau, "Political Science," in Bert F. Hoselitz, ed., *A Reader's Guide to the Social Sciences* (New York: Free Press, 1959), p. 91.
3. J. Roland Pennock, "Political Development, Political Systems, and Political Good," *World Politics*, 18 (April 1966), p. 420.
4. Karl de Schweinitz, Jr., "Economics and the Underdeveloped Economies," *The American Behavioral Scientist*, 9:1 (September 1965), pp. 3, 5; italics added.
5. Walter T. Newlyn, "The Present State of African Economic Studies," *African Affairs* (Spring 1965), p. 39.
6. Lloyd A. Fallers, "Social Stratification and Economic Processes," in

Melville J. Herskovits and Mitchell Harwitz, eds., *Economic Transition in Africa* (Evanston, Ill.: Northwestern University Press, 1964), pp. 126, 127, 129, 130.

7. Wilfred Malenbaum, "Economic Factors and Political Development," *The Annals* (March 1965), pp. 42–43.

8. Elliot J. Berg, "Socialism and Economic Development in Tropical Africa," *The Quarterly Journal of Economics*, 78 (November 1964), pp. 558–560.

9. Tony Killick, "Making Ghana Grow Again," *West Africa*, August 20, 1966, pp. 937–938; and "Ghana's Economic Legacy," *West Africa*, November 5, 1966.

10. Albert O. Hirschman, "Comments on 'A Framework for Analyzing Economic and Political Change,'" in The Brookings Institution, *Development of the Emerging Countries: An Agenda for Research* (Washington, D.C.: Brookings Institution, 1962), p. 41.

11. Morris Janowitz, *The Military in the Political Development of New Nations* (Chicago: University of Chicago Press, 1964), pp. 21, 23.

12. Harry Eckstein, *A Theory of Stable Democracy* (Princeton: Princeton University Press, 1961), p. 39.

13. Mancur Olson, Jr., "Rapid Growth as a Destabilizing Force," *The Journal of Economic History*, 23 (December 1963), pp. 530–531.

14. Everett E. Hagen, "A Framework for Analyzing Economic and Political Change," in The Brookings Institution, *Development of the Emerging Countries*, p. 37.

15. Ibid.

16. Elliot J. Berg, "The Economic Basis of Political Choice in French West Africa," *The American Political Science Review*, 56 (1960), pp. 391–405.

17. Adam Curle, *The Role of Education in Developing Societies*, (Accra: Ghana University Press, 1961), pp. 7–8.

8 Modernization: Political Aspects

The political aspects of modernization refer to the ensemble of structural and cultural changes in the political systems of modernizing societies. As an analytically separable subsystem of society the political system comprises all of those activities, processes, institutions, and beliefs concerned with the making and execution of authoritative policy and the pursuit and attainment of collective goals. Political structure consists of the patterning and interrelationship of political roles and processes; political culture is the complex of prevailing attitudes, beliefs, and values concerning the political system. The overall process of modernization refers to changes in all institutional spheres of a society resulting from man's expanding knowledge of and control over his environment.[1] Political modernization refers to those processes of differentiation of political structure and secularization of political culture which enhance the capability—the effectiveness and efficiency of performance—of a society's political system.[2]

Political modernization can be viewed from a historical, a typological, and an evolutionary perspective. *Historical political modernization* refers to the totality of changes in political structure and culture which characteristically have affected or have been affected by those major transformative processes of modernization (secularization; commercialization; industrialization; accelerated social mobility; restratification; increased material standards of living; diffusion of literacy, education, and mass media; national unification; and the expansion of popular involvement

Reprinted with permission of Macmillan Publishing Company, a Division of Macmillan, Inc., from *International Encyclopedia of the Social Sciences,* David L. Sills, editor. Vol. 10, pp. 395–402. Copyright 1968 by Crowell Collier and Macmillan, Inc.

and participation) which were first launched in Western Europe in the sixteenth century and which subsequently have spread, unevenly and incompletely, throughout the world. *Typological political modernization* refers to the process of transmutation of a premodern "traditional" polity into a posttraditional "modern" polity. (Since concrete polities are only more or less modern, the term "modern polity" is used here to refer to those polities which in the 1960s are typologically the most modern.) *Evolutionary political modernization* refers to that open-ended increase in the capacity of political man to develop structures to cope with or resolve problems, to absorb and adapt to continuous change, and to strive purposively and creatively for the attainment of new societal goals. From the historical and typological perspectives, political modernization is a process of development toward some image of a modern polity. From the evolutionary perspective, the growth process is interminable and the end state of affairs indeterminate.

Theoretical Approaches

Efforts to depict the complex characteristics of a modern polity have tended to take three forms: descriptive trait lists, single-dimension reductionism, and ideal-type continua. Several studies have combined all three approaches in variant ways.[3] The trait list approach usually identifies the major structural and cultural features generic to those contemporary polities regarded as modern by the observer.[4] These efforts have been criticized for being temporally and culturally bounded, for being excessively multidimensional, and for including some traits which vary independently of one another.[5]

The reductionist approach focuses upon a single antecedent factor, explanatory variable, correlate, or determinant as the prime index of most distinguishing feature of modernization and, by implication, of political modernity. Single characteristics which have been highlighted include the concepts of capacity or capability,[6] differentiation,[7] institutionalization,[8] national integration,[9] participation,[10] populism,[11] political culture,[12] psychological traits,[13] social mobilization,[14] and socioeconomic correlates.[15] These reductive efforts do not imply a denial of multivariate causation; rather, they reflect either the timeless quest for a comprehensive single concept of modernity or simply the desire to illuminate a previously neglected or underemphasized variable.

The ideal-type approach is either explicit or implicit in most conceptualizations of both a modern political system and the process of political modernization. Descriptive trait lists of a generically modern polity tend unavoidably to be ideal-typical; indeed, the very notion of a "modern polity" implies an ideal-typical "traditional polity" as a polar opposite, as well as a "transitional polity" as an intervening type on a continuum of political modernization. Inspired by the original simple dichotomies of Maine (status-contract) and Tönnies (*Gemeinschaft-Gesellschaft*), and more directly by the pattern variables developed by Talcott Parsons, more complex ideal-typical dichotomous schemata of variable multidimensionality have been suggested for the study of comparative politics[16] and comparative administration.[17] The essential differences between these schemata and the ideal-typical trait lists are that the attributes of the former are more logically interrelated in a unified construct and are specified for the two polar opposites (e.g., agrarian-industrial; traditional-modern). According to these schemata, the orientations governing the interactions characteristic of a traditional polity are predominantly ascriptive, particularistic, and diffuse; those of a modern polity are predominantly achievement-oriented, universalistic, and specific. Political modernization is viewed as the process of movement from the traditional pole to the modern pole of the continuum.

The three-stage (traditional-transitional-modern) approach to political modernization is vulnerable to at least three criticisms. First, like all such models used in the study of change in the social sciences, it tends to convey a false image of the traditional pole of the modernization continuum.[18] The static, sacred, undifferentiated character of chronologically traditional polities tends to be exaggerated. Many historically "traditional" political systems in fact had typologically "modern" structures, attributes, and orientations and vice versa. Indeed, the political structures of all empirical societies—historical and contemporaneous—are mixed; the degree of their modernity is determined by whichever tendency predominates within the mix. Although this fact is acknowledged, even stressed, by most users of the three-stage approach, the tendency to confuse, or at least to slur, the differences between historical and typological political modernity is a common fallacy in much of the literature. Second, this approach suggests that the movement between the two poles of traditionality and modernity is and must be irreversible, directional, and unilinear. It does not allow for political "breakdowns" in modernization,[19] for "negative" political development or "prismatic" arrest,[20] or for political "decay."[21] Third, at the modern end of the continuum, the three-stage model reinforces the image that the modernization process terminates, a notion implicit in the ordinary "present-day" meaning of the concept of modernity. It suggests the completion of a once-and-for-all and once-to-a-system process of transmutation. By implying that there cannot be any further or continuous modernization, it rules out the concept of evolutionary political modernization.

The evolutionary perspective emancipates the concept of political modernization from both its temporal (1500 to the present day) and its cultural and areal (Western world) constraints. It overcomes the implication of termination inherent in the idea of a "modern" polity and avoids the notion of "postmodern" political development. Although it does not becloud the fact that historically the major thrust in political modernization has occurred in the core area of Western Europe in its postmedieval period, it allows us to reach back to the beginning of man's organized existence and to encompass the full range of structural diversity in man's experience in governing himself. Moreover, by viewing political modernization as an ongoing and continuous process, it encourages comparative trend analysis. Such a redefinition of the concept ties in with the revival and extension of evolutionary theory in cultural anthropology[22] and in sociology.[23] Indeed, the distinction made by Sahlins between specific evolution (the historically continuous adaptation of particular societies to their environments) and general evolution (overall, but discontinuous, development in human organization as manifested in the passage from lesser to greater capacity and all-round adaptability and from lower to higher levels of integration) is particularly crucial.[24] This dual character of the evolutionary perspective makes it possible to refer, on the one hand, to the specific process of political modernization (i.e., the acquisition of typologically modern traits and capabilities) in particular concrete societies, which through specialization and adaptation may in time cease modernizing, and, on the other hand, to general political modernization, as manifested in the successive acquisition by politically organized man of enhanced and new capacity to seek, change, and attain his goals. It is, in short, a perspective that allows us to conceptualize political modernization, political development, and political growth as synonymous.

Characteristics

In the growing body of literature on modernization and development, the major characteristics most often associated with the concept of modern polity and the process of political modernization can be roughly grouped under three major headings: (1) differentiation, as the dominant empirical trend in the historic evolution of modern society; (2) equality, as the central ethos and ethical imperative pervading the operative ideals of all aspects of modern life; and (3) capacity, as the constantly increasing adaptive and creative potentialities possessed by man for the manipulation of his environment. The political modernization process can be viewed as an interminable contrapuntal interplay among the process of differentiation, the imperatives and realizations of equality, and the integrative, adaptive, and creative capacity of a political system. In these terms, political modernization is the progressive acquisition of a consciously sought, and qualitatively new and enhanced, political capacity as manifested in (1) the effective institutionalization of (a) new patterns of integration and penetration regulating and containing the tensions and conflicts produced by the processes of differentiation, and of (b) new patterns of participation and resource distribution adequately responsive to the demands generated by the imperatives of equality; and (2) the continuous flexibility to set and achieve new goals.

THE PROCESS OF DIFFERENTIATION

Differentiation refers to the process of progressive separation and specialization of roles, institutional spheres, and terms. It includes such "evolutionary universals"[25] as social stratification and the separation of occupational roles from kinship and domestic life, the separation of an integrated system of universalistic legal norms from religion, the separation of religion and ideology, and differentiation between administrative structure and public political competition. It implies greater functional specialization, structural complexity and interdependence, and heightened effectiveness of political organization in both administrative and political spheres.[26]

THE ETHOS OF EQUALITY

Equality is the ethos of modernity; the quest for it and its realization are at the core of the politics of modernization. It includes the notion of universal adult citizenship (equality in distributive claims and participant rights and duties), the prevalence of universalistic legal norms in the government's relations with the citizenry (equality in legal privileges and deprivations), and the predominance of achievement criteria (the psychic equality of opportunity to be unequal) in recruitment and allocation to political and administrative roles. Even though these attributes of equality are only imperfectly realized in the most modern polities, they continue to operate as the central standards and imperatives by which modernization is measured and political legitimacy established. Popular participation or involvement in the political system, either symbolically or determinatively, is a central theme in most definitions of political modernization.[27]

THE GROWTH OF POLITICAL CAPACITY

The acquisition of enhanced political administrative capacity is the third major feature of political modernization. It is characterized by an increase in scope of polity functions, in the scale of the political community, in the efficacy of the implementation of political and administrative decisions, in the penetrative power of central governmental institutions, and in the comprehensiveness of the aggregation of interests by political associations. Institutionalization of political organization and procedures, the development of problem-solving capabilities, centralization, and the ability to sustain continuously new types of political demands and organizations are among the varying ways in which the concept of capacity include both differentiation (secularization, functional specialization, greater structural interdependence, motivation generated by status hierarchization) and equality (liberation of human energy and talent, universalism, achievement, rationalization, and civic identity and obligation); yet the tensions and divisiveness of differentiation and the demands of egalitarianism also constitute the main challenge to the capacity of a polity. The fact that the three aspects of modernization may sometimes conflict rather than reinforce one another explains why their contrapuntal interplay is central to any discussion of the modernization process.

DEMOCRACY AND NATION-STATE

Two other characteristics commonly attributed to a modern polity are democracy and the nation-state. In some instances, Western democratic institutions are used explicitly as the empirical referents for a model of political modernity; in others such an identification is only implicit. This infusion of the concept with an allegedly culture-bound element limits the utility of the concept as a cross-cultural analytical tool. Recognition of this fact has stimulated efforts to identify and specify traits generic to those political systems generally recognized as the most modern in the contemporary world. Ethnocentrism aside, however, there are those who defend a democratic component in any model of political modernization either on ethical grounds or because it demonstrably enhances the integrative and adaptive capacity and the flexibility of a political system. This latter rationale is the basis for identifying the "democratic association" as an "evolutionary universal," a major threshold in political modernization.[28]

The nation-state is the second major controversial component in definitions of political modernization. Most studies assume that the nation-state is the essential, if not the natural, framework of political modernization. According to Black,[29] the essential effect of modernization has been the creation of national states. Indeed, "nation building" is commonly viewed as either a crucial dimension of or as a synonym for political modernization. Historically, of course, the centralized nation-state (existing or emerging) has been the empirical unit of modernization in all its aspects. Moreover, unlike democratic institutions, it is a form of political organization that has in fact become universalized. It has also been legitimated by prevailing norms of international law and organization. Therefore, it is the most convenient and logical unit for analysis in studies both of historical and of contemporary modernization. From the evolutionary and typological perspective, however, it need not and should not be included as a requisite component of political modernization.[30]

Patterns and Variables

THE AUTONOMY OF THE POLITY

A prominent theme in various strands of Western social and political thought is the dependence of the polity upon other institutional spheres. This tradition of looking at political behavior and institutions as deriving from more fundamental social, economic, or psychological factors has been fortified in the social sciences—and particularly in political science—by a variety of other influences: behavioralism, systems theory, and structural functionalism; the prominence in our image of modernization in the Western world of the laissez-faire period, in contrast with the earlier polity-dominant statist period; the pronounced economic determinism in America's post-World War II foreign aid policy, conditioned as it has been by the presumably successful democratization of West Germany and Japan; and several studies which suggest a positive correlation between political, social, and economic aspects of development.[31] In line with the continual rediscovery of lost or neglected variables in the pendulumlike evolution of the social sciences, the reaction against this polity-as-the-dependent-variable tradition is now in full swing.[32]

The need for a critical reexamination of the degree of autonomy and primacy of the polity in the modernization process has been given added impetus as a result of retrospective analysis of historical modernization in the West;[33] the dominance of the political sphere in the modernization of the Soviet Union and mainland China, as well as Japan, Turkey, and Mexico;[34] and the preeminence of the political factor in the modernization of the developing countries. In virtually all of these instances political leadership and centralized political organization have been dominant and causal, rather that derivative. There are also historical instances where substantial changes have taken place in the political sphere without correspondingly significant changes in the social and economic spheres, and vice versa,[35] thus underlining the autonomy of the polity in the modernization process. The American experience, as Huntington[36] emphasized, demonstrates conclusively that some institutions and some aspects of a society may become highly modern while other institutions and other aspects retain much of their traditional form and substance.

PATTERNS OF MODERNIZATION

The varying patterns in the relationship between the polity and the society (polity dominance, polity dependence, and polity autonomy) are only one aspect of the extraordinary diversity which has characterized the process of political modernization throughout history. There presumably is no single universal process, no uniform sequential pattern or common structural arrangement. The modernizing experience of each country is *sui generis*. According to one view, the only generalization one can make is that late modernizers "will not follow the sequence of their predecessors, but will insist on changing it around or on skipping entirely some stages as well as some 'preconditions.'"[37] Nevertheless, certain patterns have been suggested. One typology,[38] based on three criteria (the ascendence and consolidation of modernizing leadership, economic and social transformation, and the integration of society), identifies seven patterns of political modernization: (1) Britain and France, the early modernizers and models for later modernizers; (2) the United States, Canada, Australia, and New Zealand, the offshoots of Britain and France in the New World; (3) the other societies of continental Europe, in which the consolidation of modernizing leadership occurred after the French Revolution; (4) the independent countries of Latin America; (5) societies that modernized without direct outside intervention but under the influence of early modernizers (Russia, Japan, China, Iran, Turkey, Afghanistan, Ethiopia, and Thailand); and (6) and (7) former and residual colonial territories differentiated according to the existence of precolonial institutions adaptable to modern conditions. Using different criteria, another schema[39] distinguishes six clusters: (1) constitutional democracies; (2) totalitarian states; (3) indigenous revolutionary regimes such as Turkey and Mexico; (4) dictatorships in Eastern Europe, the Middle East, and Latin America; (5) authoritarian regimes in Spain and Portugal; and (6) the postcolonial new states. A third schema,[40] primarily concerned with the earlier phases of political modernization in Europe and America, distinguishes three patterns—continental European, British, and American—according to three criteria: (1) rationalized authority; (2) differentiated political structure; and (3) mass political participation. Actual or ideal-typical patterns of political modernization in late-modernizing new states as a special category have also been suggested.[41]

VARIABLES AFFECTING MODERNIZATION

Among the many variables which can affect—and which historically have decisively affected—the course of political modernization, four seem to be particularly crucial: (1) the traditional political structure and culture; (2) the historical timing of the modernization thrust; (3) the character and orientation of political leadership; and (4) the sequence in which major system-development problems or "crises" generic to the political modernization process are encountered.

Tradition Traditional institutions and values have an extraordinary resilience and persistence. "[The] form a modern society takes is the result of the interaction of its historically formed traditions with the universalizing effects of modernization."[42] For example, if prior to the modernization leap a national state, a centralized government, and a dominant value system supportive of innovation and change already exist, there can be a "reinforcing dualism"[43] between the traditional system and the modernizing process.

Timing The timing of the modernizing "take-off" is also crucial in many ways: it determines the significance of an array of other variables, such as the international environment, the range of modernizing models available for emulation, the political manipulability or obstructiveness of tradition, the degree of social and political mobilization of the population and the resultant demand load upon the polity, and the opportunities for modernizing shortcuts available to late starters favored by the so-called Law of Evolutionary Potential.[44]

Leadership The nature of a modernizing political leadership largely determines the extent to which tradition is harnessed to modernization if it is supportive or neutralized if it is obstructive. It also determines the degree to which the disadvantages of timing are minimized and the opportunities are exploited. Individual political leaders and political elites have been the prime movers in political modernization. The rate and direction of that process, as well as the political structures and culture which emerge, reflect in large measure the values and goal orientations of the leadership;

its adaptive and creative capacities; and its reaction to the modernization crises it confronts.

Crises The experience of the most highly developed contemporary polities has led to the identification of several critical system-development problems or crises which every modernizing polity encounters at least once and must cope with or surmount if it is to continue to modernize.[45] Although formulations vary, the following six problems illuminate this way of conceptualizing the political modernization process: (1) *national identity*, the transfer of ultimate loyalty and commitment from primordial groups to the larger national political system; (2) *political legitimacy*, the legitimation of modernizing elites and the authority structure of the new state; (3) *penetration*, the centralization of power, the establishment of a "determinate human source of final authority" transcending preexisting subnational authority systems,[46] the bridging of discontinuities in political communication, and the effectuation of policies throughout the society by the central institutions of government; (4) *participation*, the development of symbolic or participatory institutions and a political infrastructure to organize and channel the characteristically modern mass demand for a share in the decision-making process; (5) *integration*, the organization of a coherent political process and pattern of interacting relationships for the making of public policy and the pursuit and achievement of societal goals; and (6) *distribution*, the effective use of government power to bring about economic growth, mobilize resources, and distribute goods, services, and values in response to mass demands and expectations.

The modernization of a political system is measured by the extent to which it has developed the capabilities (symbolic, regulative, responsive, extractive, and distributive) to cope with these generic system-development problems.[47] It is argued not only that these capabilities are logically related but also that they suggest an order of development, that is, the development of one type of capability requires the development of another (e.g., increasing the extractive capability implies an increase in the regulative capability). Indeed, this approach could be the first step in the direction of a theory of political modernization, if the structural and cultural characteristics of political systems can be related to the ways in which these systems have confronted and coped with the crises common to all of them.[48]

Systematic comparative historical studies of political modernization in Western polities are increasingly feasible as a consequence of the development of data archives and the use of electronic computers in processing historical information.[49] One promising initial focus would be upon the growth in political participation: in most countries of the West the requisite political statistics are available as far back as the French Revolution. This rediscovery of the legitimacy and theoretical potentiality of the historical dimension in political research and diachronic analysis has been one of the unintended consequences of the postwar concern with the modernization of the developing countries. Continued systematic study of the evolution of the latter, together with the retrospective analysis of the political modernization of older polities, should significantly enhance our capacity not only to generalize about the past but also to suggest probabilities regarding the future.

NOTES

1. Cyril E. Black, "Political Modernization in Russia and China," in Kurt London, ed., *Unity and Contradiction: Major Aspects of Sino-Soviet Relations* (New York: Praeger, 1962), pp. 3–18.

2. Gabriel A. Almond and G. Bingham Powell, Jr., *Comparative Politics: A Developmental Approach* (Boston: Little, Brown, 1966).

3. E.g., Gabriel A. Almond and James S. Coleman, eds., *The Politics of the Developing Areas* (Princeton: Princeton University Press, 1960).

4. Ibid; Black, "Political Modernization in Russia and China"; Shmuel N. Eisenstadt, "Political Modernization: Some Comparative Notes," *International Journal of Comparative Sociology*, 5 (1964), pp. 3–24; William Kornhauser, "Rebellion and Political Development," in Harry Eckstein, ed., *Internal War: Problems and Approaches* (New York: Free Press, 1964), pp. 142–156; Conference on Communication and Political Development, Dobbs Ferry, N.Y., 1961, published as *Communications and Political Development*, ed. Lucian W. Pye (Princeton: Princeton University Press, 1963); Conference on Political Modernization in Japan and Turkey, Gould House, 1962, published as *Political Modernization in Japan and Turkey*, ed. Robert E. Ward and Dankwart A. Rustow (Princeton: Princeton University Press, 1964).

5. Robert T. Holt and John E. Turner, *The Political Basis of Economic Development: An Exploration in Comparative Political Analysis* (New York: Van Nostrand, 1966).

6. Ibid.; Gabriel A. Almond, "A Developmental Approach to Political Systems," *World Politics*, 17 (1965), pp. 183–214; Zbigniew Brzezinski, "The Politics of Underdevelopment," *World Politics*, 9 (1956), pp. 55–75.

7. Fred W. Riggs, "Bureaucrats and Political Development: A Paradoxical View," in Joseph G. LaPalombara, ed., *Bureaucracy and Political Development* (Princeton: Princeton University Press, 1963), pp. 120–167.

8. Samuel P. Huntington, "Political Development and Political Decay," *World Politics*, 17 (1965), pp. 386–430.

9. Leonard Binder, *Iran: Political Development in a Changing Society* (Berkeley and Los Angeles: University of California Press, 1962).

10. Daniel Lerner, *The Passing of Traditional Society: Modernizing the Middle East* (Glencoe, Ill.: Free Press, 1958; paper ed., 1964).

11. Lloyd A. Fallers, "Equality, Modernity, and Democracy in the New States," in Clifford Geertz, ed., *Old Societies and New States: The Quest for Modernity in Asia and Africa* (New York: Free Press, 1963), pp. 158–219.

12. Gabriel A. Almond and Sidney Verba, *The Civic Culture: Political Attitudes and Democracy in Five Nations* (Boston: Little, Brown, 1965).

13. Leonard W. Doob, *Becoming More Civilized: A Psychological Exploration* (New Haven: Yale University Press, 1960); Lerner, *The Passing of Traditional Society*; Conference on Communication and Political Development (1961).

14. Karl W. Deutsch, "Social Mobilization and Political Development," *American Political Science Review*, 55 (1961), pp. 493–514.

15. James S. Coleman, "The Political Systems of the Development Areas," in Almond and Coleman, *The Politics of the Developing Areas*, pp. 532–576; Phillips Cutright, "National Political Development: Measurement and Analysis," *American Sociological Review*, 28 (1963), pp. 253–264; Seymour M. Lipset, *The First New Nation: The United States in Historical and Comparative Perspective* (New York: Basic Books, 1960).

16. Almond and Coleman, *The Politics of the Developing Areas*; Francis X. Sutton, "Representation and the Nature of Political Systems," *Comparative Studies in Society and History*, 2:1 (October 1959), pp. 1–10.

17. Fred W. Riggs, "Agraria and Industria: Toward a Typology of Comparative Administration," in William J. Siffin, ed., *Toward the Comparative Study of Public Administration* (Bloomington: Indiana University Press, 1959), pp. 23–116.

18. Wilbert E. Moore, *Social Change* (Englewood Cliffs, N.J.: Prentice-Hall, 1963).

19. Shmuel N. Eisenstadt, "Breakdowns of Modernization," *Economic Development and Cultural Change*, 12 (1964), pp. 345–367.

20. Fred W. Riggs, *Administration in Developing Countries: The Theory of Prismatic Society* (Boston: Houghton Mifflin, 1964).

21. Huntington, "Political Development and Political Decay."

22. Marshall D. Sahlins and Elman R. Service, eds., *Evolution and Culture* (Ann Arbor: University of Michigan Press, 1960).

23. Talcott Parsons, "Evolutionary Universals in Society," *American Sociological Review*, 29 (1964), pp. 339–357.

24. See "Cultural Evolution," *International Encyclopedia of the Social Sciences* (New York: Macmillan, 1968), 5:221–228.

25. Parsons, "Evolutionary Universals in Society."

26. See "Political Organization," *International Encyclopedia of the Social Sciences*, 12:193–202.

27. See "Equality," ibid., 5:102–111.

28. See "Democracy," ibid., 4:112–121.

29. Black, "Political Modernization in Russia and China."

30. See "Nation," *International Encyclopedia of the Social Sciences*, 11:7–14.

31. Arthur Banks and Robert Textor, *A Cross-Polity Survey* (Cambridge, Mass.: MIT Press, 1963); Coleman, "The Political Systems of the Development Areas"; Cutright, "National Political Development"; Seymour M. Lipset, *Political Man: the Social Bases of Politics* (Garden City, N.Y.: Doubleday, 1960).

32. John D. Montgomery and William Siffin, eds., *Politics, Administration and Change: Approaches to Development* (New York: McGraw-Hill, 1965), especially the articles by Glenn D. Paige, "The Rediscovery of Politics," pp. 49–58, and Alfred Diamant, "Political Development: Approaches to Theory and Strategy," pp. 15–47; Herbert Spiro, ed., *Africa: The Primacy of Politics* (New York: Random House, 1966).

33. Cyril E. Black, *The Dynamics of Modernization* (New York: Harper & Row, 1966).

34. Black, "Political Modernization in Russia and China"; Tand Tsou, *America's Failure in China, 1941–1950* (Chicago: University of Chicago Press, 1963); Conference on Political Modernization in Japan and Turkey (1962); Eisenstadt, "Breakdowns of Modernization."

35. Paige, "The Rediscovery of Politics."

36. Samuel P. Huntington, "Political Modernization: America vs. Europe," *World Politics*, 18 (1966), pp. 378–414.

37. Albert O. Hirschman, "Comments on 'A Framework for Analyzing Economic and Political Change,'" in The Brookings Institution, *Development of the Emerging Countries: An Agenda for Research* (Washington, D.C.: Brookings Institution, 1962), pp. 39–44.

38. Black, *The Dynamics of Modernization*.

39. Eisenstadt, "Breakdowns of Modernization."

40. Huntington, "Political Modernization: America vs. Europe."

41. David E. Apter, *The Politics of Modernization* (Chicago: University of Chicago Press, 1965); Edward Shils, *Political Development in the New States* (The Hague: Mouton, 1962).

42. Black, "Political Modernization in Russia and China."

43. Conference on Political Modernization in Japan and Turkey (1962).

44. Sahlins and Service, *Evolution and Culture*.

45. Almond and Powell, *Comparative Politics: A Developmental Approach*; Black, *The Dynamics of Modernization*; Conference on Political Modernization in Japan and Turkey (1962); Lucian W. Pye, *Aspects of Political Development: An Analytic Study* (Boston: Little, Brown, 1966).

46. Huntington, "Political Modernization: America vs. Europe."

47. Almond, "A Developmental Approach to Political Systems"; J. Roland Pennock, "Political Development, Political Systems, and Political Goods," *World Politics*, 18 (1966), pp. 415–434.

48. Almond and Powell, *Comparative Politics: A Developmental Approach*.

49. Stein Rokkan, "Electoral Mobilization, Party Competition and National Integration," in Joseph G. LaPalombara and Myron Weiner, eds., *Political Parties and Political Development* (Princeton: Princeton University Press, 1966), pp. 241–265.

9 The Concept of Political Penetration

Political penetration is a broad organizing rubric subsuming processes associated with the formation of new postcolonial states.[1] It is a heuristic concept aggregating that ensemble of processes by which the political-administrative-juridical center of a new state (1) establishes an effective and authoritative central presence throughout its geographical and sectoral peripheries, and (2) acquires a capacity for the extraction and mobilization of resources to implement its policies and pursue its goals, however these may be determined. In both historical and comparative perspective these processes are an integral part of the more all-embracing concept of "state-formation."[2] The latter, however, includes all of those processes by which both external sovereignty (i.e., independence vis-à-vis the new state's international environment) is maximized and internal sovereignty (i.e., supremacy vis-à-vis its internal environment) is established. Although the two dimensions are empirically inseparable, due to the interpenetration of external and internal forces and influences, the emphasis in this volume is upon the creation of internal sovereignty in new states, with reference where appropriate to how the prevailing international system may condition or inhibit that process.

The Nature of the Concept

As an aggregative concept, political penetration serves as "an umbrella for a number of subconcepts which do share something in common."[3] The main subconcepts are: (1) center-formation, consolidation, and coordina-

Reprinted from L. Cliffe, J. S. Coleman and M. R. Doornbos, eds., *Government and Rural Development in East Africa* (The Hague: Martinus Nijhoff, 1977), pp. 3–18.

tion;[4] (2) structural integration of the center and its peripheries; (3) coordination of outreach structures of the center at the peripheries, and their articulation and integration with local structures at the peripheries; and (4) legitimation of the structural arrangements in (1) and (3).

Two subconcepts—one ("extraction") is implicit and the other ("legitimation") is explicit—in the foregoing formulation are in different but interrelated ways a measure of effectiveness of penetration. The object of penetration is not only to extract the requisite resources to maintain the center's presence but also to pursue other national (particularly developmental) goals. The structural arrangements for such extraction are as integral a part of the overall pattern of penetrative structure as are those concerned with regulation.[5] However, the effectiveness of the structures of regulation and extraction is significantly determined by the extent to which they have become legitimated, that is, institutionalized. Although conceptually separable, both extraction and legitimation are manifestly critical dimensions of the concept of political penetration.

The twin processes of extension of central power and the institutionalization of central structures are directed toward the progressive establishment of the central presence throughout the peripheries; yet more is demanded and required of the centers of new states of this epoch. Initially at least, and possibly for the predictable future, they are, by default or by assertion, the locus of initiative, planning, resource extraction, mobilization, and allocation for the protonational societies of which they are the political and administrative centers. As a United Nations report summarized:

> The central government of a developing country must initiate and, at least in the early stages, carry out most of the things that must be done to accelerate social and economic development. . . . the distinguishing feature of developing countries—and indeed a measure of their underdevelopment—is the degree of reliance upon the central government and more particularly upon decisions in the national capital for public services carried out locally. In countries in the earliest stages of development, the conduct of all but the most traditional affairs may be centred in the nation's capital.[6]

Political penetration is not only conceptualized as a process; it is also concerned specifically with structure. It is here that the conceptual distinction between *state*-building and *nation*-building is analytically useful, indeed essential. As Nettl argues, "If the entry of the third world onto the stage of modern socioscientific consciousness has had one immediate result (or should have had), it is the snapping of the link between state and nation. What were awkward exceptions before (Switzerland, the Soviet Union, empires generally, and so on) have now become almost a rule of nonnation-states."[7] Once this conceptual distinction is made between the essentially structural (i.e., organizational) character of *state*-building, and the essentially cultural (i.e., inculcation of values, attitudes, orientations, beliefs, and feelings) nature of *nation*-building,[8] the interdependence of these two processes, or at least their overlap, must be recognized. Indeed, one dimension of the history of the modern epoch is that of self-conscious nations (i.e., groups of people whose members feel themselves to constitute a single and distinctive terminal community) seeking to establish their own states (i.e., a sovereign single-center ensemble of authoritative structures embracing their "national" territory) under the principle of national self-determination (i.e., the ethical imperative that every nation should have its own state) or by the wielders of power in nonnational states seeking to weld together into one nation, coterminous with the boundaries of that state, the diverse nationalities over which they exercise power, whether inherited or asserted. Ex-colonial new states of this epoch, like those emerging from empires in other periods in the modern era, are engaged in the second of these two major historical processes.

The conceptual distinction between state-building and nation-building is blurred somewhat by the concept of legitimacy. The structural arrangements which coercively bind a group of people together in one state, in a world of sovereign states, and through which decisions are made from an ultimate single territorial center affecting all of the peripheries, cannot and will not become stabilized, nor endure, unless for the majority of the people—or at least for the majority of the politically conscious strata and groups—those structures are felt and believed to be necessary and right. It is in this sense that the historical concept of nation, and the more recent social scientific concept of "political community"—the objects respectively of nation-building and state-building—become both logically and empirically linked. However, Callaghy is undoubtedly correct in his assertion that "despite assertions of much of the academic literature and of African leaders themselves, state-formation, not nation-building, is the primary focus of political action and of ruling elites in Africa today."[9]

All concepts, conceptual schemes, and models have their weaknesses, but the concept of penetration seems to be particularly vulnerable and to have more than its fair share of impediments. These weaknesses and vulnerabilities must be squarely faced. First, like all such global aggregative concepts, it cannot be operationalized or used in theoretical models designed for the purpose of testing propositions; such concepts are weak in "explanatory power" and their indiscriminate use tends to degenerate into neo-scholasticism.[10] However, operational purists have noted that despite their theoretical limitations or uselessness such concepts can serve a useful pedagogical and heuristic function, evidence of which is their continued prominence in all of the social science disciplines.[11] Stein Rokkan, a scholar long concerned with the macro-micro gap, has suggested that through the development of time series data and composite indicators such summative concepts have considerable potential utility in the comparative analysis of the state- and nation-building processes. In any event, the use of a summative concept here is based not on any scientific pretentiousness but on its assumed heuristic and organizing utility in conceptualizing a broad historical process.

The second vulnerability of the concept "political penetration" is specific to it, namely, the way it has been used by one school of analysis has given it a manipulative, authoritarian, unidirectional, conservative, and elite-centric bias, or at least imagery, which has led to a positive valuation of anything an all-powerful center (and particularly the incumbent power elite) does to penetrate its peripheries. Richard Sandbrook has illuminated this particular vulnerability with great force, noting that some users of the penetration concept subtly shift from making the *empirical* point that governments seek to penetrate and control their peripheries to the imperative that the incumbent elites *should* do so.

> [T]he interest in order of those at the top is given logical precedence over the interest in social justice of those below. . . . If a central government is committed to rural development, its lack of an effective presence in the countryside will impede the implementation of progressive policies designed to ameliorate the lot of the people. But note the conditional nature of this reformulation. Penetration, the problem of central control, is not treated as a problem in its own right, but one which is dependent upon the actual commitments and performance of a regime. If political scientists are not to be simply technicians available to whoever is in power, they need to pose a prior question: penetration for what? Penetration, after all, historically has often meant greater oppression of the underprivileged strata.[12]

Kesselman asserts that the imperative of penetration as propounded by some analysts tends to be a fusion of the perspectives of powerholder and scholar: "My objection is not to describing how authorities attempt to maintain dominance, but rather to the implicit espousal of their cause."[13] The presumably analytically objective "center," it is suggested, easily becomes not only the "governing power elite," but the *incumbent* elite; the developmental imperative of effective penetration thereby becomes a justification for the preservation of the status quo.[14] Sandbrook's conditional reformulation of the way in which the penetration concept can be employed is a useful precaution.

A third vulnerability of the penetration concept arises from focusing singularly upon it as an organizing rubric; the consequence is that because one of the principal objectives of penetration is to establish political order, the latter value *ipso facto* acquires primacy. Several political developmentalists, of course, have explicitly stressed the priority and primacy of order in new states; for example:

> Given the extreme weakness of national political centres in Africa, the greatest priority from the point of view of political development may entail the reinforcement of the centres themselves. . . . The rapid extension of participation can indeed create more problems than it solves by jeopardizing the very existence of the centres.[15]
>
> . . . The primary problem is not liberty but the creation of a legitimate public order. Men may, of course, have order without liberty, but they cannot have liberty without order. Authority has to exist before it can be limited.[16]

To this genre of argument Kesselman has introduced a vigorous dissent:

> [P]olitical values do not exist in isolation from one another. The achievement of one value may facilitate or impede the achievement of others. . . . Even if one grants that order *logically* precedes liberty, this need not dictate that order *chronologically* should precede liberty. . . . Granted, political order is less secure in changing societies than in modern societies; yet so too are liberty, freedom, and other core values. A predominant concern for political order would be warranted only if it could be shown . . . that, compared to other values, it was *disproportionately* endangered.[17]

Suffice it here to disclaim that in focusing singularly upon penetration in new states no emphatic primacy or priority to the value of political order is intended.

A fourth weakness in the penetration concept, common to many concepts and models in the social sciences, is the neglect or exclusion of the international environment as a major variable in the formation and evolution of new states. In his comprehensive survey of recent literature on development as it relates to state formation Charles Tilly laments the general tendency to ignore international variables:

> The extreme concentration on the individual nation, political system, society, *or* state has drawn attention away from the international structures of power within which "development" takes place. . . . I have encountered impressively little discussion of the way the structure of the world markets, the operation of economic imperialism, and the characteristics of the international state system affect the patterns of political change within countries in different parts of the world.[18]

In focusing upon the processes of establishment and consolidation of internal sovereignty within new states as a working conception of "political penetration" there is an even greater danger of being intersystem-centric, of ignoring or being insensitive to international penetration as a variable. According to the theory of dependency and underdevelopment the state is "the instrument of a national oligarchy whose position depends on control of local land and capital—a control bolstered by the state's repressive apparatus, but exercised within stringent limits set by the outside powers to which the national economy is subordinate."[19] By the measure that such international penetration is empirically operative in a new state its intrastate penetrative processes will obviously be affected.

Despite the foregoing vulnerabilities of the concept of political penetration, there remains a need for an organizing concept to delimit a range of empirical processes associated with the formation and consolidation of the central authority of new states. If all of the dangers of bias and potential ideological use and usefulness are made explicit, penetration still remains a useful summative rubric, and usefulness is the only real test of a concept. Many of the most commonplace concepts in social science analysis, whether used by bourgeois developmentalists or the radical underdevelopmentalists, would have to be discarded if their vulnerability to valuative or ideological biases were the test of their utility.[20] Moreover, unless one is a doctrinaire philosophical anarchist, it hardly seems necessary yet once again to argue for the logical necessity and the empirical reality of a center in any form of organized human existence. The prime requisite of the existence of a political system is that there be a center where there is a "last word," whether it be that of an individual, a constitution, a legislature, or an institutionalized process for authoritative decision-making for the whole. The center is wherever this last word is situated. Without this there logically and empirically could be no political system.[21] And if there is a center there is a periphery, and between them there characteristically is some sort of structured relationship.

The Nature of the "Center" in New States

To be useful, the concept "center" must be disaggregated and placed within a working conceptual framework. For present purposes, stated rather starkly, the center in a new state is the locus of "state power," exercised through the "state apparatus" by a "state bureaucracy" ultimately controlled and directed by a "ruling group." Thus, political penetration is that process by which the most influential and powerful actors—the penetrators—in the ruling group and state bureaucracy use state power and the state apparatus both to maximize state sovereignty and to pursue the ideal and material interest both of themselves and ideally of the society over which they exercise control.

Jackson has argued that most postcolonial African societies are "one-class societies":

> This is the political-administrative class comprising all those persons who hold public and parastatal posts which confer upon occupants a measure of authority or discretion. Included among this stratum would be national politicians and party officials, police officials and military officers . . . civil servants and parastatal officials above clerical ranks, university professors . . . and generally all other persons who enjoy public employment involving some exercise of authority, actual or potential.[22]

Others have found it useful—as I have done above—to distinguish within this stratum at least two main categories: (1) the ruling group, or political class more narrowly defined (i.e., as John Saul puts it, "those who staff the state *at the most overtly political level*—including, most obviously, the President/Prime Minister, his cabinet and immediate circle of advisors, senior officials of the ruling part"),[23] and (2) the state bureaucracy viewed broadly, to include subcategories of (a) career bureaucrats, (b) managers of state enterprises, and (c) officers of the armed forces and police. These latter distinctions can be important both in terms of role function, differing institutional interest, ideological orientation, and political competition within the state apparatus.[24]

There is a lively debate on the extent to which, following Jackson, the ensemble of all of these various categories constitutes a class. The consensus appears to be that it is only a class in formation, a "protoclass," fragmented into competing factions, presenting to the analyst the task of trying, as Roger Murray put it, "to comprehend the contradictions inherent in the accession to *state power* of unformed classes."[25] This same quality of fractionalization by crosscutting tendencies characterizes all other social formations (peasantry, entrepreneurs, urban labor, etc.) which at this stage remain only classes in formation in terms of any disposition for meaningful political action or class conflict. Thus, in most new states, given the brevity of their existence, neither "centers" nor their "peripheries" are empirically composed of stable and coherent entities.

Once this inchoateness in the formation of self-consciousness among different categories of presumptive classes is noted, there can be little doubt that the center is perceived by its peripheries as dominated by a contrastively distinctive stratum, largely due to the colonial legacy. In observing the elements of continuity in fundamental perceptions between the "colonial conquest state" and its postcolonial successor, Callaghy observes:

> During the period of colonial rule, the administrative stratum was the one stratum recognized by all African groups as being a class apart. With independence, an African inheritance elite took over these positions and has used them to consolidate the emerging class interest. The political aristocracy is now the only group recognized by all Africans as a separate and dominant stratum. The members of this stratum also recognize this fact.[26]

The same point has been made even more pungently eloquent by Amilcar Cabral:

> Some independent African states preserved the structures of the colonial state. In some countries they only replaced a white man with a black man, but for the people it is the same. You have to realize that it is very difficult for the people to make a distinction between one . . . white . . . administrator and one black administrator. For the people it is the administrator that is fundamental. And the principle—if this administrator, a black one, is living in the same house, with the same gestures, with the same car, or sometime a better one, what is the difference? The problem of the nature of the state created after independence is perhaps the secret of the failure of African independence.[27]

Thus, although the center may be the arena for the struggle for status among various differentiable competing protoclasses and factions, it tends to be perceived by much of the rest of society as a single dominant stratum.

Structures and Patterns of Penetration

State power penetrates, or seeks to penetrate, a society through a variety of structures[28] which schematically would include the following:

1. Governmental structures, which are formal, presumptively authoritative, usually constitutionally prescribed, and territory-wide in purview, namely: executives, bureaucracies, armies, courts, police, parastatal agencies, public enterprises, and so on—the ensemble of which constitutes the state apparatus through which the center endeavors to establish and maintain its presence, exact compliance, extract resources, and evoke a supportive response. The ensemble also includes:
   a. structures of territorial (regional, provincial, district, village, etc.) administration, which are the outreaches of the state apparatus (including, of course, sectoral ministries) to the peripheries, some of which may historically have varying degrees of limited autonomy, depending upon the penetrative capacity, the centralizing will or the permissiveness of the center;
   b. presumptively participant structures, which can be either formal bodies (legislatures, councils, etc.) or associations, either officially created and sanctioned or tolerated by the state, and used, or not, as channels of participation (i.e., upward penetration) at best, or at least for communication or for their symbolic value;
   c. process structures for
      i. resource extraction (systems of taxation, levies, conscription, etc.),
      ii. economic control and direction (pricing and marketing mechanisms, subsidies, land registration, etc.),
      iii. patronage (patron-client systems), rewards, inducements,
      iv. manipulated elections,
      v. intimidation, punishment, coercion and repression.
2. Associational structures, which are groups formed, independently or by state direction, presumptively representing the interests of a definable group, aggregate, or protoclass (labor unions, farmer cooperatives, traders' associations, ethnic associations, etc.) or, in one-party systems, the entire society.
3. Structures of education, communication, and mass media.
4. Residual traditional structures of authority or symbolism.

The foregoing central structures of penetrations can be and are selectively perceived by those affected either as meaningful and legitimate channels of regulation and extraction, or as illegitimate sources of direction and coercion to be avoided or resisted. They may impinge only intermittently or indirectly, or not at all, as Zolberg has argued in his conception of "residual space"[29] (i.e., significant areas and activities within new states regarding which there effectively is no central penetration). The really effective structures of penetration, as perceived by and as affecting behavior at the periphery, may be partially or totally discontinuous with any center nexus, even in the most ostensibly monolithic and declaredly penetrative regimes, as Bienen has shown.[30] The range and depth of the potential penetrative power of the full panoply of structural linkages between a people and the state apparatus in a new state are overpowering; the functioning actuality in most instances is at most only an uneasy, fragile, and intermittent penetration of the strategic sectors, due mainly to the frailties of their inheritances and the special character of the dominating international environment into which they are born.

Among the several patterns of penetration which have characterized the process of state formation in postcolonial African new states, three are of particular interest, namely (1) *departicipation*; (2) *ethnic management*; and (3) *socialist transformation*. In his very insightful analysis of penetrative processes in new states, under the organizing rubric of "departicipation," Nelson Kasfir argues that "forcing people out of politics is a strategy available to the leadership in many countries for enhancing its capacity to rule and making its tenure secure."[31] Certainly the dominant political feature of the terminal colonial period in most former colonies was a vast expansion in popular participation and consciousness, and a belated effort by the departing colonial powers to erect central, regional, and local participatory structures of a presumptively democratic character. Since independence the general pattern throughout the continent has been characterized by systematic efforts to contain and to reduce participation as a means of enhancing the power of the center in general and of the existing regimes in particular:

> Departicipation is the most striking feature of postindependence political change in black Africa. . . . political structures which markedly increased participation were hastily installed in the last hectic years of colonial rule. Since independence they have been unceremoniously dismantled with the same alacrity.[32]

The main features of this continental—indeed, global—syndrome of new state formation have been covered extensively in the literature and following Kasfir's analysis need only be summarized briefly here.

1. Dismantling of federal structures (e.g., Uganda and Kenya) which

were part of the independence compromise and the diminution or extinction of powers of traditional authorities, middlemen,[33] local government bodies[34] (*corps intermédiaires*) as part of an inexorable process of progressive concentration, and monopolization of power at the center.

2. Progressive strengthening of executive power (e.g., Zolberg: "A steady drive to achieve greater centralization of authority in the hands of a very small number of men who occupy top offices in the party and government, and even more in the hands of a single man at the apex of both institutions"),[35] a process of "monocentralization" leading in most instances to what Apter has termed "presidential monarchs." The many dimensions of this process are also familiar, including progressive diminution of the powers of legislative bodies, the vast expansion in the powers of provincial and district commissioners accountable directly to presidents, and the assumption by the latter of discretionary powers of detention without trial and restrictions on movement, assembly, and the press.[36]

3. The harassment and ultimate banning of opposition parties and the steady move toward the consolidation of one-party systems;[37] the interpenetration and, in many instances, the fusion of structures of government and the party; and a terminal trend toward what Wallerstein aptly termed "inanition" and the "no-party state."[38]

4. The assertion of state control over all interest associations, particularly labor organizations and agricultural cooperatives, and their attempted conversion into "transmission belts."

5. The foregoing first-phase processes of political and administrative centralization, monocratization, and other dimensions of new state formation and consolidation reach their culmination in the establishment of military regimes, which, Kasfir notes, have become the "model form of government in black Africa."[39] Only those civilian regimes still controlled by remaining "founding fathers" (e.g., Kenyatta, Nyerere, Kaunda, Houphouet-Boigny) have been spared; but all odds are on the military becoming their successors.

The explanations advanced for this general postindependence syndrome of centralization, departicipation, monocracy and ultimate consolidation under authoritarian bureaucratic-military regimes in new states have been extensively analyzed elsewhere and certainly do not need, yet once again, repetition here.[40] The explanations include the destabilizing conditions (particularly the politicization of ethnicity) which new governments faced in the years immediately prior to and after independence, supportive or predisposing elements in traditional society, various aspects of the colonial legacy, the statist ethos and assumptions undergirding the political culture of the new governing groups, with special emphasis upon the priority of order—all being reinforced and facilitated by the intrusion of external influences and by the farily pervasive passivity and manipulability of the peasantry, the mass of the population. The end result everywhere is the preeminence of state bureaucracies, aptly summarized by one central Minister of Internal Affairs:

> Thus, one paradoxically comes back again to the administrative structures existing before June 30, 1960, that is, a central and strong authority basing itself on decentralized provincial administrations which realize through district commissioners and territorial administrators all the options of economic and social progress.[41]

The prominence, indeed in most instances the overriding determinative importance, of ethnicity as a force in African politics and in the processes of state formation—or in politics anywhere in the contemporary world—would hardly by now be disputed by any analyst.[42] There is, however, a vigorous division in interpretation between so-called "modernization" analysts and class analysts regarding the subjective or objective basis of the phenomenon. As Kasfir has summarized the division:

> Radical analysts tend to see ethnicity as a subjective, rather than an objective phenomenon. Since classes are based on objective economic relations, acting on the basis of ethnic loyalties can only be subjective. . . . ethnicity must be understood in terms of the elite (or bourgeoisie), not the masses . . . a tool used by the elite to consolidate its class position . . . [whereas] modernization analysts . . . argue . . . that ethnicity has to be understood as an objective phenomenon, characterizing the masses at the level of fundamental values.[43]

Despite this difference of view among analysts as to whether the ultimate basis of political action is class or ethnicity, the fact is that throughout Africa ethnic divisions have been and are the primary bases for the activation and escalation of the ethnic consciousness of people by elites competing for power at the center irrespective of their own sense of class identity. The nationalist movements which struggled for and won independence, and the nationalist elites which sought and achieved consolidation of their power after independence, were mainly based on *ethnic manipulation*. Ethnic identification was and remains at once the most secure base and ethnic manipulation (including "ethnic arithmetic") both the easiest and the most powerful penetrative tactic and strategy available to any politician or coalition of politicians struggling to reach, remain in, or dominate the center. And, as in Kenya, where ethnic hegemony has been achieved, it remains the ultimate weapon, as Leys has argued:

> The Kikuyu bourgeoisie were well aware that many of their special advantages depended on their political dominance within the state apparatus. So long as enough of the Kikuyu masses believed that this was also of prime importance to them, appeals to tribal solidarity would serve the double purpose of reinforcing the Kikuyu leadership's position at the centre, and repelling challenges based on class antagonism within Kikuyu society.[44]

Among all new states in independent Africa, Tanzania stands out in so many respects as exceptional in how it has endeavored both to institute new modes and structures of participation replacing those inherited at independence and to minimize and constrain ethnic manipulation as a penetrative instrument. It had certain inherited advantages at birth, as Cliffe has shown, but the critical variable has been a leadership which has been both rhetorically and genuinely deeply committed to values of participation and ethnic irrelevance.[45] But even more striking has been its uniqueness in seriously pursuing a path of socialist transformation, a model, as some would argue, of a socialist strategy of penetration for national development. However, even among its most sympathetic analysts, whether conventional or radical, there are serious reservations whether this virtually unique experiment will succeed, mainly, but not entirely, for reasons beyond its control.[46]

State-building—internally the penetration by the centers of state power to their peripheries—everywhere and throughout history has involved varying degrees and modes of coercion.[47] The more transformative and radical the structural changes being attempted the more overt and direct must be the coercion.[48] In historical perspective one of the most distinctive features of contemporary state-formation in Africa is that it is being attempted in an epoch in which coercion, although in variant forms omnipresent, is at least repugnant to dominant ethical ideals, and in a situation in which the coercive capacity of state power at the centers is relatively weak and tenuous in comparison with the functions they must perform and the goals they seek.[49] The second distinctive feature is that it is taking place or being attempted in an international environment and a situation of all-embracing dependence on that environment, which is unique in history. As Sandbrook observes, "Perhaps the main element which is unique in the contemporary situation of the underdeveloped countries as compared to Euro-America a century or so ago is the importance of the *transnational* influences upon political and economic development."[50]

These unique aspects of state-formation in our epoch clearly limit the value of historical analogies and make all the more interesting studies which reveal how penetration is being attempted and occurring, or not, in the new states with which this volume is concerned.

NOTES

1. The adjective "political" as the modifier of "penetration" is used in its most general sense, embracing all analytical aspects of "political organization" as defined by M. G. Smith: "Political organization consists in the combination and interplay of relations of authority and power in the regulation of public affairs. Briefly, the political organization is the set of arrangements by which a public regulates its common affairs. Such regulation always integrates two modes of public action, the *administrative*, which consists in the authoritative conduct of public affairs, and the *political*, which consists in the exercise and competitions of power to influence or control the course of these affairs." *International Encyclopedia of the Social Sciences* (New York: Macmillan, 1968), 12:194; italics added. Adopting this wider concept of "political" obviates the need for the more cumbersome phrase "political-administrative penetration."

2. The concept of "state" is here used interchangeably with that of "political system," it being understood that the latter refers to a unit which is member of the international states system. Charles Tilly has perceptively observed that political scientists, perhaps too precipitately, "lost interest in talking about the state as such twenty or thirty years ago," partly, as Almond argued, to "separate out analytically the structures which perform political functions in all societies regardless of scale, degree of differentiations, and culture," and partly "to extend the analytical scope of political analysis to include political culture, political socialization and similar phenomena relevant to government but outside the formal structure of government." This introduced a fluidity and problem of comparability in the political units of reference. See Charles Tilly, ed., *The Formation of National States in Western Europe* (Princeton: Princeton University Press, 1975), pp. 617–618. But, as Nettl has convincingly argued regarding the state, "the thing exists and no amount of conceptual restructuring can dissolve it." J. P. Nettl, "The State as a Conceptual Variable," *World Politics*, 20:4 (1968), p. 559.

3. Samuel P. Huntington, "The Change to Change: Modernization, Development, and Politics," *Comparative Politics*, 3:3 (April 1971), p. 303.

4. Stein Rokkan, "Centre Formation, Nation-Building and Cultural Diversity: Report on a Symposium Organized by UNESCO," *Social Science Information*, 8 (February 1969), p. 89.

5. Robert H. Jackson, "The Crises of Penetration and Extraction" (unpublished manuscript), p. 2.

6. United Nations, *Decentralization for National and Local Development* (New York: United Nations, 1962), pp. 5–6.

7. Nettl, "The State as a Conceptual Variable," p. 560.

8. Almond and Powell make this distinction: "We might view the problem of state building as essentially a structural problem. That is to say, what is involved is primarily a matter of the differentiation of new roles, structures, and subsystems which penetrate the countryside. Nation building, on the other hand, emphasizes the cultural aspects of political development. It refers to the process whereby people transfer their commitment and loyalty from smaller tribes, villages, or petty principalities to the larger central political system." Gabriel A. Almond and G. Bingham Powell, Jr., *Comparative Politics: A Developmental Approach* (Boston: Little, Brown, 1966), p. 36.

9. Thomas M. Callaghy, "Implementation of Socialist Strategies of Development in Africa: State Power, Conflict and Uncertainty" (unpublished manuscript), p. 28.

10. Social science concepts of the summative type, such as political penetration, state-formation, and nation-building, are only useful if, as Huntington suggests in "The Change to Change," p. 303, "they help to separate out two or more forms of something which would otherwise be thought of as undifferentiated." Cf. LaPalombara's trenchant self-criticism of the innovation in macroconceptual nomenclature: "[We are] armed to be sure with new terminology, but not any more successful than were the ancients in narrowing the gap between abstract formulations and theoretical realities. . . . Concept-refining very quickly degenerates into the scholastic game." Joseph LaPalombara, "Macrotheories and Microapplication in Comparative Politics: A Widening Chasm," *Comparative Politics*, 1:1 (1968–69), pp. 54–55.

11. "What, if anything, can be done with summative units when they are employed in theory building? . . . May we then employ such units in our theories with any profit of utility? My answer is no. Such units are useless in theories and theoretical models that are designed for the purpose of the testing propositions. Summative units have their function in a scientific discipline, but not in relation to theoretical models." Robert Dublin, *Theory Building* (New York: Free Press, 1970), pp. 62–63.

12. Richard Sandbrook, "The 'Crisis' in Political Development Theory," *The Journal of Development Studies*, 12:2 (January 1976), pp. 180–181. Sandbrook cites Donal Cruise O'Brien's insightful revelation of the authoritarian bias in much of the political analysis of developing countries during the 1960s: "There does emerge one major common prescriptive assumption, that the new institutional order should be the work of political elites, able and willing to impose new structures on the masses from above." Donal Cruise O'Brien "Modernization, Order, and the Erosion of a Democratic Ideal: American Political Science 1960–70," *The Journal of*

Development Studies, 8:4 (July 1972), p. 362. This same point has been made by several others, particularly Raymond F. Hopkins, "Securing Authority: The View from the Top," *World Politics*, 24:2 (January 1972), pp. 271–292, and Mark Kesselman, "Order or Movement? The Literature of Political Development as Ideology," *World Politics*, 26:1 (1973), pp. 139–154. The empirical reality of oppression historically being associated with penetration is illuminated in the study of Western state-making by Charles Tilly and his colleagues: "The European experience . . . does not show us modernizing elites articulating the demand and needs of the masses, and fighting off traditional holders of power in order to meet those needs and demands. Far from it. We discover a world in which small groups of power-hungry men fought off numerous rivals and great popular resistance in the pursuit of their own ends." Tilly, *The Formation of National States*, p. 635.

13. Kesselman, "Order or Movement," p. 144.

14. "Supposedly value-neutral models of political development possess ideological use to the extent that these reinforce or challenge . . . [the] *status quo*." Sandbrook, "The 'Crisis' in Political Development Theory," p. 181.

15. Aristide R. Zolberg, "Political Development in Tropical Africa: Center and Periphery" (unpublished manuscript). It should be stressed that Zolberg does not advocate "monolithic penetration"; on the contrary, he very emphatically rejects authoritarian measures as necessary "to maintain order and to bring about modernization in the political, the economic, and other spheres" not only because the costs would be extremely great and incompatible with African values, but also because it would probably be unsuccessful. See his *Creating Political Order* (Chicago: Rand McNally, 1966), pp. 158–161, where he recommends the political machine as possibly the most effective mode of penetration in new African states.

16. Samuel P. Huntington, *Political Order in Changing Societies* (New Haven: Yale University Press, 1968), pp. 7–8.

17. Kesselman, "Order or Movement," pp. 146–147.

18. Tilly, *The Formation of National States*, p. 620.

19. Ibid., p. 628. See also Sandbrook, "The 'Crisis' in Political Development Theory," p. 181.

20. "Nation-building," another summative concept, in Third World rhetoric is probably one of the most unchallengeable and highly valued concepts, but it was not so long ago that nationalism and nationhood (following the Nazi-Fascist extravagances) were regarded as pathologies by many who believed in world peace and the basic unity of mankind. From this perspective "nation-building," or indeed the concept of "nation-state," was viewed as retrograde. And its utility to handle emerging phenomena is not unquestioned. See Nathan Glazer and Daniel P. Moynihan,

eds., *Ethnicity: Theory and Experience* (Cambridge, Mass.: Harvard University Press, 1975).

21. The exceptions would be the so-called stateless political systems and the international political system. Our concern here is with (national) political systems of this epoch for which that statement holds true. See David Easton, *A Systems Analysis of Political Life* (New York: John Wiley & Sons, 1965), pp. 282–285; and Roger D. Masters, "World Politics as a Primitive Political System," *World Politics*, 16:4 (July 1964), pp. 595–619.

22. Quoted in Callaghy, "Implementation of Socialist Strategies," p. 22. (The reference is taken from Robert H. Jackson, "Political Stratification in Tropical Africa," *Canadian Journal of African Studies*, 7:3 (1973), pp. 381–400.) Callaghy adds that "the Road to status, power, and wealth in African states is clearly through entering this official realm, through acquiring political or administrative office. This class is created and defined by its direct and close relationship with the state. The state creates the class, and it in turn controls the state. Linkages between the ruling class and other groups in the stratification structure are primarily through the state via patron-client ties that are often ethnically based."

23. John S. Saul, "The Unsteady State: Uganda, Obote and General Amin," *Review of African Political Economy*, 5 (1976), p. 18.

Although Callaghy himself fuses the two at one point in the broad term political aristocracy, elsewhere he makes the crucial distinction: "State formation can be viewed as a three-way struggle between a ruling group, the official/administrative apparatus, and the various internal and external competing groups and organizations, each with their own ideal and material interests. . . . The dominant coalition of the state attempts to use its administrative staff to lessen or manage its dependence on groups in its environment. Paradoxically, however, the dominant coalition must also reduce its dependence on this administrative staff. This is the search for sovereignty and the three-way struggle of state formation." Callaghy, "Implementation of Socialist Strategies," p. 3.

24. Colin Leys, "The 'Overdeveloped' Post Colonial State: A Re-evaluation," *Review of African Political Economy*, 5 (1976), p. 44, argues that at least in the Tanzanian one-party case it is useful to distinguish a fourth component, namely, "the party-recruited element" brought into the state apparatus, which has "political links with workers and peasants" and which thereby "may be significant for understanding the origins and course of the struggles that do occur inside the state apparatus." Regarding ideological orientation he notes that the "officials entering the 'state enterprise' branch are especially exposed to the bourgeois values embodied in the technology, management practices, 'efficiency' ideology, etc. of the firms they take over."

25. Quoted by Saul in "The Unsteady State," p. 16. Saul stresses the ambiguity and incoherence in the process of the bureaucratic fraction of

what he calls the "petty bourgeoisie" crystallizing into a class. However, Callaghy is more certain: "This political aristocracy is also consolidating itself as a class. The political aristocracy is a class in reality, and it is becoming increasingly conscious of its existence as a class." Callaghy, "Implementation of Socialist Strategies," p. 22.

26. Callaghy, "Implementation of Socialist Strategies," p. 23.

27. Quoted in Editorial, *Review of African Political Economy*, 5 (1976), p. 1.

28. The concept "structure" is used here in its most aggregative and global sense, to include concrete membership structures (clusters and complexes of roles) such as parties, pressure groups, armies, courts, bureaucracies, etc; analytical process structures (i.e., the structure of patterned action), such as the "structure of law enforcement," the "structure of patronage," the "structure of rewards and punishments," the "structure of ideological diffusion," etc; and analytical holistic structure (patterning and interrelation of parts as dominated by the general character of the whole of reference) such as the "economic structure," the "structure of communications," etc.

29. Zolberg, *Creating Political Order*, pp. 133 ff.

30. Henry Bienen, "What Does Political Development Mean in Africa?" *World Politics*, 20:1 (1967), p. 132.

31. Nelson Kasfir, *The Shrinking Political Arena* (Berkeley and Los Angeles: University of California Press, 1976), p. 14. Kasfir argues, convincingly, that "because it is a continuous variable not necessarily related to a specified institutional complex, participation/departicipation is a more discriminating concept than the democracy/authoritarian dichotomy."

32. Ibid.

33. There seems to be little interest in the establishment of intermediate institutions, political, economic, or social. In this sense, postcolonialism has failed to transcend the "dual" political structure of colonial society. Indeed, it is arguable that the periods of decolonization and early independence have seen a consolidation of the "bureaucratic polity-implementing structures," and a steady atrophy of those structures which briefly promised some widening of popular representation and control." Martin Staniland, "The Rhetoric of Centre-Periphery Relations," *The Journal of Modern African Studies*, 84 (1970), pp. 617–636.

34. In *Politicians and Policies: An Essay on Politics in Acholi, Uganda 1962–65* (Nairobi: East African Publishing House, 1967), p. 9, Colin Leys stressed the strength of local government in Uganda in the immediate postindependence period: "Local government in Uganda was unusually strong, both constitutionally and psychologically . . . [and] is not likely to disappear completely at once." This was written just before the radical centralization measures of the Obote regime followed by the total extinction of local government by the Amin regime.

35. Zolberg, *Creating Political Order*, p. 135.

36. Kasfir, *The Shrinking Political Arena*, p. 232.

37. Ibid., p. 241. Kasfir notes, as of 1976, that "to the fourteen single-party states that had banned opposition parties by 1963 can be added the formerly multiparty states of Uganda, Kenya, Tanzania, Sudan and Zambia."

38. Immanuel Wallerstein, "The Decline of the Party in the Single-Party African States," in Joseph G. LaPalombara and Myron Weiner, eds., *Political Parties and Political Development* (Princeton: Princeton University Press, 1966), p. 208.

39. Kasfir, *The Shrinking Political Arena*, p. 324.

40. James S. Coleman and Carl G. Rosberg, Jr., *Political Parties and National Integration in Tropical Africa* (Berkeley: University of California Press, 1964), pp. 655–674; Zolberg, *Creating Political Order* (entire) and "The Structure of Political Conflict in the New States of Tropical Africa," *The American Political Science Review*, 62:1 (March 1968), pp. 70–87; and particularly Kasfir, *The Shrinking Political Arena*, pp. 227–290.

41. Quoted in Kasfir, *The Shrinking Political Arena*, p. 236.

42. Glazer and Moynihan have forcefully argued that in fact ethnic conflicts almost everywhere appear to have become the primary form in which interest conflicts between and within states are pursued for two related reasons: (1) "The strategic efficacy of ethnicity in making legitimate claims on the resources of the modern state," and (2) the "nature of inequality. . . . Men are not equal; neither are ethnic groups." *Ethnicity: Theory and Experience*, p. 11.

43. Kasfir, *The Shrinking Political Arena*, p. 68. Those emphasizing the subjective basis of ethnicity include Sklar: "Tribal movements may be created and instigated to action by the new men of power in furtherance of their own special interests which are, time and again, the constitutive interests of emerging social classes. Tribalism then becomes a mask for the class privilege"; and Mafeje: "If anything, . . . [tribalism] is a mark of *false consciousness*. . . . On the part of the new African elite, it is a ploy or distortion they use to conceal their exploitative role," quoted in ibid., pp. 67 and 68. John Saul, "The Unsteady State," p. 20, notes that there are manifestly cultural differences among African peoples, as well as uneven development between regions that do provide an objective basis for activation and escalation of ethnicity for elite self-serving goals: "It is relatively easy to induce the lower strata of any given ethnic group to interpret the essence of their backwardness as being the result of a zero-sum game over the distribution of scarce resources played out between tribes rather than being primarily a result of class division, world-wide and local."

44. Colin Leys, *Underdevelopment in Kenya: The Political Economy of Neo-Colonialism 1964–1971* (London: Heinemann, 1975), p. 205.

45. Lionel Cliffe, *One Party Democracy* (Nairobi: East African Publishing House, 1966); John S. Saul, "African Socialism in One Country: Tanzania," in Giovanni Arrighi and John S. Saul, eds., *Essays on the Political Economy of Africa* (New York: Monthly Review Press, 1973), pp. 237–335; and, most recently and succinctly, Kasfir, *The Shrinking Political Arena*, pp. 251–262.

46. One of the most penetrating critiques of the Tanzanian experiment of socialist transformation as a penetrative strategy is Michael F. Lofchie, "Agrarian Socialism in the Third World: The Tanzanian Case," *Comparative Politics*, 8:3 (April 1976), pp. 479–499.

47. Tilly, *The Formation of National States*, p. 636.

48. There tends to be a curious avoidance of the coercive implications or requisites for radical socialist transformation in African states. Callaghy, "Implementation of Socialist Strategies," p. 6, notes, for example, that Arrighi and Saul argue for the creation of "a state power dedicated to the task" but "proceed to discuss state power as if coercive capacity was not a crucial or even important element of that power." Similarly, great emphasis has been made by many analysts regarding Nyerere's refusal to use force (e.g., Lofchie, "Agrarian Socialism in the Third World," p. 488), but Leys, "The 'Overdeveloped' Post Colonial State," p. 47, notes a fine distinction between an "ujamaa," a "socialist," and a "development" village: "[Nyerere's] 1968 statement was that no one could be forced into an ujamaa village—it could not be a *socialist* village if force was used. The villages into which people have since been forced are actually termed "development villages." While the President was obviously very reluctant to use force, for any purpose, he seems to have concluded that it was justified in order to improve the ability of the government to direct an increase in agricultural production."

49. Referring to Tanzania, but of equal applicability to other new states, Nellis notes that contemporary regimes possess "no reliable coercive means of significance, no financial means of substance, and no ruthlessly efficient administrative-organizational mechanisms." John R. Nellis, *A Theory of Ideology: The Tanzanian Example* (Nairobi, New York: Oxford University Press, 1972), p. 193. In analyzing the Ugandan case, Saul, "The Unsteady State," p. 21, notes that the frailties in the system are such as not to provide sufficient state power "even to guarantee that minimum degree of stability necessary for the consolidation of a smoothly functioning neo-colonial system."

50. Sandbrook, "The 'Crisis' in Political Development Theory," p. 177, correctly argues that such transnational dimensions "must be systematically incorporated into models of development if these are to advance understanding of the contemporary situation in the Third World."

10 American Political Science and Tropical Africa

Universalism vs. Relativism[1]

James S. Coleman and C. R. D. Halisi

Probably no two of the scholarly works punctuating the past quarter century better exemplify the intellectual voyage that Africanist political scientists have taken than do Thomas Hodgkin's pioneering classic, *Nationalism in Colonial Africa* (1956), and Crawford Young's recent admirable comparative study of political economy in *Ideology and Development in Africa* (1982).[2] These two broadly comparative works reflect the major shift from the study of the processes of African self-assertion and decolonization—the quest for and acquisition of state power—which characterized the concerns of the first decade of that period, to the study of how that power is maintained and in whose interest and with what effectiveness it is exercised, foci which have increasingly become the preoccupations of the last decade.

The intention here is to examine some of the features of this intellectual trek—from first generation conventional studies of nationalism, elections, and constitutions to the current preoccupation with the state, class, and political economy—not by a travelogue of the journey, but by focusing upon an enduring issue, namely, the antinomy of universalism versus relativism.[3] The antinomy exists at two levels. The first is that of the individual scholarly endeavor and product; namely, does the product reflect (a) a generalizing and scientific mode of inquiry in which the scholar's intent and perspective is to identify uniformities and regularities—as well as differences—through systematic comparison? In short, is it *nomothetic*? Or is it (b), a mode that is *idiographic*, that is, that aims to describe and to

Reprinted from *African Studies Review* 26:3-4 (September-December 1983), pp. 25–62.

understand a phenomenon in all its configurative, situational, and cultural-historical particularity and uniqueness? The antinomy at the second and obviously related level concerns the conceptualization of the discipline by a particular set of practitioners as either (a) a social scientific endeavor aimed at generalization and universality,[4] or (b) an intellectual vocation which is essentially descriptive and interpretive of political phenomena that are inherently historically and culturally relative to a particular human group or situation.[5]

At the beginning of our quarter-century epoch one found the challenging juxtaposition of, on the one hand, an Africa which had theretofore tended to be perceived stereotypically as a continent of peoples and cultures with historical experience and a future which were largely unique to it and would remain so, and, on the other hand, an evangelical, American-dominant discipline of political science—equipped with presumptively universal categories, typologies, frameworks, and accumulated propositions for testing in new cultural settings—launched upon a global quest for generalizations confirming the unity of mankind and the universal convergence toward a common destiny. With characteristic felicity, Thomas Hodgkin sought at the beginning to find a middle way by thoughtful deference to the element of enduring validity in both poles of the relativism-universalism antinomy:

> There is some advantage in ceasing to regard Africa, as it has sometimes been regarded in the past, as a kind of "thing-in-itself," the private preserve of *Africanistes.* This implies an approach which recognizes African nationalism, in its many manifestations, as an historical movement, necessarily and characteristically African, yet revealing definite points of resemblance to the nationalisms that have emerged in other parts of the world.[6]

In the following pages we will address this antinomy by focusing first upon the shifting trends and fashions in the Africanness branch of the discipline as practiced in the United States during the quarter century under review, and then upon the process of the globalization of a presumptively universal American political science during the first phase of the period, selectively summarizing its main defining characteristics. We will next turn to the de-Americanization of and subsequent changes in the discipline, and finally, we will briefly review, in terms of the universalism-relativism polarity, some of the reactions by, and new orientations among, the emergent African political science community.

Table 9. Dominant Themes of Emphasis by American Political Scientists on Tropical Africa in Selected Professional Journals, 1953–1982

	Journal				*Decade*				*Total*	
	APSR	*WP*	*CP, CPS*	*JMAS*	*1950s*	*1960s*	*1970s*	*1980–1982*	*Number*	*Percentage*
Nationalism, parties, elections, participation	6	3	7	6	3	8	8	3	22	11.4
Traditional institutions	—	1	1	6	—	3	5	—	8	4.0
Formal institutions	—	2	4	6	—	4	5	3	12	6.2
Single parties	2	1	0	3	—	5	1	—	6	3.0
Military intervention	1	6	8	9	—	4	12	8	24	12.4
Ethnicity	2	6	6	3	—	3	11	3	17	8.8
National integration	—	—	—	9	—	3	4	2	9	4.6
Class	—	—	—	7	—	2	5	—	7	3.6
Dependency/political economy	—	3	2	6	—	—	8	3	11	5.6
Political culture and socialization	—	1	1	1	—	1	2	—	3	1.5
Political development/modernization	—	3	1	3	—	5	2	—	7	3.6
Regime consolidation, maintenance, and performance	1	0	2	8	—	—	5	6	11	5.6
Local, rural, micro, and agricultural studies	—	4	1	8	—	—	11	2	13	6.7
Intra-African relations	—	—	—	10	—	—	11	2	10	5.1
Extra-African relations	1	4	1	8	1	3	10	—	14	7.2
Political thought, theory, and ideology	2	1	2	6	1	5	4	1	11	5.6
Methodology/bibliography	2	4	2	—	3	1	2	2	8	4.1
Total	17	39	38	98	8	51	99	35	193	100.0

Note: Calculated from *American Political Science Review* (APSR), 1954–1982; *World Politics* (WP), 1953–1982; *Comparative Politics* (CP) and *Comparative Political Studies* (CPS), 1969–1982; and *Journal of Modern African Studies* (JMAS), 1963–1982. Limited to putatively American political scientists.

Trends and Fashions

In the intervening years of the fundamental pendulum swing in perspective from nationalism to political economy, there have been intermediate shifts in the dominant preoccupations of academic political analysis of the African scene. These shifts have been stimulated by and have reflected both significant changes in Africa itself and changes in modes and fashions of academic analysis.[7] The concrete changes in the African political scene itself have been remarkable for their approximate simultaneity and similarity in sequence of occurrence, as well as the generality of their patterning, all of which facilitates both rough periodization and maximal comparison. The sequence of the successive changes since the mid-1950s is well known and reflected in the dominant themes and varying emphases in the literature over the years as shown in the data in table 9. During the 1950s, nationalism, parties and elections, and ideology figure prominently; during the early 1960s, political modernization had an evanescent appeal, but in the later part of the decade issues of military intervention, ethnicity, and intra-African relations increasingly commanded the spotlight; in the 1970s, political modernization lost its vogue, intractable military rule and ethnicity continued their insatiable claims to attention, and issues of class, dependency, and "political economy," the emerging omnibus code words of the new epoch, asserted their primacy, along with the marked shift to grass roots, micro, and rural development concerns, and the insistent intrusiveness of extra-African international interventions. As the 1980s opened, one found the durable factor of military rule, as well as issues of regime maintenance, performance, and transformation, highest on the agenda. The attention and focus of the scholarly analyses of Africanist *politicologues* have indeed pursued and reflected evolving real-world trends and concerns.

The successive shifts have also reflected changes in modes and fashions of academic analysis and of the paradigms they serve. They have been affected by broad and pervasive shifts in mood resulting from the progressive waning of the Enlightenment idea of progress[8] and the pendulum swing in perceptions about "development" from the unbounded optimism of the fifties to the deep pessimism of the seventies; by fads and fashions,[9] such as the loss and rediscovery of the "state" and "political economy"; by variables and conceptualizations fashionable elsewhere (e.g., dependency, clientelism, machine politics, or corporatism) which American scholars have imported and applied in a testing manner to the African situation; and by the sheer contagion of trendiness.

Ceaseless foraging for and the career-enhancing "discovery" of an underemphasized or neglected variable in the modes of analysis of intellectual rivals characterize the profession.[10] The oscillation among variables as a consequence of this dialectical competition is one to which political science is particularly vulnerable largely because of its macropolitical disposition to apply a holistic perspective to large-scale political systems of nation-states. Continuously overwhelmed by an unmanageably large number of variables, its practitioners find that the discovery of controlled relations among them becomes virtually impossible without radical simplification and rigorous parsimony, such as a focus on segments only or a selected number of key variables.[11] The manageability dilemma political scientists face and the forced reductionism by which they seek to resolve it vastly increase their vulnerability to charges of underplaying or omitting variables which other analysts can reasonably argue are important. This results in what Fesler calls "the natural history of revolts against conventional wisdom," that is, the tendency "to make the newly discovered element [which was there all the time] the independent variable to which the earlier perceived part of reality becomes a merely dependent variable."[12] The pressure for continuous shifts in paradigms, modes of analysis, and foci of concentration in political science thus has its own dynamic, producing gyrations which make Kuhnsian paradigmatic change appear glacial by comparison.[13]

Changing modes of analysis have also been inherent in the interaction among different national intellectual traditions (e.g., American universalism, British empiricism, and French Cartesianism) as well as in the dialectic between contrasting conceptions of science and epistemology. The very characterization of science as the quest for universal knowledge which transcends all cultural, regional, racial, or ideological relativity is perceived by some as but one conception of scientific activity.[14] Academics also engage in generational conflict;[15] successive academic generations "contest intellectual terrains." Members of an upcoming generation confront received paradigms which channel and constrain their own distinctive contribution to knowledge. Fortified by an academic ethos enjoining unremitting critique of prevailing paradigms, and goaded by an insecure status which nurtures hypercriticism, there is an automatic incentive to roll over paradigms.[16] Central figures in the profession (e.g., Claude Ake, Colin Leys, Immanuel Wallerstein) can also undergo dramatic metamorphoses in interests and ideological perspectives, catalyze and acquire a following, and precipitate new orientations in scholarly activity.

Other more mundane factors have been political constraints and the accompanying self-censorship imposed upon scholarship by insecure authoritarian regimes, or the insistence that all research must be applied, practical, and relevant. John Lonsdale cites Wrigley's proposition that academic vogues can be periodized by their correlation with changes in Africa's terms of trade.[17] Even the vagaries of external funding and the priorities and preferences of its sources can exert an exogenous directional influence, encouraging some frameworks and approaches and discouraging others.[18] In any event, whatever the complex admixtures of these motivating factors, they have in varying ways affected the fluctuating concerns and frameworks of Africanist political scientists during the past three decades.

The Globalization of American Political Science

In the mid-1940s, Carl Friedrich observed that political science "is in many ways a peculiarly American discipline," adding that it played only a minor role in some European universities and none in the rest of the world.[19] In 1950 there were over 5,000 members of the American Political Science Association (formed in 1903); by contrast, in the same year there were, for example, only 50 political scientists in Great Britain, 37 in Belgium, 30 in Canada, 10 in the Netherlands, and 2 in Switzerland.[20] By 1970 it was estimated that at least three-quarters of all political scientists were in the United States.[21] This early dominance was demonstrable by all statistical indicators of professional institutionalization, namely, the scholarly production of books, journal articles, and doctoral dissertations; the number of courses taught and student enrollments; and the attendance at professional meetings, and other measures of density of interaction of practitioners. There are, of course, many peculiarly American reasons for this staggering asymmetry, most notably the vast early expansion of higher education, the fact that a large proportion of each age group enters universities, the predominance of the four-year general course for the undergraduate degree, the inclusion of political science (in the American civics tradition) within the framework of general liberal education, and the fact that upon this broad base at the undergraduate level intensely competitive and self-perpetuative doctoral programs have been built at all of America's major universities.[22] Whatever the explanation for its early and sustained quantitative growth, the fact that the worldwide academic center of gravity of the discipline was located in the United States from the beginning of the postwar period until the 1970s is incontestable.[23]

One consequence of this vigorous early quantitative development of American political science was that internationally, political science tended, like sociology, to become synonymous with "American political science."[24] Until at least the late 1960s, the globalization of political science as a separate field of study meant, in general, the Americanization of the discipline in many parts of the world.[25] Some zealous borrowers came to "out-Americanize the Americans." Indeed, as late as 1982 John Trent noted that it is "the American scientific-behavioralist approach which hold sway in the International Political Science Association."[26]

Two contrasting explanations have been offered for this uncritical diffusion. One is the argument that comparatively greater institutionalization and larger-scale output establishes "academic centrality," thereby encouraging emulation of the most fashionable model.[27] The other explains it as the result of the emergence of the United States as a world power projecting inevitably an economic, political, and cultural imperialism.[28] Mafeje argues similarly that American political science "invaded Western Europe and penetrated even communist countries. . . . To the proponents of the system, this was further evidence of the validity and superiority of the American way of life."[29] It is unclear what epistemological criteria can be used to assess the truth content of this and like propositions.

Two caveats are required at this point. One is that there has been no single national model of political science available for export. True, at the most general level of characterization, distinctions have been commonly made between American political science as a presumably undifferentiated whole, and say, the British emphasis upon history and political philosophy or the French stress upon law and institutions; but since World War II the heterogeneous American mix of feuding institutionalism, pluralism, behavioralism, structural-functionalism, rational choice, and so forth, has amply demonstrated that there has been a monolithic American political science; there have been and are a myriad of different competing orientations.[30] The second caveat is that the academic tradition in which advanced study is done does not necessarily determine the subsequent theoretical and methodological preference of a student. This is underscored by the frequency of divergence between the theories and analytical frameworks to which a student is exposed and his or her subsequent theoretical orientation or persuasion.

The traditions of political science which were diffused to the ex-colonial countries of the Third World followed the imperial connections. At least for the first postcolonial generation in Francophone countries it has clearly been the French legal and institutional tradition.[31] In Zaire, the Belgian, French, and American models of exposure all commingle. The absence of any tradition of political science in Portugal and the ideological exclusion of political science as a separate discipline in the prevailing Marxist tradition in Lusophone Africa account for its absence there. It is in Anglophone

West, East, and Central Africa that the impact of American political science has been most pronounced, alongside the initially dominant British tradition. The common English language has obviously been a major factor in accentuating this relationship.

The three main mechanisms which have exposed African political scientists to American political science, in all its heterogeneity and heterodoxy, include American teaching staff who have served in African universities, particularly in their early developmental phase; advanced training in political science which Africans have pursued in American universities; and books and articles and other professional literature in the English language. The American impact via these various channels has been highly varied. Expatriate professors had a major presence in the early stages, but in Anglophone Africa African scholars who returned from abroad with their Ph.D.s rapidly replaced them. The expatriate professoriate was financed from various local and external sources. Its nationality makeup in Anglophone Africa, unlike Francophone Africa, was very mixed: no particular nationality dominated. All appointments were made by the universities themselves. The mélange of nationalities, and within nationalities the mix of differing ideological and disciplinary orientations, inevitably assured heterodoxy; exposure to or imposition of a single national model of political science could not and did not occur.

The second and by far the most significant channel of exposure to American political science was through advanced (usually doctoral) studies at American universities. During the three-decade period 1950–1980, an estimated 143 Africans received doctorates in political science from American universities for dissertations written on an African topic. As table 10 shows, Africans acquired 34 percent of the total number of area-related doctorates awarded during the period. They pursued their studies at fifty universities and were undoubtedly exposed to the proponents and opponents of the major competing paradigms and approaches (Marxism excepted). The themes of their dissertation topics, given in the same table, show a wide diversity of interests. Comparative French and United Kingdom data in table 11 reveal equal diversity as well as significant cross-cultural commonality in subject matter.

American political science has quantitatively dominated the literature in the discipline, particularly textbooks and journals. Such studies as have been made confirm this fact. In a recent twenty-five year international survey of major changes in the discipline, Karl Deutsch cited some 445 key authors representing twenty-four nationalities.[32] American authors constituted 66 percent of the total and 91 percent of the English-language

Table 10. U.S. Political Science Doctoral Dissertations on Tropical African Topics by Subject Category, 1950–1980

	No. of disserta-tions	*Percentage for each subject*	*No. by non-Africans*	*No. by Africans*	*Percentage by Africans*
International relations/ foreign policy	118	28.4%	79	39	33.1%
Political participation	82	19.8	60	22	26.8
Central institutions	46	11.1	31	15	32.6
Local institutions	43	10.4	27	16	37.2
Political economy	41	9.9	25	16	39.0
African political thought	17	4.1	8	9	52.9
Ethnicity/race	16	3.8	12	4	25.0
Political history	10	2.4	8	2	20.0
Military regimes	9	2.2	5	4	44.4
Rural development	9	2.2	6	3	33.3
Leadership	8	1.9	3	5	62.5
Constitution studies	7	1.7	4	3	42.9
State/state formation	6	1.4	4	2	16.7
Political development	3	0.7	2	1	33.3
Total	415	100.0	274	143	34.3

Note: This table was created from a compilation of dissertations based on the annual listing of Ph.D dissertations completed at universities in the United States which appeared in the *American Political Science Review*.

subtotal. Analysis of the subject matter of this literature reveals the same range of heterodoxy and disciplinary dissonance that characterizes course and teaching orientations in the universities.

In sum, the "model of exposure" that African students encountered at an African or American university or in professional publications was probably a very heterodox one, with more confusion than clarity being imparted about the nature of the discipline of political science. This leads us to a brief summary of some of the more salient characteristics of American political science when its diffusion to Africa commenced some twenty-five years ago.

Table 11. Subject Categories of Doctoral Dissertations in Political Science on Tropical African Topics by African Students

	United States, 1950–80		*United Kingdom, 1951–79*		*France and Francophone Belgium, 1966–76*				*Total*	
	No.	*%*	*No.*	*%*	*No. (doctorats d'état)*	*No. (other[a])*	*Total No.*	*%*	*No.*	*%*
International relations/ foreign policy	39	27.7	14	34.2	13	18	31	29.8	84	29.4
Political participation	22	15.6	5	12.2	4	8	12	11.5	39	13.6
Central institutions	15	10.6	8	19.5	8	7	15	14.4	38	13.3
Local institutions	16	11.4	6	14.6	1	12	13	12.5	35	12.2
Political economy	16	11.4	1	2.4	1	3	4	3.9	21	7.3
African political thought	9	6.4	—	—	9	9	9	8.6	18	6.3
Political history	2	1.4	1	2.4	3	7	7	6.7	10	3.5
Ethnicity/race	4	2.8	1	2.4	—	4	4	3.9	9	3.1
Leadership	5	3.6	—	—	—	2	2	1.9	7	2.5
Military regimes	4	2.8	—	—	2	1	3	2.9	7	2.5
State/state formation	2	1.4	1	2.4	2	2	4	3.9	7	2.5
Constitution studies	3	2.1	3	7.3	—	—	—	—	6	2.1
Rural development	3	2.1	1	2.4	—	—	—	—	4	1.4
Political development	1	0.7	—	—	—	—	—	—	1	0.3
Total	141	100	41	100	34	70	104	100	286	100

Note: This table was created on the basis of dissertation listings in the *American Political Science Review*, in *Bulletin d'information et de liaison*, vols. 1–9 (Paris: Centre d'Analyse et de Recherche Documentaires pour l'Afrique Noire [CARDAN], 1969–78), and *Index to Theses Accepted for Higher Degrees by the Universities of Great Britain and Ireland and the Council for Academic Awards*, 29 vols (London: Aslib, 1953–81).

[a]Other: *Troisième cycle, doctorat universitaire*, and *doctorat*. Dissertations from Francophone Belgian universities were included with those of French universities. The Belgian dissertations were 11 in number and all belonged to the "other" category.

The Anatomy of American Political Science during Globalization

What prevailed as a sort of stable paradigm in American political science from the 1880s to the 1930s was shattered by the trauma of the latter decade and the ensuing World War II.[33] During the 1950s the discipline's identity crisis was further aggravated by the burgeoning pressures of three new internal movements: behavioralism, comparative cross-cultural political analysis, and area studies. One enduring element was the hold of Enlightenment political theory, as illuminated by the tendency toward a unilinear conception of political history and a teleological belief that democracy is both the inevitable direction and the end state of human history.[34] At the core of the American liberal tradition this lingering belief has had—and probably still has—a powerful influence on the American mind.[35] This was reflected once again in the hubris of the 1976 bicentennial, during which Austin Ranney, in his presidential address to the American Political Science Association, quoted approvingly James Bryce's glorification of the world's putative political model:

> The institutions of the United States . . . are believed to disclose and display the type of institutions towards which, as by a law of fate, the rest of civilized mankind are forced to move, some with swifter, others with slower, but all with unresting feet.[36]

This American ideological liberalism explains a cluster of related predispositions. One has been the evangelical commitment to the spread of democracy through the export of liberal constitutionalism and American pluralism.[37] Another has been a belief in universalism and scientism, a corresponding attraction to generalizations and grand theory, and the human tendency to believe that a generalization about one's own culture has universal validity.[38] A third predisposition has been toward a rather naive optimism and the tendency to accept rhetoric as reality;[39] once cold reality can no longer be ignored, there is then a plunge into deep pessimism.

Another oft-noted defining characteristic of the discipline in that period was the perception of politics as a dependent variable, that is, the implicit or explicit belief that extrapolitical (economic, social, cultural, and psychological) factors were determinative of political behavior and institutions.[40] Various explanations have been advanced for this bias: the incorporation into the discipline of concepts and methods from sociologists, anthropologists, and psychologists, resulting in part from their study of the rise of totalitarian political movements;[41] the influence of conservative ideas stressing the primacy of culture and nonrationality or irrationality in human affairs;[42] the dominance of holistic modes of analysis, such as structural-functionalism and systems theory, which emphasized societal constraints on the polity;[43] and the representational view of politics "according to which political actions both are and ought to be predominantly the expression of more basic underlying forces."[44] Whatever the wellspring of this socioeconomic-psychocultural determinism, the polity emerged as the dependent variable. Among its consequences was the virtual abandonment of the "state" as a conceptual variable[45] until its rediscovery by both neo-Marxists and non-Marxists alike.[46] It also reinforced an existing predisposition in American political science of that epoch to neglect almost completely purposive political leadership and political organization as variables;[47] indeed, leadership was not explicitly provided for in any of the prevailing approaches.[48]

American political science on the eve of its global diffusion had other characteristics, in addition to the biases of unilinearity and society-centrism. As the discipline evolved over the years, three idiosyncratic cleavages developed: those between political science and public administration; between political science and international relations; and between normative and empirical political theory. The first great divide—between politics and administration—was the turn-of-the-century doctrine laid down by Woodrow Wilson, the only American academic political scientist who ever became president, that politics and administration are separate studies. For the following half-century this bifurcation pervaded both the internal organization and the conceptualized self-image of the discipline.[49] The persistence of this division is illustrated by the two separate universes of theorizing and discourse which coexisted throughout the 1950s and 1960s in the work of the Comparative Politics Committee of the Social Science Research Council (purveyors of the much critiqued systems functionalism, political development/modernization, vogue, with a bias toward "inputs") on the one hand, and the Comparative Administration Group of the American Society for Public Administration (with a bias toward "outputs") on the other.[50]

The second cleavage, the one between political science and international relations, resulted from the separate development of the study of politics within countries on the one hand and the study of the relations between countries on the other. The former tended to neglect the exogenous variables of the international environment, and the latter tended to regard states—the objects of study—as the functional equivalent of interacting billiard balls. Neither included systematically within their analytical framework the interpenetration of the other's domain. The separation was furthered by America's interwar isolationism, a period during which the international environment was self-consciously suppressed as a relevant variable. Smiley argues persuasively that simply because of its size, wealth, internal specialization, and vitality, the American political science enterprise is insular.[51] Most American political scientists work in a milieu largely devoid of non-American influences, or at least of influences to which they attach weight. Moreover, for a generation the American political science community has not had "an important infusion of persons embodying other intellectual traditions." Cairns also argues that American parochialism is intensified because of its high level of institutionalization and scholarly output, the high incidence of unilingualism among its professionals, and the quality and number of its graduate school, which reduce the attractions of studying abroad.[52] This type of insularity obviously is self-reinforcing.

Even the impact of World War II and America's postwar role as "Leader of the Free World" did not perceptibly change the perspective in American political science regarding the bifurcation of political science and international relations.[53] One explanation is that in the most powerful country the international environment was not perceived as a constraint, nor were exogenous determinants believed to affect significantly the functioning of America's national political system or, by America's universalizing penchant, the functioning of any political system. It was a psychological disposition that Fulbright called "the arrogance of power," and the French refer to as *folie de grandeurs*. Only when America began to sense international environmental constraints, most notably in Vietnam and Iran, but also elsewhere, did one find a significant shift in American academic perspectives and a concerted effort to insert the international environment into the frameworks of international and comparative political analysis, thereby unleashing the new vogue and growth industry of "international political economy." The first movement in this direction carried the rubric "linkage politics"[54] and was followed by the massive swing of the pendulum to the opposite extreme, in which the international environment totally took over: the era of the Wallersteinian modern world system as the only unit of analysis had dawned.[55] Total neglect breeds total revenge.

The third bifurcation has been in political theory between a normative perspective (the critical study of the philosophies and theories of selected classical writers) and an empirical perspective (the nomothetic search for generalizations about political behavior and institutions through rigorous scientific studies). The former represents a traditional, once dominant, but still solidly recognized component of the discipline which, as a consequence of the impact of scientism, has tended to become isolated.[56] Although in some respects a false dichotomy, there has been and continues to be a widening communication gap between the normativists and the empiricists.

Another distinctive feature of mid-1950s American political science, which has persisted with little change throughout the past quarter century, was the virtual nonexistence of serious Marxist academic scholarship. A political scientist of Marxist persuasion was a rarity, as was a non-Marxist committed to principled heterodoxy and equal time for the study and understanding of Marxist analysis as an alternative perspective. Mainline political science hardly ever acknowledged the Marxist position—indeed, its very existence—until Charles Lindblom in his 1981 presidential address criticized the profession for this neglect.[57] Some of the brightest American students in the discipline, he observed, were exploring and finding intellectual nourishment from some of the neo-Marxist writers, many of whom came to the study of politics, not from political science but "from sociology, philosophy, economics, and history, as well as disproportionately from European intellectual traditions to which American political science is cool."[58]

Explanations for the ideological anti-Marxism of nearly all leading American political scientists are not found simplistically in the intimidatory effects of latent McCarthyism in American culture, nor in dominating Cold War mentality—the bias existed long before these phenomena appeared. Nor is the explanation convincingly found in significant measure in the argument that Marxism failed to take root in American society because, among other factors, "Americanism" is a political ideology with the same value content as socialism.[59] A more fundamental reason why articles by Marxists do not appear in the *American Political Science Review*, or those by mainline American political scientists in *Monthly Review* (or, for that matter, in the *Review of African Political Economy*) has been the mutual repulsion, the two-world existence, of practitioners from the two domains. Epistemologically, ideologically, and methodologically they were not attracted to each other's assumptions, frameworks, and methodologies. For Marxists, political science was superficial when detached from political economy as they defined the concept. American political scientists were equally repulsed by the ideological rigidity, sectarianism, and determinism of most orthodox Marxism. The greater flexibility of and pluralism among the neo-Marxists and the new mutual interest in the state and political economy have expanded the area of dialogue. Significantly, the ambiance of catholicity and ideological tolerance engendered by the activities of interdisciplinary, multinational area studies associations (e.g., the Twenty-Fifth Annual Meeting of the African Studies Association) have contributed powerfully to this change.

Although there were exceptions, for most American Africanists trained in mainline political science during the heyday of its globalization the neglect of Marxism by the discipline meant inadequate professional preparation in one major dimension of modern sociopolitical analysis. This professional deficiency significantly inhibited subsequent communication and understanding in scholarly dialogue between most American political scientists—and those trained in its tradition—and scholars and students (including many from Africa) socialized into the traditions of, for example, Canada, Britain, and France, where ideological pluralism has had greater legitimacy and where, as a result, serious Marxist studies have long had a home.[60]

A final aspect of the first wave of American political analysis of African political phenomena was its elite-centrism. Clearly incongruent with the society-centrism already discussed, the focus on elites was the function of the special circumstances prevailing in Africa immediately before and after independence. Although present, the study of elites had not been a central concern in American political science. When it turned attention to the non-Western world, however, elites (nationalist leaders and subsequently initial national power holders) came to center stage. They enjoyed a halo effect, if not an exaggerated charismatic aura, from the nationalist phase, and accordingly received a honeymoon to build their states and nations and develop their countries. Academic euphoria over their entering their own brave new world, reinforced by a guilt-atonement syndrome,[61] tended to mean that initially they could do no wrong, and this sentimentalism colored some analyses. In the then prevailing atmosphere of the "primacy of politics" the governing elites at the center of those states were not unreasonably viewed as the most likely strategic foci and determinants of the unfolding political drama. The historical literature on earlier modernization experiences made elites the modernizers and state builders.[62] As in all postrevolutionary new state situations, central national institutions were fragile or nonexistent, recalling Montesquieu's aphorism that "at the birth of societies, it is the leaders of the commonwealth who create the institutions." Others saw the central elites as embryonic dominant classes in formation which rightly commanded attention if power was, as it should be, a central concern of political scientists. For these and other reasons, the immediate postindependence period was predominantly elite-centric. This did not last long; predictably, there was in due course an anti-elite pendulum swing to yet one more newly discovered and underemphasized variable—to the villages, rural areas, and grassroots politics at the periphery.[63]

The foregoing are some of the more salient defining characteristics of the American discipline in the late 1950s and early 1960s as it confronted and endeavored to respond to and to absorb the three most assertive revolutions then in progress: behavioralism, a universalizing comparative politics, and area studies. Behavioralism symbolized the explicit insistence upon value-free scientism and universality. Heinz Eulau, one of its leading pioneers, argued: "Only the assumption that politics is not immune to scientific inquiry into human relations and behavioral patterns can justify the entire venture called 'political science.'"[64] Behavioralism was not a specific mode or framework of analysis; rather it was a "mood" or, as Eulau preferred, a "persuasion," which stressed scientific rigor, clarity and precision in conceptualization, an empiricism aimed explicitly at the quest for uniformities, the formulation of hypotheses, and the construction of theories of ever-higher generality. It was initially developed in the study of elections in the United States and later Europe, because individual electoral behavior was scientifically measurable through survey research and the new social science computer technology. It sought to replace the then dominant historical, legal, and institutional idiographic tradition with a unified science of society which was quintessentially universalistic and nomothetic in its intent.

The "comparative politics movement" in American political science gathered momentum in the early 1950s and was strongly influenced by the ongoing behavioral revolution in the study of American politics, most particularly by its scientism, and by the area studies movement, then undergoing rapid expansion. A growing number of students became interested in the use of the comparative method to create and test generalizations and theories about macropolitical systems on a global basis. The movement incorporated into its conceptual baggage a mélange of new concepts and approaches which were then acquiring currency. Among these were "systems analysis," "structural-functionalism," and subsequently "crises" in political development. There were several submovements in this new front seeking to interpret a changed world. The most critiqued was a vast ephemeral body of literature on "political development and modernization," the rise and fall of which Riggs has traced in detail.[65] The movement started with a number of brave principles: "Look beyond description to more theoretically relevant problems; look beyond the formal institutions of government to political processes and political functions; and look beyond the countries of Western Europe to the new nations of Asia, Africa, and Latin America."[66] Durkheim had affirmed that comparative sociology *is* sociology, because the comparative method was the scientific method of sociology. Similarly, Gabriel Almond, the pioneer in the comparative politics movement, argued that the latter was not a separate subdiscipline for the study of foreign politics (as "comparative government" had tended to be viewed), but the comparative analytic framework for the development of the discipline of political science as a whole.[67] In short, comparative political analysis is political science. Like behavioralism, which inspired it, the tenets of the new movement were nomothetic.

The frameworks and conceptual innovations of one particular cluster in the movement—the Comparative Politics Committee of the Social Science Research Council—acquired some initial notoriety. Its output in the early 1960s was an eclectic mix of synchronic "comparative statics" concepts (i.e., systems and structural-functional analysis) and diachronic "comparative dynamics" developmental concepts (e.g., change analyzed according to a traditional-modern dichotomy, or to system development problems or crises). This mix of macroanalytic concepts reflected acknowledged borrowings and adaptations from a variety of sources—the system metaphor from Easton,[68] but stretching back to antiquity (Marx, Machiavelli, Aristotle); the dichotomous tradition-modernity model from Parsons's pattern-variables (with their origins traceable to earlier formulations of Weber and Tönnies); structural-functionalism and particularly "functional requisites" adapted from Marion Levy and Francis Sutton,[69] who had drawn from Parsons, but also with roots in Radcliffe-Brown,[70] and evolutionary assumptions drawn partly and implicitly from the Enlightenment as well as from the actual history of Western state and nation formation, which postulated a process of successive surmounting of a set of logically derived functional-requisite system problems or crises (e.g., legitimacy, identity, etc.). This mix of synchronic and diachronic approaches was never melded into a coherent single framework. As Almond retrospectively acknowledged, "The concepts we elaborated and the classification schemes that we experimented with were very definitely of an ad hoc sort."[71]

The major objective sought by the comparativists at the time was the development of a framework and categories that were universally valid so as to permit comparison of all types of historical and contemporary political systems (particularly Western and non-Western) irrespective of scale, structure, or the cultural matrix within which they are found. Easton's concept of the analytic system (as distinguished from actual physical systems) was considered neutral and useful for this purpose. Also, since existing Western structures, and the categories used in their description and analysis, tended to be inherently culture-bound, it seemed persuasive to postulate instead a set of logically derived, universal functional categories applicable to all systems, from an Eskimo band to the USSR.

Those universal political functions which Almond postulated in his schema were implicitly derived from the structures of the Anglo-American polity.[72] In the same manner, the concept of a "modern" political system was a characterization of such a polity. "We were," he later explained, "aware of the fact that we were comparing non-Western political systems according to Western categories and from a Western perspective. After all, we were Westerners, beginning with the knowledge and concerns of the West, trying to understand how the newly emerging and rapidly changing political systems of Asia, Africa, and Latin America were similar to or different from our more familiar institutional systems and processes."[73] Almond's central objective in developing his universal political functions was to liberate comparative analysis from the enthnocentric bias in Western culture-bound structural categories. However, the dominant impression among critical receptors was that culturally relative (American) categories were being proposed (imposed?) a priori as universal.

The third postwar movement which challenged traditionally political science was the emergence of area studies, focusing particularly on non-Western societies, as a major feature of the American academic landscape. The story has been described elsewhere and need not detain us here.[74] Their emergence sparked a quiet but fundamental struggle within the conventional disciplines, the nature and resolution of which Robert Ward analyzed in his 1973 APSA presidential address under the rubric "Culture and the Comparative Study of Politics, or the Constipated Dialectic."[75] The crux of the issue concerned the relative merits of the historico-cultural idiographic approach to knowledge (the "thing-in-itself" caricature referred to by Hodgkin) versus the scientistic, universalizing nomothetic approach, espoused by behavioralism and the new comparative politics of the 1960s. It was, in short, the area approach versus the behavioral approach to the study of differing systems. The image of behavioralists harbored in the area studies camp was that they ignored the critical significance of unique cultural and historical contexts, proclaimed as universal their own culture-bound generalizations, and naively sought a chimerical universalism. Most mainline political scientists thus tended to believe that the development of African area studies was by definition incongruent and conflictive with the development of a generalizing nomothetic political science. We will argue with Prewitt[76] that not only is this basically a false dichotomy but that the practice of African area specialists has not conformed to the image.

The foregoing sketch of American political science during its heyday of globalization suffers a bit from caricature. The object was to underscore the contextual relativity of much of the corpus of American political science. As the sociogenesis of knowledge would suggest, it reflected in significant respects certain unique features of American national development and its implicit underlying ideologies. Even its scientism and commitment to universality are as much rooted in the persisting vigor of the Enlightenment ideas which infuse its unique liberal tradition as they are in its universalizing nomothetic compulsions as a hegemonic power.[77]

The De-Americanization of Political Science

Fairly early in the globalization process Ann Ruth Willner raised an alarm over the danger of an entire new generation of political scientists throughout the world becoming locked into a single paradigm which would be reproduced over successive generations:

> Once a theoretical framework or even a few loose concepts achieve intellectual currency, they become institutionalized. They form the patterns of regularities of belief to which successive generations of scholars and the consumers of scholarships become socialized. . . . they tend to set the course of future research.[78]

There indeed can be a strain toward institutionalization, but as we have already suggested, approach mongering and the ethos of academic polemical disputation are ironclad guarantees that the whole profession will not become prisoners, not for long anyway, of any particular framework or concept, no matter how fashionable. The dynamics of paradigmatic change alone would probably not allow any faddish dominance of American models to continue indefinitely. This has been further assured by other influences which have accelerated the de-Americanization process—the very penetrating critiques made by a wide variety of scholars (including self-criticism by practitioners themselves and their American peers, as well as critical analyses by non-American scholars), the global movement to develop national political science identities and professional associations, the movement toward internationalization of the profession, and above all, the actual performance and product of American Africanist political scientists.

Several aspects of the version of American political science which was globalized during the 1950s and 1960s were fairly immediately subjected to extensive critique, most particularly the various concepts and frameworks associated with the study of political development and modernization. In the welter of criticism, much of it incisive and poignant, three themes stand out: the limitations to "grand theory," the question of value-free scientism, and the bias of ideological conservatism. In fact, so-called grand theory is not theory at all. Having no explanatory power, it is pretheoretical. It refers to those macropolitical efforts to develop analytic conceptual schemata, which are essentially typological and classificatory in nature, as proposed by Talcott Parsons and Marion Levy for society in general and David Easton and Gabriel Almond specifically for whole political systems. Easton in fact claimed that his analytic system was no more than a conceptual framework which hopefully could help in the development of theory.[79]

The heuristic value of grand theory was faulted by some of its pioneer promulgators and others on two counts: its abstractness, and its procrustean effect of forcing aspects of reality into boxes in which they do not belong.[80] But the most telling fault was not its heuristic limitations, but its being implicitly or explicitly burdened with unilinearity, teleology, and ethnocentrism. This resulted in its being perceived by its non-American (and particularly non-Western) critics not only as irrelevant but as a display of cultural arrogance. The suggestion that there was only one path and one direction in a people's progress, that the end to which they are being drawn and finally will reach is predetermined, and that the path and end are concretely exemplified by the Anglo-American democratic polity, was not a grand design likely to commend itself as a universal proposition. A decade after the grand theory was first advanced, Gabriel Almond wrote a persuasively reasoned defense of it, but observed that "most of us who contribute to this still somewhat turgid field of inquiry have violated these tabus" (of unilinearity, teleology, and ethnocentrism).[81]

Behavioralism and the scientism of the comparative politics movement adhered to the positivist belief in the quest for a value-free social science. Africanist critics of this position[82] argue that claims to objectivity and value freedom are either mistaken or consciously biased, and that "social science must indeed stop modelling itself on a naive conception of a value-free natural science."[83] Within American social sciences this core issue has been debated without closure. Von der Muhll asked, "Why do political scientists have such difficulty in distinguishing between why we ask the questions we do and whether they have been correctly answered?"[84] In this regard Marenin has pointed out that bias is more obvious in the selection of problems and in the selection of interpretation, but that in the selection of methods, "even value-engaged theorists must argue the case for a value-free method. If they did not they would undercut their whole work. Reality must mean something; and the question of reality is one of method. On this point we are Weberians."[85]

Both David Easton's political system and Gabriel Almond's structural-functionalist approaches have been exhaustively critiqued and impugned for their alleged ideological conservatism; that is, they favor system maintenance, stability, and equilibrium,[86] and hence, the critique says, they are handmaidens of dominant elites and existing structures, which are coercive and exploitive. Even worse, these approaches are alleged to downplay or ignore the conflictual potential in society and therefore resist change and, in any event, they are said to be completely irrelevant and inappropriate in such structurally fluid and politically indeterminate situations as Africa has confronted during the past two decades in its state-building epoch. By now the arguments in the liturgy of the critique are well known.

Although the nature of the structural-functionalist approach can predispose an analyst toward conservative patterns and biases,[87] anthropologists and sociologist have long since tired of beating the dead horse of functionalism.[88] Moreover, Marxist thought is essentially functionalist, and Parsons's works include "dynamic" concepts. Leys has stated flatly, "I do not subscribe to the frequently expressed view that structural-functionalism is an inherently conservative method of analysis, nor even that it has always been used as a matter of fact to support a conservative viewpoint."[89] Moreover, Southall notes that the empirical reality of most societies is that "forces of system maintenance do predominate,"[90] which of course does not mean that they should. One critique could be that Northern ideological liberals have sought guilt atonement on the racial issue by avoiding any "conceptual terminology which, by even the most remote stretch of the imagination, could be construed as 'conservative,'"[91] and attacking any frameworks which do. The bottom line is arguably that the neglect of dynamics and change should not be blamed upon reified concepts and analytical frameworks but upon the predilections of their users.[92]

The most salient limitations for Africa of some of the analytic schema of American political science of the 1950s and 1960s could well be found elsewhere, namely, in two of the anomalies of the discipline discussed earlier: (1) in its neglect (until its recent rediscovery via political economy and public policy analysis) of the "output" side of the political system and of the dominant role of the state, particularly in a continent of pervasive statism;[93] and (2) in its neglect (until dependency theory and world systems theory became the vogue) of exogenous variables.

De-Americanization of the discipline has also been furthered by the global movement to foster national political science identities. By 1977 there were thirty-six national (single-country) political science associations and one continental (African) association.[94] National self-assertiveness is an understandable reaction to American dominance of the discipline. Significantly, the Canadian movement for developing a national sociology and political science is among the most vigorous and self-conscious. This is partly a function of heightened Canadian nationalism in general vis-à-vis its southern colossus. Proximity and the massive U.S. economic and cultural penetration of Canada are understandably goads to the establishment and rationalization of Canadian identity.

Specific factors and arguments which have contributed to the movement for the indigenization of disciplines include (1) belief in the superiority of the insider over the outsider, especially when foreign scholars are perceived as intellectual imperialists[95] or are not adequately generating society-specific data; (2) the fact that ethnocentrism in the disciplines of exporting countries inevitably stimulates counter-ethnocentrism among importers;[96] (3) the sociogenetic and relativistic argument advanced by some Canadians that there is a determinate relationship between a society's environment and culture and its social sciences;[97] and (4) for some advocates of the nationality of disciplines, professional career advantages to be gained from curtailment of the importation of foreign paradigms, particularly if foreign personnel accompany them. The crucial point to be made before we turn later to the African situation is that globally there is a reactive nationalistic and parochial strain toward some national relativism in the development of the social science disciplines, just as there exists an irrepressible countervailing strain everywhere toward universality.[98]

Image versus Reality in Africanist Political Science

A large gap has existed between the images and the realities of the field of American Africanist political science. The actual record of research, teaching, and publication of American Africanist political scientists over the past three decades puts to rest the fears[99] and refutes the stereotypes dominant in the beginning. The scholars were not captured by, nor did they become purveyors of, the modernization paradigm. Indeed, astonishingly, despite all the hullabaloo over that paradigm, and particularly structural-functionalism, it had virtually no discernible impact on political Africana which emerged during the period.[100] Illuminating the tenacity of the image-reality gap was Ake's cry of alarm over the imperialist threat the paradigm posed, and Rigg's claim that effectively it was moribund a few years earlier.[101] Young reflected, "I can't remember anyone among Africanist political scientists who was, in classroom or writing, dogmatically asserting that universal truth was to be found in these approaches."[102] The few exceptions proved the rule. No more than 5 percent of the nearly 200 articles published during the period in selected leading journals (table 9) concerned the modernization paradigm, and these were largely criticism of it. By our calculations, only one of the 286 doctoral dissertations submitted on both sides of the Atlantic during the three decades (tables 10 and 11) came close to embracing the paradigm. In a survey conducted in the early 1970s of nearly 300 American university teachers of African politics, only Zolberg's *Creating Political Order* had a significantly high number of mentions.[103] Some of the concepts and categories proved suggestive and were adapted to use, but in general, as Magid observed, most practitioners "have tended to ignore or treat lightly various methodological problems confronting . . . their own discipline."[104] In sum, the image of threat or dominance by the modernization paradigm was from the beginning a chimera.

A second persistent image which requires exposure to reality is that held by mainline political scientists, which depicts the Africanist as a narrow, atheoretical, area-bound parochialist. The reality is that the bulk of most of the influential product of American political science on Africa has been in the Hodgkinian mode mentioned at the beginning of this article, namely, the combination of the idiographic and nomothetic in recognition that both are essential, mutually enriching, and equally legitimate. The case for studying and understanding the unique and the limitations of "compulsive and mindless theorizing" has been eloquently argued by Hirschman.[105] "Hodgkin was the first [and, we would add, the enduring] paradigm-setter, and not Almond or Parsons."[106] Verba has made explicit what Hodgkin in the cited quotation implied, namely, that the dichotomy between the generalized nomothetic approach and configurative-idiographic approach is false, and that one resolution of the dilemma is found in what Verba calls the "*disciplined* configurative approach," that is, the systematic study and analysis of the unique in ways that permit and facilitate comparison.[107]

The latter approach was in fact what most of the first generation practitioners implicitly followed in building the quintessential idiographic infrastructure upon which later was progressively erected a body of area generalizations generated by intra-Africa comparisons, which in turn provided the African reservoir of data and propositions used to compare and combine with data and experiences from other areas in the development of global generalizations. Progression in the trilevel ascent from the disciplined configurative case studies of particular countries or phenomena to intra-African and then to global comparison and generalization has roughly characterized the chronology of intellectual movement and cumulative maturation during the three decades of our period. Successive engagement at each of the three levels has characterized the work of many of our colleagues.

As in the anthropological tradition of establishing one's professional legitimacy first through the production of a solid idiographic ethnography before proceeding to comparative ethnology, first-generation Africanist political scientists concentrated upon the first level of disciplined configurative single county/phenomena studies (illustrative only are such names and the countries associated with them as Apter, Abernethy, Bienen, Bustin, Coleman, Foltz, Johnson, Kilson, Lemarchand, LeVine, Liebenow, Lofchie, Marcum, Rosberg, Sklar, Whitaker, Wolpe, Young, Zolberg, and many others). During the same period "la grande comparativiste" Gwendolen Carter skillfully entrepreneured the first wave of country-study symposia, further expanding the idiographic-configurative base for broader comparisons. Then followed the movement of several of the same scholars, or newcomers, to the second level, that of intra-African comparisons in quest of area patterns. Thus, a new wave of analytic generalizing studies emerged (e.g., Zolberg and Morgenthau on the single-party syndrome, Bienen and Welch on the military, Hanna and Barkan on students, Lemarchand on political clientelism, Sklar on class, Rosberg on protest movements, Young and Kasfir on ethnicity). Comparisons and generalizing at the intra-African area level, which Lijphart and others[108] have argued can *scientifically* be most fruitful, continue unabated to the present day, refining and qualifying older nomothetic propositions and postulating new ones (e.g., Jackson and Rosberg on personal rule, Young on ideology and political economy, Bates and Lofchie on the political economy of agriculture). At the third, global level, data on the African experience have increasingly infused comparative studies aimed at universal generalization by both Africanists and non-Africanists (e.g., Young on cultural pluralism, Foltz on national integration, Bienen on urban political development, Laitin on religion, Perlmutter on military regimes, Huntington and Moore on one-party systems). Several practitioners have continued to function at all three levels; others have migrated internally within Africa (e.g., Foltz and Price to Southern Africa); and still others have migrated to other areas (e.g., Apter to Chile and from there to Japan and Zolberg to Belgium).

The cumulative result of these various intellectual voyages into ever-increasing generality and refinement though replication has been a vast expansion in our understanding of the individual peoples and phenomena of Africa in all their idiographic uniqueness, a more solid empirical

Table 12. Nomothetic vs. Idiographic Orientations of Africanist Political Scientists in Selected Professional Journals, 1950–1982

	Journal of Modern African Studies, 1963–82	*African Studies Review, 1970–80*	*American Political Science Review, 1950–82*	*Comparative Politics, 1969–82*	*World Politics, 1950–82*	*Total*	%
Nomothetic orientation							
Global generalizations (African and non-African data)	—	4	—	8	14	26	11
Intra-African area comparisons and generalizations	28	23	7	6	15	79	34
Disciplined configurative case studies[a]	29	6	8	12	5	60	26
Idiographic orientation	18	18	1	4	—	41	18
International relations	17	—	—	—	2	19	8
Political thought	7	—	—	—	1	8	3
Total	99	51	16	30	37	233	100

Note: Limited to American political scientists. Distinction between nomethetic and idiographic orientations was drawn on the basis of perusal of articles to observe explicitness of intent and effort to compare and generalize at either an African or a global level, and in the case studies, whether the descriptive and analytic categories are general-variable or idiographic in character. Assignment to the classifications are admittedly only rough and approximate, but differences are sufficiently discernible to reflect the general patterns noted. Inclusive years for each journal are the years of publication between 1950 and 1982.

[a] Source: Verba, "Some Dilemmas in Comparative Research," *World Politics*, 20:1 (October 1967), pp. 14–15.

data base for generalization about the distinguishing commonalities of Tropical Africa as an area, and the infiltration and incorporation of an ever-increasing volume of African data in the ongoing effort to identify universal patterns (the unsung-hero role of Bienen as review editor of *World Politics* should here be noted). Paraphrasing Donne's apt aphorism, we are more deeply aware that "an individual African polity is like no other polity, like some other polities, like all other polities," and that it is the task of the analyst to recognize and contribute to understanding at all three levels.

In contrast to the pejorative image of Africanist political science harbored by mainline political scientists, the reality of performance has been that over 70 percent of the studies which appeared in selected professional journals during the past three decades have reflected a strong nomothetic orientation, that is, a commitment to either intra-African or, using African data, global comparisons and generalization, and that among the individual case studies (43 percent of the total), a significant majority have been of the discipline configurative type; only 18 percent of all studies have been essentially atheoretical and idiographic in orientation (see table 12). There has also been a demonstrable infusion of African content into the expanding number of comparative studies at the global level, examples being the enrichment of global theorizing by the incorporation of substantial data on the African experience, particularly as regards ethnicity, military intervention, and personalistic rulership. This reality belies the seemingly ineradicable stereotypic image mainline political scientists have of the African area specialist. As Prewitt—another unsung hero of the foreign area studies with impeccable credentials in Americana—points out, it will take some time before mainliners in the discipline will change, but "thoughtful people are simply moving beyond the debate." By providing a deeper understanding of the place in which matters occur, he argues, area studies promises to "advance the only kind of scholarship which has a chance to instruct us about the world we live in."[109]

A third image-reality gap proved far more evanescent. Whatever biases toward a democratic evangelism and society-centrism American Africanist political scientists may have commenced with, they were moderated fairly quickly by the failure of the naive high hopes invested in independence democratic formulas, by the pervasiveness and density of Africa's statism, by the flagrant use of political power for the rapid accumulation of wealth by an emergent new class,[110] and by a cultural pluralism that rendered the then voguish political cultural approach both impractical and seemingly irrelevant.[111] By the mid-1960s disenchantment had swung the pendulum to realism, if not realpolitik, exemplified by the extraordinary influence of Zolberg's *Creating Political Order* and Huntington's *Political Order in*

Changing Societies—a shift in American political science poignantly critiqued by O'Brien.[112] The realities of Africa's new authoritarianism were sobering and conducive to Machiavellian analysis, an orientation reinforced by transformative changes in American society itself during the same period. The latter had "forced a recognition that much of the political 'science' of the previous two decades had been mere ideology and obfuscation" and that a view of politics that emphasized the "cynical pursuit of self-interest" (whether by an aggrandizing presidential monarch or a recklessly exploitive new class) had become much more attractive.[113] Concepts such as class, state, and political economy were increasingly incorporated into the vocabulary of scholars of divergent ideological dispositions. The unmentionables of 1955 had by 1980 become the staples—the universals, if you will—of Africanist discourse.

As any title count of political Africana during the past decade would readily demonstrate, political economy has emerged as the most fashionable rubric for almost any contemporary work in political science or economics. It has numerous variants; Frey identifies seven, but space does not permit their disaggregation and explication.[114] For Africanists, three versions are particularly in point:

1. The application of the tools of economic analysis to enhance the understanding of political processes, most notably "public choice" in democracies.[115] This "rationalist theory" variant—which incorporated methods and models from other sources than economics as well—emerged as the ascendant paradigm of the 1970s and early 1980s in American political science. Called by Rogowski the "fourth great scientific revolution" of this century,[116] it shifted the focus from the essentially sociological and nonrational Parsonian view of man dominated by political culture to the economic view of man as the "rational maximizer of his own advantage." Also known as "mathematical political science," its early proponents were economists (e.g., Downs, Olson, Arrow), but a new generation of political scientists now constitute the avant-garde in the discipline. However, except for Dudley on Nigeria,[117] it has had no perceptible direct impact upon African political studies, a fact which probably reinforces the ethnocentric belief among some mainliners that African area studies can make no significant scientific contribution to the discipline.

2. The study of the interpenetration of political and economic processes, either (a) *to understand and explain* (within or without holistic systems theory) the incidence or development of different kinds of political economic phenomena[118] or (b) to assess policy alternatives—also through the use of economic tools where appropriate—in order *to improve the efficacy of political choices* of decision-making regarding scarce re-

sources,[119] or, as in the case of Lindblom, to make "a prudential calculus of desirable political economic institutions and policies" in democracies.[120]

3. The neo-Marxian, *dependencia,* essentially "radical" study of the interconnectedness of political, economic, and social factors of change, among the key elements of which are (a) historical perspective; (b) interdisciplinarity; (c) holism; (d) emphasis upon underdevelopment, dependency, imperialism, and class formation and action; and (e) a radical political commitment to the advancement of the African peoples.[121]

Throughout modern history a conceptual dualism has existed in the form of both Marxist and non-Marxist versions of political economy. In the "new" political economy this continues to be reflected in the distinction between 2 and 3 above. Rarely was an American political scientist found among the first wave of those of Marxist or radical persuasion. Writing in 1976, Chris Allen claimed that "the most important material on the political economy of Africa has been, and will continue to be, produced by Marxists."[122] However, six years later Gavin Williams observed that during the first wave of political economy the term was largely a euphemism for Marxism, but now it often stands for anything but Marxism.[123] This change illuminated not only the transcendental power of a concept once it has become universally fashionable, but also a recognition of the existence of an emergent common empirical reality, namely, the inexorable drift—convergence, if you will—toward the modern state-dominated economy and society in which the market-state division that separated economics from political science has become increasingly unreal.

The Encounter of the Political Sciences of America and Tropical Africa

In this final sector of the intellectual voyage of American political science we will briefly examine its encounter over the past quarter century with the emerging political science of Tropical Africa. African political scientists have engaged in a continuous critique of the American version, directly and indirectly, as part of the general movement toward cultural decolonization of the Western overlay, the assertion of intellectual independence, and the search for authenticity.[124] They have rejected the racist contentions that they passively absorbed "Western ideas."[125] Yet their critique has not been merely reactive; it has been part of the larger process of providing a new generation of African intellectuals the capacities to discern sophisticated forms of cultural, ideological, and ethnocentric bias, and thereby to resist the "tyranny of received paradigms."[126] This fulfills an important sociopsychological function, in addition to the challenge it brings to works of caricature or inaccurate interpretation of African politics. Moreover, in contrast to the isolationism and parochialism that characterized the evolution of the American discipline, African political science has evolved in an intellectually interdependent environment in which African political phenomena could not be adequately analyzed without considering the world political configuration.[127]

A substantial consensus also exists among African practitioners that grappling with the legacy of colonialism is the starting-point for understanding the present forms of African politics. Hodgkin emphasized the pervasiveness of the colonial intrusion in observing that "the relationship between the 'imperialist' power and the African 'nation' is essentially one of 'domination,' in its political aspect, 'exploitation,' in its economic aspect, and 'racialism' . . . in its human aspect."[128] Indeed, the totality of the colonial impact on African society has been so all-engulfing that differentiation of the national origins of Western external interventions is not always made; the stigma of colonialism affects them all, including received paradigms in political science.

Some African scholars also value more highly the in-depth configurative studies produced by the first generation of American political scientists than they do later studies of a nomothetic orientation.[129] In the apt words of Eulau they judged the "empirical staples" to be more useful to them than "theoretical perishables."[130] The exigencies of both accuracy and empathy are better assured, as Hirschman has shown, through the complete immersion in the complexities and intricacies of a single culture or situation, particularly in contrast to those nomothetic exercises which are based on a weak idiographic infrastructure and thereby neglect crucial uniquenesses and the gestalt of a society or phenomenon.[131] One of the principal causes for non-African insensitivity to African realities is the failure to grasp the nuances of African culture.[132] Thus, African scholars question the premature pursuit of global generalizations and the penchant of grand theorists for broad classificatory schemata (e.g., the inclusion of Africa in the undifferentiated aggregate, "Third World").[133] This is one of many explanations why modernization theory did not gain acceptance among them.

African political scientists have generally agreed on the need to reassess the colonial experience, and in so doing, have placed emphasis on the different aspects of it. Jinadu has examined the writings of Frantz Fanon in a search for an African theory of colonial society.[134] The contradictions of the latter provide a starting point for Ake's work on the political economy of Africa.[135] The colonial experience is also a central factor in the intellectual separatism of those of "autarkist disposition" arguing that the study of Africa should be reserved for "insiders" because only they can interpret it.[136] This insider view holds that African and American scholars are "no longer located within the same universe of discourse."[137] Although no African political scientist has openly advocated the extreme relativism of the insider position, as historian Ayandele has, the logic of cultural nationalism implies a latent strain in that direction.

The issue of universalism versus relativism, either implicitly or explicitly, figures predominantly among the African critics of American political science. It bears directly upon political and epistemological questions of vital concern to them. The multidimensionality of that concern is reflected in the many perspectives from which they are engaged with the issue. They ask philosophically, can there be universal truth? Methodologically, how is such truth derived? Historically, what are the origins and evolution of ideas of universality? Psychoculturally, how does empathy condition knowing? And, sociopolitically, how does class position affect understanding? No matter what the perspective, these issues are not viewed abstractly, because ideology is regarded as a major determinant in the politics of paradigms selection.

African critiques of the American discipline fall roughly into two categories distinguished by a focus on enthnocentrism or class. Among those in the sample of critics we have selected, a correlation is discernible between ideological disposition and political orientation. Those emphasizing American ethnocentrism tend to be politically liberal (e.g., Mazrui and Dudley). Those stressing class are of two orientations—neo-Marxist (e.g., Ake) and social democratic (e.g., Ekeh, Jinadu, Oyovbaire, and Tunteng). These crude reductionist classifications are our own and may not reflect the self-identifications of the scholars concerned. The thrust of the liberal critiques is the de-westernization of the social sciences, the exposé and refutation of ethnocentrism, and the incorporation of African data on an equal basis aimed at true universalism in political science. They do not totally reject the American version but are highly critical of its application and of its empirical relativity behind an arrogant pretension of universalism. By contrast, the thrust of the neo-Marxist class critique is a total rejection of "Western" universalism (particularly the modernization paradigm) as "bourgeois social science,"[138] a belief in the essentiality of a transformation of the international capitalist system as a prerequisite of a true universality, the replacement of mystifying bourgeois disciplinary specializations by a holistic ("total history") perspective, and a belief that only a genuine *African* Marxism is capable of abolishing the epiphenomenal twin evils of ethnocentrism and racism.[139] Finally, the thrust of the class-oriented, social democratic critics differs from the foregoing in that it is noneconomistic, stressing the salience of political as well as economic criteria, and control over the means of domination as well as the means of production, in the conceptualization of class; and it is selectively eclectic regarding American political science as well as more flexible in confronting issues of race and ethnicity.

Two leading pioneers in institutionalizing political science as an academic discipline of the African continent were Ali Mazrui from the Anglophone East Coast and the late Billy Dudley from the Anglophone West Coast, both essentially products of the British tradition. In his prodigious productivity over the years Mazrui has demonstrated a deep commitment to an authentic African liberalism. He has emphasized two themes: liberal politics (hence his rejection of Marxism and his presumptive normative affinity with American political science), and authentic Africanism (hence his preoccupation with the decolonization of culture and thought, and his criticism of the ethnocentricity of the American discipline).[140] Some critics have discerned a tension between his liberalism and espousal of authenticity[141]—a tension which has not yet been resolved by the full articulation of an authentic African liberalism.[142] While some admirers note that he is the "only political scientist from Africa whom neither the right nor the left can claim as their own,"[143] another critic argues that Mazrui's anti-Marxism and cultural nationalism have led him to trivialize African politics and downgrade indigenous radical approaches.[144] A dedicated comparativist whose style has been described as "dialectical comparison through paradoxical exposition,"[145] Mazrui is emphatically nomothetic in orientation; his abiding quest is for a fusion of African and Western ideas in a universality that is truly equal in its origins.[146]

Also liberal in his commitment to democratic processes, as well as highly productive, Dudley developed an early interest in psephology and American behavioralism.[147] Yet, he was also a sharp critic of what he interpreted as ethnocentrism and relativism in American political science. He questioned the attribution of instability as an intrinsic quality of the non-Western political process, rather than as a characteristic of all governments of societies in transition, irrespective of epoch, nationality, culture or creed. He rejected modernization theory for its ideological illogicality (e.g., he saw no logical reason for the preference the theory showed for the competitive market model), and argued that the dependency approach served as useful function "in calling attention to the ideological bias of 'developmentalism' and similar conceptualization."[148] Unlike Mazrui the comparativist, Dudley remained singularly interested in the Nigerian political experience. However, like Mazrui his goal was a truly universal political science.

The neo-Marxist strand in class-oriented African critiques of American political science is best exemplified by the recent works of Claude Ake.[149] He shares with Jinadu a belief that American social science theories are ideological and reflect capitalist cultural values.[150] For Ake, political development theory is the bourgeois ideological expression of capitalism in Africa, which he identifies as the main impediment to the development of a universal social science. Those African scholars who become enamored of the paradigms of an imperialistic American social science fall into what General Obasanjo referred to as "intellectual trading outpost agents."[151] Imperialism in the guise of scientific knowledge, Ake believes, is the most subtle and pernicious form of imperialism.[152] African political scientists who are uncritical of such received knowledge suffer from "false consciousness." However, he maintains some hope that a radical social science can achieve universality.

Between the liberal and the neo-Marxist orientation there is an increasingly vocal left-centrist sector on the ideological spectrum which we have called social democratic. Its defining characteristic is a noneconomistic, essentially political, concept of class.[153] African scholars of this persuasion incline more to a singularly political analysis of the interaction between exogenous and endogenous intellectual forces that have influenced or can affect orientations in political science. Ekeh, for example, avoids what he calls "panideologism," that is, broad generalizations or categorical attributions such as the assertion that "all ideas and theories in a society are biased in favor of either the ruling class or the emerging class."[154] Similarly, Tunteng is not convinced by arguments that blame America for all the shortcomings of the discipline.[155] For Oyovbaire, foreign paradigms of whatever ideological thrust should be treated like any other imported commodity; thus in building an authentic African political science one selects imports only after critical evaluations have been made to determine what American political science, or any other variety, has to offer—a process he compares to import substitution.[156] Thus, this approach is essentially pragmatic, eclectic, and syncretic, and therefore does not a priori rule out the adoption of any particular foreign paradigm.

What is clear from the foregoing, however, is that irrespective of their ideological differences all African political scientists have been understandably united in their rejection of the modernization paradigm, which they perceive as blatantly ethnocentric. Ali Mazrui was the first to blow the whistle publicly on the social Darwinism implicit in the theory.[157] Around the same time another prominent African political scientist commented privately: "I can only explain the survival of the theory of political development in terms of the parochialism of Western scholars and the helplessness of the Third World scholars. It is a simplistic theory which quite arbitrarily picks out certain characteristics as desirable and assumes that some polities (the developed countries) more or less have them while others, the poor slobs (the underdeveloped countries), more or less lack them. The scientific value of such a theory is hard to see. What is not so hard to see is the consequence of the theory for the sense of superiority of some peoples and the sense of inferiority of others." It is this ethnocentric aspect of the modernization paradigm which helps to explain the curious persistence of the image that the paradigm was and remained dominant among American Africanist political scientists in the face of the reality already cited and documented (tables 9, 10, and 11), which indicates that it never had more than a few Africanist adherents, was virtually absent from political Africana of the past two decades, and more or less completely disappeared from the professional literature in general commencing in the early 1970s. However, its manifest vulnerability to charges of ethnocentrism and elitism made it eminently available for service as a whipping boy.

The exposure of the first and much of the second generation of African political scientists to various mixes of foreign traditions of political science in a socialization process in which they have been unencumbered by the parochialism of an inherited African political science tradition has, from one perspective, given them an extraordinary liberty to pick and choose from an embarrassment of riches. They have had an unfettered and cosmopolitan opportunity to reflect, critique, adapt, and innovate—indeed, even to reject totally and start from scratch—in the formulation of their own disciplinary identity, as well as to contribute to a more universal discipline. From another perspective, however, the experience has occurred in a protracted and asymmetrical condition of massive structural dependency, which provides the pretext and the provocation for a determined push toward greater relativism, as manifested in assertions of cultural nationalism, affirmations of the primacy of the insider, and hints at the "erection of intellectual tariff barriers against the importation of foreign paradigms and personnel."[158] The pluralistic and heterodox state of the African profession at this stage, as revealed by the differing orientations just discussed, suggests that no clear balance between universalism and relativism has yet been struck. Given the inherent nature of this antinomy, one could ask: Can it—or even should it—ever be struck?

Two tendencies in the African condition exert pressures for ever-greater relativism and parochialism. One is the incessant admonition that work of academic political scientists must be totally and demonstrably relevant for national development; the other is the ominous strain toward closure in academic freedom.[159] The former implies co-optation, sycophancy, and a daily ordeal of demonstrating and legitimating one's practical worth; the latter means the atrophying of the critical function of scholarship though self-censorship or exit. Nigeria has the largest, most heterodox, and most productive concentrations of political scientists in Africa, and perhaps, India aside, in the entire Third World. The reason is not just because it has greater wealth and population, but also because it is a freer and more open society.

Two of Africa's leading political scientists of divergent ideological orientation, Ali Mazrui and Claude Ake, have commented eloquently upon the imperative of a free society. In what we interpret as a defense of the quintessentiality of the critical function, Mazrui observed that "political science is par excellence a discipline of the open society. . . . [Because it is] the study of the sources of power and its utilization, [it] cannot thrive in societies which are too illiberal or too unwilling to talk about politics."[160] In the same spirit, Ake in his presidential address to the 1981 annual conference of the Nigerian Political Science Association counseled his colleagues that "we must take a firm stand against the abuse of power, the erosion of democracy and prevent a possible march to fascism. . . . [The] resort to massive repression and political absolutism . . . must not happen."[161]

The interdependence between a robust discipline of political science and a free society comes close to being a universal proposition. However else they may differ internally between themselves, both African and American political sciences share the belief that the existence of the discipline in any setting is inextricably linked, as both Mazrui and Ake suggest, to a society where a measure of freedom exists.

Appendix: Analytic Notes and Tables

Table 9 presents data on articles appearing in four selected key journals in American political science, including the American Political Science Association's official journal, the *American Political Science Review* (*APSR*), plus the leading international Africanist journal, the *Journal of Modern African Studies* (*JMAS*). During the three-decade period covered by the survey only 11 percent of the nearly 200 articles by American political scientists writing on Tropical Africa were published in *APSR*. This is understandable, given *APSR*'s emphasis upon pathbreaking methodological studies and a tendency to avoid subject matter articles. The articles of the period are divided almost evenly between those addressing a disciplinary constituency (*APSR*, *World Politics*, *Comparative Politics*, and *Com-*

parative Political Studies), and those aimed at an Africanist community of colleagues (*JMAS*), which division fairly reflects the duality in the professional identities and reference groups of political science Africanists. The special attractions of the *JMAS* for Africanist political scientists have been its internationality, its interdisciplinarity, its high credibility for careful, sustained, quality editing over the years, and its receptivity to heterodox subject matter.

The data also confirm the correlation between changes in the African political scene and shifting foci of scholarly analyses and publication. The 1950s were the nonage concerned with the nationalist buildup and bibliography; the 1960s continued to be concerned with nationalism but shifted to an emphasis upon one-party systems, political development, and political theory; and the 1970s focused upon military intervention, ethnicity, local micropolitics and the rural sector, and the international environment, in part in reaction to their neglect during the 1960s. The 1980s continued a concern with the military and displayed a heightened interest in regime consolidation, maintenance, and performance.

The data illuminate at least three other dimensions:

1. There was extremely limited concern (1.5 percent of the articles) with studies of political culture and political socialization during the thirty-year era, reflecting most likely the fact that the dynamic processes of formation of new national communal identities (nation-building) tended to be the central goal of politics.

2. There was only an evanescent interest in modernization and political development (seven articles, only 3.6 percent of the published total), and this existed mainly in the 1960s.

3. Within the framework of special emphases, there continued to be a professional concern with a wide spectrum of phenomena, reflecting the pluralistic nature of the discipline and of the subject matter of commanding interest.

The data in tables 10 and 11 were derived from dissertation titles only, on the basis of which they were classified into the working categories we created for this purpose—admittedly a hazardous process. The distinction "African" and "non-African" has been drawn according to whether or not the author's name appeared to be African. The statistics yielded by these procedures should thus be regarded as indicative rather than absolute.

The data reflect the comparative subject matter emphases of doctoral dissertations written on Tropical African topics by political scientists during the thirty-year period 1950–1980 in the United States and the United Kingdom, and 1966–1976 in France. Table 10 shows that 415 dissertations were completed in universities in the United States, of which slightly more than one-third were submitted by Africans completing their Ph.D. programs and presumably returning to become members of the emergent African political science communities in their home countries. Table 11 is complementary in showing the number of Africans who received their doctorates in the United Kingdom and France during the same period, again by comparable subject matter categories.

Both tables underscore the high prominence of the subject of international relations and foreign policy as the focus of dissertations in all three Northern Hemisphere countries. This probably reflects the lack of opportunity and the means of support during this period for both Africans and non-Africans pursuing doctorates in the North to engage in empirical research on political phenomena in Africa itself.

Table 11 reveals a remarkable international similarity in the relative emphasis given to different subjects, suggesting greater internationality in the discipline than the usual stereotypes imply. Dissertations done in the United Kingdom gave marginally greater emphasis to the study of formal institutions and constitutions than those written in the United States and in France. Among the total of 286 doctorates awarded Africans in the three countries only one appears to have been written explicitly on political development in the modernization framework. Assuming those who obtained their doctorates in the United States and the United Kingdom constituted the main pool from which African political scientists were recruited to staff universities in Anglophone African countries, then those trained in the United States would constitute 77 percent of the total. This surely indicates statistical dominance, but given the broad distribution of subjects of specialization it does not imply the dominance of one particular paradigm; rather, the data underscore the heterodoxy characteristic of the discipline.

NOTES

We are grateful for the valuable comments and criticisms we received from David Abernethy, Ladipo Adamolekun, Claude Ake, Archie Mafeje, Otwin Marenin, Ali Mazrui, Ndolam Ngokwey, Kenneth Prewitt, Donald Rothchild, Richard Sklar, George von der Muhll, Gavin Williams, and Crawford Young, and for the help at all stages of Norma Farquhar and Joseph Ngu.

1. The title's limiting modifiers "American" (for political science) and "Tropical" (for Africa) could be—but we hope they are not—interpreted as reflecting either an Americo-centrism or an insensitivity to pan-Africanism. Also, America refers only to the United States and does not

include Canada or Mexico. The delimitation is partly due to the article being an invited contribution in the form of a disciplinary self-critique to the 25th anniversary of the African Studies Association, whose membership is predominantly American (although the membership criterion is emphatically universalistic), and to the fact that for generally recognized reasons (linguistic limitations in Arabic North Africa and access constraints in white-dominated South Africa), the engagement of "American" political scientists from the United States has been, until recently, far more pronounced in the new states of Tropical Africa. The narrower focus underemphasizes the significant and enduring impact of the French and British traditions. Moreover, even the discussion of American political science herein is necessarily selective. Finally, the adjective "American" disguises the fact that, like the other social sciences, the discipline in all its heterogeneity has an ancestry that is not nationality-bound; it is the legatee of the ages, most recently of the massive brain drain from Europe in the 1930s and 1940s (e.g. Karl Deutsch, Carl Friedrich, Henry Kissinger, Leo Strauss, and many others).

2. Hodgkin and Young, of course, are well known for work in both fields: M. Crawford Young's *Politics in the Congo* (Princeton: Princeton University Press, 1965) remains the classic study of the rise of nationalism in Zaire, and Hodgkin was the dean among the group of British Marxists who launched the journal *The Review of African Political Economy*, a crucial medium in the vast expansion of literature emphasizing a political economy perspective in the study of African political systems.

3. The choice of the terms "universalism" and "relativism" to characterize the antinomy has been influenced by Fallers's trenchant essay on societal analysis in which he stresses the ultimately irresoluble paradox in the continuing tension in the social sciences between a universalistic, generalizing orientation inspired by the Enlightenment view of mankind as essentially unitary, and an orientation that emphasizes cultural-historical relativity which conditions human social life in general. See Lloyd Fallers, "Societal Analysis," *International Encyclopedia of the Social Sciences* (New York: Macmillan, 1968), 14:563–564. Some of the Great Debates in intellectual history (e.g., universalism of the French Revolution versus the cultural-historical relativism of the Burkean conservative reaction, or the universalism of Herbert Spencer's evolutionism and the extreme cultural relativism of Franz Boas's reaction) illuminate this inherent paradox and what we mean here by the two terms.

4. Although a social science, like any science, aspires to generalizations of universal validity, David Abernethy has reminded us that generalizations are not inherently universal; they can be more or less general or universal in their application, depending on the conditions specified by the analyst.

5. Cf. Fallers, "Societal Analysis," p. 576; and Lucian W. Pye, *Political*

Science and Area Studies: Rivals or Partners (Bloomington, Ind.: Indiana University Press, 1975), p. 6.

6. Thomas Hodgkin, *Nationalism in Colonial Africa* (London: Frederick Muller, 1956), pp. 16–17.

7. John Lonsdale, "States and Social Processes in Africa: A Historiographical Survey," *African Studies Review*, 24:2/3 (June-September 1981), pp. 143–144.

8. Gabriel A. Almond, Martin Chadorow, and Ray Harvey Pearce, eds., *Progress and Its Discontents* (Berkeley, Los Angeles: University of California Press, 1982).

9. Heinz Eulau, *Micro-Macro Political Inquiry* (Chicago: Aldine, 1969); Aidan Southall, "Orientations in Political Anthropology," *Canadian Journal of African Studies*, 10:2 (1976), pp. 42–52; Paul Streeten, "The Limits of Development Research," in Laurence D. Stifel, Ralph K. Davidson, and James S. Coleman, eds., *Social Sciences and Public Policy in the Developing World* (Lexington, Mass.: D. C. Heath, 1982), pp. 21–56.

10. Marvin Harris, *Cultural Materialism: The Struggle for a Science of Culture* (New York: Random House, 1979), p. 8.

11. See Joseph LaPalombara, "Whole Systems v. Partial Systems," in P. G. Lewis and D. C. Potter, eds., *The Practice of Comparative Politics* (London: Longmans, Green, 1973); Arend Lijphart, "Comparative Politics and the Comparative Method," *American Political Science Review*, 65 (September 1971), pp. 682–693.

12. Quoted in Glenn D. Paige, "The Rediscovery of Politics," in John D. Montgomery and William J. Siffin, eds., *Approaches to Development* (New York: McGraw-Hill, 1966), p. 50.

13. Cf. Ronald Rogowski, "Rationalist Theories of Politics," *World Politics*, 30:2 (January 1978), pp. 305–307.

14. Alvin W. Gouldner, *The Coming Crisis of Western Sociology* (New York: Basic Books, 1970); Otwin Marenin, "Essence and Empiricism in African Politics," *Journal of Modern African Studies*, 19 (March 1981), pp. 1–30.

15. Otwin Marenin, personal communication, December 15, 1982.

16. Cf. Rogowski, "Rationalist Theories of Politics," pp. 306–307.

17. Lonsdale, "States and Social Processes in Africa," p. 144.

18. Fred W. Riggs, "The Rise and Fall of 'Political Development,'" *Handbook of Political Behavior*, 4 (1980), pp. 289–347.

19. Carl J. Friedrich, "Political Science in the United States in Wartime," *American Political Science Review*, 41 (October 1947), p. 978.

20. John E. Trent, "Political Science Beyond Political Boundaries: The International Institutional Development," in Stein Rokkan, ed., *A Quarter-Century of International Social Science* (New Delhi: Concept Publishing Company, 1979), p. 182.

21. W. J. M. Mackenzie, "The Political Science of Political Science," *Government and Opposition*, 6 (Summer 1971), p. 297.

22. Ibid.

23. Edward Shils, "Tradition, Ecology, and Institution in the History of Sociology," *Daedalus*, 99 (Fall 1970), p. 763.

24. Harry H. Hiller, "Universality of Science and the Question of National Sociologies," *American Sociologist*, 14 (August 1979), p. 125; Paul Lamy, "The Globalization of American Sociology: Excellence or Imperialism," *American Sociologist*, 11 (May 1976), pp. 104–114.

25. This generalization requires immediate qualification if it implies that there was not significant prior development of political science in other national traditions. It developed under another rubric, as economics or political studies in England, and in the law faculties in France. For a recent detailed analysis of the earlier development of the discipline in all major countries of the world (although Africa is virtually excluded), see William G. Andrews, ed., *International Handbook of Political Science* (Westport, Conn.: Greenwood Press, 1982). Americanization, in addition to content, refers to the development of political science as an autonomous discipline with a rough consensus on its analytic boundaries, to its institutional departmentalization in a university setting, and to an emphasis upon the scientific-behavioralist dimension.

26. John E. Trent, "Institutional Development," in ibid., p. 36.

27. Shils, "Tradition, Ecology, and Institution," pp. 760–825.

28. Gouldner, *The Coming Crisis of Western Sociology*, p. 142.

29. Archie Mafeje, "The Problem of Anthropology in Historical Perspective: An Inquiry into the Growth of the Social Sciences," *Canadian Journal of African Studies*, 10:2 (1976), p. 317.

30. David Apter, "Political Studies and the Search for a Framework," in Christopher Allen and R. W. Johnson, eds., *African Perspectives* (Cambridge: Cambridge University Press, 1970), pp. 213–224; David Ricci, *Community Power and Democratic Theory* (New York: Random House, 1971), p. 206; Albert Somit and Joseph Tanenhaus, *The Development of American Political Science: From Burgess to Behavioralism* (Boston: Allyn & Bacon, 1967).

31. Mohamen Bouzidi, "Development of Political Science in North Africa," in Richard L. Merritt, ed., *International Political Science Enters the 1980s* (Ottawa: International Political Science Association, 1979), p. 208.

32. Karl W. Deutsch, "Political Science: Major Changes in the Discipline," in Stein Rokkan, ed., *A Quarter-Century of International Social Science* (New Delhi: Concept Publishing Company, 1979), pp. 171–172.

33. David B. Truman, "Disillusion and Regeneration: The Quest for a Discipline," *American Political Science Review*, 59 (December 1965), pp. 865–873.

34. Gabriel Almond, "Politics, Comparative," *International Encyclopedia of the Social Sciences*, 12:331.

35. Robert A. Packenham, *Liberal America and the Third World* (Princeton: Princeton University Press, 1973), pp. 18–22.

36. Austin Ranney, "The Divine Science: Political Engineering in American Culture," *American Political Science Review*, 70 (March 1976), p. 148.

37. Packenham, *Liberal America and the Third World*, p. 191.

38. Donald Smiley, "Must Canadian Political Science Be a Miniature Replica?" *Journal of Canadian Studies*, 1 (February 1974), p. 35.

39. Michael F. Lofchie, "Political Theory and African Politics," *Journal of Modern African Studies*, 6 (May 1968), p. 6.

40. Seymour M. Lipset, "Introduction," in Seymour M. Lipset, ed., *Politics and the Social Sciences* (New York: Oxford University Press, 1969), pp. vii–xxii; Eric A. Nordlinger, *On the Autonomy of the Democratic State* (Cambridge: Harvard University Press, 1981), pp. 1–41; Paige, "The Rediscovery of Politics," pp. 49–50.

41. Lipset, "Introduction," p. xi.

42. Brian Barry, *Sociologists, Economists and Democracy* (Chicago: University of Chicago Press, 1970), pp. 7–9.

43. Theda Skocpol, "Bringing the State Back In," *Items*, 36 (June 1982), p. 2.

44. Paige, "The Rediscovery of Politics," p. 50.

45. J. P. Nettl, "The State as a Conceptual Variable," *World Politics*, 20:4 (July 1968), p. 561.

46. Nordlinger, *On the Autonomy of the Democratic State;* Skocpol, "Bringing the State Back In," p. 1.

47. Paige, "The Rediscovery of Politics," pp. 49–58; Dankwart A. Rustow, *A World of Nations* (Washington, D.C.: The Brookings Institution, 1967), pp. 135–169; Robert C. Tucker, *Politics as Leadership* (Columbia: University of Missouri Press, 1981), pp. 9 ff.

48. Cf. Robert J. Jackson and Carl G. Rosberg, Jr., *Personal Rule in Black Africa* (Berkeley: University of California Press, 1982).

49. Nordlinger, *On the Autonomy of the Democratic State*, pp. 3 ff.; Herbert A. Simon, "The Changing Theory and Changing Practice of Public Administration," in Ithiel de Sola Pool, ed., *Contemporary Political Science: Toward Empirical Theory* (New York: McGraw-Hill, 1967), p. 87.

50. Ralph Braibanti, "Development Administration" (1975) (unpublished manuscript).

51. Smiley, "Must Canadian Political Science Be a Miniature Replica?"

52. See Lamy, "The Globalization of American Sociology," p. 107.

53. James N. Rosenau, *Linkage Politics* (New York: Free Press, 1969), p. 3, notes that all of the work of the Comparative Politics Committee of the SSRC ignored the impact of external variables and that although

Gabriel Almond's leading text on comparative politics did acknowledge the relevance of such variables, it did not make them actually part of the model. See Gabriel Almond and G. Bingham Powell, Jr., *Comparative Politics: A Developmental Approach* (Boston: Little, Brown, 1966).

54. Rosenau, *Linkage Politics.*

55. Immanuel Wallerstein, "Africa in a Capitalist World," *Issue*, 3 (Fall 1973), pp. 1–111.

56. Lofchie, "Political Theory and African Politics," pp. 5–6.

57. Charles E. Lindblom, "Another State of Mind," *American Political Science Review*, 76 (March 1982), pp. 9–21.

58. Cf. Trent, "Political Science Beyond Political Boundaries," p. 199.

59. Seymour M. Lipset, *The First New Nation* (New York: Basic Books, 1973), p. 178.

60. We are grateful to our colleague Richard L. Sklar for helpful clarification of several aspects of the neglect of Marxist studies in American political science. Increased mutual comprehension of and sophistication in Marxian analysis does not necessarily mean greater consensus; on the contrary, it could polarize and fragment because the ultimate issues are eschatological. Both Canadian and British political scientists have stressed the advantages their respective traditions offer for the serious study of Marxism. See Smiley, "Must Canadian Political Science Be a Miniature Replica?" p. 40; Colin Leys, ed., *Politics and Change in Developing Countries* (Cambridge: Cambridge University Press, 1969), p. 27.

61. Pierre L. van den Berghe, "Research in Africa: Knowledge for What?" *African Studies Review*, 13:2 (September 1970), pp. 333–336.

62. Cyril E. Black, *The Dynamics of Modernization* (New York: Harper & Row, 1966), pp. 71 ff.

63. Robert H. Bates, "People in Villages: Micro-Level Studies in Political Economy," *World Politics*, 31:1 (October 1978), pp. 129–149; Raymond F. Hopkins, "Securing Authority: The View from the Top," *World Politics*, 24:2 (January 1972), pp. 271–292; Mark Kesselman, "Order or Movement? The Literature of Political Development as Ideology," *World Politics*, 26:1 (October 1973), pp. 139–154; Donal Cruise O'Brien, "Modernization, Order, and the Erosion of a Democratic Ideal: American Political Science 1960–1970," *Journal of Development Studies*, 8:4 (July 1972), p. 363; Maxwell Owusu, "Policy Studies, Development and Political Anthropology," *Journal of Modern African Studies*, 13 (September 1975), pp. 364 ff.

64. Eulau, *Micro-Macro Political Inquiry*, p. 149.

65. Riggs, "The Rise and Fall of 'Political Development,'" pp. 289–348.

66. Sidney Verba, "Some Dilemmas in Comparative Research," *World Politics*, 20:1 (October 1967), p. 111.

67. Almond, "Politics, Comparative," p. 334.

68. David Easton, *The Political System* (New York: Alfred A. Knopf, 1953).
69. Riggs, "The Rise and Fall of 'Political Development,'" p. 304.
70. A. R. Radcliffe-Brown, *Structure and Function in Primitive Society, Essays and Addresses* (New York: Free Press, 1952).
71. Gabriel A. Almond, "Approaches to Developmental Causation," in Gabriel A. Almond, Scott C. Flanagan, and Robert J. Mundt, eds., *Crisis, Choice and Change: Historical Studies of Political Development* (Boston: Little, Brown, 1973), p. 2.
72. Almond, "Introduction: A Functional Approach to Comparative Politics," in Gabriel A. Almond and James S. Coleman, eds., *The Politics of the Developing Areas* (Princeton: Princeton University Press, 1960), pp. 26–57.
73. Almond, "Approaches to Developmental Causation," p. 2.
74. Pye, *Political Science and Area Studies*; Bryce Wood, "Area Studies," *International Encyclopedia of the Social Sciences*, 1:401–406.
75. Robert E. Ward, "Culture and the Comparative Study of Politics, or the Constipated Dialectic," *American Political Science Review*, 68 (March 1974), pp. 190–201.
76. Kenneth Prewitt, "Annual Report of the President, 1981–82," in *Social Science Research Council Annual Report 1981–1982* (New York: SSRC, 1982), pp. xv–xix.
77. Albert O. Hirschman, "The Search for Paradigms as a Hindrance to Understanding," *World Politics*, 22:3 (April 1970), p. 329, argues that "in so far as the social sciences in the United States are concerned, an important role has no doubt been played by the desperate need, on the part of the hegemonic power, for shortcuts to the understanding of multifarious reality that must be coped with and controlled and therefore be understood at once." Understanding social reality and its "laws of change" provide a hegemonic power, Hirschman notes, with a "quick theoretical fix."
78. Ann Ruth Willner, "The Underdeveloped Study of Political Development," *World Politics*, 16:3 (April 1964), p. 470.
79. A. James Gregor, "Political Science and the Uses of Functional Analysis," *American Political Science Review*, 62 (June 1968), pp. 435 ff.
80. Joseph LaPalombara, "Macrotheories and Microapplications in Comparative Politics: A Widening Chasm," *Comparative Politics*, 1 (October 1968), p. 54; cf. Leys, *Politics and Change in Developing Countries*, p. 6; Verba, "Some Dilemmas in Comparative Research," p. 112.
81. Gabriel Almond, *Political Development* (Boston: Little, Brown, 1970), p. 287.
82. Colin Leys, "Social Science, Natural Science and History: A Review Article," *Journal of Commonwealth Political Studies*, 9 (March 1971), pp. 66–67; Mafeje, "The Problem of Anthropology in Historical Perspec-

tive," p. 326; Richard Sandbrook, "The 'Crisis' in Political Development Theory," *Journal of Development Studies*," 12 (January 1976), pp. 165–182.

83. Leys, "Social Science, Natural Science and History," p. 67.

84. George Von der Muhll, personal communication, January 7, 1983.

85. Otwin Marenin, personal communication, December 15, 1982; cf. Streeten, "The Limits of Development Research," pp. 28–29.

86. René Lemarchand, "African Power through the Looking Glass," *Journal of Modern African Studies*, 11 (June 1973), p. 313.

87. See Almond, "Approaches to Developmental Causation," p. 7; Gregor, "Political Science and the Uses of Functional Analysis," pp. 425–438; Oran Young, *Systems of Political Science* (Englewood Cliffs, N.J.: Prentice-Hall, 1968), p. 37.

88. Southall, "Orientations in Political Anthropology," p. 45; Pierre L. van den Berghe, "Dialectic and Functionalism: Toward a Theoretical Synthesis," *American Sociological Review*, 28 (October 1963), p. 695.

89. Leys, *Politics and Change in Developing Countries*, p. 9.

90. Southall, "Orientations in Political Anthropology," p. 54.

91. Lofchie, "Political Theory and African Politics," p. 6.

92. Easton, "Systems Analysis in Political Science Today," p. 5; Oran Young, *Systems of Political Science*, p. 37.

93. Claude Ake, "Presidential Address, Nigerian Political Science Association," *West Africa*, May 25, 1981, p. 1163; M. Crawford Young, *Ideology and Development in Africa* (New Haven: Yale University Press, 1982), pp. 187–189. The colonial experience and its legacy was one of thoroughgoing bureaucratic authoritarianism and therefore it was from an African point of view, as David Abernethy has suggested to us, "so much a case of political output, and so little a case of responsiveness to African political inputs." Therefore, "an input-oriented political science is poorly 'positioned' to analyze the formative experience of modern Africa, the colonial experience."

94. Trent, "Political Science Beyond Political Boundaries," p. 196.

95. Prewitt, "Annual Report of the President, 1981–82," p. xiv.

96. Robert K. Merton, "Insiders and Outsiders: A Chapter in the Sociology of Knowledge," *American Journal of Sociology*, 78 (July 1972), p. 18.

97. Michael Stein, John Trent, and Andre Donneur, "Political Science in Canada in the 1980s: Achievement and Challenge," (August 14, 1982) (unpublished manuscript).

98. Kenneth Prewitt, "The Impact of the Developing World on U.S. Social Science Theory and Methodology," in Laurence D. Stifel, Ralph K. Davidson, and James S. Coleman, eds., *Social Sciences and Public Policy in the Developing World* (Lexington, Mass.: D. C. Heath, 1982), pp. 3–19.

99. Willner, "The Underdeveloped Study of Political Development."

100. Murray I. Fischel, "Political Science, Political Culture, and Africa," *Journal of Modern African Studies*, 16 (December 1978), pp. 679–685.

101. Claude Ake, *Social Science as Imperialism: The Theory of Political Development* (Lagos: University of Ibadan Press, 1979); Rigg, "The Rise and Fall of 'Political Development.'"

102. M. Crawford Young, personal communication, January 5, 1983.

103. Aristide R. Zolberg, *Creating Political Order: The Party-States of West Africa* (Chicago: Rand McNally, 1966). See Henry C. Kenski and Margaret C. Kenski, "Teaching African Politics at American Colleges and Universities," *African Studies Review*, 19:1 (September 1976), pp. 101–110.

104. Alvin Magid, "Methodological Considerations in the Study of African Political and Administrative Behavior," *African Studies Review*, 13:1 (April 1970), p. 75.

105. Hirschman, "The Search for Paradigms as a Hindrance to Understanding," pp. 329–343.

106. M. Crawford Young, personal communication, January 5, 1983.

107. Verba, "Some Dilemmas in Comparative Research," pp. 114–115.

108. Lijphart, "Comparative Politics and the Comparative Method," pp. 688–689; Reinhard Bendix, "Concepts and Generalizations in Comparative Sociological Studies," *American Sociological Review*, 28 (August 1963), pp. 532–538; Chalmers Johnson, "Political Science and East Asian Area Studies," *World Politics*, 26:4 (July 1974), pp. 560–575; Pye, *Political Science and Area Studies*; Ward, "Culture and the Comparative Study of Politics" pp. 190–201.

109. Prewitt, "Annual Report of the President, 1981–82," pp. xv–xix.

110. Richard Sklar, "The Nature of Class Domination in Africa," *Journal of Modern African Studies*," 17 (December 1979), pp. 531–532.

111. Cf. Kenski and Kenski, "Teaching African Politics at American Colleges and Universities."

112. See note 103, above; Samuel Huntington, *Political Order in Changing Societies* (New Haven: Yale University Press, 1968). See O'Brien, "Modernization, Order, and the Erosion of a Democratic Ideal."

113. Rogowski, "Rationalist Theories of Politics," p. 305.

114. Bruno S. Frey, *Modern Political Economy* (New York: John Wiley & Sons, 1978), pp. 37–52.

115. Barry, *Sociologists, Economists and Democracy*, pp. 99 ff; Frey, *Modern Political Economy*, pp. 66 ff; William C. Mitchell, "The Shape of Political Theory to Come: From Political Sociology to Political Economy," in Seymour Martin Lipset, ed., *Politics and the Social Sciences* (New York: Oxford University Press, 1969), pp. 105 ff.

116. Rogowski, "Rationalist Theories of Politics," pp. 296–297.

117. Billy Dudley, *Instability and Political Order: Politics and Crisis in Nigeria* (Ibadan: Ibadan University Press, 1973).

118. For example, Robert H. Bates, *States and Markets in Africa* (Berkeley and Los Angeles: University of California Press, 1981); James S. Coleman, "The Resurrection of Political Economy," *Mazawo*, 1 (June 1967), pp. 31–40 [Chapter 7, this volume; ed.]; Frey, *Modern Political Economy*.

119. Warren F. Ilchman and Norman Uphoff, eds., *The Political Economy of Change* (Berkeley: University of California Press, 1969); Donald Rothchild and Robert L. Curry, Jr., *Scarcity, Choice, and Public Policy in Middle Africa* (Berkeley: University of California Press, 1978).

120. Charles W. Anderson, "The Political Economy of Charles E. Lindblom," *American Political Science Review*, 72 (September 1978), p. 1012.

121. Giovanni Arrighi and John Saul, eds. *Essays on the Political Economy of Africa* (New York: Monthly Review Press, 1973); Dennis L. Cohen and John Daniel, eds., *Political Economy of Africa* (London: Longmans, Green, 1981); Richard Harris, ed., *The Political Economy of Africa* (New York: John Wiley & Sons, 1975); Editorial, *Review of African Political Economy*, 1 (1974), pp. 1–8.

122. Chris Allen, "A Bibliographical Guide to the Study of the Political Economy of Africa," in Peter C. W. Gutkind and Immanuel Wallerstein, eds., *The Political Economy of Contemporary Africa* (Beverly Hills: Sage Publications, 1976), p. 291.

123. Gavin Williams, personal communication, December 21, 1982.

124. See Leo Spitzer, "Interpreting African Intellectual History: A Critical Review of the Past Decade, 1960–1970," *African Studies Review*, 15:1 (April 1972), pp. 113–118.

125. Thomas Hodgkin, "The Relevance of 'Western' Ideas for the New African States," in J. Roland Pennock, ed., *Self Government in Modernizing Nations* (Englewood Cliffs, N.J.: Prentice-Hall, 1964), pp. 50–80.

126. See *Nigerian Journal of Political Science*, 2 (1980), p. 9.

127. Immanuel Wallerstein, "Left and Right in Africa," *Journal of Modern African Studies*, 9 (May 1971), p. 10.

128. Thomas Hodgkin, "A Note on the Language of African Nationalism," in Kenneth Kirkwood, ed., *St. Anthony's Papers Number X* (London: Chatto & Windus, 1961), p. 23.

129. *Nigerian Journal of Political Science*, 2 (1980).

130. Eulau, *Micro-Macro Political Inquiry*, p. 387.

131. Hirschman, "The Search for Paradigms as a Hindrance to Understanding."

132. Robin Horton, "African Traditional Thought and Western Science," *Africa*, 37 (January 1967), p. 50.

133. Carl E. Pletsch, "The Three Worlds, or the Division of Social

Scientific Labor, circa 1950–1975," *Comparative Studies in Society and History*, 23 (October 1981), pp. 569–590.

134. Adelel Jinadu, *Fanon: In Search of the African Revolution* (Lagos: Fourth Dimension Publishers, 1980).

135. Claude Ake, *A Political Economy of Africa* (Nigeria: Longman Nigeria Limited, 1981), p. 68.

136. E. A. Ayandele, *The Educated Elite in the Nigerian Society* (Ibadan: Ibadan University Press, 1974), p. 3.

137. Merton, "Insiders and Outsiders," p. 59.

138. Otwin Marenin, "Essence and Empiricism in African Politics," *Journal of Modern African Studies*, 19 (March 1981), p. 7

139. Yolamu Barongo's edited volume entitled *Political Science in Africa: A Critical Review* (London: Zed Press, and Ibadan: Progressive and Socialist Books Depot, 1983) for the first time provides a collection of contributions by primarily African scholars offering neo-Marxist analyses of the development of political science in Africa. One essay by the influential Nigerian Marxist Eskor Toyo—an active analyst of Nigerian, African, and international developments for well over thirty years—reinforces our contention that many African Marxists consider ethnocentrism to be an outgrowth of capitalism. He argues that it is more important to demonstrate the theoretical deficiencies of Western social science than to focus simplistically on the unsurprising ethnocentric myopia of Western intellectual tradition. The least conscious forms of Western social science ethnocentrism are the most important, according to Toyo, precisely because these can more clearly be "associated with certain other defects within the metropolitan social science itself." See Eskor Toyo, "Non-Ethnocentric Flaws in Competing Non-Marxist Paradigms of Development," in ibid., p. 156.

140. See Marenin, personal communication, December 15, 1982.

141. Jitendra Mohan, "A Whig Interpretation of African Nationalism," *The Journal of Modern African Studies*, 6 (October 1968), pp. 343–409.

142. Marenin, "Essence and Empiricism in African Politics," p. 6.

143. L. Julie Wei, "Ali Mazrui: A Confluence of Three Cultures," *Research News*, 33 (April-May 1982), p. 40.

144. Thomas Hodgkin, "Intellectual Gymnast," *New Society*, 45 (July 13, 1978), p. 86.

145. Marenin, "Essence and Empiricism in African Politics," p. 6.

146. Ali A. Mazrui, "The Making of an African Political Scientist," *International Social Science Journal*, 25:1/2 (1973), pp. 101–106; idem, *Political Values and the Educated Class in Africa*, (London: Heinemann, 1978).

147. Billy Dudley, *Parties and Politics in Northern Nigeria* (London: Cass, 1968); idem, *Instability and Political Order*; idem, *An Introduction*

to Nigerian Government and Politics (Bloomington: Indiana University Press, 1982).

148. Dudley, *An Introduction to Nigerian Government and Politics*, p. 19.

149. Ake, *Social Science as Imperialism*; idem, *A Political Economy of Africa*.

150. Jinadu, *Fanon: In Search of the African Revolution*, p. 239.

151. Quoted in Segun Osoba, "The Deepening Crisis of the Nigerian Bourgeoisie," *Review of African Political Economy*, 13 (December-September 1978), p. 64.

152. Ake, *Social Science as Imperialism*.

153. Sklar, "The Nature of Class Domination in Africa."

154. Peter Ekeh, "Colonialism and the Two Publics in Africa: A Theoretical Statement," *Comparative Studies in Society and History*, 17:1 (1975), p. 94.

155. Kiven Tungten, "Pseudo-politics and Pseudo-scholarship (in Africa)," *Transition*, 8:41 (1972), p. 26.

156. S. Egite Oyovbaire, "The Tyranny of Borrowed Paradigms and the Responsibility of Political Science: The Nigerian Experience," in Yolamu Barongo, ed., *Political Science in Africa: A Critical Review* (London: Zed Press, and Ibadan: Progressive and Socialist Books Depot, 1983), pp. 239–254.

157. Ali Mazrui, "From Social Darwinism to Current Theories of Modernization," *World Politics*, 21 (October 1969), pp. 69–82.

158. Von der Muhll, personal communication, January 7, 1983.

159. Sarfatti Magali Larson, *The Rise of Professionalism: A Sociological Analysis* (Berkeley: University of California Press, 1977), p. 63.

160. Quoted in Akiiki B. Mujaju, "Political Science and Political Science Research in Africa," *African Review*, 4:3 (1974), p. 341.

161. Ake, "Presidential Address," p. 1163.

3

UNIVERSITIES AND DEVELOPMENT IN THE THIRD WORLD

11 The Academic Freedom and Responsibilities of Foreign Scholars in African Universities

On the Nature of Academic Freedom

"Academic freedom," Eric Ashby asserts, is "an internationally recognized and unambiguous privilege of university teachers."[1] Is this proposition confirmed by experience to date as regards the academic freedom of the foreign scholar in African universities? This is the central empirical question. Or is it merely a culture-bound affirmation of a normative ideal which it is hoped might be instituted as a universal right of university teachers, irrespective of citizenship status, tenure of appointments, and the political and university systems in which they serve? Indeed, is it an ideal which can be realized, however imperfectly, or in any event, ought to be categorically affirmed as a privilege of foreign scholars serving in universities anywhere? These are among the questions Ashby's proposition provokes, and which require, at the outset, some disaggregation of the meanings and interpretations of such a highly normative and emotion-ridden concept, whose genesis and sustenance are undeniably *sui generis* to a particular cultural and historical experience.

Webster's two-dimensional definition is a useful starting point: academic freedom is the freedom of a teacher "to teach according to personal convictions about what is or appears to be the truth," and of researchers and students "to learn and inquire fully in any field of investigation," in both cases "without fear of hindrance, dismissal, or other reprisal." However, some argue that this is not an absolute personal privilege of a member of an academic community; rather, it is a specification of the functional requisite of effective performance of a particular societal role, namely,

Reprinted from *Issue* 7:2 (Summer 1977), pp. 14–33, with the author's postpublication corrections.

"that freedom of members of the academic community . . . which underlies the effective performance of their functions of teaching, learning, practice of arts, and research. The right of academic freedom is recognized in order to enable faculty members and students to carry on their roles."[2] Clearly, this is a "functional requisite" freedom, not a "human rights" freedom.

There has been a tendency to distinguish, both in convention and in commentary, between what might be called "classical institutional" freedoms and "civic participation" freedom. The guidelines of the American Association of University Professors (AAUP),[3] which are among the few explicit compendia on the subject, specify:

1. Within the university, freedom from institutional restraints as regards (a) research and publication of research results, and (b) presentation of subject matter or competence in the classroom (i.e., the classical institutional freedoms).[4]

2. Outside the university, freedom from institutional censorship or discipline when a teacher or researcher speaks or writes as a citizen (i.e., civic participation freedom). This extra-university right of "academics to carry on the same kinds of political activities as other citizens"[5] is hardly a special privilege; it only means that an academic has no special civic disability.

Presumably, within the African university, expatriate professors are entitled to the same academic freedom as indigenous professors; however, *outside* the university, the presumption is that "civic participation" freedom is *confined* to *citizens* of the country, within the limits of the civic liberties allowed by its laws, which by definition means it does not automatically exist for foreign professors.

The necessity for conceptually distinguishing *academic freedom* from *institutional autonomy* has been frequently stressed.[6] The latter includes the freedom of a university to select students and staff, to set standards and decide to whom to award its degrees, to design its own curriculum, and to decide how to allocate among its various activities such funds as are made available to it. However, logically there is an obvious interdependence, and empirically it has been made ominously clear that although some of the most serious challenges to academic freedom can come from within universities themselves, institutional autonomy (i.e., freedom from external control) is a first line of defense for protecting academic freedom. Vice Chancellor Alex Kwapong has made the point forcefully:

> A university which is a mere tool of government and a mere department of government ceases to be a university as the term is accepted and understood. A university must not only serve but also

> must challenge through critical and independent thought the orthodoxies of the moment, dissent being a necessary feature of academic integrity. . . . Hence the need for the necessary element of self-management—in the determination of curriculum, the appointment of its staff, the management of its teaching and research—which is a *sine qua non* for the essential end of academic excellence and success.[7]

Autonomy does not—cannot—mean complete independence. In almost all societies, universities acknowledge that they are financially accountable, and among the world's variety of academic traditions there is a vastly increased recognition of an accountability to "public definitions of purpose and function as well."[8] This is undoubtedly linked with the worldwide diminution of the autonomy of universities, even where it has been most highly protected, as a result of increased intervention by public authorities demanding central planning and coordination, greater accountability and efficiency in the use of resources, and more explicit commitment to societal problems and development.[9] Cognizance of this global process of redefinition and diminution of institutional autonomy, and potentially of the academic freedom it protects, is clearly relevant to an understanding of the fragility of these privileges in African universities.[10]

It is also useful conceptually to distinguish *civil liberties* from *academic freedom* and *institutional autonomy*. Civil liberties embrace that ensemble of freedoms and rights that are, or ought to be, respected and guaranteed by governments, including the freedom of speech and political discussion, organization, and activity. It is possible for a measure of academic freedom to exist in a university—either through official indifference or explicit permissiveness—at the same time that there are extremely limited civil liberties in a country; the converse could also prevail, although they are mutually reinforcing areas of freedom and tend generally to go together.

The existence and the degree of respect for all three freedoms—academic, institutional, and civic—are relative to the historical circumstances of each country. In particular, the nature of the national political system and the degree to which the freedoms have become institutionalized in conventions and structural arrangements which command the respect of public opinion and public authorities of that country. Ashby has shown how modes and structures of university governance transferred from Europe to Africa can have unintended effects opposite from those envisaged by the founders.[11] By definition, conventions (rules, customs, beliefs widely accepted and established by long usage) are unique to each society and therefore nontransferable.

Academic freedom, however its definition in an African context may be circumscribed, is subject to dynamic and evolving forces at work in the relationships between universities on the one hand and their governments and social and economic environments on the other; in the relationships within universities among administrators, professors, and students; and the quest for legitimacy on the part of universities and for stability and survival on the part of governments. These evolutionary forces produce certain patterns of response among expatriate professors and pose for them, as well, a variety of dilemmas, both moral and professional, in their efforts to define their roles. The struggle for academic freedom will increasingly be fought by the African professoriate which will have implications for the way in which expatriates become involved in the issue.

On the Nature of African Universities

There is now a fairly extensive literature on the genesis, structure, and explosive development of African universities during the past three decades.[12] We are here concerned only with how four selected features generic to those universities, as they have evolved, affect, or could affect, the academic freedoms and responsibilities of expatriate professors.

UNIVERSITY-STATE RELATIONS

At the time most of the present African universities were established (shortly before or not long after the independence of their countries), a variety of factors combined to create and maintain a distance between the universities and the new African governments during the first independence decade:

1. The initial patterns of university governance were explicitly designed by the founders to create exactly the distance which the varying imported traditions of institutional autonomy had evolved.
2. The establishment of close metropolitan dependency relationships, especially in the recruitment of expatriate staff, but in other regards as well (e.g., the U.K. special relationships formula and the Dakar-Paris and Louvain-Lovanium axes), and initial heavy funding of both capital and recurrent expenditures by external Western and international donor agencies.
3. The singular concentration upon the "replacement function" (accelerated Africanization of the public services) which perpetuated and reinforced the Eurocentric orientation of the new universities and led as well to almost uncontrollable expansion.[13]
4. The comparative political quiescence of the first wave of African

students with very little doubt on their part—or anybody else's for that matter—about gaining elite status upon graduation, and with a socialization during lower educational levels which predisposed them, in any event, to quiescent predispositions described by Prewitt and Barkan.[14] This meant initially that in many, but certainly not all, African countries university students as a category tended not to be perceived as a serious threat by governing regimes.

5. The overwhelming expatriate domination of the command posts in the administration and academic departments and in the senior ranks of the professoriate; indeed, it was a domination which extended to most university decision-making bodies. The ideological and political disposition and orientation of this initial transitional expatriate ruling class, to which many of the first generation of African academics were allied, was essentially conservative and avoided involvement with or threat to the political regimes (i.e., student political quiescence was reinforced by professorial political quiescence). As de Kiewiet concludes:

> Out of timidity, or a respect for the phenomenon of political independence, the academics of the sixties tiptoed around controversial issues involving the claims or the attitudes of governments. Thomas Balogh described this as an "uncritical and ultrapolite acceptance of whatever [emerges] as a consequence of the administrative educational and socio-economic failing of defunct imperial systems." . . . In their first form the universities held intellectual attitudes, and followed rules of academic procedure that separated them from some of the most important realities of their environment.[15]

By the end of the 1960s and as one entered the 1970s many changes, in gestation for some time, were producing a radically altered and much more intimate pattern of university-regime relationships, the essence of which was a progressive and substantial diminution of university autonomy. In all new states there has been a seemingly inexorable and inevitable movement toward more authoritarian, unitarian, etatistic, and nationalistic political systems than were originally envisaged by independence constitutions; the one-party and military takeover syndromes have now been extensively covered in the literature.[16] The latent tension inherent in university-government relationships everywhere is particularly deep in new states, and even more so in the case of insecure authoritarian civilian or military regimes.[17] At the core of this tension is the intrinsic unacceptability, indeed intolerability of the claim for *any* autonomy by *any* structure, sector, or activity within a society governed by such a regime, and the likelihood and actuality of its eruption into outright confrontation. The latent power of this inherent tension was increasingly strengthened by several factors and developments:

1. The persistently heavy, if not dominant, presence of expatriates (predominantly from the former colonial power), reinforced by African professorial colleagues (whom they selectively recruited) of essentially the same conservative persuasion because their own intellectual formation was in similar universities abroad and their own professional identities and reference groups remained there. Governing elites, in varying intensity,[18] resented being preached to by expatriates and their allied African colleagues about the categorical necessity of university autonomy. This concept was based upon an externally derived imperative that a university has a dual loyalty "on the one hand to the community it serves, on the other hand to the international fraternity of universities."[19] The smouldering university-regime differences were exacerbated by a mixture of anti-intellectualism and a deeply nationalistic frustration; there was an infuriating need to endure the continuing presence of a subtly defiant "expatriate enclave" that strained toward being a state within a state asserting a competing citizenship in a "republic of learning."[20] As Colonel Acheampong reportedly once demanded, "What are our universities for, anyway?"

2. The regimes' overriding concern for stability and their own survival heightened the inherent suspicion that universities were the main actual or potential sources of hostile criticism and serious opposition, as well as political instability.[21]

3. The first phase of student quietism gave way to increasing demonstrations and protests, culminating in the closing down of eleven universities in 1971 ("the year of the students"). The reaction by governments was drastic everywhere, in some cases draconian (i.e., Zaire, Senegal, Ethiopia, Zambia, and Nigeria). The causes were varied, ranging from ordinary "barracks gripes" to explicitly antiregime demonstrations. In some instances the precipitant was a deeply felt foreign policy issue in African affairs (or difference with the regime regarding its foreign policy position). A reinforcing factor in many instances was a growing perception of saturation—and hence diminution—of postuniversity employment opportunities; the "replacement function" of universities was increasingly being fulfilled. In Francophone Africa, a common feature was protest against the continued heavy dependence upon and control by the French metropolitan university system and the cultural domination it represented, both symbolically and actually.[22] In several instances the continued presence of expatriate professors (or those of certain types) was the object of complaint by the students; in others expatriates were blamed (and

deported) by regimes for allegedly misleading the students (Ghana, Zambia, and Zaire).[23] There was no common pattern.

4. A striking feature of the no-nonsense, nonnegotiable, and fairly drastic responses by the challenged regimes (whether of the radical or conservative variety) was their unequivocal support of university administrations against the students. In some instances, this reflected common agreement among public and university authorities regarding the frequently unreasonable, self-serving, amenities-refinement motivations for student protests (viewed obviously from the perspective of the wide gap between their relatively pampered lifestyle and the extreme poverty of the peasant masses, but not of the gap between that of the students and the elegant lifestyle of the governing elite and bureaucratic bourgeoisie, the reference group of the students). The relative quiescence and silence of the professoriate, both expatriate and national, facilitated this university-government common front. Perhaps more significantly, however, by the early seventies the central authorities in the top command posts and decision-making bodies of the universities were either appointees of, or deferential to, the governing regimes.[24] In any event, among the consequences of the widespread student challenges to regimes during the late sixties and early seventies was a stronger regime suspicion of universities as bases of opposition and discontent, a greater questioning of the fundamental purposes of universities, and a deeper penetration by regimes into vital areas of decision-making previously within the sacrosanct realm of university autonomy.[25]

The propensity for regimes increasingly to extend their control over universities has been vastly enhanced by the fact that they are extremely high-cost institutions. Both absolutely and relative to the cost of other institutions, and through seemingly uncontrolled expansion, universities have become financially almost prohibitive. The halcyon first phase of their development was marked by massive external assistance for higher education, the unquestionably transcendent priority of Africanizing high-level manpower positions in the society, and the initial independence endowment of financial reserves in many countries. In the early days opportunity costs and cost-benefit considerations were largely ignored. However, commencing in the early seventies university budgets were subjected to ever greater scrutiny and control by governments. This was partly because the pressures to fulfill the replacement function were beginning to dissipate (although these were increasingly countered by new and expanding political pressures from the hordes of secondary school graduates clamoring for university entry irrespective of the graduate job market), but mainly because of a disastrous deterioration in the general economic situation for reasons well known. Increasing government control was also due to the emergence of a far higher priority claimant in the allocation of national revenues, namely, the military establishment (whether self-service when in power or as a feared and pampered force by civilian regimes).[26]

The financial dependence of African universities upon governments not only renders them vulnerable to intervention and control on budgetary matters by political leaders and civil servants with anti-intellectual prejudices, but it underscores their total dependence in general upon the state. As Vice Chancellor Kwapong noted:

> Universities in these countries are public institutions . . . created on public initiative and, as a result of public policy, are charged with urgent public national responsibilities. . . . [In contrast] there is the very important private sector of universities in the United States and Europe which exists outside the public government structure. . . . these old and prestigious institutions exercise this push or pull toward autonomy and academic freedom, but so do the great public institutions that have been modeled upon and have developed more or less as public versions of these private institutions.[27]

The university-state intimacy in most African countries is reinforced by the singularity, centrality, and visibility of *the* national university. Its problems and crises become major national political issues and many have been inescapably drawn into the vortex of partisan politics.[28]

Closeness has also been deliberately fostered in the inexorable movement toward each country having its own national university. However overpoweringly rational and logical (in an economizing sense) the argument may have been for "regional" universities (most notably the University of Dakar serving functionally much of Francophone West Africa, and the University of East Africa serving constitutionally the three countries of East Africa), it was both natural and inevitable for each country to establish its own national university as an instrument in furthering movement along its distinctive path of national development.[29]

THE PRIMACY OF UNIVERSITY ADMINISTRATORS

Although the inherited traditions of university governance presumed primacy of academics and academic bodies, it was the university administration which was the first component of the presumptive university community to be Africanized. This occurred extremely rapidly in most instances, particularly in Anglophonic Africa, mainly because of the belief—long a part of the British tradition (in Britain as well as in her dependencies)—that any good arts (or better, classics!) graduate is qualified (indeed, best qualified) to be an administrator. This conception prevailed as well in the public service. Beshir notes as regards the University of Khartoum that at the time of the creation of an independent University of Khartoum in 1956 the executive decision-making regarding academic affairs was in the hands of expatriates, and that the Sudanization of the university administration was given priority for both practical and logical considerations because "Sudanese qualified to take over the senior administrative posts were available" but "there were few Sudanese who were sufficiently qualified for the academic staff."[30] Within four years the university administration was completely Sudanized, yet twelve years later a majority of the professors in the University were still expatriate, although 80 percent of the total staff was Sudanese.

It has been suggested by Chagula that one of the reasons for accelerated Africanization of the senior administrative staff in universities was to avoid a possible misinterpretation by governments that expatriate pronouncements on controversial subjects constitute the views of the universities.

> It is partly to avoid situations such as this that it was rightly decided several years ago that the senior administrative staff in each college should be nationals of one of the East African countries. For they should be best qualified to advise and guide the largely expatriate academic staff in various matters pertaining to relations between the college on the one hand and the governments and the public on the other.[31]

Among the consequences of this imbalance between an expatriate dominant academic component and a national dominant administrator component in the internal authority structure of most universities has been an internal tension of varying intensity between the components with the consequent absence of any sense of university community. It has also meant the early establishment and subsequent consolidation and acceptance of the primacy of the university administration. Virtually everywhere, the center of gravity in decision-making has tended to become lodged in the administration, and although there are numerous examples of extraordinarily able and efficient administrators, in many cases an administrative "command ethos" has developed. This has frustrated the emergence (or extinguished the existence) of any strong institutional loyalty on the part of an increasing number of alienated academics. An illuminating exception, among others, has been the impressive experience of the University of Ibadan in which "the internal control of university affairs remained solidly in the hands of academics as opposed to administrators."[32]

Top university administrators have pursued different strategies of defense for their institutions in confrontations with governing regimes. They are inescapably placed in an ambivalent position; the most responsible and effective course of action is often ambiguous. Whether subservient or allied to the political elite, or simply honest believers that a nonconfrontation strategy is not only realistic but more effective, most have pursued a strategy of trying to defuse government-universities crises by working quietly behind the scenes and not defiantly resisting government actions. Few have emerged from the torturous experience with the plaudits of their expatriate critics. There have been two notable exceptions. One was the impressive struggle by Dr. Conor Cruise O'Brien, expatriate vice chancellor of the University of Ghana, to preserve the autonomy of his university against the ominous threats of the Nkrumah regime during the period 1962–1963.[33] The other was the defiant defense, under strong pressure from Sierra Leone's first military regime, of the autonomy and principle of academic freedom at Fourah Bay College, the University of Sierra Leone, by its citizen principal, Dr. Davidson Nicol. Dr. Nicol's report of his confrontation speaks for itself:

> The college, as a whole, did not welcome the formation of an army-police regime as a government and strongly insisted that there should be an immediate return to civilian rule. . . . In a letter to the press [the principal] . . . clearly stated that as a university college we were unable to declare loyalty to the regime as other groups had done and were doing. . . . The principal was called before a full meeting of the army and police officers of the NRC and . . . asked to withdraw his remarks in the press by another letter but he refused categorically. . . . [They then demanded an assurance] that no criticism of the regime would be made by the principal. The latter refused to give this assurance, asserting again that the reputation of a university institution for maintaining the fearless and eternal nature of truth could not be compromised or surrendered however great the pressure of expediency or of contemporary events. The possibility of detaining the principal in prison was apparently seriously discussed at this and subsequent meetings but was never carried out.[34]

Dr. O'Brien, a scholar-statesman of international stature, was among the last expatriate university heads to serve in Africa. Dr. Nicol, an internationally recognized scientist, was apparently untouchable, not only in his own right, but also as head of Black Africa's oldest university (1827), a commentary on the resilience of a national structure which has become solidly institutionalized.[35] In any event, the record of the past decade reveals no similar cases of such open, spirited resistance as was displayed by these two top university administrators when faced by a challenge from a regime. Recent experiences, such as those of the University of Zambia and Ahmadu Bello University, reveal a different and far less outspoken strategy of institutional defense.

FRAGILITY OF THE LEGITIMACY OF NEW UNIVERSITIES

There is undoubtedly no other structure established in new states less amenable to legitimation and institutionalization than the modern university. No other major structure is so exotic and foreign in its cultural conceptions; in its dependence on external contacts and professional relationships; the proportion of foreign personnel who occupy roles in it; the agonizing slowness with which those roles can be and are Africanized (be it noted that everywhere, governments have tended to give Africanizing the academic staff of universities the absolutely lowest priority); its inherent resistance to adaptation; and in the difficulty it has in validating its worth to the nation on a cost-benefit basis. Strong African vice chancellors have waxed eloquent on this painful dilemma:

> These new institutions have to work their passage and thus they are without the legitimacy and authenticity born of long performance and traditional acceptance. This is an important factor. The lack of legitimacy of the new institutions means that factors which are taken for granted in older places are called into question. This is even more complicated when [they] have to rely mainly upon foreigners and foreign institutions.[36]

> The modern university scholar is an entirely new type of person in Nigeria, not identified with any traditional role. The condition for such a type to flourish, such as academic freedom, is therefore an entirely new conception . . . [that] has still to justify itself in the Nigerian context. . . . The really cogent arguments for academic freedom . . . although applicable to Nigeria, are derived from other situations. The scholar has not yet fully arrived in Nigeria, and the advantages to be gained by giving him freedom are not yet obvious.[37]

> The idea of the university is tolerated but not truly accepted in Africa, either by the masses who pay taxes, or by the political leaders who dispense the taxes. . . . The problem of indigenizing

> our universities goes beyond the question of the relevance of the curricula. It involves the whole question of identity and continuity with African tradition.[38]

The history of institution-building teaches at least two fundamental points. One is that when new structures of any kind are established they become institutions only through leadership pursuing policies aimed at their progressive legitimation. And since the dawn of nationalism, and no less in the contemporary African situation, that legitimating leadership must be indigenous. Expatriates can help to create *structures* (i.e., presumptive institutions), but they cannot themselves build *institutions* in other lands; even their physical presence can at best inhibit the process, and their activist presence or protracted occupancy of command positions can be the kiss of death.[39] The second point is that institutionalization is a long, slow, highly chancy, nonunilinear process of progressive habituation to and heightened valuation of structure, in which luck is a major ingredient. African universities are extraordinarily fragile, nonlegitimated structures both because they are perceived as still mainly foreign and because of the brevity of their existence. Foreign professors who come to African universities with the determination and belief that in directing roles they personally can build institutions—as distinguished from subtle and unobtrusive facilitation of their emergence—are pursuing a chimera.

PERMISSIVE AUTHORITARIANISM

In a surprising number of countries in the Third and Fourth Worlds one finds a curious combination of political authoritarianism and a considerable degree of de facto freedom for teaching and research in universities. There are obvious exceptions (e.g., contemporary Ethiopia and Uganda), and it is a limited freedom in the narrow sense of nonintervention into what goes on in the classroom or the research seminar, as distinguished from the broader conception of human rights and civil liberties which generally exist precariously or not at all. A decade ago Ashby noted:

> There have occasionally been complaints and tensions about the teaching of some academics, but we doubt whether there are any well-authenticated cases of teachers being victimised for opinions they have expressed in the classroom. . . . [However] if the definition of academic freedom is broadened to cover the right of academics to hold political opinions distasteful to the government, then cases have occurred.[40]

Cases have indeed occurred in the decade since, but it is difficult in most instances to establish conclusively from the evidence available whether punitive or intimidatory actions against expatriate professors were incidents of *academic* restrictions or violations of human rights. In the former case, professors were "teaching according to personal convictions about what is or appears to be the truth," *in the classroom*, in which case they suffered a clear denial of academic freedom; in the latter case, actions against professors were based on their extramural political activities which governing regimes found unacceptable for *raisons d'état*, whereby there was a denial of civil liberties and human rights. The significant feature of the two celebrated cases of 1976—the detainment and subsequent deportation of five expatriate lecturers by the University of Zambia and the reported intimidation of eight expatriate lecturers at Nigeria's Ahmadu Bello University—was in both instances the vagueness or silence regarding the precise offenses allegedly committed. It was never made explicit by governmental or university authorities in either case whether the actions against the victimized expatriates were for intramural or extramural expressions or activities. This may itself be a significant commentary on the extreme reluctance of authoritarian regimes and hypercautious university officials to admit openly to deprivations of academic freedom.[41]

The fact that authoritarianism—and increasingly its military variety—is becoming a prevailing form of political regime in Africa hardly needs documentation. Neither is it necessary to document the relative frailty of the machinery for the enforcement of human rights in new states; the Winter 1976 *Issue* confronted this sensitive problem with candor and objectivity.[42] What is difficult to demonstrate is that this authoritarian orientation is accompanied by overt and explicit denial of freedom within academe. Such denial may be omnipresent as a threat, and actualized in confrontation situations, but the anomaly of an ostensibly permissive authoritarianism vis-à-vis academe prevails. How is this explained? One clue may be found in the special nature of what Crawford Young has called "the remarkable phenomenon of minimal coercion authoritarianism," in which the mechanism of control is not terror, nor large-scale repression and imprisonment, but a repertoire of informal techniques of control and pressure (e.g., co-optation and rewards mixed with the threat of withdrawal of resources and status).[43] The authoritarian socialization of the colonial epoch, the still vivid memories of the failure of early postindependence democratic experiments, adroit management and manipulation of ethnicity, and the absence of any perceived alternatives are possible reinforcing or predisposing factors making minimal coercion sufficient for regime survival. Also, most authoritarian regimes, particularly of the military variety, are putatively nonideological; thus what is taught or researched in the universities is in some cases not perceived as threatening to any explicit ideological rationalization of a regime's legitimacy.[44]

There is also the understandable effort by authoritarian regimes to minimize or avoid international criticism and censure, which overt and explicit denials of academic freedom to expatriate professors would assuredly provoke, at least from some external circles. Such sensibility obviously varies in its significance and weight, as well as manifestation, among regimes as well as among differing circumstances and authorities in one regime; its restraining power can be both exaggerated and underrated. Many contemporary authoritarian regimes came to power faced with fairly well-developed universities which embodied the ethos, structures, and procedures associated with university autonomy and academic freedom of Western university traditions; they had as well vigorous social science departments. Overt denials of already existent academic freedoms are far more visibly provocative and morally censurable than implicit denials achieved largely by avoiding the problem *ab initio* (e.g., the creation of its own university by an authoritarian regime in which the social sciences are excluded altogether, as in the University of Malawi).

Universities, more than other national structures, are linked in a variety of ways to an international network of national and international institutions and to an international scientific community. National universities are unique sources of dignity and pride, as well as instruments for and symbols of co-equal participation in the world community. Notwithstanding the anti-intellectualism of some military regimes, education in Africa has remained supremely valued, and normally, pride of place goes to a national university, the apex of the national education system and reputedly the prized gate to upward mobility. Even the semiliterate dictator Field Marshal Idi Amin appears to have taken great pride in wearing his academic gowns at convocation ceremonies as Chancellor of Makerere University, and Emperor Bokasa I has graced his national university with his name. Moreover, despite the general *faiblesse* of human rights in new states and the ambivalences about how much they really care for international opinion, or for that matter universities, authoritarian regimes have been seemingly reluctant to demean their national universities in the eyes of the world by overt denials of academic freedom to resident expatriate professors. Other, more subtle, devices have been available, such as the threat of nonrenewal of contracts to hyperactive expatriates. Indigenous professors generally have not enjoyed the same relative invulnerability, subject as they are to the array of informal coercive mechanisms authoritarian regimes can employ to maximize the quiet self-censorship of the indigenous professoriate.

Another range of explanations for permissive authoritarianism is that such regimes are either ignorant of or insensitive—or possibly even indifferent—to any threat from the results of so-called sensitive research or from the free classroom discussion of ideas and realities. At the crudest level the argument would be that the authoritarian leaders neither read the literature nor understand the issues involved. Also, the immediacy of any threat is possibly judged by them to be so remote as not worth the efforts required to control it, or the likely opprobrium such efforts would evoke. More convincing would be the explanation that monitoring research and teaching require the sophistication, determination, and resources of a totalitarian regime, none of which is possessed by existing "minimal-coercion" authoritarian regimes. As Leys notes, "It is not really possible for outside bodies to control research very closely, and on the whole governments do not try to."[45] Indeed, permissiveness toward academe could serve the purposes of authoritarian regimes in a positive sense, as Robert Arnove has argued:

> It is a curious situation that regimes like those of Brazil tolerate the writings of radical social scientists. . . . Either the regimes are ignorant of this literature, which has received international recognition—an unlikely case—or the writings of these individuals pose no serious threat to the political system. The research is not threatening probably for two reasons: (1) it is not intelligible to the masses, for certainly, if the same sentiments were expressed not in academic journals—but from a street corner or as part of a political movement which mobilized large numbers—the individuals would be jailed or exiled; and (2) the regime itself benefits from the knowledge generated, while simultaneously enhancing its international image of permitting academic freedom.[46]

Moreover, most regimes are aware of the suppressive power of co-optation, one of the most effective instruments of minimal-coercion authoritarianism. Presumptively, most students—even those being exposed to and accepting the most radical ideas—will ultimately join or accommodate to the regime in one way or another, as they overwhelmingly have done, because of either the absence of other career opportunities or the seductive rewards that accompany accommodation. This also explains the special intolerance of such regimes regarding the indigenous professors who refuse to accommodate.

Beyond all of the foregoing possible interpretations of the curious coexistence of political authoritarianism and a de facto measure of academic freedom in African universities there remains the immeasurable but undoubtedly substantial degree of self-censorship by the expatriate university professoriate. As Leys argues, "Most of the constraint arises from the self-censorship of academics failing to tackle subjects which they . . . think will give rise to controversy."[47] Conclusion: Authoritarianism is permissive because the professoriate is deferentially self-restrained.

The reasons for such restraint among expatriates are manifestly varied. The range of self-serving concerns is wide; they include the elementary desire to have and keep a job (i.e., to avoid deportation and to ensure contract renewal), the hypothesized psychic need for "guilt atonement" (see van den Berghe, below), careerism in an academic market normally less competitive than at home, and all of the other attractions of being "Tarzan," so brilliantly described by Paul Theroux.[48] Self-restraint can also be the result of that sense of deference and nonintervention considered proper for a foreign visitor, of a distaste for neo-missionarying, or of a reluctance to make quixotic demands for standards inapplicable to or unrealizable in the local context. Or they are concerned about their careers in their own countries, either because they are sent by their governments or because they are afraid of not being able to gain reentry into their own university system.

Self-censorship in teaching and publication can also be rationalized by some as prudent for the duration of expatriate service and data-gathering, confident that one's scholarly courage can be vindicated by full and frank dissemination of the truth as one sees it once one has left the country. Others may feel constrained by the technical assistance organizations which finance their appointments,[49] even when it is stressed that their identification must be with the university in which they serve and the role they undertake to perform. There are still others where the question of self-restraint does not arise; either by nature or persuasion they avoid conflict; or they conceive their function to be purely technocratic and wish to be left alone to do their thing, or they are totally indifferent to the moral, professional, and institutional issues and dilemmas involved. Finally, self-censorship for some reflects a reluctance to be prescriptive or advocatory (either directly or through conclusions which inescapably emerge from objective analysis) where personally they do not have to suffer the ultimate consequences. Paul Streeten has described the dilemma of this restraint, observing that it is something about which he is personally schizophrenic:

> Assume a careful analysis leads to the conclusion that a radical redistribution of assets and power is a condition of progress. Can we then tell citizens of other countries to adopt these radical

> changes which may require a revolution? At the level of independent, objective analysis, there is nothing wrong with saying such changes are necessary, where they are seen to be. But for an outsider to say this may be condemned not only as an easy option (nothing is easier than to be radical for another country), but also as counterproductive. These changes, by definition, are going to hurt some people. . . . What some may regard as supporting and well-wishing outside pressures, others will see as the kiss of death, or at least an embarrassing embrace. So here is the dilemma. Honest research bids us expose the political constraints and point to the radical solutions, but it may be both improper and counterproductive for foreigners to recommend painful and possibly bloody domestic reform.[50]

What are the tolerable limits of self-restraint consistent with commitment to the quest for truth, to scientific objectivity, and to speaking the truth as one sees it? This is indeed the quintessential dilemma of the expatriate professor.

THE DILEMMAS OF A RESPONSIBLE EXPATRIATE PROFESSOR

"It is a significant and melancholy fact," Ashby lamented in 1970, "that neither the American Association of University Professors (AAUP) nor the British Association of University Teachers have clearly enunciated the responsibilities of the academic profession, though they have a good deal to say about the profession's rights."[51] Actually, that very year, in the sobering aftermath of the campus revolutions of the late sixties, the AAUP endeavored to clarify its baseline position set forth in the 1940 Statement of Principles on Academic Freedom and Tenure by its "1970 Interpretative Comments," in which it stressed that "membership in the academic profession carries with it special responsibilities."[52] Two of these are positive responsibilities, namely, a university professor's "particular obligation" to (1) "promote the conditions of free inquiry and to further public understanding of academic freedom," and (2) to "show respect for the opinion of others." Two other responsibilities are essentially restrictive qualifications to total academic freedom, namely, (3) in the classroom, "the teacher should be careful not to introduce into his teaching controversial matter which has no relation to his subject" (qualified in 1970 to stress that "controversy is at the heart of free academic inquiry" and that the intent was to "underscore the need for the teacher to avoid persistently intruding material which has no relation to his subject"), and (4) outside the classroom to "make every effort to indicate that he is not an institutional spokesman."[53] This restatement was made within the framework of (a) the 1967 U.S. Supreme Court decision that academic freedom is a right protected by the First Amendment of the U.S. Constitution and (b) the AAUP observation that its specification of rights and responsibilities is not a "static code but a . . . framework of norms to guide adaptations to changing times and circumstances."[54] This curious juxtaposition of a categorical imperative with an acknowledged temporal and situational relativity in its application is characteristic—and perhaps inherently so—of all commentary on and analyses of this dilemma-laden subject.

Taking into consideration the foregoing only known written specifications of the responsibilities corollary to academic freedoms, but mindful that they are emanations of a particular culture and therefore not universally prescriptive, our purpose here is to examine selectively the nature of the presumed responsibilities of expatriate professors in African universities. This will be done under three rubrics: (1) respect for the idea of the "developmental university"; (2) protection of the political neutrality of the university; and (3) effective role performance.

THE DEVELOPMENTAL IMPERATIVE

In the early 1960s most African universities were either only in gestation or in the first phase of their own establishment. Although their initial charge was to concentrate on producing quantitatively the high-level manpower required to fulfill the replacement-of-expatriates function, there were already indications of a large presumptive "developmental" responsibility. At the 1962 UNESCO (Tananarive) Conference on the Development of Higher Education in Africa, this larger and more ambitious charge was that they become "the main instrument of national progress."[55] Increasingly, insistence upon the "development" mission of the university has become ever more prominent in the rhetoric about higher education in Africa. Thus, on its creation in 1963 the University of East Africa was enjoined to "apply itself to the formidable problems that best us in East Africa, political, economic, social and cultural, and contribute to their solution. . . . Above all the University should be relevant to our situation."[56] The exhortation that an African university must be demonstrably relevant for and totally committed to national development has now become so incessant and all-engulfing that it saturates all speeches, studies, debates, and discussion of the raison d'être of the institution. In part this may only reflect a more general African phenomenon, what Carl Widstrand has called "development by exhortation." Of course, this insistence that a university be "relevant" is a global phenomenon, albeit with variant meanings; indeed, as Shils notes, "ever since the nineteenth century and above all in the United States [there has] been a demand that the universities should cease to be 'ivory towers' and should contribute directly to the well-being of their societies."[57] However, during the past decade the development-relevance imperative for African universities has probably reached its apotheosis, articulated as vigorously—possibly more so—by outsiders as by African leaders themselves. In any event, an expatriate professor is expected to be "developmentally" oriented.

At first glance it seems difficult to refute the logic of the "developmental university," namely, the proposition that such an extraordinarily high-cost structure embracing and concentrating most of the scientific and intellectual resources of a country should be made maximally relevant to the practical problems of development. There are other reinforcing reasons as well, as Leys and Shaw have noted:

> The value of the "developmental concept" and the cluster of altered ideals which it stands for, must not be underrated. It provides a powerful slogan for Vice Chancellors and others struggling to bring about institutional changes. . . . It enables them to defend themselves against the criticism of being indifferent to urgent national needs, of pursuing useless knowledge at great cost and of being insufficiently sympathetic to the policies of the government. It earns sympathy among aid donors, too, to justify aid for higher education in relation to aid for other things. It permits imaginative experimentation and allows donors, too, to justify innovations in their aid patterns. In general it tends to expose established practices to critical review.[58]

Some of the most penetrating critics of the obsessive concern with the development-relevance imperative (e.g., Edward Shils and Colin Leys, each from somewhat different perspectives) acknowledge its importance in African countries as a means of furthering the legitimation of the universities.[59] The main argument has been how extensive and direct the commitment to vocational and development functions should or can be, and, more fundamentally, what "development" is all about.

The assumption by an African university of an explicit responsibility for helping to solve problems of national development generates or aggravates problems and dilemmas which affect its own development. Obviously, undertaking such a responsibility heightens its political vulnerability because it reduces (indeed, it could reduce to extinction, that is, the university could become a department of government) the necessary distance between the university and the state.[60] What is tolerable closeness?

Clearly, this can only be answered within the context of the distinctive pattern of university-state relationships of each country. But there is a real dilemma: a university can maintain the minimum freedom and autonomy requisite for effectiveness only if it deeply involves itself in concrete development functions to demonstrate its relevance, which engagement *ipso facto* jeopardizes its freedom and autonomy. Harland Cleveland has quoted the conversation of two Asian university presidents on this point: one opined, "The marriage with Caesar *must* be consummated. . . . there's no alternative." "Agreed," replied the other. "But the question is, how many times a week?"[61]

Undertaking heavy development commitments also created what Leys and Shaw have called "functional overload and incompatibilities":

> Most of the new functions to be added to the traditional functions of universities under the developmental approach will fail to be performed by the academic staff responsible for these traditional functions. . . . Some of the new functions may well be performed less well than if they had been entrusted to other agencies while some of the old ones frequently suffer. Probably the first casualty is original research. . . . The "developmental" university offers severe temptations to its staff to devote energy to things for which they are not necessarily well qualified . . . and not doing what at least no one else is paid to do, namely writing serious books about their subjects.[62]

Such commitments also overload an already heavily burdened university administration which in many instances, due to the omnipresent shortage of administrative skills and experience, further reduces the effectiveness of the university in performing *any* of its functions—traditional or developmental. Thus, there is a second dilemma: a university can acquire desperately needed credibility and thereby accumulate legitimacy (thus fortifying its autonomy and academic freedom) only by undertaking developmental functions, which because of both academic and administrative "overload" cannot be performed effectively, and which inescapably require an expansion in the number of expatriates,[63] neither of which is likely to be conducive either to an image of credibility or to a growth of legitimacy. Francis Sutton's caution is in point: "We are learning in the advanced countries that too much can be expected of universities and there is danger in imposing weighty expectations on struggling new ones in social environments where they have yet no settled place."[64]

The arguments that serious efforts to implement the "developmental university" are likely to be self-defeating strategies (i.e., that they will make universities "handmaidens" or "departments" of governments, denying them the minimum requisite freedoms to be genuine universities, and that they encourage them pretentiously to undertake inherently incompatible and nonperformable functions) are only statements of hypothetical probabilities; they have not yet been verified. The initial efforts to implement the "developmental university" concept at the University of Dar es Salaam, as well as numerous other experiments examined in a recent broad comparative study, suggest that fairly significant university involvement in development activities is not incompatible with the continued existence of considerable academic freedom and the adequate performance of traditional university functions.[65]

However, one cannot ignore the fact that the "developmental university" ethos, with its insistence upon applied research and direct involvement in concrete problems of societal development, can be incongruent with the research norms and competencies which most expatriate professors bring with them. As regards norms, these could include a strong belief that quintessentially academic freedom is the individual freedom of a scholar to do "his own thing," or that preoccupation with applied research is basically demeaning to a scientific discipline. As Streeten argues, objecting to the imperative that research must be, and must be seen to be, in the service of the host country and its people, the primary obligation of the researcher is "to advance the subject, therefore [his responsibility] is to the international fraternity of scholars, whether inside or outside of the host country."[66] As regards competency, not many expatriate scholars, particularly from the United States and Europe, have acquired a competence, through either their training or experience, to carry out applied developmental research, let alone to guide, instruct, and direct others how to do it.[67]

A third dimension of the "developmental university" movement is the fundamental rethinking and change in perception which has occurred in recent years regarding the causes of underdevelopment and what constitutes the meaning and the measure of development. The nature of this change and its consequence for universities in Africa was crystallized in a provocative speech by Colin Leys at a meeting of Commonwealth vice chancellors in 1971:

> Throughout the underdeveloped world a confrontation is developing between two opposed views of the causes of underdevelopment and the goals of development. The established view . . . sees the

> causes of underdevelopment in terms of accidents of history and geography which made some countries start out late on the path of modernisation and economic growth. . . . they are seen as suffering from constraints which must be overcome by the supply of missing *inputs* such as capital or education or management skills. . . . The opposing view is essentially Marxist in its intellectual origins, though by now it is tending to command a substantial non-Marxist following. It sees underdevelopment as a specific condition of the ex-colonial countries corresponding to, and making possible, the development of the capitalist countries in the West. . . . Capitalism is rejected as being simply not available [to them] as a basis for development; it is seen as being a world system which by its very nature allocates to the underdeveloped countries a permanent place at the bottom of the ladder. From this point of view . . . it is only a short step to identifying the universities, to the extent that they still transmit a predominantly Western culture, as institutions for transmitting to the rising elite a culture which endorses capitalism, and hence as major *instruments of underdevelopment* along with foreign companies and the rest of the neo-colonial apparatus.[68]

Leys argues that the old concept of universities as "instruments of development," rooted as it is in a linear theory of development in which one fills "missing components" or overcomes obstacles and impediments, comes "dangerously close to a surrender of their very identity as centres of fundamental thinking and intellectual leadership." These functions, if exercised, could "call in question the whole basis of the symbiosis between them and their governments which was so carefully cultivated in the last ten years."

This confrontation between two perspectives (the linear developmentalist versus the nonlinear dependency perspective) is reflected in a vigorous ongoing debate among academics in African universities. In this dialogue, members of the expatriate social science professoriate are understandably in the eye of the storm. The debate has resulted in a categorization and stereotyping of scholars according to their theoretical approaches, conceptual frameworks, modes and tools of analysis, teaching methods, content of courses, and the subject matter and methodology of research—all are presumptively "perspective-bound."[69] The debate has introduced a far sharper and more simple criterion for discriminating between what is relevant in teaching and research and what is not. A researcher who conducts research the results of which could be ameliorative of the existing state of affairs can be viewed as a mere "system tinkerer," consciously, or unwittingly, supportive of existing repressive regimes in particular, and of the whole dependency system in general.[70] As Paul Streeten has put it:

> On the linear, missing components view, research . . . can contribute bits of knowledge and thereby remove a particular constraint. On the neo-Marxian view, research may itself be part and parcel of the international oppressive or at least impeding system, depriving the developing countries of brains, or diverting the attention of their brains to irrelevant problems or inducing them to produce apologies for their ruling class and the unjustifiable world system.[71]

The tendency toward simplism in the developmentalist/dependency dichotomy regarding "relevant" scholarship suggests Eldridge Cleaver's dictum that "if you're not part of the solution, you're part of the problem."[72]

Leys notes that the radical perspective, although intellectually rooted in Marxism, is not confined to Marxists. "A growing number of non-Marxists," Streeten agrees, "have come to attribute a large part of underdevelopment to the existence and the policies of the industrial countries of the west, including Japan and the Soviet Union."[73] Indeed, so-called "radicals" are, like everyone else, broadly distributed along a spectrum on the dependency dimension, and the Marxians among them are fragmented often very sharply on the ideological dimension. It is a perspective which has been reinforced by a concern over what is believed or proven to be a link between some expatriate academics and neo-imperialists or Western intelligence activities.[74] However, the "handmaiden to Caesar's" orientation of an expatriate professor in an African university need have nothing to do with any ideological orientation; on the contrary, as van den Berghe has argued, it can simply be a racial hangup:

> Most white American scholars carry with them a burden of collective racial guilt. . . . The way to atone for the past and present sins of our "race" and to absolve ourselves of the charge of neo-colonialism, we are told, is to "serve the needs of Africa," to do research defined as relevant by Africans, to contribute to the development of African universities. . . . Translated in practice, these ostensibly impeccable precepts mean that Western scholars in Africa must serve the interests of the black mandarinate which succeeded the European administrators in office. They must become the handmaidens of the new ruling class, or at least refrain from rocking the boat, just as they did under the colonial regime before. . . . One of the subtle effects of this guilt atonement syndrome is the "double standard in reverse. . . . Liberals" are so afraid of being branded as racists that they simply suspend critical judgment in regard to Af-

> rica, which means that they abdicate their responsibility as scholars.[75]

The influence of the radical critique and of dependency theory within African universities was initiated by expatriate academics and to a considerable extent has been mainly sustained by them in some African universities. The developmentalist/dependency debate has been conducted most vigorously at the University of Dar es Salaam; in some universities (i.e., Nigeria and Ghana) it has not been prominent at all. Whether of the Leys, van den Berghe, or other variety, the critique has been a salutary influence on attitudes and perspectives regarding the role of foreign professors in African universities. It has raised the critical moral issue of whether and to what extent applied policy-oriented research by a foreign professoriate can strengthen and perpetuate oppressive regimes as well as an international system of rich/poor relationships and underdevelopment, or at best is no more than frivolous amelioratory system-tinkering of not even marginal consequence. Certainly, it is demonstrable that engagement in policy-oriented, applied, developmental research on certain subjects (particularly economics) inevitably decreases the distance from Caesar (who is either the physical source of the requisite statistics and other data or the donor of research access to it) and *ipso facto* increases markedly the degree of expected if not prescribed self-censorship in both research publications and classroom lectures.[76] This is not to argue, however, that any research relevant for policy need proceed from a particular evaluative perspective or induce self-censorship; a scholar can simply neutrally report his data, the policy relevance of which may be subsequently perceived and highlighted by others.

Among expatriate scholars the radical critique has undoubtedly stimulated significant self-scrutiny, possibly self-reproach among some. Others have succumbed to a variant of the "guilt atonement syndrome": to paraphrase van den Berghe, "liberals" are now so afraid of being branded linear developmentalists, or neo-imperial agents, or handmaidens of oppressive Caesars, that they simply suspend critical judgment and jump on the currently voguish radical bandwagon. Intrauniversity threats to academic freedom—subtle or frontal intimidation by colleagues and/or students—are sometimes far more serious than those from outside.[77] In balance, however, the critique has forced a fundamental reappraisal of the whole concept of what constitutes development, of just how much cant there is in the rhetoric of the "developmental university," of what is the role of a university in a developing country, and what indeed are the "developmental" responsibilities of expatriate professors.

PROTECTION OF INSTITUTIONAL NEUTRALITY

The political neutrality of the university is both logically and empirically a precondition, the price it must pay, for whatever autonomy it is permitted to enjoy. Even a modicum of autonomy, Perkins notes, requires that a university "maintain some degree of neutrality in partisan and social controversy . . . [if it] is to be a critic of accepted values and ideas as well as a developer of new ones."[78] Radical critics have much more to gain than to lose by protecting their university's political neutrality. Universities, Barrington Moore notes, "constitute a moat behind which it is still possible to examine and indict the destructive trends . . . in society."[79] As we have seen in most new states, the moat is very shallow and easily bridged, and once destroyed probably will not soon or easily be rebuilt. The burden of avoiding provocations which could lead to the destruction of existing university autonomies by hypersensitive and unsympathetic regimes reacting to confrontation rests heavily upon all members of the university community.

How can an expatriate professor affect the institutional neutrality of a university? Prominent among the caveats in the literature is that a professor should disassociate himself from his university in his extramural utterances and activities. From the perspective of the general public such disassociation is perhaps far more difficult to grasp in newer countries because of the exaggerated esteem which attaches to the educated person, an awe which frequently borders on credulity as regards the professorial spoken or written word. As well, an expatriate, being a noncitizen and usually physically differentiable, commands greater visibility in extramural commentary. These and other considerations suggest that if, at his own risk vis-à-vis the government of the host state, an expatriate wants to engage in extramural commentary and activities—and in general expatriate professors have tended to think it more prudent and helpful to their universities not to do so—then he has a presumptive special responsibility to scrupulously emphasize that he is not an institutional spokesman. Arguments for such constraint are *ipso facto* arguments against an expatriate professor, particularly in the social sciences, engaging in "community service" activities (public lectures, debates, etc.), or participating in extension, "continuing education," and other outreach programs of a university—activities which would appear to be at the very heart of any meaningful conception of a "developmental university."

A second caveat designed to project a university's neutrality, already noted earlier, is that the price for academic freedom within the classroom is that a professor must avoid persistently intruding controversial material which has no relation to his subject or professional competence, or using the classroom as a political base for espousing a single particular political ideal.[80] The problem with this caveat is its evasion of the fact that the subject matter of the social sciences and the humanities is inherently or inescapably controversial, and that it is the professional responsibility of the competent social scientist and humanist to illuminate controversy. As Max Weber argued in his celebrated essay "Science as Vocation":

> The primary task of a useful teacher is to teach his students to recognize "inconvenient" facts—I mean facts that are inconvenient for their party opinions. And for every party opinion there are facts that are extremely inconvenient, for my own opinion no less than for others.[81]

Pursuing this point, Martin Trow notes that "a major function of quantification in the social sciences is that it embodies impersonal procedures that ensure the collection of negative as well as supporting evidence for whatever 'party opinion' we hold at the moment."[82] The key consideration, of course, is that for all practical purposes the problem of academic freedom in the classroom (and its corollary, the problem of institutional neutrality) is created mainly by the social sciences and humanities being true to themselves in uncongenial milieus. This exists anywhere, but it is most poignantly the case for the expatriate social scientist and humanist in a university in an authoritarian new state.

An expatriate professor confronts another dilemma directly related to the problem of institutional neutrality, namely, ethnic balance versus merit as the governing criterion in the appointment and advancement of existing or prospective indigenous members of academic staff. The overriding importance of ethnic divisions and of ethnicity as the bases of politics in most of Africa's new states has been thoroughly documented and analyzed.[83] Ethnicity as the determinative element in relationships and action characteristically pervades not only the national political systems, but all major national structures (bureaucracy, army, policy, parastatal organizations, and the national university); indeed, such structures frequently are simply microcosms of the ethnic conflicts in the country at large.[84] For a variety of historical and cultural reasons, frequently gross ethnic imbalances characterized the composition of the elite strata of those structures at the time of their creation, and unless explicit countervailing actions are taken, the inexorable tendency is for such imbalances to cumulate and expand. This is particularly true in a structure such as a university which, left to itself, inherently favors the advancement of those ethnic groups within the population which are advantaged in terms of the dominant objective criterion for upward mobility within a university (i.e., earlier educational opportunity and achievement).

The initial ethnic imbalances in the African professoriate in African universities are well demonstrated by the predominating groups (e.g., the Creoles in Fourah Bay, the Ga and Ewe in the University of Ghana, the Yoruba in the University of Ibadan as well as Ahmadu Bello University, the Baganda in Makerere, initially the Luo and the Baluhya in the University of Nairobi, the Wachagga and Wahaya in the University of Dar es Salaam, and the Baluba, Bakongo, and peoples from the Bandundu Region in the National University of Zaire). Where the ethnic composition of the dominant power elite has been different from that in the university there has been a tendency to establish control over the university through its administration (usually by ethnic appointments congruent with that of the power elite) and the pursuit of variants of an ethnic balance policy aimed at retarding the further expansion of the predominant ethnic element in the professoriate, while at the same time accelerating the advancement of underrepresented ethnic groups, most particularly that of the power elite. In those surprisingly few cases where the dominant ethnic group has been identical in both the political and university systems, the existing ethnic imbalance has tended to be perpetuated. In any event, whether righting or strengthening an imbalance, the fact is that ethnic considerations frequently, if not normally, intrude themselves, and most forcefully when decisions have to be made regarding admission, grading, and award of degrees to students, and the appointment and advancement of members of the African professoriate.

The dilemma of the expatriate professor is all too clear: "ethnic balance" is a political desideratum whereas, above all other institutions, universities are presumed to function exclusively according to the norms of academic collegiality in decision-making, and of demonstrated merit as the sole criterion for advancement. The manifold pressures upon an expatriate professor can emanate from all directions—from administrative officials commanding "ethnic balance," from the senior members if the dominant ethnic group struggling to maintain their dominance, and from the hapless best performers and highest potentials (of whatever ethnic group) pleading for enforcement of the criterion of merit. The dilemma is most acute when those academically most meritorious are deliberately penalized and held back on ethnic grounds in preference to others who are demonstrably mediocre or outrightly marginal. The expatriate professor, particularly in situations of polarized ethnicity, is the only neutral objective observer able to press the case of the most meritorious, and it is manifestly his professional and moral responsibility to do so.

Yet the importance of the other horn of the dilemma cannot be ignored. In a multiethnic society, where ethnicity persists either as an objective force in its own right, or as a force manipulated by opportunistic power seekers, no purportedly "national" structure can become institutionalized and acquire the neutrality requisite for its academic freedom if it is, and is seen to be by the bulk of the population, a preserve of one or two ethnic groups. Here the imperative of achieving and preserving institution neutrality requires an explicit policy of reducing unhealthy existing imbalances through active identification, recruitment, and promotion of excellence among the underrepresented groups. It follows that consistent pursuit of "constrained maximization" by an expatriate professor (i.e., recognition of certain constraints on his/her activities and a striving for the greatest amount of freedom and best quality of output consistent with these constraints) would prescribe that he/she be sensitive to the desideratum of ethnic balance and work with and seek to promote excellence among disadvantaged ethnic groups.[85]

A third dilemma for an expatriate professor arises when there is a fundamental threat to the university as an institution. Individualism is at the core of academic freedom, but the defense of a university *qua* university is generally accepted as a corporate responsibility of the university community. Vice Chancellor Ajayi observed, "Universities must show that they value autonomy enough to defend it and make sacrifices if need be to preserve their essential nature . . . [but this is only possible] through the creation of virile academic communities."[86] Unanimity among all components of the academic community (administration, professoriate, students) can be a powerful force against a threat to a university as a corporate group. The example of Fourah Bay College described previously by Dr. Nicol has already been cited. However, once the threat occurs the usual pattern has been early fragmentation among and within the different components: administrators have usually turned to behind-the-scenes negotiations; while expatriate and national professors, as well as students, have split among those who withdraw from any involvement, those who reluctantly support the strategy of the administration as the only realistic option, and the diehard confrontationists. Because of the special vulnerability of the national professoriate, as well as students, the espousal and leadership of the confrontationist strategy have frequently fallen to a core of expatriate professors and the more defiant among the students. The demonstration of solidarity by a wider transnational African academic community has also never occurred, not only because such a community does not exist but also because of the strength of the principle of nonintervention in contemporary inter-African affairs. The legacy of such wrenching and fragmenting experiences has usually weakened even further whatever nascent sense of university community might have existed before the crisis.

Once again the nature of the dilemma is clear, but what the expatriate responsibility should be in such situations is not at all unambiguous, either tactically or morally. Experience in another setting led one veteran to caution realism:

> The universities, of course, must resist moves that would destroy them. Yet, they cannot afford to be doctrinaire on these grounds; they will frequently have to bend with the social hurricanes, or they will be uprooted. In bending, however, they should keep in mind that they do so only for purposes of survival, not because the principle of institutional neutrality has been invalidated.[87]

Realism would also suggest that in a confrontation between an authoritarian anti-intellectual regime and the university of its country, the university (and the country) will probably lose, and for the university the loss will be that precious little autonomy and neutrality it inherited and nurtured from an earlier period, and which, if the boat is not rocked, it might still retain. The counter to this is the insistence that under any and all circumstances the principle of institutional autonomy must be defended. In practice, human nature being what it is, expatriate professors under crisis have distributed themselves along a broad spectrum from the totally uninvolved cynics to those irrepressible cause-prone quixotes who have manned the barricades.

MAXIMUM EFFECTIVENESS IN ROLE PERFORMANCE

Academic freedom has been justified as a requisite for the effective performance of a professorial role; it is only reasonable that academic responsibility, the *quid pro quo* of that freedom, be specified in the same terms. It would follow that the fundamental responsibility of an expatriate professor is to be maximally effective in his professorial role within the constraints of the empirical situation in which he serves. The measure of his effectiveness would be the extent to which he (1) practices and promotes academic freedom within those constraints; (2) demonstrates a sensitivity to and a humility regarding the inherent biases, the temporal and territorial limitations, and the culture-boundedness of his own discipline, his perspectives, and all of the intellectual baggage he brings with him; and (3) tolerates, indeed encourages, heterodoxy and intellectual pluralism in his own discipline and in the African university in which he serves. In short, an academically responsible expatriate professor is one who is true to the ideal of academic freedom and to science as a vocation, and has, as well, an uncontrollable passion to be replaced as soon as possible by his African successor.

Realistic Promotion of Academic Freedom The responsibility to practice and to promote academic freedom is a bounden duty of all scholars serving anywhere, including, of course, expatriate professors in African universities, not only because such freedom is a fundamental requisite for the effective search and exposition of the truth—a common good and the raison d'être of their profession—but also because of the basic unity of scholarship throughout the world. Ideally, the practice of such freedom is to refuse to accept constraints on one's own quest for and exposition of the truth and to insist that the same right be accorded to all other scholars. The promotion of such freedom involves taking an open, principled stand whenever it is threatened, and as an educator to further the understanding of its essentiality for the common good in whatever quarters required. Some go further, and argue that an expatriate scholar has a special responsibility to carry the burden of protecting and furthering academic freedom. As one leading African scholar put it:

> There is a tendency to regard the expatriate professor as an "impartial" referee or judge in the internal feuds between political protagonists. . . . There is an increasing expectation that the expatriate scholar should, because of his relatively greater political immunity, embody and actively stand for the norms of academic freedom as well as scientific rationality, which so many African governments violate in the name of "political" rationalities of various brands.

Indeed, van den Berghe argues that it is "doubly incumbent on the expatriate" to engage in sensitive ("dangerous to vested interests") research because of his relatively greater impunity; an indigenous scholar would "find himself in jail or exile."[88] Expatriates are expendable; the worst that can happen to them is deportation. The differential fate of expatriate and indigenous academic persons in the recent University of Zambia case illustrates this point.

Given the constraints upon freedoms within which many African universities must function, what should an expatriate professor who values academic freedom do? Those of the Theroux persuasion would argue that he should not remain in a country where there are limitations upon his freedom.[89] A variant of this stand would be for an expatriate not to accept an appointment in a university where such constraints exist. Here the problem is that, for reasons already discussed, no African university has admitted nor is likely to state that it denies academic freedom; in any event, it is normally governments which deny and intimidate, not universities, except as their administrations give way under irresistible government pressure. In any event, a strong humanitarian case could be made for expatriate professors serving in universities struggling under repressive regimes to "stay in there" (e.g., Makerere University in Amin's Uganda) and continue to help nurture whatever preservable precious traditions and ideals there are. The argument would be that the institutions themselves are innocent and will be desperately needed in any hopefully more promising future.

The 1940 AAUP Statement of Principles of Academic Freedom provided that "limitations of academic freedom because of religious *or other aims* of the institution should be clearly stated in writing at the time of the appointment."[90] This interesting provision suggests that by accepting de facto limitations on freedom American academe has not been doctrinaire on the issue: academic freedom has in practice been accepted as relative; it has not been demanded as an absolute right everywhere and under all conditions. Limitations have been explicitly acknowledged as tolerable, provided they are specified in writing in advance of an appointment. Even without such advance precautionary notice, however, one could argue that any expatriate who values academic freedom and accepts an academic appointment in an African university without informing himself beforehand of the limited state of freedom therein should neither have sought nor received an appointment in the first place; but having done so, he should resign à la Theroux once the constraints prove intolerable. That act itself would dramatize the discharge of his responsibility for personally practicing academic freedom.

There is evidence that the implicit—if not explicit—requirements for maximally effective role performance in some African universities are increasingly being viewed as relative to particular local conditions. At the University of Dar es Salaam, for example, it is generally understood that one of the requirements for the appointment of an expatriate professor is that the candidate have a sympathetic predisposition—some would argue a total commitment—toward Tanzania's particular sociopolitical system and aspirations, namely, its variant of African socialism. In principle this would appear not to differ at all from the implicit appointment, promotion, and tenure requirements heretofore—and many places still—prevalent in

American church-related (and not a few secular) universities. The discriminatory criterion need not be interpreted as an insistence upon ideological (or religious) conformity as such, but a simple role effectiveness within the constraints of the institution and its environment. As one analyst put the point, expatriates "should basically be in agreement with the ideology of the recipient country, if for no other reason than that of safeguarding themselves against charges of sabotage and of acting as agents of imperialism or neo-colonialism."[91] Scholars who are adherents of academic freedom and the intellectual pluralism it implies are likely to regard such an argument repugnant.

Commentary on the ambiguities and dilemmas of realizing the ideal of academic freedom in developing countries tends to reflect a sort of schizophrenic ambivalence between the need to uncompromisingly affirm the imperative of academic freedom in categorical clarion-call terms and the equally imperative need for realism in demanding its application in the world as it is. An example:

> The scholar, in presenting the results of his work, will not be concerned with tact, tactics, or diplomacy. He will not keep silent merely to spare feelings and he will not mince words. It would be a form of inverted snobbery and condescension if scholars from developed countries thought it necessary to treat "sensitive" problems of the developing countries with kid gloves . . . [but] sensitivity and imaginative understanding are essential in social studies and tactics are in order if implementation is desired.[92]

Note the interesting juxtaposition: tact, tactics, and diplomacy are repugnant to scholarship, but they are in order if scholars are to be maximally effective. Categorical affirmation is the catharsis which makes accommodation and compromise psychologically tolerable and morally excusable. Obviously, something has to give, and the characteristic resolution of the dilemma—and the only alternative to principled declination or resignation of an appointment—has been tact, tactics, and diplomacy, or in other words, a measure of restraint and self-censorship.

The principal challenge, then, to the responsible expatriate professor who has decided to work within the less than perfect (freedom-wise) academic setting is, in the interest of science, to exploit to the fullest, and expand wherever possible, such limited areas of freedom as do exist for whatever reason: default, inattention, or explicit permissiveness. One of the most common "tactics" of maximizing effectiveness is teaching by analogy. The concrete cases of references used as illustrations to teach and analyze even the most sensitive subjects (e.g., the basic structure of societies, including systems of social, economic, and political stratifications, the genesis and evolution of one-party systems, etc.) do not include the host country, but those of the same type, that is, its analogue. Confrontation is minimized, deportation possibly avoided, and the intelligent students get the message.

Sensitivity to Bias Expatriate professors, like all scholars, have a professional responsibility to seek, identify, and acknowledge the biases inherent in all concepts, models, theories, and even methodologies, including particularly those in their own intellectual baggage. This responsibility—and the humility and empathy it compels—is one of the most difficult to exact and fulfill. Yet for an expatriate in an African university it is an especially insistent one for at least three reasons: the nature of the professor-student role relationship in which the expatriate is always the superordinate possessed of all the indoctrinating and coercive influence inherent in that role; the tendency, largely due to the inherent colonial educational system, for many African university students to prefer dictated lectures, easily memorized handout syllabuses, unambiguous single "official answers," and examinations that reward regurgitation; and the fact that the expatriate is functioning in a cultural and historical situation totally different from the one which he has personally experienced and on which his own knowledge, cultural assumptions, categories, and perceptions, and general intellectual apparatus are based. There is something incongruous and presumptuous in the unqualified claim for freedom "to speak the truth as one sees it," when at most the truth can be only partial, therefore inadequate, possibly irrelevant, and most certainly biased.

There is no need here to inventory in detail the long list of putative biases in the theories, concepts, analytical schema, course content, reading lists, and research agendas of expatriate professors who have held (and continue to hold) appointments in African universities during the past two decades. The charges have been made almost exclusively against "Western" scholarship because of the obvious monopoly "Westerners" have exerted either as expatriates in African universities or as professors in the Western universities where the overwhelming majority of the African professoriate have received their advanced training.[93] This massive predominance accentuates Western academic vulnerability to the charge of bias diffusion; however, the source of the charge has been mainly Western self-criticism sparked by Western intellectual pluralism.

Prominent among the various biases of which Western expatriate professors are the putative carriers and diffusers are that their concepts, models, and paradigms can and do serve purposefully or unwittingly ideological purposes, that is, defense of the status quo and the interests of neo-imperialism and the dominant classes;[94] that their single disciplinary specialization and form of academic organization, derived from and perpetuated by bourgeois capitalism, are obstacles to the development of a meaningful interdisciplinary and holistic perspective;[95] that their scientific baggage is, in any event, inappropriate to and largely inapplicable to the "utterly different circumstances of developing societies";[96] and that the biases are not limited only to the social sciences and humanities (where they are admittedly more pronounced), but include all fields of learning (e.g., bias toward acute curative medical treatment rather than disease prevention and mass delivery of health care, bias in engineering against labor-intensive intermediate technology, bias in agriculture against small-scale peasant farming systems, etc.).[97]

In a penetrating critique of some of these charges Streeten concludes that "it is quite legitimate [in the service of universal truth] to criticize orthodox Western models for their excessive claims, for their 'intellectual imperialism,'" for the "seepage of bias into analysis," and for "concepts, models, and paradigms that are irrelevant, unrealistic, or ideologically biased."[98] From his analysis and that of others, two caveats emerge. One, of course, is that ideological bias is inherent in all human thought, and that even after the most rigorous analysis, massing of evidence, and explicit articulation of value premises, bias can be reduced, but not completely eliminated. Secondly, there is the danger of overreactive self-castigation which would lead to the advocacy of another typically Western product, the doctrine of nontransferability:

> There is a short step (it might be argued) from the doctrine of the need to evolve alternative styles of thinking to the doctrine of "separate but equal" and from thereto apartheid. It is quite easy to give the call for alternative systems of thought a nasty racialist ring. The doctrine of non-transferability may be interpreted as an unpleasant form of Western neo-colonialism.[99]

In balance, the dialectic of bias exposure and correction which has been provoked by the encounter of the Western expatriate professor with African universities has been a positive contribution, hopefully toward a more comprehensive theory of human society and more universally valid categories. It has also enabled all involved to go through the catharsis of a fundamental rethinking of their disciplines.[100]

Support for Heterodoxy and Heterogeneity of Personnel A third responsibility of an expatriate professor inescapably thrusts itself to the fore as a sequel to the foregoing discussion of bias, namely, the essentiality of his support for intellectual heterodoxy as well as heterogeneity in the nationality of members of the expatriate professoriate. Neither heterodoxy nor heterogeneity alone is sufficient; one does not assure the other; both are valuable. A responsible expatriate would vigorously encourage both. Helen Kimble has noted that

> academic "non-alignment" is no longer interpreted in terms of sending as many students to Moscow and Peking as to Manchester and Princeton; it is rather a matter of recruiting an international—one might almost say interdenominational—staff for the universities already rooted in African soil, where socialist and "capitalist" professors are already working side by side. Perhaps their students will be able to adopt an eclectic viewpoint, drawing on the most helpful aspects of both traditions.[101]

Since 1967 this policy has been consciously pursued at the University of Dar es Salaam, and as Court points out, although heterogeneity "has occasionally caused problems in consistency of Faculty offerings it has been more than compensated for by the educational benefits to students from being exposed to a range of perspectives."[102] It was also the declared objective of Professor Ali Mazrui as Dean of Makerere's Faculty of Social Sciences. It is the only sure means for the continuous exposure of bias. Moreover, diversity both in ideas and partial truths, and in the foreign origin of their exponents, renders psychically a bit more tolerable the continued dependence on expatriate professors.

There have been and are strong influences opposing and resisting intellectual diversity; it is a state of affairs that must be explicitly and continuously pursued as a fixed principle. The strain in human organizations is toward orthodoxy, that is, for existing members or those who control recruitment to strengthen the numbers of those who are ideologically congenial through selective recruitment or proselytism. The Western ideal of the university, however, is an explicit strain toward heterodoxy. However, there is a strong presumption and no little evidence that the selection and appointment of expatriate academics in the early development of many African universities, controlled as they were mainly by overseas recruitment of the former colonial power, were significantly skewed, both ideologically and nationality-wise, against heterodoxy and heterogeneity. The later radical and Marxian presence and influence in this expatriate professoriate has been directed toward righting the balance, and in this respect it has been a salutary pressure toward intellectual pluralism.[103]

There are those, of course, who believe that a university is or should be an ideological institution, that is, that intellectual orthodoxy and not pluralism is the *sine qua non* of effectiveness. As Ward noted, there exists the "notion that African universities must be strongly committed to the predominant social and political ideologies of their respective nations and that such a commitment is difficult if not impossible to carry out when these universities are heavily staffed by expatriate faculty."[104] Until now this view has not gained hold; where they exist, ideological institutes have been set up outside of universities. This could be because expatriate university professors were indeed rightly judged to be of doubtful effectiveness as teachers of African ideologies, or because the state and party could only have unfettered control over an entirely separate structure, or because of respect for the university—or for all three reasons. In Tanzania, one of the few African countries where ideology has been taken very seriously, there can be little doubt that an abiding respect for the university and for what it stands—including particularly academic freedom and intellectual pluralism—by its chancellor (who is also head of state and party, and one of Africa's greatest scholar-statesmen) has certainly been a decisive factor.[105]

THE FUTURE OF THE EXPATRIATE PROFESSOR

The expatriate professor in African universities was always intended to be only a transitional phenomenon. According to prevailing norms, one of the principal criteria of an expatriate's effectiveness has been the speed with which he was succeeded by his African replacement. Africanization of the professoriate has been and remains a priority objective of those universities, although, as noted earlier, not necessarily of governments. In summarizing the conclusions of a workshop of the Association of African Universities in 1972, Professor Yesufu reported that as a matter of policy "localization should aim roughly at filling up to 90 per cent of the staff positions with indigenes of the country in which the university is located, and 10 per cent by expatriates."[106] Except for the smaller recently created universities, most African universities have had from fifteen to twenty-five years to work toward this objective. Very substantial external assistance has been provided from a variety of agencies to accelerate the process. Thus, one would have thought that issues concerning the expatriate professor, including his academic freedoms and responsibilities, were more or less dated and that any analysis and commentary is essentially retrospective. Yet one confronts the startling fact that the overall continental estimate of 50 percent Africanization of universities is probably on the high side, and that in some universities the proportion of Africans has actually even declined in the past few years.[107] Thus, despite earlier assumptions that expatriates constituted a species destined for early extinction (except for Yesufu's 10 percent target to preserve international contacts and to avoid total provincialism), the actual need for them is in fact declining agonizingly slowly.

The explanations for this rather disheartening situation are now clear, although the causes themselves remain fairly intractable. One explanation is the continuous expansion in both the number of new universities and in the scope of and number of students in existing universities, both phenomena due in part to the unremitting political demands for higher education. The most dramatic example is the decision to establish seven new Nigerian universities, the staffing of which (together with some older ones) would require 1,500 additional expatriate staff before 1980.[108] A second explanation is the omnipresent pressure to establish, as early and completely as possible, advanced postgraduate degree programs in African universities. This is an understandable and necessary trend, although it vastly increases the number of expatriates required because in some fields senior experienced African scientists and scholars competent to give quality postgraduate instruction, at least over the next several years, are simply not available; more expatriates must be recruited. Thirdly, there is an internal brain drain from the universities to financially more attractive public or private careers, or, as in Tanzania, university professors are assigned to development roles in the public service considered to be of higher priority by their national governments. The ranks of some departments approaching complete Africanization have been nearly depleted. This problem is compounded by external brain retention or competition either because of more immediately attractive positions (North American universities and international agencies being the strongest rivals), particularly in contrast to the penury in resources, the disesteem in status, and the lack of professional opportunities Africans face in some African universities; also, because of a scholar's ideological antipathy to, fear of, or refusal to serve under the oppressive regime in his home country. The tragedy of Makerere is a case in point.

Thus, there will undoubtedly be for some years a continuing, although declining need for expatriate professors. Their academic freedoms and responsibilities will remain active and important issues, particularly if there is further erosion of basic freedoms and human rights in the new states of Africa. However, for at least two reasons confrontation crises and self-censorship dilemmas could well attenuate. One of these is that most universities have pursued, necessarily and understandably, a policy of Africanizing as rapidly as possible all academic authority positions (deanships, headships of departments, directors of institutes, etc.) irrespective of the degree of Africanization of the professoriate itself. This has resulted in a vast reduction in the presence, and hence the visibility, of expatriates in the key academic authority roles and decision-making bodies of the universities (senates, councils, boards, etc.); by equal measure, the likely direct expatriate involvement in delicate issues of university-state relationships has diminished.

The second reason is the change that has occurred in the type of expatriate professor that is required and desired. Except for the selective development of postgraduate and other special programs, and certain specializations (e.g., linguistics, management and administration, econometrics, statistical analysis, survey technology, and data processing, namely, the "harder" social sciences), law and the humanities and the social sciences are disciplines that are further along toward achieving the goals of optimal Africanization, hence the need and demand for expatriates in those fields has markedly declined and will continue to do so.[109] For example, only 11 percent of the expatriates required by the expanded Nigerian university system are to be recruited for the arts and social sciences. The vacant positions in those fields in the new Nigerian universities, plus a few universities outside Nigeria, could probably be filled from among the significant number of qualified Nigerian professors now teaching in universities in North America. The overwhelming priority need in Nigeria and elsewhere in Africa is for expatriates in the physical and natural sciences and in professions such as medicine, agriculture, and engineering. The subject matter of these fields of learning is not inherently controversial, or certainly not in the same volatile and sensitive sense as the humanities and social sciences. This diminution in the presence of the expatriate humanist and social scientist and the heightened accent upon the apolitical technocrat and hard scientist portend a progressive reduction in the area of possible friction between the expatriate professor and African regimes on issues of academic freedom.

The progressive disappearance of the expatriate professoriate in the humanities and social sciences—usually the front-line disciplines required by their subject matter to defend academic freedom more vigorously—means a shift in the burden of that defense to their far more vulnerable African colleagues who have replaced them. Yet the moral burden remains universal and collective. As Streeten has argued, the pursuit of knowledge unites scholars around the world, and

> it is this unity of scholarship that gives us the right, beyond a general appeal to human rights, to send petitions to foreign gov-

ernments to protect the life and work of colleagues in danger of being imprisoned or tortured for their ideas.[110]

NOTES

1. Eric Ashby, *Universities: British, Indian, African: A Study in the Ecology of Higher Education* (Cambridge: Harvard University Press, 1966), p. 293.

2. Quoted in ibid., p. 291.

3. Quoted in W. K. Chagula, "Academic Freedom and University Autonomy in the Economic, Social and Political Context of East Africa," *Minerva*, 6:3 (Spring 1968), p. 415.

4. See Edward Shils, "The Enemies of Academic Freedom," *Minerva*, 12:4 (October 1974), p. 405: "The objects of that freedom were activities which were specifically academic—teaching, training, and research—and which took place within universities."

5. Ibid., p. 414.

6. Ashby, *Universities*, pp. 290–343; Chagula, "Academic Freedom and University Autonomy," pp. 409–414; Zelman Cowen, "Institutional Autonomy and Academic Freedom," and Alex Kwapong, "University Autonomy, Accountability, and Planning," in International Council for Educational Development (ICED), *Higher Education: Crisis and Support* (New York: ICED, 1974), pp. 43–62. As Ashby stated (p. 290), "It is a commonplace of history that an autonomous university can deny academic freedom (as Oxford did in the early nineteenth century) and a university which is not autonomous can safeguard academic freedom (as Prussian universities did in Humboldt's time)."

7. Cited in ICED, *Higher Education*, p. 174.

8. Barbara Baiord Israel, *Can Higher Education Recapture Public Support* (New York: ICED, 1974), p. 36. In a statement issued by British vice chancellors in 1947 they said that "the universities entirely accept the view that the government has not only the right, but the duty to satisfy itself that every field of study which in the national interest ought to be cultivated in Great Britain is in fact being cultivated in the University system." Cited in A. M. Carr-Saunders, "Britain and Universities in Africa," *Universities Quarterly*, 19 (June 1965), p. 231.

9. In the Carnegie Commission's report on the *Governance of Higher Education* it was noted that "the greatest shift of power in recent years has taken place not *within* the campus but in the *transfer* of authority from the campus to outside agencies." Cited in Cowen, "Institutional Autonomy and Academic Freedom," p. 46.

10. C. Vann Woodward argues in "The Erosion of Academic Privileges and Immunities" that the diminution in both institutional autonomy and academic freedom has in some measure been the result of neglect and

indifference, but also "betrayal within the walls of the academy." *Daedalus*, 103:4 (Fall 1974), p. 34.

11. Ashby, *Universities*, pp. 336–337.

12. Eric Ashby's pioneering study is the most comprehensive analysis to date. Other selected works include Francis X. Sutton, "African Universities and the Process of Change in Middle Africa," in Stephen D. Kertesz, ed., *The Task of Universities in a Changing World* (Notre Dame: University of Notre Dame Press, 1971); Roger J. Southall and Joseph M. Kaufert, "Converging Models of University Development: Ghana and East Africa," *Canadian Journal of African Studies*, 8:3 (1974), pp. 607–626; T. M. Yesufu, ed., *Creating the African University* (Ibadan: Oxford University Press, 1973); C. W. de Kiewet, *The Emergent African University: An Interpretation* (Overseas Liaison Committee, December 1971); Benoit Verhaegen, "L'Université dans l'Afrique Indépendante," *Cultures et Développement*, 1:3 (1968), pp. 555–583; L. Gray Cowan, "Government and the Universities in Africa," *U.S. Library of Congress Quarterly*, 27 (July 1970), pp. 197–205; David Court, "The Experience of Higher Education in East Africa: The University of Dar es Salaam as a New Model," *Comparative Education*, 2:3 (October 1975), pp. 193–218. The most detailed study of the anatomy of an African university is Pierre L. van den Berghe's *Power and Privilege at an African University* (London: Routledge & Kegan Paul, 1973).

13. The various aspects of this "replacement function" have been examined by Sutton, "African Universities and the Process of Change in Middle Africa," pp. 349 ff., and Court, "The Experience of Higher Education in East Africa," pp. 197–201.

14. Kenneth Prewitt, "University Students in Uganda: Political Consequences of Selection Patterns," and Joel D. Barkan, "Elite Perceptions and Politics in Ghana, Tanzania, and Uganda," in William John Hanna, ed., *University Students and African Politics* (New York: Africana Publishing Company, 1975), pp. 167–186 and 187–214. It should be stressed that this relative quiessence was not universal; it was more strikingly evident in the new states which emerged from former British and French colonial Africa. There are several notable exceptions, in particular the effective resistance of Sudanese students at the University of Khartoum to the Abboud regime commencing in 1958, and the high degree of politicization and activism among Congolese (Zairian) students between 1964 and 1970.

15. de Kiewet, *The Emergent African University*, p. 49.

16. Aristide R. Zolberg, "The Structure of Political Conflict in the New States of Tropical Africa," *American Political Science Review*, 6:1 (March 1968), pp. 70–87; idem, "The Military Decade in Africa," *World Politics*, 25:2 (January 1973), pp. 309–331; and James S. Coleman and Carl G.

Rosberg, eds., *Political Parties and National Integration in Tropical Africa* (Berkeley: University of California Press, 1964).

17. Verhaegen, "L'Université dans l'Afrique Indépendante," pp. 557–558: "Adapter l'université aux besoins et aux exigences immédiates de la société est donc une entreprise impossible, si, au préalable on n'admet pas que les relations entre université et société sont dialectiques et conflictuelles, surtout dans une société longtemps sujette à des processus de changements induits de l'extérieur et où les intellectuels sont mis en demeure de repenser des institutions à l'établissement desquelles ils n'ont pas été associés."

18. The variation in intensity has been a function in part of the educational level and makeup of the governing group. As L. Gray Cowan, "Government and the Universities in Africa," p. 198, has noted, "The majority of the nationalist leaders who formed the first postindependence governments were men whose education had been limited to secondary school. They tended to regard the university with a mixture of awe and even some slight fear, since they felt inferior to the staff and even to the students." de Kiewet, *The Emergent African University*, p. 51, observes that political leadership of this character "found it difficult not to be anti-intellectual, especially when the rules of university conduct were laid down *ex cathedra* by expatriate academics." In contrast, he observes, "African political leaders whose intellectual formation had taken place either abroad or under predominantly metropolitan influence, were initially disposed to accept the university as it presented itself. Their attitude was reinforced by the presence within government of expatriate bureaucrats, advisors, and technicians."

19. Ashby, *Universities,*, p. 222.

20. Representative of this sentiment was a policy statement of one Nigerian political group cited by Eric Ashby, ibid., p. 322: "Every time suggestions are offered by outside bodies for certain actions to be taken by the University College for the good of Nigeria the reply invariably comes that the University College is an 'autonomous institution' which would not submit to 'dictation by any outside body.' This sort of reply is, of course, sheer nonsense because no estate within a State can be absolutely autonomous."

21. Among insecure regimes there tends to be a strong suspicion that university staff and students are inherently heretical in their political convictions and that they are disposed to strongly resist any move toward closer integration of universities with public authority, even if in fact there is considerable deference existent. See Ali A. Mazrui and Yash Tandon, "The University of East Africa as a Political Institution," *Minerva*, 5:3 (Spring 1967), 384; and Verhaegen, "L'Université dans l'Afrique Indépendante," p. 557.

22. Colin Legum, *Africa: The Year of the Students* (London: Rex Collings, 1972), p. 2.

23. Ibid. Deportations of expatriates occurred in Zaire and Zambia (including the Canadian first vice chancellor of the University of Zambia); however, Tanzania refrained from taking action against two activist expatriates in the demonstrations at the University of Dar es Salaam (a Canadian political scientist and a Guyanan historian), and finally abandoned the deportation actions against a Kenyan student leader (ibid., pp. 8–14). The response of the Ugandan vice chancellor to the student charges that the expatriate staff was frustrating Ugandanization was: "My own experience is that in most cases it is the university that fights to keep [the expatriates] because of the absence of Ugandans at that level, rather than that the expatriates fight to stay because they are anxious to establish themselves elsewhere before it is too late to do so" (ibid., p. 15).

24. Increasingly, vice chancellors and members of governing bodies were appointed because of their identity with or deference to the governing regime, a phenomenon particularly illuminated by appointments of the first African vice chancellors and University Councils of the University of Nairobi, Makerere University Kampala, and the University of Dar es Salaam. However, there are notable exceptions illuminated by the courageous affirmation of fundamental principles in the speech made by Vice Chancellor Ajayi at the 1972 workshop of the Association of African Universities. See J. F. A. Ajayi, "Towards an African Academic Community," in Yesufu, *Creating the African University*, pp. 11-19.

25. Harlan Cleveland, *Education Is Development, and Vice Versa* (New York: Institute of International Education, 1975), p. 6, has noted the uniquely exasperating nature of the challenge of student demonstrations to authoritarian regimes: They must "reckon with many different constituencies. . . . Control is not difficult as long as the constituency to be controlled is itself organized in ways the regime can understand. But student power is often a baffling scene of shifting leadership, unplanned demonstrations, and unpredictable targets." Howard Elliott has suggested that one variable influencing a government's approach to academic freedom is the political strength of students, either because they are well organized or because they are held in awe by the people. Experience at the University of Lovanium, Makerere University, and others would support this argument.

26. "Evidence suggests that most of the pressures for a high level of material support of the armed forces in Ghana, the Congo, and Ethiopia, have come from the top political leaders who recognize that a satisfied army is as essential to their continued political control as it is to state security," Ernest W. Lefever quoted in Zolberg, "The Military Decade in Africa," p. 317. The reason for the extraordinarily high cost of African universities (small size in terms of numbers of students, high staff/student

ratios, high public utility costs, high equipment costs, and high staff expenses—particularly for expatriates) are analyzed in Kwapong, "University Autonomy," pp. 57–58, and also in Colin Leys and John Shaw, "Problems of Universities in Developing Countries" (mimeo), May 1967.

27. Kwapong, "University Autonomy," pp. 56 and 60. Government financing and control over universities is also the dominant pattern in Europe, but as Ashby has shown, mechanism and conventions have developed over the years which have provided a protective shield, although this itself is eroding or under challenge in many respects. Ashby, *Universities*, p. 341, quotes T. H. Silcock as suggesting that "universities might be more secure as functional organs with a defined influence within the state structure than as separate institutions needing constitutional defences." Cleveland, *Education Is Development, and Vice Versa*, p. 7, notes: "Financing the piper *does* in practice entitle the political authorities to call the tune on (a) how many of which categories of its constituents get into the universities, (b) what kinds of academic training and research are essential to development (as defined by the authorities), (c) how much money will be available for the holders of university credential."

28. Court, "The Experience of Higher Education in East Africa," p. 206; and Ajayi, "Towards an African Academic Community," p. 14.

29. de Kiewet, *The Emergent African University*, pp. 53–54; Roger Southall, *Federalism and Higher Education in East Africa* (Nairobi: East African Publishing House, 1974).

30. Mohammed Omar Beshir, "Higher Education for Development: Case Study, University of Khartoum" (ICED, April 1975), pp. 2–3.

31. Chagula, "Academic Freedom and University Autonomy," p. 415.

32. van den Berghe, *Power and Privilege at an African University*, p. 263, notes that "there are powerful restraints against letting internal conflicts turn into an attack against the University itself. Vis-à-vis the larger society, the University is a solidary group." The lines of cleavage among various components of universities have varied, both temporally and among different systems. At the University of Dar es Salaam, for example, the cleavages that later emerged were national (administrator and academic) versus expatriate (irrespective of nationality) and Marxist/non-Marxist.

33. In his final report, Dr. O'Brien stated: "For a university, autonomy is not an end in itself. It is simply the guarantee and the protection of the freedoms of thought and speech, of reading and writing, which are essential for the maintenance of high educational standards. As long as that autonomy is intact, critical and independent thought remains relatively secure; but if that autonomy is once breached, then elements inimical to such values may easily establish themselves in control and change the whole character of the University." See Dennis Austin, "Et in Arcadia Ego: Politics and Learning in Ghana," *Minerva*, 13:2 (Summer 1975), p. 244.

34. Davidson Nicol, "Civic Responsibility and Academic Freedom in Africa," *Minerva*, 7:1–2 (Autumn-Winter 1968), pp. 76–77.

35. The institutional autonomy and academic freedom in Africa's older universities (Fourah Bay, University of Ghana, University of Ibadan, University of Khartoum, and Makerere University) is undoubtedly less fragile than those of newer universities; the passage of time, the socialization and habituation of at least two generations; and the weighty respect they command as national institutions make them less vulnerable. The recent capitulation of the regime of Siaka Stevens to the students of Fourah Bay College regarding the holding of new elections in Sierra Leone is a fresh demonstration of the power of that honored university.

36. Kwapong, "University Autonomy," p. 59.

37. E. Njoku, "The Relationship between University and Society in Nigeria," in *The Scholar and Society*, entire issue of *Science and Freedom* [Manchester], no. 13 (1959), p. 82.

38. Ajayi, "Towards an African Academic Community," pp. 12-13.

39. Kamla Chowdhry, "Strategies for Institutionalizing Public Management Education: The Indian Experience" (mimeo), p. 21, brilliantly illuminated the critically determinative role played by early leaders in the institutionalization of new educational structures of exotic origin, endorsing the basic philosophy underlying the Max Planck Institutes in Germany, namely, "The Kaiser Wilhelm Society shall not first build an institute for research and then seek out the suitable man but shall first pick up an outstanding man and then build an Institute for him." Cowen, "Institutional Autonomy and Academic Freedom," p. 205, rightly stresses that the special disabilities of the new universities are but one aspect of the deeper "national crisis of the legitimization of authority through which all the new states of Africa are now passing."

40. Ashby, *Universities*, p. 320. The early celebrated cases of expatriate expulsions were Professor Terence Ranger, then lecturer in history at the University College of Rhodesia and Nyasaland, victimized by the white Rhodesian government for his opposition to racial segregation (Ashby observed, ibid., "It is ironic that the most shocking examples of scorn for the integrity of universities on the African continent should have come from white governments in Rhodesia and South Africa, not black government"); and John Hatch, former director of extramural studies at Fourah Bay College, deported for a derogatory article in a U.K. journal about the Sierra Leone government; see Nicol, "Civic Responsibility and Academic Freedom in Africa," p. 81. In both cases university authorities vigorously protested the actions by governments. Edward Shils, "The Enemies of Academic Freedom," p. 407, observes that "in the United States a large proportion of the infringements of the freedom of academic persons in the period from the 1890s to the 1930s had to do with actions and expressions, outside academic institutions, of views regarding current political, social,

and economic questions. In the state and major private universities, remarkable few . . . had to do with academic activities proper, namely, research and teaching."

41. The five expelled University of Zambia expatriates apparently confronted only hints that there was involvement in a "Red plot," "foreign interference and subversive elements," and the like, but no evidence was produced. This all occurred during the heat of the Angolan war and the intervention by South Africa in that conflict, on which the Zambian government had an anti-MPLA, pro-UNITA position. The Ahmadu Bello crisis involved physical attacks on expatriate members of staff and allegations of conduct "at variance with the mood of the Nation," but no specific charges were ever produced, and the university administration reportedly undertook no vigorous efforts to clarify the matter. Again, this occurred in the emotion-ridden aftermath of the tragic assassination of General Murtala Mohammed.

42. *Issue: A Quarterly Journal of Africanist Opinion*, 6:4 (Winter 1976), especially pp. 3–13.

43. M. Crawford Young, private communication.

44. Nzongola Ntalaja has cogently argued that since ideology is inherent in all political structures the distinction between ideological and non-ideological regimes is not particularly useful. A counter to this is that an ideology that is explicit and prescriptive does provide a basis for identifying and punishing overt challenges to it which a latent or unarticulated regime does not.

45. Colin Leys, "The Role of the University in an Underdeveloped Country," *Education News* [Canberra], (April 1971), p. 18. A distinction should be made here between expatriate professors holding appointments at African universities (for which research access in most instances is indeed relatively open) and visiting expatriate scholars who must obtain visas and research clearance in advance. In these latter cases controls are much more rigorous, but the record in most countries is one of considerable permissiveness, punctuated by occasional capricious closure.

46. Robert F. Arnove, "The Ford Foundation and 'Competency Building' Overseas: Assumptions, Approaches, and Outcomes" (mimeo), p. 24.

47. Ibid., p. 18.

48. According to Theroux, "Tarzan Is an Expatriate," *Transition*, 7:32 (August-September 1967), p. 14, the expatriate professor ("Tarzan") comes to Africa for any one (or all) of several reasons: "an active curiosity in things strange; a vague premonition that Africa rewards her visitors; a disgust with the anonymity of the industrial setting; a wish to be special; and an unconscious desire to stop thinking and let the body take over."

49. Philip G. Altbach, "Education and Neocolonialism," *Teachers College Record*, 72:4 (May 1971), p. 551; and Jennifer C. Ward, "The Expa-

triate Academic and the African University," *Africa Today*, 18:1 (January 1971), p. 36.

50. Paul Streeten, "Some Problems in the Use and Transfer of an Intellectual Technology," in International Bank for Reconstruction and Development (IBRD), *The Social Sciences and Development* (Washington, D.C.: IBRD, 1974), pp. 40–41.

51. Eric Ashby, "Four Views of Academic Freedom," *Minerva* 8:2 (April 1970), p. 314.

52. *AAUP Bulletin*, (Summer 1974), p. 271.

53. Ibid., *passim*, pp. 270–272.

54. Ibid., p. 271.

55. UNESCO, *The Development of Higher Education in Africa* (1963), p. 13.

56. See Court, "The Experience of Higher Education in East Africa," p. 196.

57. Edward Shils, "The Academic Ethos Under Strain," *Minerva*, 13:1 (Spring 1975), 13.

58. Leys and Shaw, "Problems of Universities in Developing Countries," p. 5.

59. Edward Shils, "The Implantation of Universities," *Universities Quarterly*, 22 (March 1968), p. 163: "It is perfectly clear that if universities contribute to the well-being of their societies as well-trained persons, knowledge and mastery of their physical and biological environment, useful services and good advice, they will acquire appreciative friends outside the university who will understand that a university must have a life of its own if it is to do these things well." See also Leys, "The Role of the University in an Underdeveloped Country," pp. 12 ff.

60. Court, "The Experience of Higher Education in East Africa," p. 212: "[A] degree of distance seems essential if a university is to retain the flexibility it needs not simply to serve already defined and agreed on developmental tasks but to contribute what it is in a unique position to supply, namely, the constant re-examination and redefinition of the nature of underdevelopment and the task of development."

61. Cleveland, *Education Is Development, and Vice Versa*, p. 7.

62. Leys and Shaw, "Problems of Universities in Developing Countries," p. 18. Leys and Shaw stress "community service" functions as the main content of the "developmental" role.

63. See Court, "The Experience of Higher Education in East Africa," pp. 201–204: "There is absolutely no question that the expansion of developmental responsibilities, if taken seriously, necessitates a marked increase in and retention of the number of expatriates, particularly in applied (developmentally oriented) social science research institutes and centers." See also James S. Coleman, "Some Thoughts on Applied Social

Research and Training in African Universities," *The African Review*, 2:2 (1972), pp. 289–307.

64. Sutton, "African Universities and the Process of Change in Middle Africa," p. 403.

65. On Tanzania, see Court, "The Experience of Higher Education in East Africa," pp. 206–217; and de Kiewet, *The Emergent African University*, pp. 55–58. In the Tanzanian case Nyerere has argued that there is no incompatibility between complete objectivity and commitment to the development needs of society. See Julius K. Nyerere, "The University in a Development Society," *Présence Africaine*, no. 6 (1967), pp. 3–10. The results of the border multicountry study are contained in Kenneth W. Thompson and Barbara R. Fogel, *Higher Education and Social Change: Promising Experiments in Developing Countries*, 2 vols. (New York: Praeger, 1976).

66. Streeten, "Some Problems in the Use and Transfer of an Intellectual Technology," p. 51.

67. See Court, "The Experience of Higher Education in East Africa," p. 203.

68. Leys, "The Role of the University in an Underdeveloped Country," p. 14.

69. For a penetrating critique of how a particular analytical framework can reflect a particular perspective and can affect both political analysis and political action, with particular reference to the system-functional approach, see Richard Sandbrook, "The 'Crisis' in Political Development Theory," *The Journal of Developmental Studies*, 12:2 (January 1976), pp. 165–185.

70. John Saul, quoted in Court, "The Experience of Higher Education in East Africa," p. 206, has cautioned about the danger of scholars engaging in system tinkering for repressive regimes: "All too often technical advice, narrowly defined, is being made available to elites who are not prepared to make the structural transformations necessary to development; at best, therefore, [a university research institute] may reinforce and legitimize a mood conducive to mere tinkering with the system, at worst it may provide active assistance to classes concerned with buying time for the system (and their own stake in it) by efficient management and marginal readjustment."

71. Streeten, "Some Problems in the Use and Transfer of an Intellectual Technology," p. 8.

72. Gary Wasserman, "The Research of Politics, the Politics of Research," *East Africa Journal*, 7 (November 1970), p. 12.

73. Streeten, "Some Problems in the Use and Transfer of an Intellectual Technology," p. 7.

74. See, for example, Africa Research Group, *African Studies in America: The Extended Family* (Boston: Africa Research Group, 1968); Ronald

H. Chilcote and Martin Legassick, "The African Challenge to American Scholarship in Africa," *Africa Today*, 18:1 (January 1971), pp. 4–13; Robert Molteno, "The Role of Certain North American Academics in the Struggle against the Liberation of Southern Africa" (mimeo); Altbach, "Education and Neocolonialism," pp. 543–558; and *Final Report of the Select [Church] Committee to Study Governmental Operations with Respect to Intelligence Activities* (Report No. 94–755 of the U.S. Senate) (Washington, D.C.: GPO, 1976), pp. 179–191.

75. Pierre L. van den Berghe, "Research in Africa: Knowledge for What?" *African Studies Review*, 13:2 (September 1970), pp. 333–334.

76. The early experience of the Institute for Development Studies in the University of Nairobi illuminated the dilemma of the applied, developmental, social science researcher as regards publication of research results. Considerable self-censorship was clearly expected; indeed, on certain subjects prior approval of government was required before publication or other dissemination. This was understandably the source of considerable anguish and sharp debate as to the tolerable limits of self-censorship. However, the same constraints existed as regards the applied social science research units at the University of Dar es Salaam, which curiously did not seem to evoke among critics the same concern. This suggests that opprobrium for closeness to Caesar and self-censorship in his cause depends upon the character of the Caesar in question, and not necessarily upon the transcendant imperative of academic freedom.

77. The intimidatory power of fads and fashions in scholarship as well as the vogue of an ascending ideological perspective having the appearance of being the source of personal and professional legitimation is a common phenomenon in the pendulum swing between alternating emphases on particular variables, values, or approaches to comprehension of reality. But it is, of course, through the dialectic that we can get closer approximations of the truth. See Streeten, "Some Problems in the Use and Transfer of an Intellectual Technology," p. 8.

78. James A. Perkins, "Reform of Higher Education: Mission Impossible?" ICED Occasional Paper No. 2 (June 1971), p. 4.

79. Quoted in Julius Gould, "Reflections after the Storm," *Minerva*, 11:2 (April 1973), p. 272.

80. Ibid., p. 271.

81. Quoted in Martin Trow, "Higher Education and Moral Development," *AAUP Bulletin*, 62:1 (April 1976), p. 22. Court, "The Experience of Higher Education in East Africa," p. 216, has observed that "the best way in which the university can contribute to the alleviation of inequality, one of the paramount goals of development, is to train students in the analytical capacity to describe and expose its different manifestations."

82. Trow, "Higher Education and Moral Development," p. 23.

83. The most comprehensive treatment of African ethnicity from a

global comparative perspective is M. Crawford Young, *The Politics of Cultural Pluralism* (Madison: University of Wisconsin Press, 1976). The universality of the explosion of political ethnicity is well argued in Nathan Glazer and Daniel P. Moynihan, *Ethnicity Theory and Experience* (Cambridge: Harvard University Press, 1975). For the debate on the objective or subjective bases of political ethnicity see Nelson Kasfir, *The Shrinking Political Arena* (Berkeley: University of California Press, 1976), especially pp. 47–90.

84. van den Berghe, *Power and Privilege at an African University*, pp. 36–44.

85. Howard Elliott suggested the term "constrained maximization" and observed that an African government can decide what it wants from its educational system and if it prefers to sacrifice quality for equality that is part of its social welfare function; expatriate professors working for that system have no basis for moralizing about the educational strategy selected.

86. Ajayi, "Towards an African Academic Community," pp. 12-13.

87. Perkins, "Reform of Higher Education," p. 5.

88. van den Berghe, *Power and Privilege at an African University*, p. 13.

89. Ward, "The Expatriate Academic and the African University," p. 19.

90. *AAUP Bulletin*, (Summer 1974), p. 270; italics added. The 1970 Interpretive Comments by the AAUP stated, as regards this clause, that "most church-related institutions no longer need or desire the departure from the principle of academic freedom implied in the 1940 Statement, and we do not now endorse such a departure" (p. 271).

91. See Yashpal Tandon, ed., *Technical Assistance in East Africa* (Uppsala: Dag Hammarskjold Foundation, 1973), p. 13. Tandon attributes this argument to Reginald Green.

92. Streeten, "Some Problems in the Use and Transfer of an Intellectual Technology," p. 22. "Tact and diplomacy are, of course, necessary if recommendations are to be adopted by governments. But this must not affect the content of basic research, partly because it offends against the principles of scholarship and partly because policies based on blinkered analysis are bound to fail. . . . some sycophantic or 'diplomatic' work is at bottom patronising and hence equally insensitive" (p. 19).

93. Guy C. Z. Mhone, "The Case against Africanists," *Issue*, 2:2 (Summer 1972), p. 10: "Africanists are, by virtue of their predominance in the modern intellectual tradition of Africa, guilty of perpetrating the predominance of Anglo-American (or Western) biases in Africa's modern intellectual thought."

94. Sandbrook, "The 'Crisis' in Political Development Theory," p. 168, notes: "It is not a little ironic that social scientists, while denying that

their own models of society have ideological implications, are prone to emphasize the ideological nature of opposing paradigms." In addition to Sandbrook's excellent analysis of the hidden ideological element in presumably value-free paradigms, see Chilcote and Legassick, "The African Challenge to American Scholarship in Africa," pp. 9–10; Altbach, "Education and Neocolonialism," pp. 548–552; van den Berghe, *Power and Privilege at an African University*, pp. 9–12; Ali Mazrui, "From Social Darwinism to Current Theories of Modernization," *World Politics*, 21:1 (October 1968), pp. 69–83; Martin Carnoy, *Education as Cultural Imperialism* (New York: David McKay, 1974); and John Loxley, "Technical Assistance, High-Level Manpower Training and Ideology in Tanzania," in Yashpal Tandon, ed., *Technical Assistance in East Africa* (Uppsala: Dag Hammarskjold Foundation, 1973), pp. 65–82. At p. 79 Loxley argues: "Socialist economists make their ideological considerations explicit and attach great importance to them, but the ideology of orthodox western European or North American economists is none the less real for being unstated: it is implicit in their tools of analysis."

95. Benoit Verhaegen, "Interdisciplinarité et science bourgeoise," *Revue de l'Institut de Sociologie* [Université Libre de Bruxelles], 1–2 (1975), pp. 198–202.

96. Streeten, "Some Problems in the Use and Transfer of an Intellectual Technology," p. 10: "[Western] alien concepts and models determine inappropriate policies and either divert attention from the real problems or become apologies for existing power structures. Excessive sophistication, esoteric irrelevance, ignorance and false beliefs conveyed by these doctrines are opportunistic and serve vested interests. . . . The paradigms of 'Western' social science serve as blinkers or escape mechanisms, preventing scholars and policy makers from seeing and acting upon the strategic fronts."

97. van den Berghe, *Power and Privilege at an African University*, p. 10; cf. Peter J. Donaldson, "Foreign Intervention in Medical Education: A Case Study of the Rockefeller Foundation's Involvement in a Thai Medical School," *International Journal of Health Sciences*, 6:2 (1976), pp. 251–270.

98. Streeten, "Some Problems in the Use and Transfer of an Intellectual Technology," p. 11, *passim*. Yesufu, *Creating the African University*, p. 56, also suggests that such bias is probably ineradicable: "The foreign academic, however objective he might be, is bound to be handicapped in his understanding of the social environment, and in his interpretation of the local cultures and traditions."

99. Streeten, "Some Problems in the Use and Transfer of an Intellectual Technology," p. 21.

100. van den Berghe, *Power and Privilege at an African University*, p. 10.

101. Helen Kimble, "On the Teaching of Economics in Africa," *The Journal of Modern African Studies*, 7:4 (1969), p. 738.

102. Court, "The Experience of Higher Education in East Africa," p. 214.

103. Orthodox (i.e., scientific) socialists, like orthodox "liberal" scholars, can, of course, push for their own orthodoxy even in a university; however, because they tend to be more explicit regarding their ideology their pressure for orthodoxy seems to command greater visibility. Thus, in proposing a new M.A. program in economics for the University of Dar es Salaam, one incumbent expatriate economist stressed that "it would be imperative that they [i.e., the expatriates] should not only be experienced and 'highly qualified' but also committed to socialism." And the chief academic officer of the university was criticized for the fact that "the verbal commitment to recruit socialist teachers is not matched by any action to ensure the implementation of that commitment as far as expatriates are concerned." See Loxley, "Technical Assistance, High-Level Manpower Training and Ideology in Tanzania," pp. 78–80. Many radicals would argue that intellectual pluralism is itself an orthodoxy.

104. Ward, "The Expatriate Academic and the African University," p. 34.

105. See William Tordoff and Ali A. Mazrui, "The Left and the Super-Left in Tanzania," *The Journal of Modern African Studies*, 10:3 (October 1972), pp. 427–446.

106. Yesufu, *Creating the African University*, p. 57; he added that "as much as possible a large proportion of the expatriates should come from other African universities."

107. Court, "The Experience of Higher Education in East Africa," p. 200. According to his calculations in 1975, out of the total number of establishment positions, Africans occupied 32 percent at the University of Nairobi, 25 percent at the University of Dar es Salaam, and 43 percent at Makerere University.

108. Kenneth Prewitt persuasively argues in a private communication that social science technology continues to change. To keep African universities abreast of current techniques in data collection and data analysis, for instance, "will require the continued presence of expatriates. . . . the difference between the social sciences and natural sciences is less great than you might imagine. And just as, for a long time to come, African universities will have to be brought up to date on the newest work in microbiology or chemistry, so will they need to be brought up to date on the newest work in econometrics, statistical analysis, data processing."

109. *Brief from National Universities Commission Staff Scouting Team to North America* (June/July 1976), p. 6.

110. Streeten, "Some Problems in the Use and Transfer of an Intellectual Technology," p. 22.

12 Zaire: The State and the University

James S. Coleman and Ndolamb Ngokwey

Zaire is in many respects typical, in other respects *sui generis,* among postcolonial new states. But even in its exceptionality, it could be argued, it largely manifests in extreme form characteristics common to other new states. Most of the new states have shared a common syndrome—indeed, a near simultaneity of experiences during this century. However, compared with Zaire, few other countries have suffered a precolonial capitalist exploitation so harsh, predatory, socially disorganizing, and unrestrained; a colonial system of bureaucratic authoritarianism so massive, deeply penetrative, paternalistic, and insulated from external monitoring; a colonial educational system so pyramidally flat, utilitarian in the service of colonialism, and monopolistically dominated by missionaries in close alliance with the colonial state; an externally oriented economic system of such excessive concentration of income and economic power in the hands of a colonial power and gigantic metropolitan financial groups and mining enterprises, and of such widespread use of forced labor in the mining industry and compulsory cultivation of export crops; a nationalist agitation period so brief and explosively pandemic; a democratic experiment immediately before independence of such fleeting brevity and politicized ethnicity; an indigenous leadership so denied of experience and unprepared for independence; an imperial evacuation so precipitate and ill-planned; an initial postcolonial period of such Hobbesian chaos, secessionism, and external manipulation; and the subsequent postcolonial agony of a protracted and seemingly interminable personalistic and patrimonial autocracy by one of Africa's most durable presidential monarchs. Other

Reprinted from R. Murray Thomas, ed., *Politics and Education: Cases from Eleven Nations* (Oxford: Pergamon Press, 1983), pp. 55–78.

new states have shared approximations or equivalents of some such experiences, but none has had the full ensemble to which Zaire seems to have been singularly fated. Ironically, even as regards its physical size—the largest country in Black Africa, tenth largest in the world—its extraordinarily rich resource base, and the amount of its external debt, Zaire's exceptionality is insistently defined by superlatives. This led one of Zaire's distinguished social scientists to introduce himself at an international conference with the words, "I come from that other planet called Zaire."

The colonial legacy and the pattern of evolution since independence have obviously affected very significantly the nature of the Zairian state, its university, and the relationships between the two. After briefly summarizing the profiles of Zaire's political and university systems, it is our intent, within that context, to examine three selected issues of crucial significance to their relationships, namely, (1) the nature of university autonomy and academic freedom and the mechanisms employed by the state to ensure its dominance; (2) the existence of regional imbalances in the quantitative and qualitative levels of educational development and the political effort to regulate access to education in order to rectify such imparities through an officially imposed quota system; and (3) the political pressures and resultant efforts by the state to introduce greater relevance and practicality in the university curriculum, in its degree structure, and in its academic product in the interest of national development. We will conclude with a brief assessment of the ways in which the university and the state dealt with these issues.

Zaire (then Congo) became independent on June 30, 1960, and was immediately plunged into a mélange of serious and protracted crises: provincial secessions, ethnic conflicts, interparty struggles, rebellions, mutiny in the armed forces, and extreme governmental fragility—all aggravated by the intrusion of international economic and political interests. The Congo became synonymous, internationally, with postcolonial chaos. On November 4, 1965, Colonel Mobutu took power in a bloodless *coup d'état* and began a process of national pacification, unification, and stabilization. He launched campaigns for the development of a new work ethic and against rampant corruption, nepotism, and tribalism. Major monetary and politicoadministrative reforms were instituted and wrought much improvement. The strength and determination of the new regime were dramatically demonstrated nationally by public hangings of opponents and internationally by a showdown with Belgian industrial and financial companies controlling the mining industries of the Katanga.

Adroitly and unremittingly, the new regime pursued a policy of centralization and concentration of power, as evidenced by the dissolution of parliament, the suppression of the position of prime minister, the abolition of all labor unions and political parties, and the creation of a single national party with compulsory membership—the Mouvement Populaire de la Révolution (MPR). A personality cult was developed around the president. This was made *de jure* by the Constitution of 1974, probably one of the most remarkably candid constitutional explications of monism existent:

> In the Republic of Zaire, there exists one sole institution; the Mouvement Populaire de la Revolution. . . . [It] is the Nation politically organized. . . . [Its President] is by right President of the Republic and enjoys the full exercise of power. He presides over the Political Bureau, the (MPR) Congress, the Legislative Council, the Executive Council, and the Judicial Council. . . . [He] names and dismisses the Regional Commissioners . . . the bench and prosecuting magistrates. He is the Supreme Commander of the Armed Forces. He names and dismisses the officers of the armed forces . . . [and] the executive level public servants of the Administration.[1]

"L'état c'est moi" is a Mobutuism; Louis XIV only asserted it first. Cardinal Richelieu and Napoleon would also find it familiar; all *corps intermédiaires* are divisive and therefore intolerable. These include political parties, ethnic associations, student organizations, labor unions, and, of course, autonomous universities. Monism abhors pluralism.

It is within the foregoing political framework that Zaire's university system has evolved. However, the creation of that system is best understood against the background of two striking features of the whole Belgian Congo colonial system of education: (1) its virtually total domination by Belgian Catholic missions and (2) its explicit anti-elitism, vocationalism, and utilitarianism. The overwhelming preeminence of state-subsidized Belgian Catholic missions over unsubsidized (until 1948) mainly non-Belgian Protestant missions reflected a calculated official policy of favoring "national missions" for the purposes of colonial security and Belgian national interests. Until World War II both the Belgian government and the colonial government of the Congo "assumed virtually no operational responsibility for African education."[2] The few such *écoles officielles* as were opened were staffed by Catholic teaching orders.[3] Even the large mining and agricultural companies gave exclusive control of their schools to Belgian Catholic missions. And between its founding in 1954 and the eve of its final nationalization in 1971, eleven years after independence, Zaire's first and main university—Lovanium—was under the total domination of the Catholic University of Louvain.[4]

Until the mid-1950s there was a virtually exclusive emphasis upon mass primary education, conceived of as both utilitarian and terminal. The extreme shallowness of the educational pyramid at independence is illuminated by the percentage of school-age population enrolled in schools at the three levels: primary, 98.26 percent; secondary, 1.7 percent; and postsecondary, 0.04 percent.[5] The extraordinary emphasis upon the primary level has been justified by its practitioners as being required to provide a large educated base in order to ensure the quality of the elite to be selected from it.[6] In fact, the policy was explicitly anti-elitist: "Pas d'élites, pas d'ennuis" (no elites, no problems). Instruction was in the vernacular, not only for broader diffusion of Christianity but to avoid what was considered useless elitist pretensions and aspirations. As then envisaged, the avowed aim of education was "to produce better Africans, and not copies of Europeans who could never be more than humans of a third category."[7] The same terminative and anti-elitist principles also applied to such postprimary and secondary education as existed. At independence, the vast majority in postprimary schools (75 percent) were terminal in the purely vocational and utilitarian lower secondary levels: "the state, the large companies and the missions saw little need for education beyond these schools which were sufficient for their purposes."[8] Only a small fraction were enrolled in schools having the complete secondary cycle, which could have been preparatory for university education if such had been available, but was not available until 1954.

Not only was the university nonexistent in the Congo, but there was an explicit policy of preventing the training of Congolese in Belgian universities or any others abroad. Only very reluctantly did the colonial authorities finally respond to the combined pressure of the Congolese "*évolués*," some professors of the Catholic University of Louvain, certain missionaries, and the demonstration effect of dramatic events elsewhere in Africa undergoing rapid liberation. In April 1954 they authorized the opening of Lovanium University on the outskirts of Leopoldville. From the very beginning, the new university was clearly marked by its total dependence upon the parent university of Louvain, by the dominance of the Catholic Church, by the resultant tension between the state and the church over its control, and by the tiny number of Congolese admitted for university-level study. In 1955, one year after Lovanium was created, a Socialist-Liberal government succeeded the Christian Social Party in Belgium and created the nonconfessional Official University of the Congo in Lubumbashi, modeled after, and closely linked with, Belgium's state universities of Ghent and Liège. Zaire's third university—the Free University

Table 13. Enrollment Increases in Republic of Zaire, 1950–1977
(Numbers of students)

	1950	*1960–61*	*1965*	*1971–72*	*1977*
Secondary Level	4,004	38,000	118,078	297,556	643,675
University Level	0	419	1,107	9,558	13,399

Sources: H. Kitchen, ed., *The Educated African* (New York: Praeger, 1962), p. 193; E. Bustin, "Education for Development, National University of Zaire: A Review" (unpublished manuscript, 1979), p. 65.

of the Congo—was established in Kisangani in 1963, the culmination of protracted efforts by Protestant missionaries; its links were primarily with the Free University of Amsterdam.[9]

For fifteen years after independence in 1960 the government of the Congo continued to rely upon missionary organization for the operation of the primary and secondary levels of the educational system, although in 1961–1962, under the strong influence of UNESCO, several major changes were introduced, including the requirements that French be the language of instruction in all primary schools. In 1967, a national state examination was established for high-school graduates, the successful passing of which gave entitlement to university admission. In 1971 the three widely dispersed universities, together with all other postsecondary institutions in the country, were incorporated into a single monolithic National University of Zaire (UNAZA). One decade later, in 1981, these latter major changes were reversed. The "institutes" were separated from UNAZA and the latter was, in turn, disintegrated into its three former constituent universities.

Apart from these dramatic structural changes and reversals, there have been three major interrelated developments in Zaire's educational system since independence. One of these has been the explosive expansion in school enrollments, particularly at the secondary and university levels, as table 13 shows, reflecting the uncontrollable escalation in social demand. A second development has been the complete abandonment of the Belgian colonial principle and practice of making primary and most of secondary education terminal for all but the very few. As elsewhere in the developing world, Zaire has been severely afflicted with Dore's "diploma disease," in which the sole function of primary education is perceived as being preparation for the secondary level, and the latter in turn prepares solely for the university level; any form of education short of that which leads to a university degree is regarded as categorically unacceptable—a death-blow to one's self-esteem and life chances.[10] The third development has been an inexorable, self-reproducing degradation of the quality of education at all levels.

With this brief explanation we now turn to an examination of the three issues in state-university relationships previously identified—university autonomy and academic freedom, regional imbalances and politically imposed quotas, and the imperative of relevance and practicality.

University Autonomy and Academic Freedom

Although Zaire obtained its formal political independence in 1960, it did not achieve formal university independence until 1971, the year of the creation of the National University of Zaire (UNAZA). Lovanium University, Zaire's first university, remained a veritable state within a state, a satellite of Louvain University in Belgium, whose constitution, standards, curricula content, and ethos it replicated under the dynamic and dominating rectorship of Monseigneur Luc Gillon. Throughout its life it was Zaire's premier university, staffed overwhelmingly by Belgian professors, and insulated almost totally from effective control or influence by the colonial state until 1960, or by the Zairian state until 1971.

This autonomy and distance from the state was a calculated objective, as noted by one of Lovanium's founders, Guy Malengreau:

> We must form a Catholic elite and assure its social and political education by having it participate under our direction in our colonial undertaking. . . . To this elite we must open the doors of higher education, always under the condition that this education cannot be trusted to a state agency, which under the pretext of neutrality and of freedom of choice would create only a nursery for rebels.[11]

Despite the fact that by 1971 a full 80 percent of the operating budget of Lovanium and the universities in Lubumbashi and Kisangani was covered by the Zairian government, the three universities remained fairly autonomous under their respective charters and external linkages. While recognizing their obligation to respect the state, the principle of institutional autonomy and freedom from government intervention was vigorously affirmed by the universities, and reasonably respected by the new state in the earlier years.

The principle of academic freedom for faculty and students was also an integral part of the ethos of the universities in their inception and early years of operation. Academic freedom here refers to freedom of teachers to teach what they believe to be the truth, the freedom of students to choose what they wish to learn, and the freedom of both to engage in research without fear of hindrance, dismissal, or reprisal. At the birth of Lovanium for example, heterodoxy was explicitly stipulated. There existed no obligation on the part of either faculty or students to have a "positive engagement" regarding Catholicism either as a faith or as a church, and it was not to be regarded officially as a Catholic University.[12] Immediately before independence in 1960 the expatriate professors at the Official University of the Congo in Elizabethville (now Lubumbashi) proposed that among the independence accords between the governments of Belgium and the future Democratic Republic of the Congo there should be one explicitly protecting the existing academic freedom of the professoriate (presumably from the new government), indeed, that it should specify that the university remain a Belgian institution "put at the disposition of the Congo for a period of time."[13] The Protestant origin of the Free University of the Congo, and the consequent heavy American and Dutch presence, likewise assured the prominence of the principle of academic freedom as known and respected in those countries whose universities served as models.

As noted elsewhere, a variety of factors present in most African countries during the independence decade of the 1960s combined to create and maintain a distance between the universities and the new African governments—the initial inherited or emulated patterns of university governance were explicitly designed by the founders to create such a distance; the close metropolitan dependency relationships, especially in the recruitment of expatriate staff (e.g., the Louvain-Lovanium axis was matched by the U.K. special relationships, the Dakar-Paris linkage) and in developmental assistance; the singular concentration upon the "replacement function" (accelerated Africanization of the public services) perpetuated and reinforced the Eurocentric orientation; the command posts in the administration and academic departments and in the senior ranks of the professoriate were overwhelmingly dominated by expatriates.[14] These factors tended to promote on the part of the universities an essentially conservative posture, the primacy of universalism and the maintenance of international standards, and an avoidance of involvement with or threats to the new African regimes; and initially at least, a more or less indifferent or deferential, if not reverential, attitude toward the universities on the part of the new regimes. Also, in most countries—but, interestingly, not in Zaire—African university students of the first wave were comparatively quiescent politically, assured as they were of automatically gaining elite status upon graduation. Toward the end of the 1960s this quiescence disappeared and everywhere the distance between state and university began rapidly to narrow.

Even though the government was not the target of their agitation, the radicalization of the Zairian university students at Lovanium during the 1960s led inexorably to increased state intervention and control over the university, and ultimately over the students themselves, in the end resulting in a total loss of institutional autonomy and a progressive erosion of academic freedom. In March 1964, the General Association of Students of Lovanium (AGEL) launched a bitter strike which lasted a full week, involved the entire student body, and paralyzed life on the campus. Central to their demands were the Africanization of the university and student participation in university governance. The strike failed miserably, but it served the ominous purpose of opening the door to a loss of university autonomy. As Ilunga notes:

> Things changed after the student strike. . . . The academic authorities, who for a long time had taken refuge behind the principle of university autonomy and maintained a haughty attitude of isolation and independence, were forced by events to seek the backing of the national political authorities, who were the only ones capable of protecting them from the student challenge. All too willing to be called to the rescue of an institution which they little understood . . . the Zairian authorities gradually took advantage of the situation to extend their control over the university.[15]

The same scenario repeated itself on the Lovanium campus again in 1969 and yet again in 1971. The first event provided the pretext for an *Ordonnance-Loi* of 1969, which stipulated that the rector and the vice rectors of the universities be appointed by the President of the Republic and that professors be appointed by the Minister of Education. The events of 1971 provoked the *coup de grâce,* the radical nationalization of all three universities and their reconstitution as a single National University of Zaire under the total control of the central government.

The nationalization and political subordination of Zaire's universities in 1971 was not an isolated retaliatory action aimed at solving at once the irritants of student activism and external domination of Zaire's universities; rather it was the culmination in the educational sector of a general process of secularization, centralization, and concentration of power in all sectors, already described.

Although centralization of power was an all-engulfing process to which the educational system—like all other sectors—would inevitably have to succumb, several additional elements operated to reinforce the rationale for the creation of a monolithic, multicampus, single-faculty, nationwide system of higher education. One was the political opportunity provided to transfer the agitation-prone faculties of social sciences and humanities (*sciences sociales et lettres*) to Lubumbashi, 1500 miles from Kinshasa, the more ignitable and vulnerable political center of the country.

A second element was the opportunity that the wholesale restructuring of the system provided for economizing and rationalizing the development of Zairian higher education. Since 1968 the government of Zaire had endeavored to establish, rationalize, and consolidate a national system of university education. This was pursued through an Inter-university Commission established by the Ministry of National Education in that year. Repeated—but largely abortive—efforts were made to use the Ministry's power of resource allocation to enforce greater rationality, coherence, and economy through nonduplication of faculties.

A third reinforcing element was the growing realization that the traditional Eurocentric type of education being imparted at all three universities was largely irrelevant and failed to prepare graduates with those skills, knowledge, and orientations that a developing society required. The existing universities were largely resistant to any fundamental adaptation of curricular or degree structures aimed at greater relevance and practicality. Only drastic surgery, it was reasoned, could bring about the necessary reorientation. Thus, the strong nationalist desire to terminate continued external domination of the universities and to accelerate Zairianization of the professoriate; the political imperative of dispersion, if not rustication, of activist students; and the urgency of achieving a more cost-effective, economizing, rational, relevant, and practical system of higher education—all of these elements provided powerful reinforcement for and justification of the Mobutu regime's independent drive for the centralization of power in Zaire.

The creation of UNAZA in August 1971 was among the last efforts in the restructuring and final consolidation of the monistic state. The process of centralization of all major structures within the state was replicated within the university; the latter became an isomorph of the former. The institutional autonomy possessed and exercised by its three predecessor universities disappeared with UNAZA's establishment as their incorporating successor. True, initially the Conseil d'Administration (Board of Trustees) of UNAZA was nominally endowed with all of the powers previously enjoyed by the *conseils* of the three incorporated predecessor universities, and four distinguished foreigners were made members.[16] However, in due course the Minister of Education was made President of the Council and the four external members were eliminated. At the daily operating level a measure of institutional discretion in certain routine, nonstrategic functional areas was permitted to exist, either by default or indifference, or because of the regime's incapacity to monitor the massive and complex monistic university structure it had created. Nevertheless, the power of the President and his Minister of National Education to intervene, and to direct or veto any matter, was omnipresent, and through repeated demonstrations, increasingly evident to all. The primacy of political authority was very clearly asserted. All important decisions affecting UNAZA were made either by Presidential Legislative Ordinance (*Ordonnance-Loi*) or by executive order emanating from the State Commissioner for Higher Education (*Arrêté Départmental*).[17] The rector became a powerless figurehead.

During the decade of UNAZA's existence various mechanisms were employed by the regime to perfect and ensure its continued control. Prominent and most effective among such control stratagems were the domination and manipulation of university administrators, the selective and rotating co-optation by the regime of members of the professoriate, and the co-optation of student leaders and neutralization of student organizations.

Although the inherited traditions of university governance presume the primacy of academics, in most new African states it has been the university administrators who have emerged as dominant. Zairian academics had already been introduced to the authoritarian administrative style of the first Belgian rector of Lovanium. However, after its creation the "command ethos" even more pronouncedly pervaded the functioning of UNAZA: the imperious edict of the administrator everywhere became the dominant mode. At least four factors help to explain this development. (1) The administration was the first component of the university to be indigenized; within a very short period there was nearly total Zairianization of the *postes de commande* in UNAZA, a necessary and understandable affirmation of Zairian independence. (2) There was the assumption that any reasonably intelligent person could be an administrator; no specialized advanced training, such as that required of academics, was expected, nor was there peer review or need for professional recognition. (3) Administrators controlled the purse strings; academic department heads and deans of faculties had extremely limited budgets for discretionary expenditures, resulting in their almost total dependence upon the whims and favors of administrators. (4) Finally, it was through the administrative cadres that the regime could control the university; therefore it was determined to assure their primacy. The loyalty and compliance of the university administrative class were secured by two stratagems used extensively by the President in all sectors. One was the calculated placement of persons from his own region (Equator) either in command positions or, where a facade of ethnic balance in top positions was desired, in immediate secondary positions. A second was the deliberate cultivation of a climate of insecurity, uncertainty, and dependence through frequent (usually annual) and unpredictable rotation of persons in and out of administrative command positions, thereby making it impossible for any one of them to build and sustain a personal empire and constituency.

Co-optation of members of the university professoriate has long been one of President Mobutu's most artfully effective devices for neutralizing dissent and opposition or commanding support and even adulation. Selective rotating appointments of Zairian professors to high positions in government or the party—appointments which could not be refused—not only brought status, a vastly higher salary, and much coveted perquisites, but also, to many recipients, opportunities for a certain amount of peculation within an established system of institutionalized corruption.[18] Invariably, those selected would cling to their professorships because the duration of appointments of co-optation are capriciously indeterminate and usually relatively brief; room must be made for those awaiting their turn for the once-in-a-lifetime opportunity to peculate freely in order to accumulate some working capital, acquire a house and car, and start a business. Indeed, the effectiveness of this device in encouraging political quietism has rested as much upon keeping alive the hopes of those awaiting their turn as it has upon satiation by those already co-opted.

The seduction and the leverage of co-optation have been vastly enhanced by the progressive degradation of the professional and personal lives of the members of the university professoriate. Throughout the 1970s the academic profession became less appealing, as evidenced by its declining ability to attract qualified people and by the migration of academics to other sectors within Zaire or abroad. Zairian professors increasingly faced an almost total lack of the most elementary supporting services and infrastructure (chalk, paper, research funding, library acquisitions, etc.). Throughout the 1970s the salaries of the highest ranking Zairian members of the professoriate were only a fraction of those of the most senior employees of governmental and parastatal agencies, with whose emoluments they had previously been assimilated. Although the government endeavored to rectify this imbalance from time to time, its efforts appeared to have little practical effect. Once at the top of the pyramid of occupational prestige, the professoriate plummeted to a disesteemed and degraded status in the self-image of many of its members. It became a milieu of dearth and penury in which only the men of power and corruption and their associated wealth commanded the valued material conditions of life. Inescapably many—but not all—of its members became even more demoralized and vulnerable to, and ripe for, co-optation.

Students have been equally amenable to co-optation. When President Mobutu came to power in 1965 the Congolese university student movement had become highly radicalized, and was initially ambivalent toward him: it was suspicious of his American connections and his role in the First Republic, yet it was attracted to his unitarian, centralizing, and nationalistic orientations, as well as to his appeal to technocratic competence.[19] Once again Mobutu turned to the university-educated elite to staff the central government, bringing freshly graduated students—including particularly student leaders—into the presidency.[20] By 1969, however, student-regime tension has become very high, leading to overt political protests in 1969 and 1971 and violent repression by the regime, followed by the abolition of all student groups and their replacement by the Jeunesse du Mouvement Populaire de la Révolution (JMPR), the youth wing of the sole legitimate Zairian political party charged with mobilizing the nation's youth behind the person and policies of Mobutu.[21] Systematic co-optation of radically inclined student leaders into posh JMPR leadership positions since 1971 has been the main stratagem of neutralizing student activism. However, this co-optation carrot has been complemented by the stick of the threat, or the actuality, of repression, the most memorable and draconian being the conscription of the entire student body into the army in 1971. Notwithstanding these containment measures, widespread student strikes exploded in April 1980 and continued in direct defiance of a presidential ultimatum. These strikes involved secondary- and primary-school students as well as those at the university, and were explicitly expressive of larger political issues.

These devices for manipulating the various strategic elements in the university effectively guaranteed regime control over the functioning of the university; they also obviously served as effective restraints on professorial and student academic freedom. Prior to the nationalization of the universities in 1971 the ethos and norms of academic freedom prevailed; after the birth of UNAZA, however, the presence of the regime on the campuses and in the classroom became increasingly visible and weighty through watchful administrators and student informants. There was no overt censorship, nor ideological prescription. However, anticipation of being graced by rotation into a high administrative role in the university through the annual *remaniement* (reshuffle), or by direct co-optation into the regime itself, plus the threat of *licenciement* (termination) were powerful goads to professorial self-censorship. However, as in other minimal-coercion authoritarian regimes in African new states, there is relatively little overt and explicit denial of freedom within academe. As noted elsewhere, such denial may be omnipresent as a threat, and actualized in confrontation situations, but the anomaly of an ostensibly permissive authoritarianism prevails.[22]

The quiet self-censorship, and teaching of politically sensitive subjects by analogy, induced by the seductions of co-optation or the threat of its being withheld or other resources and status denied—even quiet termination arranged—appear tolerably effective for the containment of any serious open opposition from the professoriate. Moreover, such regimes try to minimize or avoid international criticism and censure; national universities are unique sources of pride, as well as instruments for and symbols of coequal participation in the world community. Also, monitoring university teaching and research requires the sophistication, the determination, the massive weight of a continuous presence, and the resources of a totalitarian regime, which neither the Zairian nor most other authoritarian regimes possess. So long as the professoriate does not blatantly express criticism or dissent regarding the regime to a larger audience outside the classroom or through the mass media, the authorities appear to be indifferent, because the threat is judged by them not to be worth the effort required to try to control it.

However, all Zairian academics are sensitive to the omnipresent potentiality of repressive action against them under the present regime.[23] The President has emphasized a special Rousseauistic conception of freedom, the idea that freedom is found in obeying the laws of the state. Freedom to do as one likes is "*licence*," an abuse of liberty; true freedom requires discipline.[24] The Zairian professoriate recently witnessed the application of this idea in the actions taken by the regime following a 1980 conference at N'Sele at which they were encouraged to speak freely and frankly, and did so. Some conferees were intimidated, others were co-opted into silencing and rewarding positions; the final conference report was drastically edited to reflect the regime's views and not the criticisms voiced by the professors.

Regional Imbalances and the University Quota System

Regional imbalances in educational opportunities originated from the uneven penetration of colonization, particularly of missions, and from the differential response of local populations. The uneven penetration was due to geographical, demographic, economic, cultural, and linguistic factors. Indeed, geographical access, climatic conditions, and the general salubrity of an area largely determined the choice of sites for the implantation of missions, the continuity of the presence of missionaries, and the expansion of their activities in that area. The missions also favored areas that were densely populated and had widely spoken common languages for evangelistic and instructional purposes. The educational impact of a mission varied according to the type of congregation running it, its emphasis upon education, and its resources in personnel and funds. The commitment of the Jesuits in the former Leopoldville province (now Bandundu and lower Zaire regions) and the Scheutists in the former Kasai province largely account for the present disparities, as illuminated in table 14.

Differential response of the local populations is another variable. Success in the establishment of schools also depends greatly upon the reactions of the local communities for which the new institutions are intended. Such reactions may be influenced by cultural variables—the community's means of production, its sociopolitical organization, and/or by the values held by its members. Although the role of culture in predisposing both individuals and communities to adopt or resist schools is undeniable, most studies do not go beyond impressionistic and stereotypical descriptions.[25] Furthermore, an overemphasis on the cultural barriers to the successful implantation of schools overlooks the fact that missions were not equally effective everywhere; as mentioned earlier, they were not even present everywhere.

However caused, over time these initial ethnic and regional imbalances had a cumulative, self-reproducing effect. As a result, the educated elite stratum of the emergent Congolese society was dominated by a few ethnic groups. The policy of regional quotas was introduced to remedy these imbalances.

The system of regional quotas for admission to the university was officially introduced in 1971 with the creation of UNAZA. But concern over the ethnic and regional disparities underlying this policy existed long before that and was even voiced in colonial times. As early as 1958, when a Congolese educated elite was still nonexistent,[26] Van Bilsen suggested in his plan for educational development that the eventual elites should come from all ethnic groups and strata of the population in order to ensure "equilibrium." A decade later, in a comprehensive survey of the Zairian educational system in 1968, Rideout and his colleagues underscored the regional differentials and the special priority which should be given to projects which tend to reduce the disparities of opportunities, although they did not recommend quotas.[27]

Table 14. Regional (Ethnic) Imbalances in Education in Zaire

	Percentage of total population, 1975[a]	*Percentage enrolled primary school, 1974–75*[b]	*Percentage enrolled primary teacher training, 1973*[c]	*Percentage enrolled for state examination, 1981*[d]	*Percentage professoriate, faculty of economics, 1978–79*[e]	*Percentage professoriate, faculty of social science, 1977–78*[e]
East Kasai	7	100	19	22	30	26
West Kasai	8	52	8	9	10	13
Lower Zaire	7	85	12	7	20	10
Bandundu	14	76	11	14	13	13
Shaba	13	71	12	10	11	14
Kivu	17	50	8	11	10	16
Upper Zaire	15	49	13	4	3	3
Equator	12	46	7	6	3	5
Kinshasa	7	—	10	17[f]	—	—

[a] Source: J. Boute, "La Population du Zaire d'ici à 1985," *Zaire-Afrique* (1979): 7.

[b] Source: Département de l'Education Nationale, Direction de la Planification, *L'Enseignement au Zaire à la veille du plan national du développement* (Kinshasa, 1977), vol. 1. The percentage shown is the total actually enrolled out of the total eligible school-age population (ages 6–11).

[c] Source: T. E. Turner and M. C. Young, *The Rise and Decline of the Zairian State* (1981). Primary teacher training colleges are among the principal sources of new entrants into the university; enrollments are therefore indicators of continued reproduction of imbalances.

[d] Source: Afrique-Actualités, *Zaire-Afrique* (1981), p. 156. Those enrolled in state examination indicate the number who are in their terminal year of secondary education.

[e] Source: E. Bustin, "Education for Development, National University of Zaire: A Review" (unpublished, 1979), p. 72. Imbalances are greatest among lower ranks of the professoriate.

[f] Source: A majority of those enrolled for the state examination in Kinshasa probably came from Lower Zaire, Bandundu, and Kasai regions.

Apart from the political goal of minimizing and/or defusing the interethnic or interregional conflicts that might be caused by gross inequalities in educational development, the quota system was also justified in terms of an overall political philosophy of educational democracy and justice, offering equal opportunities to all. Social justice in general, and more specifically in education, has been a recurrent theme in President Mobutu's speeches and in the resolutions and directives of the party.[28]

Regional quotas are officially applied in three areas: the admission of students to the university, the hiring of teaching assistants, and the distribution of scholarships for graduate study abroad. The application of regional quotas in the hiring and promotion of senior members of the faculty (associate professors and professors) is somewhat hindered by the availability of positions to be filled. Thus in the following discussion, we will be mainly concerned with the application of regional quotas in those domains where scarcity of positions has prompted the government to intervene and control access.

In the name of regional balance, qualified students of well-represented regions have been denied entry to the university, while lower academic standards have been applied to admit candidates from underrepresented regions. Likewise, in the hiring of teaching assistants, qualified candidates from certain regions have been turned away while academically questionable candidates from higher priority regions were hired.

The same regional criterion is used in the allocation of scholarships for graduate studies abroad. This is true of scholarships offered by those external donors required to operate through the Zairian government (private foundations excepted), as well as of those offered by the Zairian government itself. It is significant in this regard that K. I. B. Nguz, the former Prime Minister of Zaire, gave as one of the reasons for his recent resignation the fact that the President's followers were trying to discredit him by circulating rumors to the effect that he had distributed hundreds of scholarships for graduate studies in the U.S. to students from the Kasai region.[29] The truth or falsity of this allegation is less important for our purposes than the emphasis placed on the ethnic manipulation of scholarships—an indication of the prominence of the ethnic factor in Zairian political culture.

The goals of the regional quota policy and the means to attain them have not always been unambiguously or consistently defined. It is not clear, for example, whether the rationale of the policy is to impede further education of the ethnic groups which dominate the educated elite, mainly the Baluba and Bakongo, or to promote the advancement of underrepresented groups, mainly those of the provinces of Upper Zaire and Equateur, the latter being the region of provenience of the President and of the political and military elite surrounding him, or perhaps to provide an equal number of openings for each of the nine administrative regions of the country.

Another problem in the application of the policy of quotas is that although the quotas are officially defined in terms of administrative regions, in fact, the system has strong ethnic overtones. Regional quotas are often perceived as aiming essentially at restraining the Bakongo and the Baluba and promoting the President's own ethnic group. Furthermore, within a region, the educational development of the various ethnic groups may be uneven. For that reason, some members of groups submerged within a region against which quota limits are applied (e.g., the two Kasai) resent being penalized just because they happen to live in those regions, particularly in view of the fact that their groups constitute an underrepresented minority.

Young notes that in 1972 at the campus of Lubumbashi, "only 2% of the first year students came from Equateur region," one of the regions the quota system aimed at favoring.[30] Similarly, the Baluba of Kasai, the Bakongo of Lower Zaire, and the Kikongo-speaking groups of Bandundu still constitute the dominant majority of the professoriate, as table 14 shows. The predominance of these regions is likely to continue for a while, considering, for example, that for the Faculty of Economics, 85 percent of the doctoral candidates being trained abroad are indigenous to those regions.

These numbers indicate clearly that the policy of quotas has not solved the problem of regional imbalances. Focusing on the admission of students to the university, let us examine why the quota system has not worked. First of all, there is the very magnitude of the social demand for education, as table 13 shows. This demand is stronger precisely in those regions which are supposed to be curbed by the quota policy.

Irregular admissions which do not comply with the regional quota policy contribute to the perpetration of regional and ethnic imbalances. Students succeed in getting around the regulations through their personal social networks, by assuming another identity, and by bribery. Through the informal networks, strong pressures are exerted on the authorities of the university to admit students outside of the quotas. These pressures may come either from within the university (e.g., when a university authority recommends to the registrar the admission of his brother-in-law in spite of the quotas) or from outside the university (e.g., when a high-ranking officer of the army recommends the admission of a cousin of his third wife).

Some students who do not have an influential personal network, or whose network fails to get them admitted to the university, may resort to bribing key employees of the registrar's office with cash payments or may promise to give up the first two months of their scholarships if they are enrolled. The device of gaining admission through a change of name and region of origin is facilitated by the ease with which identification papers can be obtained in Zaire, and by the new ideology of cultural authenticity, which ordered the rejection of "imported" Christian names and the adoption of new Zairian ones. Students from Kasai are adept at this type of ruse.

As these examples indicate, irregular admissions may involve all levels of the university hierarchy as well as holders of power and influence in the wider sociopolitical arena. Because of the high value attached to education, every effort is made to get into the university. Payanzo, a Zairian sociologist, notes a disproportionate representation of students from small and larger urban centers to the detriment of those from the rural areas.[31] The concentration of schools in cities can partially account for this observation. But, following our foregoing argument, it can also be explained by the fact that students from cities are more likely to have an extended and influential personal network assisting their admission and to know how to get around the university bureaucracy. As the popular idiom puts it, "they see more clearly" (*bamona clair*) and they can always find a way to solve their problems (*se débrouiller*).

Members of ethnic groups the quota system is supposed to restrict are found in large numbers in most major cities. For example, the Kikongo-speaking peoples of the Lower Zaire and Bandundu regions constitute the overwhelming majority of the population of Kinshasa, the capital city, and the Baluba are present everywhere in large numbers. The presence in centers of power and the ability to manipulate the system and to use one's influence to further the interests of one's people are also important variables undermining the quota system.

These are the main factors which have hindered the strict application of the quota policy. Not only has this policy not reached its goals, it has also given rise, as an unintended outcome, to a heightened sense of ethnic and tribal identity; it has created feelings of oppression and frustration among some ethnic groups; it has contributed to the development of a pervasive sense of distrust toward the academic institution; and it has helped to justify other abuses and breaches of regulations within that already fragile institution.

The Political Pressure for Relevance

The National University of Zaire, like most universities in the new states of Africa, was born in an era when the ethos of "developmentalism" was at its apogee. Universities were not excluded from its normative dictates. Indeed, the 1963 UNESCO Conference on the Development of Higher Education in Africa concluded that "universities are the main instruments of national progress."[32] They must be demonstrably relevant for and totally committed to national development. This has meant a radical change in the concept of purpose and the nature of the curriculum—indeed, the entire spirit—of the traditional models of university education inherited from Europe; for Zaire this meant a transformation of the Belgian model. Relevance above all meant for the student greater practicality and experiential learning regarding the "real problems" of development.

Initially, the major source of exhortation to greater developmental relevance was the international donor community. Throughout the 1960s they had given the highest priority in their aid of the development of LDC (Less Developed Country) universities for the local production of the high-level manpower required both to replace the departing expatriate colonial administrators and to staff the expanding governmental and parastatal agencies charged with developmental missions. However, by the late 1960s and early 1970s rates of return analysis and other indicators began to signal possible overinvestment in seemingly unproductive universities. One response was to exert greater emphasis and pressure on the universities to demonstrate their developmental relevance.[33] However, independent of the needs of the donor community to fortify their rationale for continued support of university development, national political leadership in new states became ever more acutely aware of both the practical irrelevance and the unbearably high cost of higher education in the face of a politically uncontrollable explosion in social demand for it.[34] The fact that the politically exigent task of expatriate replacement had largely been accomplished by the early 1970s, the emergence of burgeoning numbers of unemployable university graduates with knowledge and skills of limited marketability added urgency to the demand for relevance.

Three main components of relevance can be distinguished in the educational philosophy of Zaire: socioeconomic relevance defined in terms of practicality and professionalization; cultural relevance referring to *authenticité* or cultural revival and identity; and political relevance defined as good citizenship and commitment to the political goals of the regime.

The concern for practicality and professionalization developed to remedy what was perceived as a basic inadequacy of the university in helping to meet the pressing needs of the country. Key indicators were the amazingly high rate of attrition not only at the university but also throughout the whole educational system[35] and the continuing shortages in technically qualified human resources. As a Zairian vice minister of education put it: "The educational system was training useless or immediately non-usable individuals."[36] This lament is not a new theme in the educational philosophy of Zaire; in fact it has inspired most of the reforms of the educational system and has often been used as exhortation in the political rhetoric of the party. Nor is this concern uniquely Zairian, as already noted.

The concern for cultural relevance derived from the belief that the university was not only not contributing to the development of Zaire's national culture, but that it was transmitting values alien to the country and inimical to a truly Zairian cultural identity. Here again, although the immersion of the university in its cultural environment was particularly emphasized throughout the seventies during the heyday of *authenticité*, the regime's doctrine of cultural nationalism and identity, the idea has long been current in both political and academic milieux. Verhaegen argued that the fundamental task of a truly African university was "to contribute to the development of scientific knowledge and to teach about the cultural and social roots of African societies."[37]

The third component of relevance has been the twin political imperatives of structural integration of the university into the centralized state apparatus, previously discussed, and the inculcation of a commitment by its members (administrators, professors, and students) to the political goals of the regime.

The principle of relevance was a dominant theme in all discussions leading up to the major university reform of 1971. Specific new measures designed to increase the relevance of higher education included the restructuring and reorientation of the *graduat* cycle (the first two years of the university), the fostering of increased enrollments in the natural and physical sciences, the creation of an institute of continuing education, and curricular revisions.

The reform of the *graduat* cycle sought to create a unified cycle for the campuses and the specialized vocational institutes of UNAZA in order to make lateral transfers between the two possible. It also sought greater practicality and professionalization in order that the *graduat* degree could be respectably terminal, that is, that "the training given the students in any particular cycle should be such to qualify them for a useful role in society upon its completion."[38] In order to realize this goal, a third year was added to the *graduat* cycle in 1976 and the whole cycle "professionalized" by curriculum revisions and the introduction of a one-month internship and a report thereon.

The 1971 reform reaffirmed the imperative of developing the technical disciplines and natural sciences, and sought to achieve this through the requirement that candidates for admission to the university coming from the scientific sections of high school be automatically enrolled in the "hard" sciences. By way of inducement, the monthly stipends of students enrolled in these higher priority disciplines, in the *instituts supérieurs*, and in education were initially double the stipends of students in the humanities and social sciences. Continuing education (*éducation permanente*) was also stressed at the congress and presented as one way the university could contribute to the "culture and training of the general population," and accordingly a university center for this function was created, the Centre Interdisciplinaire pour le Développement de l'Education Permanente (CIDEP).

It was also recommended that curricular revisions emphasize courses on African and Zairian cultures, history, and languages, as well as civics, in order to educate a new type of Zairian "whose personality reflects African values of solidarity and of respect for elder persons and authorities."

All of these innovations and reforms have failed to bring about the much desired relevance. Despite the compulsory enrollment and preferential treatment of students in the physical and natural sciences, the majority of students were still found in the humanities and social sciences.[39] Even though there was a slight shift toward the hard sciences of the period 1971–1977,[40] it was nullified by the rate of attrition. The latter is largely due to the general degradation in the quality of high-school education and resultant decline in enrollments in the scientific subjects.

Efforts to professionalize the *graduat* cycle, and also render it acceptably terminal, also failed. Afflicted by the "diploma disease" and lured by the prestige primacy of the *licence* (B.A.), most of those completing the *graduat* cycle resolutely persisted to obtain the coveted *licence*. Very few transfers of students between the campuses and institutes occurred. Curricular revisions were minimal or merely cosmetic, the professoriate having neither the experience, nor the means, nor the time to make them. Lack of funding and ineffective planning hampered the internship program. Small wonder then, that in February 1980, President Mobutu terminated the unification whose rationale was precisely to ensure greater practicality in university studies.

Neither has CIDEP as a center for continuing education and vocational training been able to achieve its goals. Courses are taught by the same university professors, using the same *ex cathedra* teaching methods they use at the university. The majority of students are dropouts from high school, institutes, or the university. Hence, an institution aimed at providing continuing education has become a parallel university granting diplomas to those who do not meet the requirements either to have access to or to graduate from the university.

The failure of efforts to achieve greater professionalization and relevance has been acknowledged by President Mobutu himself. Indeed, in a major speech, following the Shaba I war, he noted: "In spite of the enormous sacrifices made by the state for this sector [education], the results reached are not yet satisfactory. . . . The National University of Zaire is supersaturated by a student population whose training does not always correspond to the demands of the job market."[41] In fact, the failure of the quest for relevance is not limited only to its socioeconomic aspects but extends as well to the cultural and political dimensions as defined by the regime. The abolition of the National University of Zaire in 1981 can be seen as the official acknowledgement of the failure of the 1971 reforms.

Numerous factors can account for this failure. The foregoing analysis has already mentioned a few of them (e.g. ceaseless improvisation, insufficient funding, inadequate organization, and outmoded teaching methods). The inertia of the university bureaucracy and the cynicism with which many Zairians have come to consider political decisions, reforms, and counterreforms—all certainly have contributed to frustrate the various efforts to introduce drastic changes. At a more fundamental level, there are certain inconsistencies in the philosophy of relevance itself. Indeed the three dimensions of relevance are not always compatible. For example, in the name of cultural relevance, the humanities and social sciences with a particular focus on Africa and on Zaire were to be promoted, but the imperative of socioeconomic relevance called for policies favoring the natural and physical sciences. Similarly, cultural relevance would inevitably point to greater humanistic understanding of Zaire's cultural diversity and pluralism, just as an accent upon social science research would stress freedom of inquiry and exposition; however, the imperative of political relevance, as viewed by the regime, placed primacy upon uniformity, conformity, monism, and discipline. The ideology of relevance applied to frail new universities imposes upon them a heavy functional overload which is patently compounded when the demands upon them are so inherently contradictory.

Conclusions

The analysis of the relationship between the university and the state in Zaire underscores the fragility and vulnerability of the former, as well as the limitations of the latter. The frailty of university vis-à-vis the state is a function of many factors characteristic of ex-colonial new states such as Zaire—the university's foreignness as an exotic import coupled with its seemingly inherent resistance to adaptation and reform; its continued susceptibility to expatriate dominance or influence after most other structures have been nationalized; its insistence upon continuing special relationships with the external world, including what is seen as a divided loyalty between the state and an international fraternity of science and scholarship; its total financial dependence upon the new state for which it is an extremely high-cost affair and to which it is unable to justify its worth on any demonstrable cost-benefit basis; and, above all, its existence as a sanctuary for dissent and criticism and lurking opposition to the regime. Unlike those institutionalized universities whose existence predated their states (e.g., Fourah Bay in Sierra Leone, the University of Khartoum, and Makerere in Uganda) UNAZA totally lacked any accumulated and autonomously derived legitimacy. From its inception it was the sole creature and instrument of the Mobutu state; such modicum of autonomy or academic freedom it enjoyed was on sufferance from and at the pleasure of the head of state. He could create it and dismantle it by a mere *Ordonnance-Loi*, which he did.[42]

The fact that the university is intrinsically weak because of its total dependence upon the state does not mean that the state is intrinsically strong, despite its centralization, monism, control over all physical means of coercion, and declared authoritarianism in the name of the people. Much of it is sheer bravado. As Turner and Young noted:

> This image of the omnipotent state must be at once rectified by recognition of its limited competence. "Mobilization" is episodic and largely ritual. . . . The actual behavior of the state apparatus bore little relationship to its formal schemas, official norms, and proclaimed purposes. The succession of developmental blueprints were quite beyond the capacity of the state to implement. . . . An often vast chasm separates the ambitious edicts and power claims of the state from the institutional competence of its apparatus.[43]

And so it has been with the Zairian state's relationship to its national university. Juridically the state has had the power, and on occasion it has exercised it, to act as if the university did not have a shred of autonomy, or its faculty and students an iota of academic freedom. In practice, however, we have found that in the interstices, in the residual space not penetrated by the state, its presence is little or only intermittently felt. Efforts to inculcate an ideology of Mobutuism in the university were ridiculed and came to naught. Similarly, the politically imposed quota system failed to correct regional imbalances and levels of enrollment. All of the exhortations of N'Sele conferences, the Party manifesto and resolutions, the *Ordonnances-Lois* and the *Arrêtés Départmentaux* have been of little avail in altering the curriculum, the degree structure, or the actual content of courses in the direction of any meaningful relevance. Just as the bravado of "Zairianization" and "radicalization" (nationalization) of the economy and the primary and secondary schools led in due course to "retrocession," so the centralization of all postsecondary education under "UNAZA" led in due course first to the separation of the institutes from it, and then finally to the dissolution of UNAZA itself into semblances of its three original universities. "Leviathan, closely inspected, is unclothed."[44]

The failure of the present regime to establish effective institutions is only symptomatic of the deeper sources of its *faiblesse*, which derive from the inherent limitations of personalistic patrimonial regimes in the running of a modern state. In such regimes ultimately all resources are directed toward a single national objective, the survival and aggrandizement of the presidential monarch. As we have seen, the mechanisms the incumbent President has employed to ensure this included ceaseless rotation of all officeholders within, as well as out of and into, the state apparatus; appointment of persons to positions of responsibility on the basis of personal loyalty or sycophancy; and distrust of or indifference toward a regularized system of generation and application of information and intelligence aimed at more rational public policy decisions. There are many obvious dysfunctional consequences of such a mode of statecraft, but among them three stand out: (1) the prevalence of an atmosphere of pervasive distrust and cynicism among the populace toward the regime as well as within the presidential entourage itself; (2) the rarity, because of its sheer futility, of a sense of responsibility (*conscience professionnelle*) regarding one's task or role on the part of those in responsible positions; and (3) because of the endless flux and capriciousness, the virtual impossibility of institutionalizing any structure whether it be the university or the state itself.

Although the university has been the hapless victim of the capricious whim of the present regime, there are at least four countervailing constraints serving to moderate state power. One is the residual awe and respect—juxtaposed against a fear and/or contempt—by Zairian leaders for university professors and graduates, who can "manipulate the symbols and the jargon of modernity . . . [and who are] invested with a legitimacy derived from an independent, internationally accepted source, whereas the politicians are always aware of the fact that their own 'legitimacy' rests upon such questionable bases as military force, co-optation, kinship with the President, credibility with foreign groups or a combination of those factors."[45] A second and related constraint is the regime's ceaseless quest for its own legitimacy; it needs its own theoreticians, who can provide intellectual rationalizations for its decisions. Members of the professoriate can serve this purpose and from time to time have given such support, most notably in the formulation and diffusion of the ideology of *authenticité* and Mobutuism. Thirdly, many university students and professors are close family members or relatives of members of the top political elite; indeed, a major segment send their children and relatives to UNAZA. Thus, they have a direct and intensely vital interest in UNAZA's effective functioning and in the quality of education it imparts. Finally, there is the extremely high social value attached to higher education in the eyes of the population at large. Every family wants to have at least one university graduate among its members. This pervasive high valuation of the university by the mass of the people throughout the developing world must be reckoned with by even the most authoritarian regimes. It explains in part why a quota system or any other form of university containment is a politically risky and delicate, if not ultimately unenforceable course of action.

This influence of the society at large upon the university underscores a final point, namely, that the university in fact tends very much to be a microcosm of that large society, reflecting its change processes, conflict patterns, and structural crises.[46] We have noted the isomorphic replication in the university of the centralizing and authority-concentrating processes in the evolution of the Mobutu state, the reproduction in the university of the country's regional and ethnic imbalances in education and social structure, the repetition within the university of the same societal syndrome of lurching from one grand architectonic *organigramme* to another, and the mirroring in the university of the national political culture of corruption and the ceaseless process of personnel circulation. These replications in the university of societal characteristics were undoubtedly most pronounced in a monolithic national university system such as UNAZA, whose singularity, centrality, and visibility made insulation difficult. As UNAZA disintegrates into a more pluralistic pattern it will be interesting to observe whether the permeability of the successor structures diminishes as a result.

NOTES

1. T. E. Turner and M. C. Young, *The Rise and Decline of the Zairian State* (1981, in press), 1:2. [Substantially revised and published as Crawford Young and Thomas Turner, *The Rise and Decline of the Zairian State* (Madison, London: University of Wisconsin Press, 1985); ed.]

2. Ibid., 2:2.

3. Lord Hailey, *An African Survey*, rev. ed. 1956 (New York: Oxford University Press, 1957), p. 1206.

4. B. LaCroix, "Pouvoirs et structures de l'Université Lovanium," *Cahiers de CEDAF*, 2–3, Série 2 (1972).

5. G. Hull, "Government Nationalization of the University: A Case Study of the Republic of Zaire" (unpublished manuscript, 1973), p. 14.

6. Bureau de l'Enseignement Catholique (B.E.C.), *Où en est l'enseignement au Congo?* (Léopoldville: Bureau de l'Enseignement Catholique, 1970), p. 15.

7. Lord Hailey, *An African Survey*, p. 1209.

8. M. D. Markowitz, *Cross and Sword: The Political Role of Christian Missions in the Belgian Congo, 1908–1960* (Stanford: Hoover Institution Publications, 1973), p. 67.

9. Hull, "Government Nationalization of the University," p. 12.

10. R. Dore, *The Diploma Disease: Education Qualification and Development* (London: George Allen & Unwin, 1976), pp. 4-5.

11. Quoted in K. Ilunga, "Some Thoughts on the National University of Zaire and the Zairian Political Dynamic" (unpublished manuscript, 1978), p. 5.

12. LaCroix, "Pouvoirs et structures de l'Université Lovanium," p. 36.

13. Hull, "Government Nationalization of the University," p. 11.

14. James S. Coleman, "The Academic Freedom and Responsibilities of Foreign Scholars in African Universities," *Issue*, 7:2 (1977), 15. [Chapter 11, this volume; ed.]

15. Ilunga, "Some Thoughts on the National University of Zaire," p. 6.

16. *Annuaire Général de l'Université Nationale du Zaire 1972–1973* (Kinshasa: Presses Universitaires de Zaire, 1972), pp. 13–58.

17. E. Bustin, "Education for Development: National University of Zaire: A Review" (unpublished manuscript, 1979), p. 65.

18. D. Gould, *Bureaucratic Corruption and Underdevelopment in the Third World: The Case of Zaire* (Oxford: Pergamon, 1980).

19. Turner and Young, *The Rise and Decline of the Zairian State*, 5:32.

20. J. C. Willame, "The Congo," in D. K. Emmerson, ed., *Students and Politics in Developing Nations* (New York: Praeger, 1968), p. 49.

21. M. G. Schatzberg, "Fidélité au Guide: The J. M. P. R. in Zairian Schools" *Journal of Modern African Studies*, 16:3 (1978), pp. 417–419.

22. Coleman, "The Academic Freedom and Responsibilities of Foreign Scholars in African Universities," pp. 18–19. [Chapter 11, this volume; ed.].

23. Amnesty International, *Human Rights Violations in Zaire* (London: Amnesty International), 1980.

24. Mobutu, "Discours du Président Mobutu Sese Seko adressé aux Cadres du Parti à N'Sele le 4 janvier 1975" *Etudes Zairoises,* 1:1 (1975), pp. 103–104.

25. G. Feltz, "Un Echec de l'implantation scolaire en milieu rural," *Canadian Journal of African Studies,* 13:3 (1980), pp. 441–459.

26. A. A. J. Van Bilsen, *Vers l'Indépendance du Congo et du Rwanda-Urundi* (Kraainem: Van Bilsen, 1968), p. 152.

27. W. M. Rideout, Jr., D. N. Wilson, and M. Crawford Young, *Survey of Education in the Democratic Republic of the Congo* (Washington, D.C.: American Council on Education, 1969), p. 2.

28. *Manifeste de la N'Sele,* May 20, 1967, p. 24.

29. K. I. B. Nguz, "Pourquoi je suis parti," *Jeune Afrique* (1981), p. 18.

30. M. Crawford Young, "La Faculté des sciences sociales à l'UNAZA: Réflexions autour d'un mandat," *Etudes Zairoises,* 1 (1978), p. 156.

31. N. Payanzo, "Political and Professional Attitudes of Zairian University Students," in J. Paden, ed., *Values, Identities and National Integration: Empirical Research in Africa* (Evanston, Ill.: Northwestern University Press, 1980), p. 339.

32. UNESCO, *The Development of Higher Education in Africa* (Paris: UNESCO, 1963), p. 13.

33. F. C. Ward, *Education and Development Reconsidered* (New York: Praeger, 1974.

34. C. Comeliau, "L'Université nationale du Zaire in 1974: un diagnostic," *Zaire-Afrique* (1974), p. 15.

35. J. Studstill, *Student Attrition in Zaire* (Ann Arbor: University Microfilms, 1980).

36. B. Verhaegen, *L'Enseignement universitaire au Zaire* (Paris/Bruxelles/Kisangani: Harmattan/CEDAF/CRIDE, 1978), p. 78.

37. Ibid., p. 89.

38. Université Nationale du Congo, "Rapport général des travaux du ler congrès des professeurs nationaux de l'enseignement supérieur et universitaire à la N'Sele, du 17 au 31 juillet 1971."

39. G. Hull, *Nationalization of the University in the Republic of Zaire* (Ann Arbor: University Microfilms, 1974), p. 359.

40. Bustin, "Education for Development."

41. Mobutu, *Discours du 1 juillet 1977* (Kinshasa: Institut Makanda Kabobi, 1977), p. 10.

42. "Décision d'état No. 09/CC/81 sur l'enseignement supérieur et universitaire," *Journal Officiel*, 12 (1981), pp. 41–42.

43. Turner and Young, *The Rise and Decline of the Zairian State*, 1:13.

44. Ibid.

45. Bustin, "Education for Development," p. 53.

46. M. Crawford Young, "The African University: Universalism, Development, and Ethnicity," *Comparative Education Review*, 25:2 (1981), p. 46.

13 The Idea of the Developmental University

The Changing Idea of the University

It was Abraham Flexner who stressed the relativity of the idea and functions of a university to the ethos of an epoch. "A university is not outside, but inside the general social fabric of a given era. . . . It is not something apart, something historic, something that yields as little as possible to forces and influences that are more or less new. It is on the contrary . . . an expression of the age."[1] From its medieval origins the idea of the university has indeed reflected many epochal changes. In his analysis of the evolution of that idea Clark Kerr identified three ideal types: the "idea of the university" of Cardinal Newman (an idea militantly hostile to utilitarianism, stressing teaching and a liberal education and opposing research and service); the "idea of the modern university" of Abraham Flexner (the then dominant German model of the advanced research university, equally hostile to public or societal service); and his own "idea of the multiversity"—the omnifunctional American university which essays to be all things to all people, including particularly service to society. What has gained prominence during the past two decades is a fourth variant, the idea of the developmental university, an institution that in all its aspects is singularly animated and concerned, rhetorically and practically, with the "solution" of the concrete problems of societal development.

While this study focuses mainly on the concept of the developmental university which has prevailed in Third World countries in recent years, the idea of the developmental university can be traced to three earlier

Reprinted from Atle Hetland, ed., *Universities and National Development: A Report of the Nordic Association for the Study of Education in Developing Countries* (Stockholm: Almqvist & Wiksell International, 1984), pp. 85–104.

traditions. One is in the land-grant movement of the mid-1860s in the United States—the world's first "new" nation—which dictated that the university should be directly engaged with the "persistent and significant problems of society."[2] A second tradition was that of Japan, the first old nation in the non-Western world self-consciously to launch itself upon a path of forced modernization. The foundation law of Japan's first national university, established in the 1880s, prescribed that the university "must assume the function of 'teaching, and researching into the inner mysteries of, those branches of scholarship and the arts which are of essential importance to'—not society but the state, and the state, moreover, which had adopted 'development' through the importation of foreign forms of 'civilisation and enlightenment' as a high-priority national goal."[3] The third tradition is that of the Soviet Union and countries which have patterned their universities after the Soviet model. It stressed the rigorous fit between the university product and manpower requirements projected in successive Five-Year Plans, and the use of the university as an instrument both to right inequalities in society and to socialize students into the ideology of the regime.[4] Thus, the concept of the university as an instrument for societal development is not a new one; it found expression in varying ways in earlier modernizing societies of both a democratic and authoritarian persuasion.

In no previous epoch, however, has the imperative of developmentalism been so insistent. The exhortation that universities in Third World countries must be demonstrably relevant for and totally committed to national development has become so incessant and all-engulfing that it saturates all speeches, studies, debates, and discussion of the *raison d'être* of the institution. One of the more eloquent exhorters is President Julius Nyerere of Tanzania:

> The University in a developing society must put the emphasis of its work on subjects of immediate moment to the nation in which it exists, and it must be committed to the people of that nation and their humanistic goals. . . . We in poor societies can only justify expenditure on a University—of any type—if it promotes real development of our people. . . . The role of a University in a developing nation is to contribute; to give ideas, manpower, and service for the furtherance of human equality, human dignity and human development.[5]

The litany stressing the primacy of the university's developmental function is expressed throughout the Third World. At the 1962 UNESCO (Tananarive) Conference on the Development of Higher Education in

Africa, universities were charged to become "the main instrument of national progress."[6] In Southeast Asia, the Regional Institute of Higher Education and Development (RIHED), based in Singapore and also sponsored by UNESCO, has as one of its two missions the enhancement of "the contributions of higher education to the social and economic development of the countries of the region."[7] In June 1980, a planning group met in Caracas, Venezuela, under the auspices of the Organization of American States because of a shared concern that universities "are not playing a role in the economic and social development of the American republics that is commensurate with their capabilities." Indeed, some new universities created in this epoch have the developmental imperative written into their founding documents. Thus, the University of Juba, Sudan, was charged to fulfill not ten, but only nine commandments:

> The University of Juba shall be an Instrument of:
>
> National Integration
>
> Social Integration
>
> Socio-Economic Development both for the Southern Region and for the Nation at large
>
> Environmental enlightenment and Action
>
> Cultural and technical enlightenment to the whole of the Southern Region
>
> Modernization in University Education
>
> Democratization of the University Organization, Admission and Administration
>
> Horizontal transfer of modern technology and a vehicle of vertical transfer of improved indigenous technology
>
> Regional and International co-operation and understanding.[8]

These are only representative examples of the highly normative and prescriptive nature of the idea of the developmental university and of the almost unlimited expansion in the range of societal functions it is expected to perform.

What is the explanation for the remarkable global diffusion of this voguish concept of the function of the university? There have been at least four sources of inspiration or pressure for a developmental emphasis in the universities. One is the voluntary and spontaneous sense of civic or national responsibility of university authorities and members of the professoriate, expressed individually or collectively, that the intellectual and physical resources of the university should be placed at the service of the nation, to the extent that this is compatible with the teaching and research functions of the university. Attitudes on state-university relations vary considerably, and undoubtedly there are some among the professoriate—including those of a deep civic consciousness—who believe that on grounds of principle a distance must be maintained for the good of both the state and the university, just as did Cardinal Newman and Dr. Flexner.

A second source is the government, whether it be prescribing national service for university students aimed at inculcating development orientations, in-service training programs for civil servants or diplomatic personnel, or the commissioning of contract research and consultancies on specific development problems. Here there is also high variability. The high degree of lateral mobility which has existed from the beginning between the Government of Tanzania and the University of Dar es Salaam is an example of closeness.

A third source is defensive self-preservation by the university inspired to take a developmental posture because of its vulnerability in the allocation of resources by the government. Logically and morally it is difficult to challenge the proposition that such an extraordinarily high-cost structure, embracing and concentrating most of the scientific and intellectual resources of a country, should be made maximally relevant to the practical problems of development.[9] During the first phase of the postcolonial epoch new universities were among the favored objects of foreign assistance; thus, the full extent of their high cost was somewhat hidden. Only when foreign aid to universities rapidly began to be phased out in the early 1970s, simultaneous with continued escalation of social demand for higher education, did the full magnitude of the cost of higher education, and the consequent vulnerability of universities, become starkly evident.

The intellectual and scientific resources of most new states tend to be concentrated in their universities, frequently in their single national university, rather than distributed among a variety of structures. Scholars and scientists tend to gravitate to university careers, certainly in the critical initial years of national development. Financial constraints usually dictate a single national concentration of those resources. This *faute de mieux* monopoly of the new nation's scientific talent by the universities made them obviously vulnerable if they did not, rhetorically at least, declare their commitment to a developmental role. This was made all the more necessary because with few exceptions universities were public institutions supported entirely by public funds, and in most instances members of the professoriate had the actual or assimilated status of civil servants. Thus, independently of any principled commitment to a service function, developmental rhetoric and posturing were enjoined by the imperative of institutional defense and survival. As Leys and Shaw have argued:

> The value of the "development concept" and the cluster of altered educational ideals which it stands for, must not be underrated. It provides a powerful slogan for Vice Chancellors and others struggling to bring about institutional changes in universities overseas. It enables them to defend themselves against the criticism of being indifferent to urgent national needs, of pursuing useless knowledge at great cost and of being insufficiently sympathetic to the policies of the government.[10]

Indeed, the Commonwealth Secretary-General admonished the Conference of Vice-Chancellors of Commonwealth Universities at their 1979 Jamaica meeting that their universities were vulnerable, and in institutional self-defense a developmental posture was essential.

> The demands of education on scarce national resources are being more rigorously assessed against the competing claims of other sectors. . . . [Also] an emerging issue is the distribution of educational expenditure between the primary, secondary and tertiary levels of the educational pyramid. In both respects, the pressure for reallocation of resources works against the universities. . . . Elitism [is a stick] likely to be wielded more frequently unless universities are demonstrably more successful in proving their relevance to the felt needs of their communities. . . . It would be unsafe any longer to take it for granted that the case for the traditional university is accepted as axiomatic. . . . Every facet of university activity will come under questioning and appraisal. Validity and relevance will need to be established and confirmed again and again. If our universities are to hold their own . . . in the competition for resources, they must be able constantly to demonstrate that they deserve to be esteemed.[11]

The fourth source of pressure toward university developmentalism, adding its weight to that of the national governments and the universities themselves, was the international donor community. The idea of the service function of the university had figured prominently in the aid program of the United States Agency for International Development (USAID) from the early 1950s onward in that the land-grant college was the model used. During the following two decades its grants for university development in the LDCs exceeded $1 billion. However, as the 1960s—the decade of high-level manpower—came to a close there was increasing disenchantment with universities within the donor community. The politically exigent replacement-of-expatriate function in the ex-colonies was fulfilled or approaching completion. The first development decade, which had banked so heavily upon human capital theory and high-level manpower as the critical variable in modernization, was increasingly judged to have been a failure. Studies on the social rates of return on investments in primary education versus higher education proved consistently and convincingly that the returns were much higher for the former. The "trickle-down" theory of development just had not worked; indeed, the elite-mass gap had widened. In certain fields there was perceived to be an overproduction of university-trained manpower. The worldwide sweep of university-student radicalism during the late 1960s everywhere accelerated the retreat from and eroded the support for higher education. By the early 1970s the older donor agencies were critically reviewing their aid policies regarding university development; two of the largest and longest involved (USAID and the Ford Foundation) decided to disengage completely from general support for university development and progressively to phase out selective support.[12] The British government, the other major donor agency which had been heavily committed in aid to universities, launched a critical reappraisal which led to major revisions of policy set forth in two White Papers, the second of which, in 1975, was revealingly entitled "The Changing Emphasis in British Aid Policy: More Help for the Poorest." By the mid-1970s the pendulum had shifted to this new emphasis in the policies of virtually all members of the donor community, as well as the World Bank, as reflected in its 1974 Education Sector report. The Rockefeller Foundation, the donor agency which most single-mindedly concentrated upon university development over a two-decade period, finally decided in 1977 to phase out its Education for Development Program over the following five years.

A dominant lament in the donor reappraisal of the early 1970s was that universities and their products did not demonstrably relate to development and had not adapted themselves so as to realize their developmental potential.[13] Those agencies which continued to believe in the centrality and the critical importance of universities, despite the frustrations and disappointments they had engendered, undertook to continue selective support to those institutions which offered promise of a developmental orientation. Thus, although USAID did drastically reduce support of overall university development, it launched a policy of focused support for those elements of institutions which were "highly significant to national development . . . [and took] a problem-solving approach to both internal university problems and problems of their societies."[14] The Rockefeller Foundation changed the name of its program to "Education for Development" in 1973 to underscore its developmental emphasis. Other donors, through various mechanisms (e.g., Canada's International Development Research Centre

[IDRC], the Swedish Agency for Research Cooperation with Developing Countries [SAREC], the Norwegian Agency for International Development [NORAD], and the Netherlands Universities Foundation for International Cooperation [NUFFIC] and its associated agencies), also stressed development in linkages created with LDC university-based applied research institutes. Explicit developmentalism became *de rigueur*: the "developmental university" had come of age.

The ethos and rhetoric of developmentalism, of course, saturates all Third World things. Public administration in the South has become "development administration," and studies of the South and its problems are everywhere known as "development studies." "Development" has become the most overused word—if not euphemism—in almost any language, reflecting not an empirical process or actuality, but an aspiration, a normativeness about not what was happening, but what ought to happen in the Third World. Undergirding and perpetuating all of this was no little Northern guilt over the history of Northern domination of the South, as well as the continuing dependency and widening gap in that awesomely asymmetrical relationship, but also an enduring faith in the idea of progress in the Third World itself, a quite inexplicable phenomenon given the disappointing rates of material improvement that were occurring on all sides. This is all the more poignant considering the gloom, pessimism, and "zero growth" mentality associated with the growing disbelief in progress and moral disorientation in the increasingly affluent North. Crawford Young has an interesting explanation for this curious paradox. Referring to Raymond Aron's observation that societies do not measure themselves against their past but against their ambitions for the future, Young argues:

> We would amend this observation by noting that the future, for advanced industrial societies, is an uncharted sea. For the Third World, the standard of measurement is advanced industrial society itself, with its unparalleled abundance. . . . The agenda of progress is starkly clear: to match the material accomplishments of the first two worlds. This elemental fact explains why an idea of progress is both so universal, and so material. . . . The very existence of the empirical referent serves to override doubts as to whether "progress" is attainable or good.[15]

The Protean Concept of Development

If a university must be developmental, then there must be some consensus on what development means. However, we now all recognize the highly subjectivist nature of this very protean concept. As Dore observed, "'Development' means movement towards a good society and every man is entitled to decide for himself what sort of society he thinks good."[16] During the halcyon and optimistic 1950s and early 1960s when much of the world was emerging from colonialism and entering the world stage as independent nation-states there appeared to be a general consensus—albeit vague and unreflective—on its meaning. In those days it meant nothing less than the new entrants becoming as rapidly as possible replicas of the advanced industrial countries—the "underdeveloped" becoming like the "developed." That this idea was not a monopoly of the arrogant capitalist West was underscored by Karl Marx's observation in *Das Kapital* a century earlier: "The country that is more developed industrially only shows, to the less developed, the image of its own future."

The reaction against this simplistically unilinear and inherently ethnocentric concept is now well known and need not detain us here. Critics tended to fall into two groups: the rejecters and the revisionists. The former insist that the whole idea of development (and more particularly its synonym "modernization") is unsalvageable. As Colin Leys put it, "The main problem is that the ideas produced in the 1950s and 1960s were incorrect at any time. To the extent that they are still with us, they are misleading, not because they are out of date, but because they embody fundamental mistakes. What is most important now is to exorcise these ideas."[17] However, the majority of the critics have been revisionists. Dudley Seers challenged both the then fashionable indicator of "economic growth" as well as the surrender to subjectivism and offered a definition in terms of social indicators or quality of life. In conceptualizing development, he argued:

> Does this mean that we are each left to adopt our own personal set of values? This is fortunately not necessary. Surely the values we need are staring us in the face, as soon as we ask ourselves: What are the necessary conditions for a universally accepted aim, the realization of the potential of human personality? . . . The questions to ask about a country's development are therefore: What has been happening to poverty . . . to unemployment . . . to inequality? If all three of these have become less severe, then beyond doubt this has been a period of development for the country concerned.[18]

Juxtaposed against this revisionist concept of objectively measurable development was the theory of underdevelopment and dependency which had been in gestation for some time. As described by Leys:

> It sees underdevelopment as a specific condition of the ex-colonial countries corresponding to, and making possible, the development of the capitalist countries of the West. . . . Capitalism is rejected as being simply not available as a basis for development; it is seen as being a world system which by its very nature allocates to the underdeveloped countries a permanent place at the bottom of the ladder. From this point of view . . . it is only a short step to identifying the universities, to the extent that they still transmit a predominantly Western culture, as institutions for transmitting to the rising elite [in the Third World] a culture which endorses capitalism, and hence as major *instruments of underdevelopment* along with foreign companies and the rest of the neo-colonial apparatus.[19]

In tracing the evolution of the concept of development over the past three decades we can identify four successive principal themes: (1) the ethnocentric notion of development as synonymous with westernization; (2) the economistic notion of development as economic growth, a more sharply focused, "critical variable" version of (1); (3) development as the measurable amelioration of poverty, unemployment, and inequality under the rubric of "the realization of human personality"; and (4) development as a basic structural transformation from an "interdependence based on hierarchy and Western charity to an interdependence based on symmetry and mutual accountability."[20] The only alternative to capitulation to sheer subjectivism in dealing with this protean concept is to state a working definition of how it will be used here. For present purposes a developmental university is one which endeavors, in such ways as it can, to promote development as defined in (3) and (4) above.

The Functions of a Developmental University

The range of functions assigned to a developmental university by its proponents tends to be quite formidable. They go far beyond the trilogy of teaching, research, and service; or at least under those rubrics is included a comprehensive array of undertakings. An illustrative list would include the following:

Teaching Curricular and degree innovations, and novel modes of instruction, aimed at making the entire university learning experience more relevant to the indigenous culture and the practical problems of development. Teaching through research and national service schemes is introduced to inculcate greater practicality, relevance, and development orientations and perspective. University-based in-service training programs, as well as community outreach training programs, become part of the regular curriculum.

Research Establishment of organized applied research units and encouragement to members of the professoriate to undertake applied research projects desired by the development ministries of governments on concrete problems of and technological constraints upon development.

Service Encouragement and facilitation of members of the professoriate to participate in public policy formulation at national, regional, and local levels through membership on planning or decision-making evaluations and contract research. Establishment and operation of programs in community health outreach, agricultural extension, adult education, extension classes, and diffusion of knowledge through the mass media.

In furthering the performance of the foregoing functions the ideal developmental university would also pursue the following policies, among others: (1) ensure that the development plans of the university are integrated with or linked to national development plans; (2) coordinate its efforts with public and private action agencies, including other postsecondary institutions and other levels of education; (3) accord recognition to members of the professoriate who engage in developmental activity as regards their promotion and retention; (4) provide the requisite infrastructure for outreach and developmental activities; and (5) emphasize the developmental role of the university in public pronouncements and policy statements by university authorities.

It is in the performance of its primordial function of production of educated citizens qualified to fill the specialist roles in the numbers required by society that the developmental university, like the traditional university, faces its greatest challenge. Throughout the developing world the extreme imbalance in student enrollments and production of graduates as between science and technological subjects on the one hand, and humanities and social sciences on the other, persists as a seemingly intractable problem. In Zaire, for example, despite compulsory enrollment and preferential treatment for students in the physical and natural sciences, the majority of students were still found in the humanities and social sciences.[21] This is a generic problem of the Third World, and even exists (albeit to a lesser degree) in the socialist societies of the Soviet Union and Eastern Europe. As Connor has observed, despite the authoritarian direction and command nature of the system:

> The image of socialist higher education . . . needs some revision . . . with reference to the assumed close congruence between the distribution of training by disciplines and the perceived economic needs of the countries. . . . Real problems exist in linking the "output" of higher educational institutions to the available spaces in the national economy. . . . The "flow" is not so clearly in the science-technology direction as many who see socialist education systems as development "successes," in comparison with African Asian systems, seem inclined to believe. . . . Socialist countries face an unresolved issue in motivating graduates to go "where they are needed."[22]

The experience of the Soviet Union also has demonstrated that no matter how efficiently manpower planning is carried out it is not likely to "ensure the education of the appropriate numbers of individuals with particular skills unless it is reinforced by the resort to financial incentives. . . . Incentives are just as necessary to an effective manpower policy as are universities and national development plans."[23] All of which is to say that even the most zealous developmental university in the Third World is not likely to perform its traditional manpower production function without external intervention as regards both the incentive structure and some sort of officially operated effective control system over enrollments and career paths. Few countries, if any, have the organizational capacity to institute and maintain such a system. Indeed, without the capacity of a totalitarian system the expansion of the educational systems at all levels is virtually uncontrollable. Citing Rado's conception of the explosive model of educational growth, Foster observed that

> far from leading to a decline in the demand for education, decreasing opportunities for educated youth lead to further *expansion* in demand. If a primary *education* alone does not bring occupational access, then individuals will demand post-primary schooling. If, as a result, post-primary education expands, unemployment among secondary school leavers will increase, leading in turn to an expanding demand for higher education. And so it goes on, the genie is out of the bottle.[24]

Another special function assigned to the developmental university in many countries has been the furtherance of national integration by means of ameliorating or eliminating inequalities, either ethnic or regional, or, in socialist systems, those of a class character. With few exceptions all new states are multiethnic, as are indeed virtually all nation-states in the modern world; it is the ethnically homogeneous nation-state that is the rarity, a fact which the explosion of ethnic consciousness in our current epoch has demonstrated so vividly. For reasons historical (uneven penetration of Western influences) and cultural (uneven receptivity to such influences), most new states emergent from colonialism are characterized by pronounced imbalances in the levels of educational development among the different ethnic groups making up their populations. These inherited imparities tend, inexorably, to cumulate and reproduce themselves over time, unless explicit steps are taken to correct them. The imposition of university admission quotas favoring the disadvantaged or underdeveloped groups has been among the devices used in several cases (e.g., Zaire, Cameroon, Malaya, India, etc.). Evidence from Zaire and India suggests that universities are not effective instruments for solving problems of national integration. In Zaire, the quota system not only failed to achieve its righting function, but it left a legacy of heightened ethnic consciousness and tension. In India the effort to introduce university quotas favoring the *harijans* (untouchables) has not worked; indeed, the policy of positive discrimination had to be abandoned due to the entrenched opposition of all the higher castes who felt their power and status being eroded. However, in the Soviet Union and Eastern Europe the policy of positive discrimination in favor of peasants and workers to right class inequalities in access to university education has unquestionably resulted in substantial democratization. Nevertheless, as Connor has shown, these advances have not produced equality of educational access if measured by the proportions of students of different social origins in universities; the children of the intelligentsia are overrepresented by about three times, and the more prestigious science faculties have disproportionate enrollments of persons of nonmanual background.[25]

The universality of the problem of compelling or inducing universities to be effective instruments for reducing fundamental class inequalities in society is further demonstrated by the massive efforts of the federal government of the United States in the late 1960s and early 1970s to increase equality of opportunity. The hope, as Clark Kerr retrospectively observed, was to draw equal proportions of students with high academic ability from all levels of family income. After billions of dollars applied to this objective, progress in increasing attendance from low-income groups was meager. True, university attendance by minorities was substantially increased and more money was brought into higher education, but there was little change in the composition of the student body in terms of source of students by level of family income.[26] The experience underscores the limits to solving a societal problem by throwing large sums of money at it, the difficulty governments have in nonauthoritarian systems in challenging the autonomy and meritocratic standards of universities (where, of course, such exist), and the enduring reproductive power of class inequalities.

Through extreme measures some rectification of imbalances may be possible over the long run, but there remains the question of the short-run political tolerability of such measures, as well as the fact that fundamental group inequalities in a society tend to be powerfully self-perpetuative and the fragile and vulnerable apex of the educational system is not the place where they will be resolved. A university is reflective of a society's social, ethnic, and class structure, not its corrective.[27] Moreover, it may well be that if a society's goal is heightened capacity for more rapid economic technological and scientific development there should be no discrimination against the advantaged groups, an observation which raises once again the functionalists' argument for inequality.

In some cases the special function of political socialization into the ideology of the governing regime has been assigned to a developmental university. President Suharto is attempting this in Indonesian universities. President Mobutu made an abortive effort to introduce his ideology of *authenticité* and later Mobutuism in the National University of Zaire, but it was received with derision. Under the pressure of a group of nine entirely expatriate Marxist staff members at the University of Dar es Salaam, Tanzania, a conference was held in March 1967 which recommended that it was the responsibility of the university "to impart political education . . . [and] the emphasis should be on the teaching of Tanzanian socialism as seen against the African and international background." It also recommended that the university should ensure that "the majority of its academic staff and all its teachers of the social sciences are sympathetic to Tanzanian socialism."[28] However, no exclusive definition of socialism was prescribed. In due course, Marxists far to the left of President Nyerere, under the mantle of socialism, proceeded to criticize Tanzania's neo-colonial status and continued dependence upon the international capitalist world. Ultimately the President was provoked to condemn the radicals for all of their "revolutionary hot air." The radical left endeavored to make the university into a socialist institution in which there could be political and ideological indoctrination; the President, although a declared socialist, resisted their efforts.[29] The consensus of most analysts of the role of formal educational institutions in political socialization is that at the university level the effect is virtually nil. Basic attitudes, orientations, and behavioral dispositions are formed much earlier; enforced indoctrination at the university level is more likely to provoke boredom, derision, or hostility to the subject matter.

The Limitations and Obstacles Confronting a Developmental University

We have said that the logic of a university becoming involved in development problems and programs is hardly challengeable. The real issue is what are the tolerable and feasible limits of involvement consistent with the university's basic mission of teaching and research. There are several limitations and obstacles which any university in a Third World country faces in trying to be developmental; a few of these will be briefly surveyed here.

GOVERNMENT'S COMMITMENT TO DEVELOPMENT

David Court has made the obvious but central point that the kind of development role that the universities are able to play "depends in large measure on the interest of government in solving developmental problems."[30] In the immediate euphoric postindependence period in most new states the political leadership enjoyed a halo effect, a brief halcyon honeymoon, having been victors in a highly moral struggle for liberation; seemingly they could do no wrong, and their motives were considered selfless and noble. Their rhetoric was accepted as fact, and affected not insignificantly the nature of analysis at the time, which now seems rather naive. Subsequent events and the self-serving, exploitive, and sometimes evil behavior of some have, unfortunately, caused the pendulum to swing to the other extreme; now they can do no right. The fact is that like leadership elsewhere in history and in the contemporary world, it is of mixed quality, and certainly of mixed motivation and multiple priorities. Colin Leys made the point well:

> Politicians do vary in determination, honesty, singleness of mind, and so on. But, speaking generally, political leaders do not *want* one particular goal beyond all others. . . . There are political leaders of poor countries such as Batista or Sukarno, who are *not* really interested in economic development. Most, however, desire it; but most are pursuing other goals at least equally keenly and seldom hesitate to subordinate economic development to these other ends. Their commitment to development is strictly instrumental and far from occupying a paramount place in their priorities, it is apt to have a fairly modest one.[31]

Among the highest priorities of many are survival, continuation in power, and self-enrichment, all decidedly inimical to development. In the kleptocracy of President Mobutu and his genre, for example, it is inconceivable that the National University of Zaire—created in 1971 with the full plenitude of developmental rhetoric—could make any contribution to development other than training critics of his regime. Indeed, there is the ominous danger that co-opted members of the Zairian university professoriate, as in a host of repressive and technocratic regimes in the Third World, could provide services which operate to perpetuate the tenure of the incumbents.

UNIVERSITY AUTONOMY AND THE CRITICAL FUNCTION

Fundamental to a university being a university is that there be a measure of autonomy and distance from government requisite for the performance of the teaching and research functions. Yet ever greater closeness and accountability to government is the inevitable consequence of developmentalism. Weiler suggests that autonomy and accountability may be inherently irreconcilable, that President Nyerere's expectation from the university sets an unrealistically high standard, namely, that it give "both a complete objectivity in the search for truth, and also commitment to our society—a desire to serve it. We expect the two things equally."[32] The victim of that closeness that developmentalism dictates could be that precious irreplaceable and unique critical function of the university. Cooptation into policy positions in government or of consultancy of contract research undertaken as salary supplementing activity by the professoriate can have a subtle self-censoring, silencing effect.

The preciousness of the critical function for society and its development has often been underscored. Sydney Webb, the socialist founder of the London School of Economics, was a radical reformer deeply committed to the essentiality of that function even in the face of criticism from such Fabian friends as George Bernard Shaw, who accused him of creating a "mere academic institution." Webb's retort was that

> as he knew, I was a person of decided views, radical and socialist, and that I wanted the policy that I believed in to prevail. But that I was also a profound believer in knowledge and science and truth. I thought that we were suffering much from lack of research in social matters, and that I wanted to promote it. I believed that research and new discoveries would prove some, at any rate, of my views of policy to be right, but that, if they proved the contrary I should count it all the more gain to have prevented error, and should cheerfully abandon my own policy. I think that is a fair attitude.[33]

More recently, from the other end of the ideological persuasion, the free-market and Nobel laureate Chicago economist, Theodore W. Schultz, lamented the decline in scholarly criticism of economic doctrines and society's institutions by economists and affirmed that "one of the primary functions of at least a sub-set of economists, whose freedom of inquiry is protected by their university, is to devote their talent to comprehensive social and economic criticism."[34]

COMPETENCE OF EXISTING PROFESSORIATE TO BE DEVELOPMENTAL

The existing professoriate in most universities were never trained to think, act, or teach developmentalism. Put bluntly, unless they retool themselves—and here both time and motivation make it most unlikely—it would be "the blind leading the blind." This applies equally to most of the foreign expatriate staff at LDC universities who preach developmentalism, few of whom have the experience or background to teach it. As Babs Fafunwa of Nigeria put it:

> The local staff member differs only in color, not in attitude, from his expatriate counterpart. Both were probably trained in the same overseas institution, and both have imbibed the same idea of what a university is in affluent society. Their research orientation and their attitude to teaching and curriculum are those of a developed economy.[35]

The obstacles to self-reform or self-retooling are formidable; indeed, the incumbent first generation may simply be non-self-reformable. Understandably, the egos, the self-esteem, and the professional self-image of members of the existing professoriate are very much at stake; they have an overpowering interest in defending and protecting—indeed perpetuating—the type of training that they know and from which they derive their professional legitimacy. Moreover, as Court has noted, there has been no dramatic alternative model of what a different kind of university, and particularly a developmental university, might look like.[36]

Beyond these considerations is the inherent conservatism regarding structural change in the university of most members of a university, irrespective of the penchant of some for trendy rhetoric and ideological radicalism. In assessing the major efforts in the 1960s and 1970s to bring about academic reform, defined as "intended internally originated academic structural change," Clark Kerr concluded that in the end about 90 percent of those efforts were abandoned or so weakened as to disappoint their authors.[37] The conservatism of an established university professoriate anywhere is reinforced by its tendency to rely on "consensus and on the opinions of the older members" in making decisions, by the facts that there are "no rewards to the faculty members who seek innovation, only the burden of long, drawn out, and often disappointing consultations," and that in actuality, most academic reforms are initiated by students (who are notably inconstant, subject to rapid turnover, and prone to fads) or by administrators (who are constrained by the conventions of academic primacy).[38] For these and other reasons universities tend to be particularly impervious to changes in structure, ethos, conventions, and new orientations in their mission.

THE FACT OF TRADITIONAL UNIVERSITY FUNCTIONS

There is the very real danger of functional overload, because, as Leys and Shaw have stressed, most of the new developmental functions have to be performed by the same professoriate as the traditional functions.[39] One of the new functions, contract research, has become a seductive, rapidly expanding, richly rewarding, salary supplementing activity absorbing a large part of the time and energy of members of the professoriate in many new states, including Kenya, Nigeria, Indonesia, and the Philippines, as examples. Those who commission contract research are all heavily involved in developmental activities (local governments, international organizations, regional development banks, nongovernmental organizations, consulting companies, and private foundations). Its benefits, as Court has shown, are the greater exposure of the professoriate to practical real-life problems of development. It also sometimes accords the researcher high status and public recognition. And it enables the university to retain talent which otherwise might become part of an internal or external brain drain.[40] But the costs to the university, and to the individual, are not unsubstantial; indeed, they are worrisome. It has commercialized scholarship (consultancies sometimes pay $300 per day); the locus of research initiative is external to the scholar and the university; it leads to extensive overcommitment and wide diffusion of interest and attention, frequently resulting in superficiality; professional norms have eroded because the scholar's reference group is no longer his peers but external agencies; basic research is largely abandoned; and, above all, teaching and university service are neglected.

Commenting on the University of Dar es Salaam, undoubtedly one of the most innovative and developmentally oriented universities in the Third World, Court remarks:

> This university is refreshing in its willingness to innovate and depart from inherited tradition, but the outside observer is left with a

> nagging feeling that the very single mindedness necessary for this level of "development" achievement has at times required the sacrifice of some of those things which are universal to universities.[41]

An observer of Gadjah Mada University of Yogyakarta, Indonesia, similarly noted that "to an outside observer it is clear that the participation of both staff and students in 'ongoing development projects' is close to being excessive. . . . So, although it may seem curious, the conclusion here is that the need is to temper development orientation with recommendations for the maintenance and growth of intellectual capital."[42] A similar observation was made by an analyst of the University of the Philippines:

> There remains however the question of whether a university can have too much of a developmental orientation, however desirable such an orientation may be in abstract terms. . . . There is little time or material incentive for independent critical analysis of the needs and problems of the society, which still remains the most important public service the academy can perform.[43]

Concluding Observations

This paper has deliberately focused upon some of the problems and limitations of the so-called developmental university. There have been some impressive examples of developmental contributions universities have made without compromising their basic mission; indeed, they have been enriched by them. The change in orientations produced by the National Service experience of students at Haile Selassi I University is a case in point; similar reports of other experiments are equally encouraging.[44] Twenty case studies of other types of developmental activity by universities have been examined in the two-volume study by Kenneth Thompson and his colleagues.[45] Nevertheless, the dangers of overdevelopment are very real. Not only can the quality of performance of traditional functions be seriously compromised (teaching, research, and the critical function), but the quality of performance of the new developmental functions could be equally compromised through "oversell," with the resultant disesteem and contempt for universities as an institution.

A second point is the prematurity of assuming too readily a developmental role before the institution itself is solidly established and institutionalized. As Francis X. Sutton observed some years ago, "We are learning in the advanced countries that too much can be expected of universities, and there is danger in imposing weighty expectations on struggling new ones in social environments where they have yet no settled place."[46] A similar point was made by Kenneth Thompson in his observation that "the long road to education for development passes through the development of educational institutions. No one has yet found a shortcut or detour."[47] This two-stage argument that the institution must be built first before it is endowed with a just bearable functional load is reinforced by an illuminating recent study by a leading practitioner in the transfer of the land-grant university tradition to the developing world. In dispelling a variety of myths about the land-grant university experience, he noted that it was not until well into the twentieth century (more than fifty years after they were established) that the land-grant colleges became a significant force in national development in the United States: "The colleges' *own* development had to precede their impact on national development. That is an oversight often found among admirers in the developing countries who are looking for importable ready-made, time-defying instruments of progress."[48]

A final point concerns the dominant belief that the university must become an omnifunctional developmental institution, that it should assume responsibility for all functions. To the extent that this is based on one of the original inspirations of the developmental university movement, namely, that universities had to demonstrate their relevance and posture developmentalism in order to save their budgets and their status, then the false pretenses this entails are bound ultimately to be exposed. The fact is that in other times and at other places both traditional and developmental functions were adequately performed by other structures. There have been epochs in which what are now considered some of the university's central functions were carried out elsewhere. From the sixteenth to the eighteenth century, for example, universities were not in the forefront of intellectual activity; indeed, during the Enlightenment most progress in the sciences, philosophy, and other areas of inquiry was achieved outside the universities. The French Revolution abolished all French universities; professional schools for medicine and law, and the *grandes écoles*, which ever since the Revolution have educated France's most prestigious categories of high-level manpower, were established as completely separate institutions.[49] In the Soviet Union and all countries under its influence advanced research is carried out in Academies of Science, completely separate from the universities. In Brazil today some of the most significant research and advanced training (including the award of degrees) is conducted in institutes separate from universities. In their own self-interest, universities in the Third World (and elsewhere as well) might critically examine and continuously monitor what functional load they can realistically and responsibly assume and ensure that their performance of whatever mix and magnitude of traditional and developmental functions they select to take on is both manageable and creditable.[50]

NOTES

1. Quoted in Clark Kerr, *The Uses of the University* (New York: Harper & Row, 1963), p. 4. As F. Cyril James put it, "Each generation—in each country of the world—must ask, and answer clearly in terms of its own problems and its concept of social development: What is the function of the university?" "A Note on the Nature and Functions of the University," in Howard Hayden, ed., *Higher Education and Development in Southeast Asia* (Paris: UNESCO, 1966), p. 491.

2. Eric Ashby, *Universities: British, Indian, African: A Study in the Ecology of Higher Education* (Cambridge: Harvard University Press, 1966), p. 279. See also Mary Jane Bowman, "The Land-Grant Colleges and Universities in Human-Resource Development," *Journal of Economic History*, 22:4 (December 1962), pp. 523–545. Edward Shils, "The Academic Ethos under Strain," *Minerva*, 13:1 (Spring 1975), p. 13, notes that "ever since the nineteenth century and above all in the United States there has been a demand that the universities should cease to be 'ivory towers' and should contribute directly to the well-being of their societies."

3. Quoted in Ronald Dore, *The Role of the Universities in National Development* (London: Association of Commonwealth Universities Occasional Paper, July 1978), p. 9. Japan's reformist Minister of Education, Arinori Mori, dictated that "learning must be exclusively for the sake of the state. The basic mission of the Imperial University is to train intellectual leaders ready to meet the needs of the State. . . . What is to be done is not for the sake of the pupils, but for the sake of the country." Quoted in Herbert Passin, "Japan," in James S. Coleman, ed., *Education and Political Development* (Princeton: Princeton University Press, 1965), p. 305.

4. International Bank for Reconstruction and Development (IBRD), *Education Reform in the Soviet Union: Implications for Developing Countries* (Washington, D.C.: IBRD, 1978).

5. Julius K. Nyerere, "The University's Role in the Development of New Countries," Keynote Address, World University Service Assembly, Dar es Salaam, Tanzania, June 17, 1966.

6. UNESCO, *The Development of Higher Education in Africa* (Paris, 1963), p. 13.

7. Robert J. Keller, "The Role of Higher Education in National Development in Southeast Asia," *Higher Education*, 6 (1977), p. 489.

8. El Sammani A. Yacoub, ed., *The University of Juba: Background, Concepts and Plan of Action* (Khartoum: University of Juba, 1976).

9. James S. Coleman, "The Academic Freedom and Responsibilities of Foreign Scholars in Africa Universities," *Issue* 7:2 (Spring 1977), p. 21.

10. Colin Leys and John Shaw, "Problems of Universities in Developing Countries" (photocopy), May 1967, p. 5.

11. Shridath S. Ramphal, Keynote Address, Conference of Vice Chancellors of Commonwealth Universities, Mona, Jamaica, March 26, 1979.

12. USAID university development projects declined from a high of seventy-five in 1966 to only ten in 1978; the Ford Foundation shifted in the early 1970s from university development to education research and planning; the number of education program officers overseas dropped from forty-four in 1971 to seven in 1979.

13. F. Champion Ward, ed., *Education and Development Reconsidered* (New York: Praeger, 1974). This is a report of a meeting of the heads of thirteen major donor agencies in 1972 to reassess the education-development nexus.

14. USAID, *Priority Problems in Education and Human Resources Development: The Seventies* (Washington, D.C.: USAID, 1970), pp. 22–23.

15. M. Crawford Young, "Ideas of Progress in the Third World," in Gabriel A. Almond, Marvin Chadorow, and Roy Harvey Pearce, eds., *Progress and Its Discontents* (Berkeley: University of California Press, 1982), p. 99.

16. Dore, *Role of Universities*, p. 8.

17. Colin Leys, "Challenging Development Concepts," *IDS Sussex Bulletin*, 11:3 (July 1980), p. 21.

18. Dudley Seers, "What Are We Trying to Measure?" in Nancy Baster, ed., *Measuring Development: The Role and Adequacy of Development Indicators* (London: Frank Cass, 1972), p. 22.

19. Colin Leys, "The Role of the University in an Underdeveloped Country," *Education News*, 13:1 (April 1971), p. 14.

20. It is interesting to note that in his thoughtful study, Professor Dore listed ten functions of a university in contributing to national development and *none* of them was directly related to the "service" function. His ten functions are: knowledge transmission, mental development, national prestige enhancement, value affirmation, social control, social criticism, knowledge production, social order maintenance, rationing by licensing professions, and screening of talent. *Role of Universities*, pp. 9–11.

21. James S. Coleman and Ndolamb Ngokwey, "Zaire: The State and the University," in R. Murray Thomas, ed., *Politics and Education: Cases from Eleven Nations* (London: Pergamon Press, 1983), p. 27 [Chapter 12, this volume; ed.].

22. Walter D. Connor, "Education and National Development in the European Socialist States: A Model for the Third World," *Comparative Studies in Society and History*, 17:3 (July 1975), pp. 342–343.

23. James, "A Note on the Nature and Functions of the University," p. 492.

24. Philip Foster, "Dilemmas of Educational Development: What We Might Learn from the Past," *Comparative Education Review*, 19:3 (October 1975), p. 378. Dore refers to this phenomenon as an aspect of the "late development effect" and what he calls the "qualification-escalation ratchet" mechanism: "If you have set your sights—or if your parents have set your sights for you—on a modern sector job, and if you find that your junior secondary certificate does not get you one, there is nothing to be done except to press on and try to get a senior secondary certificate, and if that doesn't work to press on to the university." *The Diploma Disease: Education, Qualification and Development* (London: George Allen & Unwin, 1976), p. 72.

25. Connor, "Education and National Development," pp. 330–332.

26. Clark Kerr, "'The Uses of the University'—Postscript 1982," *Change*, 14:7 (October 1982), pp. 28–29.

27. M. Crawford Young, "The African University: Universalism, Development, and Ethnicity," *Comparative Education Review*, 25:2 (June 1981), p. 46. Young argues that the university in a new state tends very much to be a microcosm of the larger society, reflecting its change processes, conflict patterns, and structural crises.

28. "Draft Recommendations of the Conference on the Role of the University College, Dar es Salaam, in a Socialist Tanzania," *Minerva*, 5:4 (Summer 1967), pp. 538–559.

29. Robin Brooke-Smith, "The Politics of High Level Manpower Supply in Tanzania," *Comparative Education*, 14:2 (June 1978), p. 149. Ali Mazrui and Yash Tandon noted in their review of the Tanzanian case that "a university cannot be a university in the sense we are discussing—however vital its involvement in the public life of the country—and also be an ideological institute." "The University of East Africa as a Political Institution," in Kenneth Prewitt, ed., *Education and Political Values: An East African Case Study* (Nairobi: East African Publishing House, 1971), p. 176.

30. David Court, "Higher Education in East Africa," in Kenneth W. Thompson, Barbara R. Fogel, and Helen E. Danner, eds., *Higher Education and Social Change: Promising Experiments in Developing Countries*, 2 vols. (New York: Praeger, 1976–77), 2:475.

31. Colin Leys, "Political Perspectives," in Dudley Seers and Leonard Joy, eds., *Development in a Divided World* (London: Penguin, 1971), pp. 110–111.

32. Hans N. Weiler, "The Hot and Cold Wind of Politics: Planning Higher Education in Africa," in Samuel K. Gove, ed., *Higher Education's Political Economy, State, National and International Issues*.

33. Quoted in Ralf Dahrendorf, "The Role of the University in Devel-

opment: Some Sociological and Philosophical Considerations," in N. T. Chideya, ed., *The Role of the University and Its Future in Zimbabwe* (Harare: Harare Publishing House, 1982).

34. Theodore W. Schultz, "Distortions of Economic Research," *Minerva* 17:3 (Autumn 1979), p. 464. Schultz was particularly lamenting the extent to which academic economists were becoming preoccupied with the "fashionable concepts of targeted and 'mission-oriented' (i.e., 'developmental') research," which he believed to be "subterfuges for intrusion" by government and a constraint upon criticism.

35. A. Babs Fafunwa, "The Role of African Universities in Overall Educational Development," in Thompson et al., *Higher Education and Social Change*, 2:512.

36. Court, "Higher Education in East Africa," p. 474.

37. Kerr, "Postscript 1982," p. 27.

38. Ibid.

39. Leys and Shaw, "Problems of Universities," p. 6.

40. David Court, "Scholarship and Contract Research: The Ecology of Social Science in Kenya and Tanzania," in Laurence D. Stifel, Ralph K. Davidson, and James S. Coleman, eds., *Social Sciences and Public Policy in the Developing World* (Lexington, Mass.: D. C. Heath, 1982), pp. 125–166.

41. David Court, "Higher Education in East Africa: A Review of Rockefeller Foundation Assistance," August 1979, Rockefeller Foundation Archives, New York, pp. 143–144.

42. Albert Nyberg, "Education for Development: Gadjah Mada University, Indonesia," August 1979, Rockefeller Foundation Archives, New York, p. 40.

43. Carl Landé, "Education for Development: University of the Philippines," March 1980, Rockefeller Foundation Archives, New York, p. 93.

44. David C. Korten and Frances F. Korten, "The Impact of a National Service Experience upon Its Participants: Evidence from Ethiopia," *Comparative Education Review*, 13 (October 1969), pp. 312–322.

45. Thompson et al., *Higher Education and Social Change.*

46. Francis X. Sutton, "African Universities and the Process of Change in Middle Africa," in Stephen D. Kertesz, ed., *The Task of Universities in a Changing World* (Notre Dame: University of Notre Dame Press, 1971), p. 403.

47. Kenneth W. Thompson, "Developing Education v. Education for Development," *Annals*, 424 (March 1976), p. 25.

48. Eldon L. Johnson, "Misconceptions about the Early Land-Grant Colleges," *Journal of Higher Education*, 52:4 (1981), p. 341. Interestingly, one of the critical obstacles the land-grant colleges failed in their performance of their developmental role was the absence of experienced, qualified professors in agriculture who could teach the subject: "But in all

states, the unpromising state of agriculture as a profession or science was a serious obstacle. Professors of agriculture could not be found because the subject did not yet exist." Ibid., p. 340.

49. Ezra N. Suleiman, *Elites in French Society* (Princeton: Princeton University Press, 1978), p. 51.

50. A. Bartlett Giamatti, president of Yale, recently advised that academic scientists should not become deeply involved in research projects sponsored by private companies seeking to use university-based research for their own purposes. "Such involvement," he said, "risks putting one's students and research associates in ambiguous circumstances, such that the graduate or postdoctoral student would not know, when working with a professor, for whom the student was working—the university, the professor or the company." Peter David, "Business and Academic Work 'Don't Mix,'" *Times Higher Education Supplement*, December 24, 1982, p. 6.

Index